C000175522

KEYGuide

The AA KEYGuide Brittany

By Lindsay Hunt and Laurence Phillips

Contents

KEY TO SYMBOLS

- Map reference
- Address
- Telephone number
- Opening times
- Admission prices
- Bus number
- Train station
- Métro
- Ferry/boat
- Driving directions
- Tourist office
- Tours
- Guidebook
- Restaurant
- Café
- Shop
- Toilets
- Number of rooms
- No smoking
- Air conditioning
- Swimming pool
- Gym
- Parking
- Other useful information
- Shopping
- Entertainment
- Nightlife
- Sports
- Activities
- Health and beauty
- For children
- ★ Walk/drive start point
- ▷ Cross reference

HOW TO USE THIS BOOK

Understanding Brittany is an introduction to the region, its geography, economy and people. **Living Brittany** gives an insight into Brittany today, while **The Story of Brittany** takes you through the region's past.

For detailed advice on getting to Brittany—and getting around once you are there—turn to **On the Move**. For practical information, from weather forecasts to emergency services, turn to **Planning**.

Out and About gives you the chance to explore Brittany through walks and drives.

The **Sights**, **What to Do** and **Eating and Staying** sections are divided geographically into four regions, which are shown on the map on the inside front cover. These regions always appear in the same order. Towns and places of interest are listed alphabetically within each region.

Map references for the **Sights** refer to the atlas section at the end of this book or to the individual town plans. For example, St-Malo has the reference 203 L8, indicating the page on which the map is found (203) and the grid square in which St-Malo sits (L8).

UNDERSTANDING BRITTANY

Superb coastal scenery, splendid seafood and an enviable heritage of castles, churches and *villes d'histoires* or *petites cités de caractère* (historic towns and villages) make excellent reasons to visit Brittany. All these things can be found in other parts of France. What the English-speaking world finds, perhaps subconsciously, in Brittany's distinctive 'otherness' are deep cultural and geographical bonds stretching back way beyond the Conquest. Its very name means 'Little Britain', signifying a microcosm of *Grande Bretagne* across the waters of the Channel. In these ragged coastal extremities, Celtic exiles from the British Isles sought asylum and brought their faith during the Dark Ages, supplanted from their homeland by Norse and Anglo-Saxon invaders. Today, thousands of us return on well-traversed migration routes for timely top-ups of Brittany's restorative charms.

LANDSCAPE AND ENVIRONMENT

Brittany is the most westerly point in Europe, its Finistèrian capes stretching far into the Atlantic. The ancient Gauls divided Brittany into two parts, Armor (the sea country, meaning 'the coast'), and Argoat (the forest country, meaning 'the interior'). Modern Brittany, shorn since 1973 of its southeastern *département* of Loire-Atlantique, now contains only about 5 per cent of France's mainland territory. Yet it has over a third of the entire French seaboard, frayed and fretted all around its edges into a jagged fringe of bays, headlands, reefs and islands. Sinuous coastal inlets and estuaries, drowned after the last Ice Age, strike deep into its low-lying interior, much of which consists of an undulating plateau of nondescript granite-strewn moorland chequer-boarded by sunken rivers and drystone walls or banks. But the great forests that once covered large parts of the Argoat have now dwindled to odd remaining patches of woodland, mainly around Paimpont, Huelgoat and Quimperlé. Elsewhere the countryside is taken up by carefully managed farmland, where artichokes or brassicas grow in serried perfection.

Brittany's diverse habitats include dunes, salt-marshes, sea cliffs, reed beds, mudflats and heath, making it a haven for many species of animals, birds, plants and seaweeds, and paradise for anyone interested in natural history. The seas around the Breton coast are rich in marine life, especially around the Ouessant–Molène archipelago, which forms part of the Armorique Regional Nature Park. Dolphins, seals and sea-otters can be seen in the Mer d'Iroise, while the Atlantic salmon finds its way across vast ocean tracts to spawn in Brittany's estuarial rivers.

Threats to the Breton coast and countryside arise mainly from pollution caused by periodic oil-spillages from passing tankers (*Amoco Cadiz* still strikes a note of doom into Breton hearts), and by nitrate run-off from artificial fertilizers and animal slurry entering waterways and washing into the sea. This sometimes causes abnormal growths of seaweed or plankton in summer, turning areas of some beaches into foul-smelling compost heaps and producing toxins in shellfish.

ECONOMY

Fishing, farming and tourism are Brittany's most important industries, though newer pursuits such as high-tech telecommunications are replacing traditional livelihoods such as ship-building and shoe manufacturing in some areas.

Brittany is France's most productive fishing region, still a significant source of income in many coastal communities. As everywhere in Europe, pressures to conserve declining fish stocks are affecting the catch. Several of Finistère's ports still dispatch seine-netting ships with refrigerated holds in search of tuna off the West African coast, or hunt for cod around Iceland or the Bay of Biscay, but increasingly, inshore crustacean fishing and fish-farming have replaced the great ocean-going trawler fleets of old. Oyster- and mussel-raising have become big business in several coastal areas, while lobster and crayfish are captured offshore and placed in holding tanks or *viviers* to reach maturity. Fish-canning is still an important industry in southern Brittany, while seaweed is harvested and processed for a great variety of uses on Brittany's north coast.

Roughly two-thirds of the Breton countryside is cultivated. Brittany accounts for a large proportion of France's total agricultural output, specializing in early vegetables (particularly cauliflowers and artichokes), cereals, and fodder crops. One of the most productive market-gardening areas is known as the Ceinture d'Orée (Golden Belt) around St-Pol-de-Léon. Dairying and pig-rearing are also major sources of revenue. The climate doesn't suit vines, but cider orchards still paint the lush valleys of the Rance and the Odet with springtime blossom. Brittany's cattle and pigs account for about 20 per cent of France's dairy products, and about half its pork. Roughly one-third of the Breton workforce is involved in food production in some way: The vote of the small farmer is highly influential in this part of France.

Seagulls flying away from breaking waves in the Channel (left), the unmistakable silhouette of Mont-St-Michel at sunset (centre), and the Medieval Festival in the town of Moncontour (right)

CULTURE AND SOCIETY

Modern Brittany consists of four *départements*: Morbihan, Finistère, Côtes d'Armor and Ille-et-Vilaine. After an administrative reshuffle, Loire-Atlantique (the area around Nantes), historically part of the old Duchy of Brittany, was reassigned to the neighbouring region of Pays de la Loire. Historically and culturally, however, it still feels like part of Brittany, and many of its inhabitants still retain a strong emotional attachment to the old Duchy, which persisted as a separate entity until 1532.

The Breton flag: a symbol of the region's distinct identity

Brittany (Breizh in Breton) has its own language, a Celtic variant closely allied to Welsh or Cornish. Despite valiant efforts to keep the Breton language alive through educational and media projects, less than half of today's inhabitants can speak it, and very few use it as an everyday language.

Breton music, however, is thriving, encouraged by a revival of interest in folk traditions, and a lively round of festivals, concerts and summer events. All through the holiday season, the strains of woodwind instruments like the *bombarde* and the *biniou* can be heard, played by community pipe-bands. At these festivals, traditional costumes are often worn, with brightly embroidered aprons and elaborate headdresses *(coiffes)* of picot lace and starched linen. The Breton flag flies everywhere to reinforce regionalism. Known as *Gwenn ha du* (white and black), its stripes represent the ancient bishoprics of Upper and Lower Brittany, while the ermine symbol evokes the historic Duchy of Brittany.

Folklore and traditions play a great role in Breton life even today, and the tourist authorities make much of the legends of the Round Table around the Forest of Brocéliande (Paimpont), where King Arthur's court set out to search for the Holy Grail. The region of Cornouaille is associated with the Tristan and Isolde legend, and with the story of the lost city of Ys, drowned by Dahut, the wicked daughter of King Gradlon. In rural churches, *memento mori* or *danse macabre* frescoes, and representations of Ankou, the Breton incarnation of death, reminded many generations of God-fearing peasants of their mortality.

Brittany is still a fervently Catholic part of France, its shrines and parish closes cared for and its churches well attended, especially on the many saints' days and *pardons* commemorated in every community. Many Breton saints were Celtic evangelists who arrived from British shores in the 5th and 6th centuries.

BRITTANY'S *DÉPARTEMENTS*

MORBIHAN

The shallow, enclosed Golfe du Morbihan ('little sea') gives its name to this *département*. The beach resorts on Brittany's sunny south-easterly shores attract many holidaymakers. Of Morbihan's two largest conurbations, the historic walled city of Vannes is the more interesting; war-torn Lorient is mostly a modern, industrialized rebuild. Conversely, the tantalizing megaliths at Carnac and Locmariaquer stretch back far into the mists of time.

FINISTÈRE

Brittany's 'Land's End' is a large and varied area with north-, west- and south-facing shores, and an unspoiled rural hinterland dominated by the Armorique regional park. The surf-pummelled extremities of Crozon and the Pointe du Raz contrast with mirror-calm estuaries and sheltered beaches. Finistère is distinguished by its rich cultural heritage and idiosyncratic parish closes; local festivals showcase the region's traditional costumes, music and language.

CÔTES D'ARMOR

The medieval gem of Dinan is unquestionably one of Brittany's star attractions, as are the splendid stretches of coast around Cap Fréhel (The Emerald Coast) and Ploumanac'h (the Pink Granite Coast). Several superb marinas attract keen sailors, and the sandy beaches of Le Val-André and Sables-d'Or-les-Pins are hard to match.

A bagpipe player at Roscoff (above), and a girl in Breton costume in Pont l'Abbé (left)

ILLE-ET-VILAINE

Most visitors pass through this northeastern frontier zone at some point, many via the handsome ferry port of St-Malo, or through the lively regional capital of Rennes. Haute-Bretagne (Upper Brittany) is the Gallo- or French-speaking part of the region, its distinctive qualities guarded since medieval times by the mighty fortresses of Vitré and Fougères, and the ethereal island abbey of Mont-St-Michel on the Normandy borders.

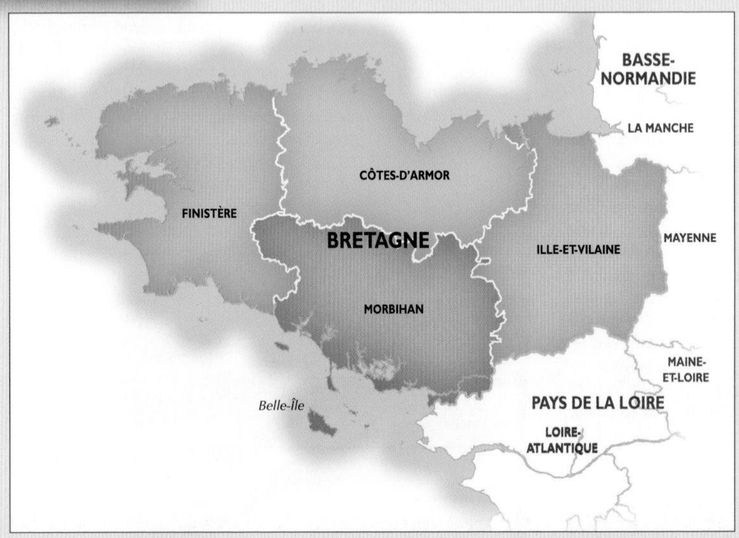

THE BEST OF BRITTANY

A two-tiered display of fruits de mer *(above)*

MORBIHAN

Belle-Île-en-Mer (▷ 37): Don't miss pretty Sauzon and the needle rocks of Port-Coton on Brittany's biggest island.

Carnac (▷ 38–9): The purpose of Carnac's strange lines of standing stones is still a baffling mystery.

Domaine de Kerguéhennec (▷ 43): This classic 18th-century château is now used as a modern sculpture park.

Golfe du Morbihan (▷ 40): This landlocked lagoon is a paradise for boat trips and birdlife.

Josselin (▷ 44): See Josselin's mighty castle floodlit at night from the Hôtel du Château.

Quiberon (▷ 47): Try some wind-and-water sports on the west-facing Plage de Penthièvre.

La Roche-Bernard (▷ 47): For the meal of a lifetime, book into the Auberge Bretonne in this pretty, petite *cité de caractère*

An old boat on the river Moros in Concarneau (above)

The Lagatjar Alignements on the Crozon peninsula (above), and playing an old Celtic instrument at Locranon

FINISTÈRE

Armorique Regional Nature Park (▷ 61, 64, 65, 69): This conservation zone encompasses a huge variety of wildlife.

Concarneau (▷ 60): Climb the ramparts of the Ville Close, visit the Musée de Pêche and the *criée* (fish auction), and take a boat trip to the Îles de Glénan.

Le Conquet (▷ 61): Follow the lighthouse trail along North Finistère's Côte des Abers.

Douarnenez (▷ 62): Visit Port-Rhu and the boat museum on Douarnenez harbour.

Guimiliau (▷ 63): Admire one of Brittany's most striking parish closes—a *tour-de-force* of Renaissance sculpture, both inside and outside the church.

Locronan (▷ 67): Visit the craft studios of this historic village.

Morlaix (▷ 68): Walk across the viaduct for a fantastic overview of the town.

Océanopolis (▷ 54): Peer through this window on the waterfront at one of Europe's largest and liveliest aquariums.

Pointe du Raz (▷ 71): Walk out to this dramatic coastal promontory to watch the tides race past the mysterious Île de Sein.

Pont-Aven (▷ 72): Wander through the Bois d'Amour to find the inspirational crucifix of Gauguin's *Christ Jaune* in the Chapelle de Trémalo.

Quimper (▷ 74–5): Buy some pottery in Cornouaille's historic capital.

Roscoff (▷ 76): Visit the subtropical gardens in Roscoff and the Île de Batz.

St-Pol-de-Léon (▷ 77): Try local artichokes grown locally in Brittany's Golden Belt.

Oceanopolis at Brest (below)

The coast at Pointe du Raz (above)

A display of faïence at Quimper (below), and artichokes from St-Pol-de-Léon (right)

THE BEST OF BRITTANY

CÔTES D'ARMOR

Cap Fréhel (▷ 80): This rugged headland marks the climax of the dramatically beautiful Emerald Coast.

Côte de Granit Rose (▷ 81): Walk the customs officers' watchpath through this rocky coastal wonderland.

Dinan (▷ 82–4): The cobbled streets and timbered buildings of this medieval gem are unforgettable.

Île de Bréhat (▷ 85): This reef-ringed island full of flowers makes the perfect away-day near Paimpol.

Le Radome (▷ 88): The Musée des Télécoms charts the history of long-distance message-relay, in a setting both historic and futuristic.

Tréguier (▷ 91): Head for this handsome old river port on summer Wednesdays for its lively market day in the square dominated by one of Brittany's finest cathedrals.

Le Val-André (▷ 92): Sand doesn't get much better than the glistening beaches in this resort.

Le Vapeur de Trieux (▷ 88, 150): A steam-train excursion between two charming historic towns is a great way to explore the scenic Trieux Valley.

A game of boules at Erquy (above), and buying oysters in Cancale (below)

The lighthouse at Île de Brehat (above)

ILLE-ET-VILAINE

Cancale (▷ 94): Try some fresh oysters from the market at the old fishing port of La Houle.

Dinard (▷ 95): Walk the Promenade du Claire de Lune for magnificent estuary views.

Fougères (▷ 97): The intact walls of Fougères' medieval fortress make a fine sight reflected in the River Nançon.

Hédé (▷ 98): Take a towpath walk along the Ille-et-Rance Canal to watch boats sail through the lock staircase at La Madeleine.

St-Malo (▷ 106–8): Climb the ramparts and circumnavigate the corsairs' home port, preferably at sunset.

Le Vivier-sur-Mer (▷ 109): Find out all about mussels at the Maison de la Baie, and take a tractor tour around the *bouchots*.

Ladies in traditional lace headdresses preparing for a parade at Pont l'Abbé (below)

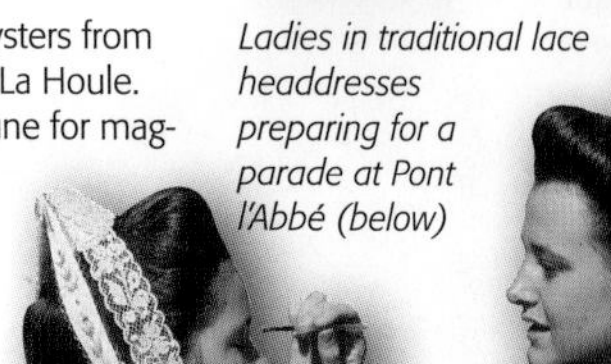

A crêpe and a cup of local cider (right)

TOP 5 EXPERIENCES

Attend a festival or *pardon* Folk events in traditional Breton costume are especially memorable. You may also hear Breton spoken.

Eat some pancakes Brittany's speciality fast-food comes in many guises.

See the parish closes These idiosyncratic expressions of religious art are among the most distinctive treasures of the region.

Take a boat trip Experiences vary from a motor launch excursion to an ocean voyage on a fully rigged, 18th-century-style sailing ship.

Try some seafood Visit a *criée* (fish auction), then sample an *assiette de fruits de mer* in a local restaurant.

Detail of a mounted figure at the Playben Calvary (left)

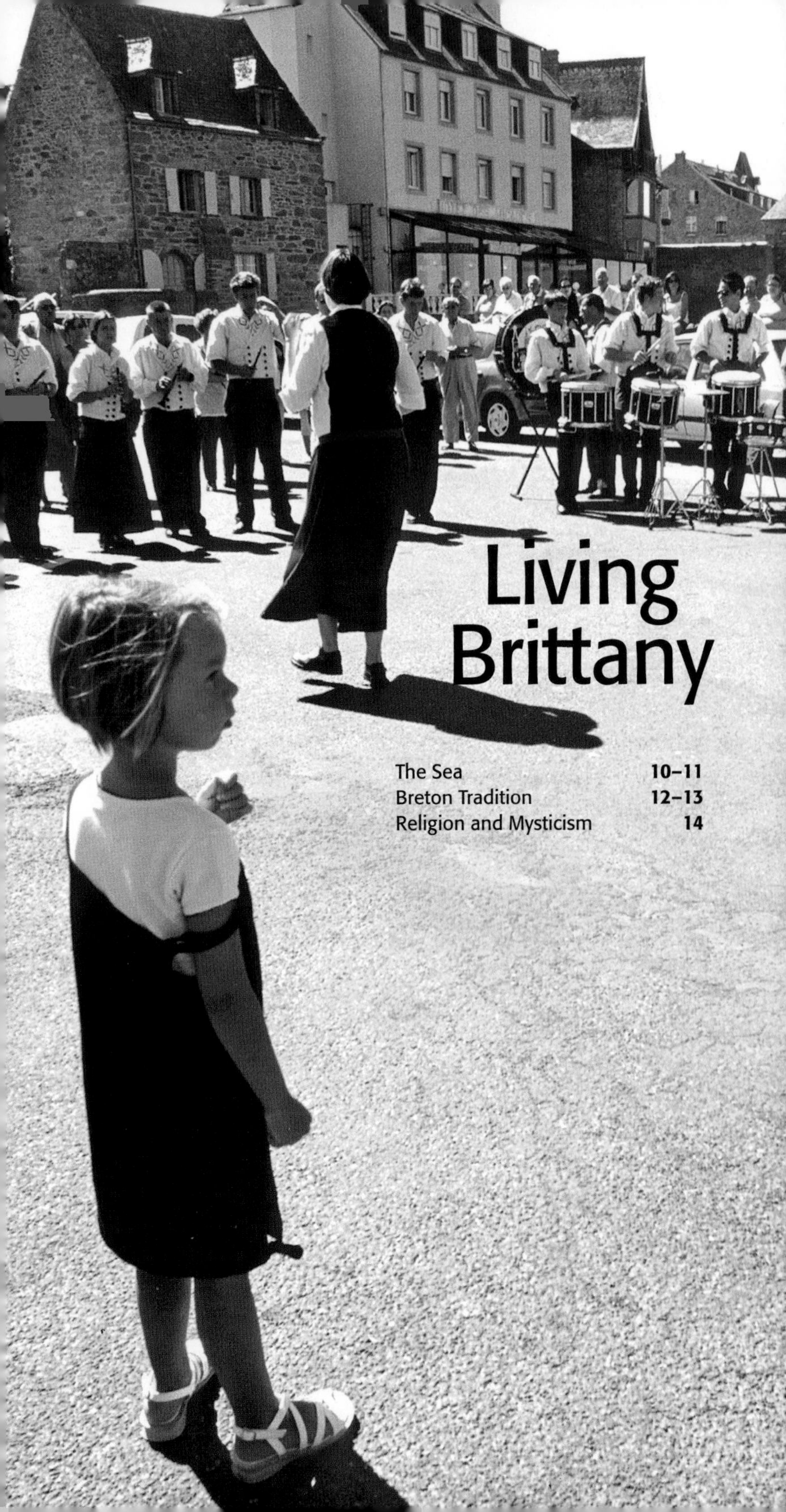

Living Brittany

Seafood platter (left), a comorant on seaweed-covered rocks (above), eating an oyster (right), and sails at Peros Guirec (below)

The Sea

A seal off the Breton coast (above), Dame Ellen MacArthur (right), and freshly caught crabs (below left)

The era of corsairs and privateers may be past, but modern Brittany still looks towards its distinctive coast for its identity. Beaches, coves and harbours have evolved to the needs of tourism. Their charm is the fact they are no mere historical curiosities, since fishing continues to be the principal maritime trade. Offshore fish-farming is the 21st century's newest approach to meeting market demand, with salmon-farming from platforms out at sea, such as Salmor off the coast of Morlaix.

The second half of the 20th century saw renewed interest in the sport of sailing, with sailing clubs, training facilities and competitions thriving across Brittany. The Glénans archipelago gave its name to Les Glénans, an association founded in 1947 by former resistance fighters and sailors, which is now France's biggest sailing school.

Modern Brittany is a major manufacturing and research base for the boating industry, with yacht-building and sail-making key to the local economy. Not surprisingly it has developed as an important stage in many international sporting events, with the Route de Rhum race departing from St-Malo every four years, and the same port gaining further fame as the finishing post of the Québec–St-Malo transatlantic race.

A Noble Adventurer

Brittany has always respected strong women and adventurous sailors, and in Dame Ellen MacArthur the region found a 21st-century heroine. The English yachtswoman regularly sets sail from Breton ports, and thousands turn out on the quay-sides to welcome her whenever she returns. Her historic 44,012km (27,354-mile) solo circumnavigation of the globe in 71 days and just under 15 hours was declared a world record as her 22.5m (75ft) trimaran *B&Q* passed the Finistère island of Ouessant in February 2005. Four months later, MacArthur and *B&Q's* next record came when she crossed a 160km (100-mile) stretch of the English Channel between Plymouth and Roscoff in just over 6 hours and 20 minutes.

Seagull in flight (above), and the lighthouse at Sauzon-Port, Belle-Île (below)

Fresh seafood (above), and young razorbills on the Côtes-d'Armor (right)

The salt pans near Guérand (above), and the aftermath of the *Torrey-Canyon* disaster (left)

The Black Tides

Not everything that the sea has brought to the Brittany coast has been welcomed. At the end of the 20th century a succession of shipwrecked tankers smeared beaches and wildlife with oil as the region faced its toughest ever environmental crises. The first oil spills to contaminate the area spread across the Channel from the *Torrey-Canyon* disaster in English waters in 1967. A decade later the *Amoco Cadiz* produced black tides closer to home. Then, at the turn of the millennium, the wreck of the *Erica* created further damaging oil slicks. After each of these disasters huge international clean-up operations worked to save bird and marine life and clean up the beaches. After extensive lobbying from France and other countries, the EU finally banned single-hull oil tankers from European ports in 2003.

Salty Success

The image of distressed sea birds in the aftermath of oil spills may have overshadowed one of Brittany's ecological success stories—one that has brought many species of bird back to the coast. The saviour of endangered wildlife is natural salt. For centuries *paludiers* (farmers) worked the salt-marshes of the Guérand peninsula until the tradition all but died out, overtaken by industrial production by the 1960s. However, since the 1980s, with fashionable restaurants demanding authentic sea salt, interest in the industry has revived. Now a one-year training course has been established, and the average age of the *paludier* is under 40. The marshes are worked organically and by hand, and this, together with the area's protected status, has brought 170 species of migrating and breeding birds to the area, including egrets, herons, harriers and plovers.

Weeding the Future

The alchemy of the 21st century is *algologie*—turning seaweed into money. Once considered a poor man's harvest, the humble seaweed may hold the key to beauty, long life and even the economic future of Brittany. In the 1990s a research establishment was created in Pleubian, on the Côtes d'Armor, where scientists research more than 600 species of pure unpolluted weed found in local waters. Researchers have found different properties in marine plants found close to the shore and those growing further away in deep water. The CEVA Technical Research Centre on the Pen Lan peninsula looks at the cosmetic applications of nutrients from the weeds. Although thalassotherapy (treatments using seawater) was first offered in Roscoff in 1899 by Dr Roger Bagot, it's taken another century for fashion to catch up.

The Last Heroes

In the era of automated navigation, Brittany's manned lighthouses remained a forgotten aspect of France's maritime heritage until the great storms of 1989. As tempests raged over the seas, Breton photographer and sailor Jean Guichard took his famous series of pictures of the last offshore lighthouse keepers of Brittany. His Phares dans la Tempête photographs have been reproduced around the world in magazines and posters. At the height of the storm, as waves battered the top of the Jument lighthouse, Guichard snapped keeper Théodore Malgorne opening the door to watch his home completely engulfed by spray. Now just three offshore lighthouses remain inhabited: Jument, Kéréon and Vieille.

Festival dancers parade at Landerneau (above), traditional Breton bagpipes (below left), and traditional Breton costume (below)

Breton Tradition

As befits a region with a passion for its own cultural identity, Bretons guard their traditions ardently. Sea shanties are sung in festivals along the Finistère coast with an almost religious fervour; legends of magic and mysticism are kept fresh with constant retelling; and even agricultural customs are adhered to with an almost obsessive fervour. On the island of Ouessant, the distinctive local sheep—tiny creatures with brownish wool—are allowed to roam freely, grazing on whatever salty grass they can find. Each February, sheep-marking ceremonies see them allocated to named farmers.

Integration with the rest of France is regarded with suspicion. A fiery spirit of cultural independence burns strongly. At the turn of the 21st century, the movement to raise the profile of the Breton language was boosted with TV and radio broadcasts in the indigenous tongue and classes in schools in a region that had been losing a worrying proportion of native speakers each year. Much of this backlash was reaction to a deliberate attempt by the state to eradicate the language and downgrade its status to a patois in the post-war years. Right-wing Breton nationalism and anti-French feeling had been associated by politicians with the sympathies of some Breton political groups to the German occupation, and Breton was banned in schools in 1947.

Celtic Invasion

Anyone who believes that the last Celtic invasion of the Brittany coast took place in the 5th century has had their eyes tightly shut during the month of August. The annual Interceltic Festival in the port of Lorient is the biggest gathering of Celtic peoples in the world, with some 4,000 musicians and representatives of national associations in the official parade of the Celtic Nations in 2005 and more than half a million revellers taking part in some 200 events over 10 days. The festival is famous for uniting Scots, Irish, Welsh and Cornish celebrants from the British Isles, Galicians from Buenos Aires, Scottish settlers from Canada and Australia and plenty of Boston Irish.

A young girl parading at Pont l'Abbé (left)

A local flag of Brittany (left), and English morris dancers entertaining the townspeople at St-Malo (right)

A Druid ceremony (above), a Breton cross at St-Cado (right), and a flag from a medieval festival (below)

Merlin's tomb at Concoret (above), Tristan and Isolde (right), and an onion Johnny (below)

The Price of Integration

In 2005, newspapers warned of an anti-British backlash as Bretons revolted against English newcomers buying homes in Brittany. The protests in Bourbriac drew much attention, with media estimates that as many as a third of local residents were Brits. The truth was more modest: 50 full-time ex-pats and 50 holiday-home owners had sparked the reaction from A-Stroll (Breton for 'together'), a local political group. In reality, the anger was directed more at the property market. The incoming foreigners were inflating house prices, and A-Stroll was more concerned at the cultural effects of the break up of local families, priced out of their home towns, than the dangers of Anglo-Saxon influences.

The Pagan Option

Bretons are known for taking their Celtic origins very seriously, but perhaps the most passionate would be the two or three dozen souls who meet each summer in a meadow in Brasparts, Finistère, for the ancient feast of Lugnasad. These are members of Brittany's contemporary Druid community. To pay homage to the god Lug, they gather in a circle of stones on the third Sunday in July for a ceremony led by Gwenc'hlan Le Scouezec, the fifth Great-Druid of La Gourzes de Bretagne. No strangers to criticism, La Gourzes' Druids nonetheless hold their ceremonies in public and are happy to welcome new members, Christians and pagans alike. Gwenc'hlan Le Scouezec, author of a dictionary of Celtic traditions, makes only one stipulation—would-be members must be able to speak Breton.

From Linens to Yarns

Brittany is a region of storytellers. Anywhere with Merlin, Tristan and Isolde as local gossip fodder is bound to develop a talent for spinning a yarn. In 1989, oral tradition gave way to the printed word. Bécherel, north of Rennes, became France's first 'Book Town'. Established by the Savenn Douar association, the concept evolved through the 1990s into bibliophile heaven. Bécherel now has 15 bookshops, bookbinders and professional calligraphers, and a vast book market on the first Sunday each month. Having gently slumped into near obscurity since its heyday as a 17th century linen and textile market, the revival of fortunes is credited to modern capitalizing on the Breton love of a good yarn. Twice yearly, the pleasure of reading gains carnival proportions with book festivals over Easter and the second Saturday in August.

Johnny Knows his Onions

If you overhear elderly men slipping occasional fluent English into Breton conversation in a Roscoff bar, don't be surprised. For generations, Roscovites knew more about England they did about France. Since the 1820s, local lads crossed the Channel to sell *troches*—tresses of onions. Battalions of 'Johnnies', as they were called, set up warehouses and sold door to door, bicycling British country lanes and bringing back English language and customs to a region that had so far managed to avoid many French influences. Today, a few Roscoff Johnnies still board the ferries to serve their loyal customers (▷ 76).

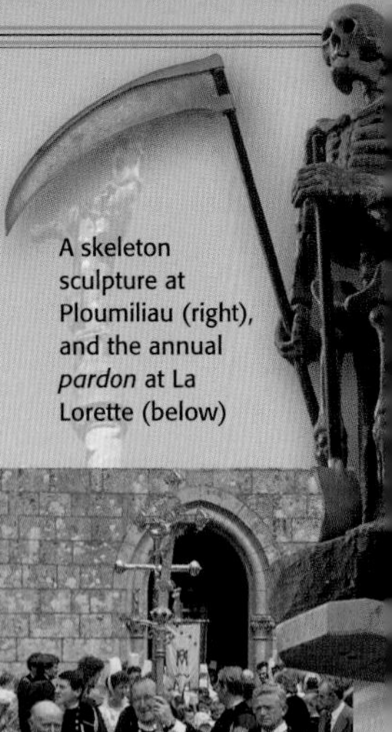

The blessing of the motorbikes (left)

A skeleton sculpture at Ploumiliau (right), and the annual *pardon* at La Lorette (below)

The Pleyben Calvary (right), and a skull from Ossuary Parish Close, Lanrivain (below)

Religion and Mysticism

From Lace to Leathers

While lace headdresses, and starched collars may be traditional costume at most *pardons* in Brittany, since 1979 the dress code at Porcaro, in Morbihan, has tended towards leather with metallic accessories. Some 6,000 gleaming chrome motorbikes hit the town each 15 August for the unique *pardon* of La Madone des Motards, Our Lady of the Bikers. The blessing ceremony sees a statue of the Virgin carried through Porcaro by celebrants whose denims and T-shirts reflect the blue-and-white vestments of the parish priest.

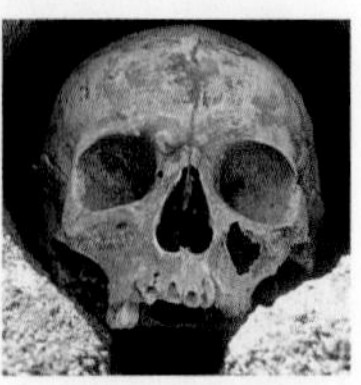

Brittany's calendar is dotted with *pardons*, days of splendid procession and devotion celebrating patron saints. Thousands of people may take to the streets or the quaysides for the biggest traditional *pardons* of St. Yves at Treguier and St. Jacques in Locquirec.

While steeped in Catholic tradition, the custom of the *pardon* also reflects secular life and modern issues. Since the 1950s, July has seen an annual joint Islamic-Christian *pardon* at Vieux Marché to celebrate understanding between faiths.

Nothing illustrates the influence of the church on daily life in Brittany more than the parish close. Around the village cemetery evolved a distinctive cluster of buildings, including the charnel house. Calvaries, monuments depicting stories from the Passion, once illustrated outdoor sermons.

Fount of Devotion

Breton inclination towards romance and magic has affected its approach to religion over the centuries. When Christianity finally reached the region it too was obliged to cater towards the local penchant for the mystic. Bretons had long worshipped 'miraculous' springs, which gushed mineral waters to cure all ills. Despite a condemnation by the church in AD658 of the worship of fountains, the healing qualities of water are still regarded with awe. Thus, over the years, the church appropriated springs and built chapels to patron saints at the sites. So St. Mériadec is credited with the deafness cure at Pontivy and St. Clair's water is said to restore sight at Reguigny.

A Breton Druid

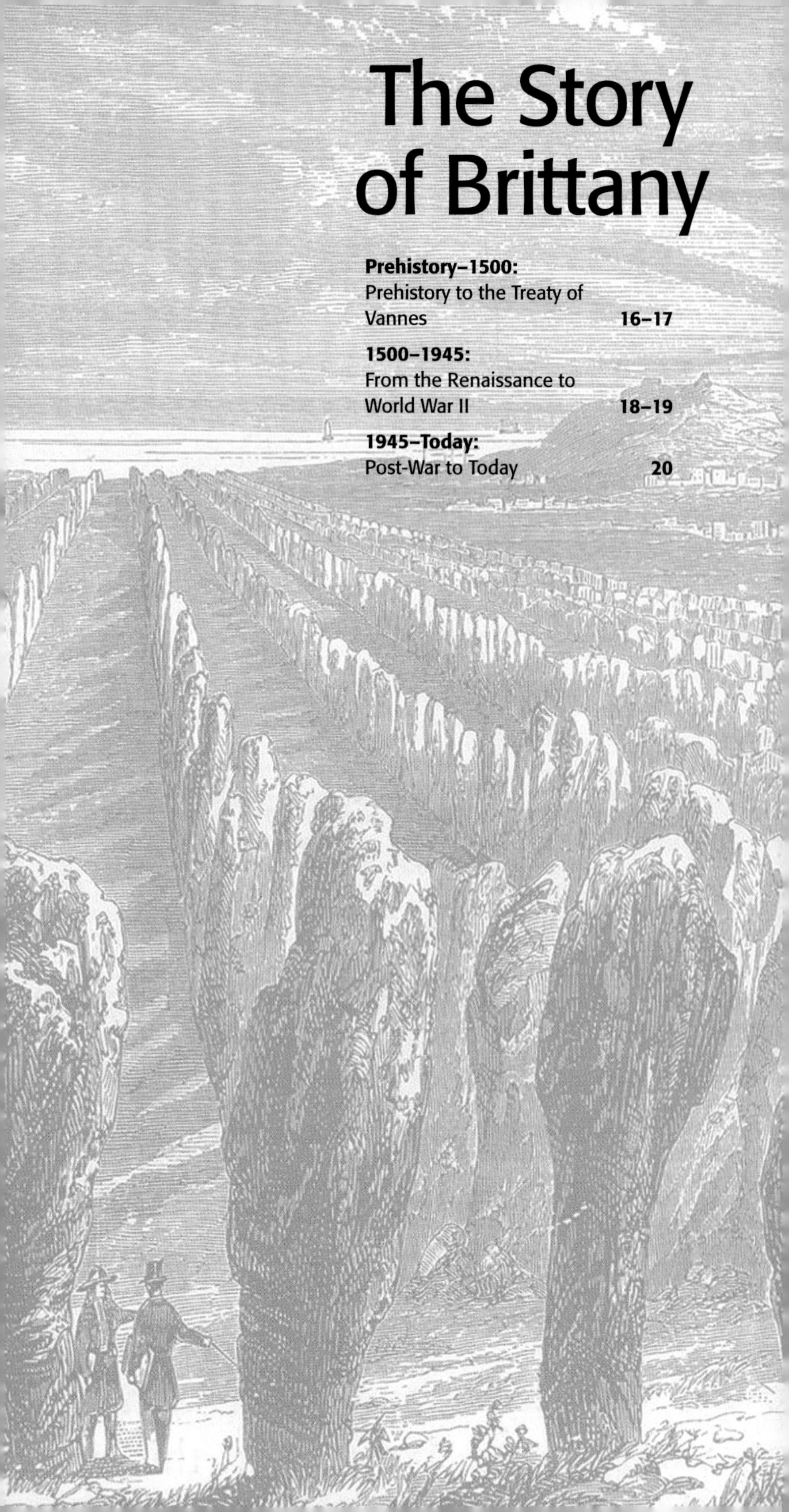

The Story of Brittany

Prehistory to the Treaty of Vannes

Brittany is renowned for its standing stones, or menhirs, which mostly date to the Neolithic period (c3000BC), yet little is known about the people who erected them. During the Bronze Age new settlers appeared; these early Celts called their land Armor—the land of the sea. In AD55, Julius Caesar invaded, marking the beginning of four centuries of Roman rule. In AD460 a fresh wave of Celtic immigration began as Angles and Saxons forced the Romans out of Britain. Thus Little Britain, or Brittany, was born.

Brittany fell easy prey to the Franks in AD799, when Charlemagne seized control, and installed his own governor, Nominoë. He, however, expelled the Franks and united the diverse Breton communities under his rule. Under his son, Erispoë, the duchy was upgraded to the status of kingdom.

The first half of the 10th century saw violent Viking invasions, eventually quelled in AD939 by the last Breton king, Alain Barbe-Torte. The house of Montfort inherited the title in 1365 and a period of stability saw close association with France. On the death of François II, the duchy passed to his daughter, Duchess Anne of Brittany, whose daughter, Claude, gave Brittany to France with the Treaty of Vannes in 1532.

An early Celtic Breton settler

From a Vassal to a King

Even kings can learn lessons in humility. Louis I of France nominated Nominoë, Count of Vannes, as first Duke of Brittany in AD826. The duchy came with strings attached, as the new duke was obliged to swear allegiance to Louis, and ruled Brittany as a vassal of the French crown. In AD841 Louis died, to be succeeded by his son, Charles the Bald, and relations between the duke and the new ruler of France lacked the respect that had marked the previous reign. Nominoë refused to bow before the new king and proclaimed Brittany an independent state. When Charles attempted to bring him to heel, France was routed in the Battle of Ballon and, in AD846, it was Charles who had to recognize Brittany as an independent kingdom.

The coronation of Charles the Bald

3000BC

Julius Caesar (left), an illustration of the original arrangement of the stones at Carnac (below), and Romans fighting Gauls (right)

The Miracle of the Honest Lawyer

History books are filled with accounts of lawyers and saints, but very few sainted lawyers. St. Yves, still fondly remembered in Brittany today, was a man of the law with the common touch. He died in 1303 and among his epitaphs were the lines *'Erat Brito, advocatus, et non latro. Res miranda populo!'* ('He was a Breton and a lawyer, but not dishonest—astonishing!') After serving as a judge in Rennes, he returned to his homeland, the Côtes d'Armour, and worked alongside Alan de Bruc, Bishop of Tréguier. As a judge he was known as the pauper's advocate and even took up cases of the downtrodden in other courts than his own. The famous epitaph came from his skill as persuading litigants to settle out of court and not spend money on lawyers.

St. Yves depicted in a stained glass window

Beware the Screaming Blonde

Among the religious icons in Fougères' 15th-century church of St. Sulpice are reminders of secular heroines. An image etched into the stained-glass windows is a declaration of the town's founding fathers' fairy ancestry. A blonde woman with the tail of a serpent can be seen, reflecting the legend of Melusine, who killed her father and was cursed to turn into a snake every Saturday. She married Raymond of Poitiers on condition that he would never see her on a Saturday and brought him great wealth and power, building castles overnight and giving him many children. One Saturday Raymond peeked, Melusine turned into a serpent and disappeared—henceforth to be heard shrieking whenever death awaits one of her descendents.

Melusine, the Screaming Blonde

Wives Behaving Badly

After centuries of warring, violence and Viking pillaging, it was no wonder that good behaviour was not among the key traits of medieval life. Thankfully, Brittany created one of the first self-help manuals to keep decent people on the straight and narrow. Thanks to Etienne de Fougères, Bishop of Rennes, after 1175 Bretons had the benefit of his *Livre des Manières*, an invaluable handbook of contemporary etiquette. As well as pointing out the correct way to behave, Etienne's writing gives a fascinating glimpse into the tricks of wives behaving badly. According to the bishop, wayward wives with an urge to stray from their marriage vows would feign illness in order that their husbands would recommend a pilgrimage to Santiago de Compostela—promising plenty of opportunity to dally with lapsed celibates en route.

Serial Child Bride

By the age of 14, Anne of Brittany was already on her second marriage. What turned the daughter of a duke into a serial child bride? Answer: inheriting a duchy at the age of 11. Before her father François II died in 1488, he had promised that his daughter would not marry without the approval of the French Crown. Of course, Brittany was an attractive dowry and many European rulers realized the advantages of wedding 11-year-old Anne. Austria, England and Aragon sent forces to protect the young duchess. Eventually, in 1490, Archduke Maximilian of Austria married the 13-year-old by proxy. French military power led Anne to annul the marriage, and wed Charles VIII of France in 1491. When Charles died childless, Anne, veteran wife at 22, married his successor, Louis XII.

Anne of Brittany (above), and a scene from her life (left)

1500

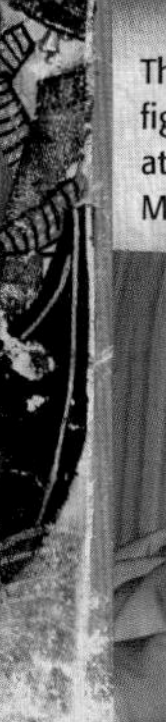

The Lords of Aubigby (above left), the recumbent figure of St. Yves at the cathedral of St. Tugdual at Tréguier (below), and a calendar showing Melusine flying over Château de Lusignan (right)

From the Renaissance to World War II

The 16th century saw Brittany looking to the wider world, with explorers, privateers and merchant fleets setting out from St-Malo. Most famously Jacques Cartier discovered Canada. In 1610 Cardinal Richelieu became governor of Brittany under Louis XIII, and concentrated on upgrading the region's naval defences. He was followed in the mid-17th century by Louis XIV's governor Colbert, whose efforts to raise funds for his extravagant monarch led to the imposition of various unpopular taxes, culminating in the Stamped Paper Revolt in 1675 against Colbert's decree that all legal transactions should use stamped paper (on which duty was payable). Although the revolt was crushed the region remained in a state of seething resentment. Any hopes that the French Revolution would improve Brittany's situation were speedily dashed—the Breton language was banned and Brittany itself split into five new *départements*. Under these conditions a loyalist counter-Revolutionary group known as the Chouans attracted local support. The Chouannerie were quashed in 1804, and the remainder of the 19th century was a time of cultural endeavour rather than martial activity: Pont-Aven became an artists' haven and writers Chateaubriand and Jules Verne put Brittany on the literary map.

After World War I, the economy was in the doldrums, and separatist organizations sprang up. Yet when the Nazis arrived in 1940 Brittany put up a spirited resistance, despite some Breton politicians being openly supportive of Hitler's regime.

FRANCE LIBRE

Cartier's Diamonds not a Boy's Best Friend

Jacques Cartier may have found Canada while hunting for the Northwest Passage to Asia, but the St-Malo-born sailor did not have the same good luck when it came to discovering precious metals and diamonds. In the 1530s he explored Newfoundland, and heard many native stories about fabulous treasures north of the settlement. He returned in 1541 to seek an incredible fortune in a land known as Saguenay. Alas the 'diamonds' and 'gold' he discovered were merely quartz and iron pyrites, better known as fool's gold.

A wax model of Cartier and a native Canadian

1500

A tower at St-Malo's castle (left), the site of the former residence of Jacques Cartier (below), and the Pont-Aven artists (right)

The Pirate Priest

When a shipbuilder's son fails as a priest, what better career than becoming a respectable pirate? After centuries of long wars with its neighbours, France discovered a profitable alternative to the navy—self-employed pirates. Rather than declare outright war, France commissioned merchant sailors to seize with impunity cargoes from merchant ships of rival nations. The king issued Letters of Marque to a number of privateers, or corsairs, who sailed from St-Malo to take on the English, Spanish and Dutch. Before the legendary 19th-century adventurer Surcouf, Brittany's hero was Duquay Trouin (1673–1736), whose debauched lifestyle abruptly ended his training for the priesthood. Instead, at 16, he put to sea and by the age of 36 he had been ennobled for his exploits.

Bridge to the South Seas

The estuary of the river Aven may seem an unlikely gateway to the South Seas, but for artist Paul Gauguin, Pont-Aven was the first step to Polynesia. In the late 1880s, the extraordinary light of this town of watermills and cheery taverns attracted a group of artists keen to explore new possibilities beyond the recent Impressionist movement. The Pont-Aven school was led by Gauguin, who seized upon the potential for vivid colours in his two-dimensional portrayal of local figures bathed in the clear light of Finistère. From Pont-Aven, Gauguin moved to Pouldu in 1889, and 6 years later took the decision to follow the light to the Marquess Islands, where his famous Polynesian canvasses owed so much to his earlier paintings of the women of Brittany.

The Owl and the Pimpernel

Ironically for a region that had spent so many years fighting against the kingdom of France, Brittany nurtured a strong royalist resistance to the Revolution. After the execution of Louis XVI in 1793, the Chouannerie monarchist guerrilla movement had a strong base in the region. The movement found its name in the fighters' practice of signalling with the call of an owl *(chouette)*. The Chouan rebellion lasted 11 years, but became enshrined in literary legend. Balzac had a huge success with his novel *Les Chouans* (1829). The movement was further glamorized by the ultimate royalist romancer of popular fiction. In 1919 Baroness Orczy followed her best-selling yarns about the Scarlet Pimpernel with *The Man in Grey*, billed as episodes of the Chouan conspiracies.

A War of Independence

The surge in Breton nationalism in the 20th century dates to the trench warfare of World War I. One million Bretons went to the fronts at Verdun and the Marne and a quarter were killed, more than twice as many as any other region. Since this was the first time that many of them had actually mixed with the French, the language and cultural differences were drawn into sharp focus, leading some commentators to conclude that the soldiers from Brittany were considered peasant canon fodder. This attitude helped to foster the political attitudes of the century that followed. The Partie National Breton (PNB) was founded in 1919, boosted by both the reaction to World War I and the success of nationalists in Ireland.

Model of a corsair at Roscoff

Gaugin, leader of the Pont-Aven school

The Scarlet Pimpernel

Detail of the blue-and-white Breton flag

Detail of a painting by Gaugin (left), Guards in The Great War (above), a Résistance poster (right), and a sign commemorating the Battle of the Atlantic (below)

Post-War to Today

The castle at Nantes (above), and the Musée des Telecoms at Pleumeur-Bodou (left)

The elements have determined much of Brittany's recent history. Winds and water wreaking havoc on land and sea: Argoat woodlands devastated by hurricanes in 1987 and maritime disasters and oil spills from the *Torrey-Canyon* in 1967 to the *Erica* in 2000 (▷ 11). Breton cultural identity has been very much in the foreground of political life. The Comité d'Études et de Liaison des Intérêts Bretons was founded in 1951 to protect the local economy, and bilingual French and Breton road signs were introduced in the region in 1985. Businesses began relocating to Rennes from 1962, when President de Gaulle commissioned a giant Citroën factory, and business parks have flourished since the 1980s. Major construction projects have included the Rance tidal barrage and Monts d'Arrée nuclear power station in 1966, and the Iroise and La Roche-Bernard bridges in the mid-1990s.

The Breton who Would be France's Leader

For a region virtually defined by its fierce spirit of independence, 2002's presidential elections brought a double irony. Not only was there a serious chance of a Breton-born candidate—Jean-Marie le Pen—becoming president of the Republic, but the candidate himself was the most vociferous French nationalist of his generation. National voter apathy and disillusionment with the candidates for the mainstream party meant that the usually fringe far-right Front National party was runner-up in the first round of the election. In order to ensure that the Front's controversial leader, le Pen, did not win the final poll, liberals, socialists and even communists found themselves voting for the less unpopular conservative Jacques Chirac.

Oops, There Goes the Capital

Many visitors believe Nantes is capital of Brittany: original home to the Breton Parliament and Henri IV's Edict of Nantes. Yet not only is Rennes the actual capital, but in 1971 Nantes left Brittany altogether to became capital of the Pays de la Loire region. Since the Revolution, Nantes had its differences with the rest of Brittany, fervently anti-Royalist and drowning monarchist rebels in the Loire. The city was first declared non-Breton in 1941 by the Vichy government, and in 1971 Nantes joined the newly created *département* of Loire-Atlantique. However, ask supporters of football club FC Nantes Atlantique where their loyalties lie and they will tell you they are proud to be Breton.

1945-Today

Breton nationalists demonstrating (right)

Jean-Marie Le Pen with his daughter (above), and the dam alongside the power station in the Rance estuary (right)

On the Move

ARRIVING

By Air

Patterns of air travel to northwestern France have fluctuated over recent years. After a period of rapid expansion, when low-cost operators began using several small regional airports, the network suddenly contracted. This hit the short-break market and left many holiday-home owners stranded with no direct local flights. Now the picture seems to be changing again as new operators step in to fill the gaps.

There are a few smallish airports in Brittany, but at present they handle few direct international flights. To get there by air from long-haul destinations such as North America or Australasia you generally have to route your journey via Paris, France's main air-gate, and take a connecting domestic flight. Lyon, Marseille, Nice and Nantes also have internal air-links with Brittany. However, it may be cheaper to fly to London and continue your journey from there.

Most flights from long-haul destinations will be routed via Paris

- From the UK, there are a few direct scheduled flights to Brittany. Low-cost airline Flybe currently operates to Brest and Rennes from Southampton and several other UK airports. Ryanair operates from London to Dinard. Channel Island operator Aurigny also flies to Dinard from various UK locations via Jersey and Guernsey. British Airways and Air France both fly directly from London to Nantes, an easy distance from southern Brittany with good rail connections. There's an Aer Arann flight to Lorient from Galway and Waterford in Ireland. Charter flights also use these and various other smaller airports in northwestern France.
- Paris has three airports. Busiest and most widely used for international traffic is Roissy–Charles de Gaulle, 23km (14 miles) from the heart of the city. It has three terminals, all efficiently connected with each other and with

AIRPORTS AND PORTS

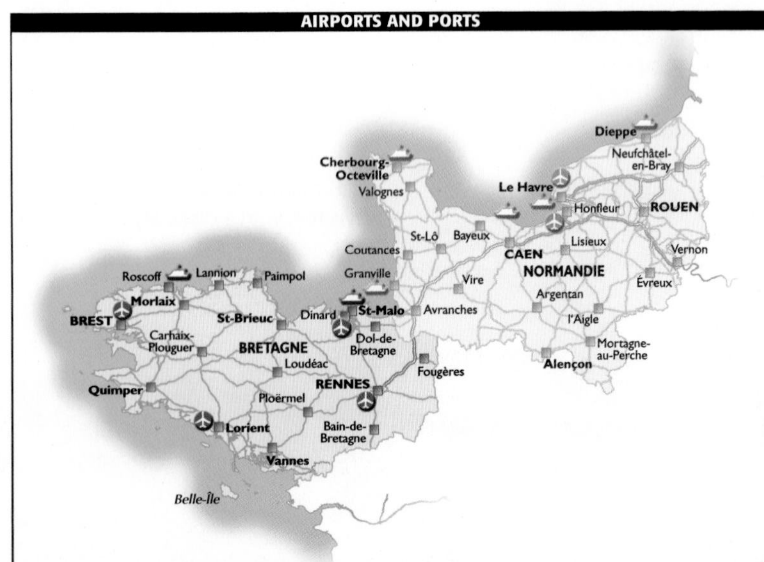

central Paris and its main railway stations by bus or train (RER Line B). The smaller Orly airport, 14km (8.5 miles) south of central Paris, takes mainly domestic but also some international flights. Its two terminals are linked by bus and train with central Paris, and also Gare Montparnasse, from which trains depart for Brittany. Beauvais Tillé airport is a much smaller and more remote airport 90km (56 miles) north of Paris. It is used by a few low-cost airlines, including Ryanair.

- From Paris, internal flights with Brit Air (Air France's domestic subsidiary) serve the Breton airports of Brest, Lannion, Lorient, Quimper and Rennes.
- It is generally more convenient, just as quick, and almost certainly cheaper to continue your onward journey to Brittany by train or rental car from a Parisian airport. Brittany is about a 3-hour drive from Paris; the quickest route is via the A11 to Le Mans (Autoroute de l'Ouest), then the A81 and N157 to Rennes.
- Exceptionally low fares generally imply some degree of inconvenience in terms of flight times, baggage allowances or airport location. Check whether prices quoted include departure tax, fuel surcharges, and what penalties are involved if you have to change your booking.

AIRPORT CONTACTS

General airport information	www.worldairportguide.com	
Information on all French airports	www.aeroport.fr or www.frenchairports.com	
PARIS		
Roissy–Charles de Gaulle	01 48 62 22 80	www.adp.fr
Paris Orly	01 49 75 15 15	www.adp.fr
Beauvais Tillé	0892 682 066	www.aeroportbeauvais.com
Orlybus	01 40 02 32 94	
Paris Métro and RER information	0892 687 714	www.ratp.fr
Air France bus to Paris	0892 350 820	www.cars-airfrance.com
BRITTANY		
Taxi fares are approximations, and vary greatly between midweek and weekend, and day and evening.		
Brest–Guipavas	02 98 32 01 00	(9km/5.6 miles NE; Bibus No. 24–Place de la Liberté; taxi about €17)
Dinard–Pleurtuit	02 99 46 18 46	(5km/3 miles SW on D168; TIV bus links from Dinard and St-Malo railway station; taxi fare about €15 to Dinard, or € 25 to St-Malo)
Lannion–Trégor	02 96 05 82 22	(4km/2.5 miles N on Trégastel road; CAT bus No. 15; taxi fare about €10)
Lorient-Lann-Bihoué	02 97 87 21 50	(10km/6 miles NW; CTRL bus; taxi fare €15–20)
Quimper–Cornouaille	02 98 94 30 30	(7km/4 miles SW; QUB bus No. 25 towards Ti Lipig; taxi fare €18)
Rennes–St-Jacques-de-la-Lande	02 99 29 60 00	(6km/4 miles SW on D777; bus No. 57–Place de la République; taxi fare €15)
PAYS DE LA LOIRE		
Nantes–Atlantique	02 40 84 80 00	(12km/7 miles SW; TAN AIR bus service connects with main flights from railway station/Place du Commerce; taxi fare €25)

ON THE MOVE

By Rail

EUROSTAR

- From London, up to 16 Eurostar trains per day pass through the Channel Tunnel into France. Journey time to Paris (Gare du Nord) is 2 hours 35 minutes on the fastest services. St. Pancras will take over from Waterloo as the London Eurostar terminal in 2007.
- Some trains stop en route at Ashford (UK), Calais–Fréthun (France) and Lille, where the line splits, one branch heading for Brussels, the other for Paris.

Onward Travel

- To travel to Britanny, leave the Eurostar at Lille and catch a high-speed TGV Atlantique Ouest connection directly to Rennes (3 hours 50 minutes) or Quimper (6 hours 50 minutes). This will save you the bother and expense of crossing Paris.
- If you are travelling through Paris, trains to Brittany depart from Paris's Gare Montparnasse. From Gare du Nord, take Métro Line 4 (Porte d'Orléans) to Montparnasse-Bienvenue.

The world-renowned TGV

By Car

If you are taking your car from the UK to France you can either catch a ferry to a choice of ports on France's northwestern coast or take the Eurotunnel shuttle train through the Channel Tunnel. Driving to France from neighbouring countries on mainland Europe is straightforward on a comprehensive system of *autoroutes* (motorways).

FERRIES

Numerous cross-Channel ferries link France with the UK. To reach Brittany by sea, you must first decide whether you prefer a short crossing to Dunkirk, Calais or Boulogne, followed by a lengthy road journey through France, or a longer ferry route across the western Channel directly to a Breton port.

- It is generally a little cheaper to take a short crossing and drive down. For obvious reasons the longer sea crossings are more expensive, but don't forget you save time and energy, as well as the cost of fuel, motorway tolls, meals en route and possibly an overnight stop. From Dunkirk, Calais or Boulogne, allow 5–6 hours to reach the Brittany border, using motorways where possible.
- The cost of crossings varies widely depending on time, day and month of travel, but fares are generally lower if you book well in advance. You may get an additional discount by booking online. You must pay in full by the booking deadline to qualify for any cheap fares.
- Look out for special offers, and good-value minibreak deals for stays of limited duration (for example five- or nine-night stays). Expect to pay somewhere between £50–£100 standard return for a car plus up to five passengers on a short crossing and anywhere between £150–£350 on a longer crossing. Inexpensive ferry deals are sometimes advertised in British newspapers.

• Ferry Savers 0870 990 8492; www.ferrysavers.com can book crossings with all the principal operators.

- Before setting off, telephone or check websites to confirm any last-minute change of sailing time, as printed ferry brochures may not always be up to date. Most companies require you to check in at least 45 minutes before departure, although extra security checks may mean you have to arrive earlier. In any case, allow plenty of time. Don't fill your fuel tank to the brim just before boarding. Have your tickets or reservation number and passport handy when you reach the check-in barrier.
- Modern ferries are efficiently stabilized for a smooth ride; many have been upgraded or refurbished and are usually bright and comfortable. All have on-board shops, bars, cafés or restaurants, exchange facilities, telephones, recreational areas and lounges. You can pay for anything you need in either sterling or euros (check exchange rates), or by credit card. All carry vehicles as well as passengers, but LPG vehicles may be excluded for safety reasons.
- Access to the car decks is restricted during the crossing, so make sure you take everything you need during the voyage (including some warm clothing if you want a breath of air on the outer decks). Don't leave valuables in your car. Lock up with the car in gear and the handbrake on, but don't engage the alarm system if you have one fitted. Before you leave your vehicle, take note of which car deck you are parked on, and which door or stairway is your nearest access point.
- It is worth reserving a cabin to ensure a decent rest if you are taking a lengthy overnight crossing to St-Malo or Roscoff. A basic two-berth cabin costs around

One of Brittany's many busy ferry ports

FERRY CONTACT DETAILS		
Brittany Ferries	08705 360 360 (UK)	www.brittany-ferries.com
Condor Ferries	0845 345 2000	www.condorferries.co.uk
Hoverspeed	0870 524 0241 (UK)	www.hoverspeed.com
Irish Ferries	01 610 511 (Ireland)	www.irishferries.com
Norfolkline	0870 870 1020	www.norfolkline.com
P&O Ferries	08705 20 20 20 (UK)	www.poferries.com
Seafrance	08705 711 711 (UK)	www.seafrance.com
SpeedFerries	0871 222 7456	www.speedferries.com
Transmanche Ferries	0800 917 1201	www.transmancheferries.com

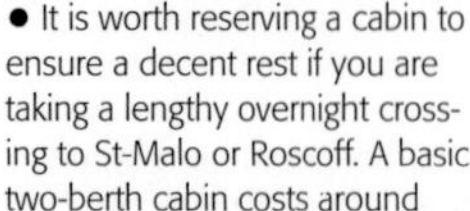

Autoroute toll roads are indicated by a Péage sign

£40 extra. All are well designed with comfortable bunk beds, private bathroom and clothes hanging space.

TAKING YOUR PET

UK visitors are allowed to take cats and dogs to France, subject to compliance with the DEFRA PETS scheme. You need the following documentation:

- Before setting off—a valid DEFRA-approved pet passport or veterinary certificate showing that your pet has been microchipped, vaccinated and blood-tested for rabies antibodies (allow at least seven months before travel to arrange all this).
- On your return—a valid DEFRA-approved pet passport or certificate showing that your animal has been treated against ticks and fox tapeworm not less than 24 hours and not more than 48 hours before returning to the UK. The timing of your return journey is therefore critical.
- Animals are not allowed on ferry passenger decks and must remain in your vehicle. Allow good ventilation and plenty of bedding. Escorted visits to the car deck may be made at specified times during the voyage.
- If documentation is not in order, your pet could be refused re-entry to the UK and placed in quarantine at your expense.

SAILING ROUTES

All sailing times are approximate and may take longer in bad weather.

- Norfolkline operates from Dover to Dunkirk (journey time 2 hours). If you don't mind the extra driving time and distance, this no-frills service is very good value, but don't forget the cost of additional motorway tolls.
- P&O Ferries and SeaFrance sail from Dover to Calais (journey time 70 to 90 minutes). The Hoverspeed catamaran cuts the journey to 50 minutes, although it is more prone to cancellations owing to bad weather.
- SpeedFerries operates a new fastcraft service between Dover and Boulogne (journey time 50 minutes), with startlingly competitive fares. An extra ferry on this route should reduce delays and cancellations due to technical problems.
- Transmanche Ferries operates a year-round conventional ferry service (journey time 4 hours) between Newhaven and Dieppe.
- Brittany Ferries sails from Portsmouth to Caen (journey time 6 hours); from Poole to Cherbourg (journey time 4 hours 15 minutes; Fastcraft 2 hours 15 minutes, summer only); from Portsmouth to St-Malo (journey time 8 hours 45 minutes); and from Plymouth to Roscoff (journey time 6 hours)
- Condor Ferries operates seasonal sailings between Weymouth/Poole and St-Malo via Jersey and Guernsey (journey time 4 hours 30 minutes)
- Irish Ferries sails from

Many visitors prefer the freedom of driving in Brittany

Cork/Rosslare to Roscoff (journey time around 12 hours).

EUROTUNNEL

Eurotunnel is a shuttle train transporting vehicles and passengers from one end of the Channel Tunnel to the other.

- The UK terminal of the Channel Tunnel lies between Dover and Folkestone. Leave the M20 at junction 11A and follow the signs.
- Drive your vehicle on to the shuttle train as directed, and you will be whisked under the Channel in just 35 minutes to the French terminal at Coquelles, near Calais.
- Eurotunnel shuttle trains depart up to five times per hour, 24 hours a day, 365 days a year; the price is charged per vehicle (reserve ahead). LPG and CNG vehicles are not currently allowed on Eurotunnel services.
- French border controls take place on the UK side, saving time when you arrive in Calais.
- You are advised to stay with your vehicle during the journey, although you can go to the toilet or walk about within the air-conditioned carriage. During the journey you can listen to the on-board radio station. Staff are available if you need any help. If you want to sit inside your vehicle, open the windows to minimize the effects of pressure changes within the carriage.

Open-top motoring through a scenic country route

Onward Travel

- The quickest way to reach Brittany from Calais is to take the A29 towards Le Havre, avoiding Rouen. South of the Seine, the A13 takes you to Caen, and from here the A84 (known as the Autoroute des Estuaires) leads on to Rennes.
- You will have to pay *autoroute* charges (a *Péage* sign will warn that you're approaching a toll road). There is a hefty toll to cross the massive Pont de Normandie suspension bridge near Le Havre (have your euros ready; cards are not accepted). You can, of course, avoid motorway charges altogether by sticking to alternative and possibly more scenic routes, for example along the coast. Roads in Brittany are all toll-free.

Eurotunnel contact details
08705 35 35 35 (UK)

MAIN ROAD NETWORK

GETTING AROUND

Driving in northwest France

Driving is the best way, indeed the only practical way, to tour rural areas of Brittany in any reasonable time-span. It is less enjoyable in larger cities such as Brest, where the traffic is heavy, the one-way systems confusing and parking sometimes difficult and expensive. Coastal resorts can also present driving headaches in high season. The roads in France are always dreadfully busy at the beginning of the summer school holidays (mid-July), and again when the holidays end at the beginning of September *(la grande rentrée)*. Try to avoid travelling during these periods.

BRINGING YOUR OWN CAR

Legal Requirements

- Private vehicles registered in another country can be taken into France for up to six months without customs formalities.
- You must always carry the following documentation: a current passport or national ID card, a full (not provisional), valid national driver's licence (even if you have an International Driving Permit), a certificate of motor insurance, and the vehicle's registration document (as well as a letter of authorization from the owner if the vehicle is not registered in your name).
- Check your motor insurance is valid for driving in France, and against damage in transit, for example on the train or ferry when your car is not being driven. Third-party motor insurance is the minimum requirement in France but fully comprehensive cover is strongly advised.
- Spot checks take place and you may be asked to produce your documents at any time. To avoid a police fine and/or confiscation of your car, be sure that your papers are in order.
- Display an international sticker or distinguishing sign plate as near as possible to the national registration plate at the rear of your car. If you don't, you risk an on-the-spot fine. Since March 2001 registration plates (Euro-Plates) displaying the Euro-symbol of an EU country mean displaying a conventional sticker or plate is unnecessary when driving in the EU, but it is always safer to display one.

CAR RENTAL COMPANIES

Company	Telephone number	Website
Avis	0820 050 505	www.avis.com
Budget	0825 003 564	www.budget.com
Europcar	0825 352 352	www.europcar.com
Hertz	01 41 91 95 25	www.hertz.com
Sixt	0820 007 498	www.sixt.com

- To avoid dazzling oncoming drivers you should adjust the headlights of left-hand-drive vehicles for driving on the right. On older cars, use simple headlamp beam converters that stick onto the glass. But don't use these on cars with halogen headlamps—check in your car handbook or with your dealer. If your vehicle has Xenon or High Intensity Discharge (HID) headlamps, check with your dealer, who may need to make the adjustment.
- Don't forget to remove the beam converters (a good time to do this is while you're waiting in the homebound ferry queue) or have your headlamps reset as soon as you return home.

Breakdown Cover

If you are taking your own car, make sure you have adequate breakdown cover for your trip to France. For information on AA breakdown cover, call 0800 444 500 or visit www.theAA.com.

RENTING A CAR

- Most major car rental agencies have offices at airports, main railway stations and in large towns and cities throughout France.
- Renting a car in France can be expensive due to high taxes. Arranging a fly-drive package through a tour operator or airline from home is generally a less expensive option. SNCF, the national railway company, has inclusive train and car-rental deals from mainline stations.
- To be able to rent a car in France you must be at least 20 years old and have held a full driver's licence for at least a year. However, some companies either do not rent to, or else add a surcharge for, drivers under the age of 25. The maximum age limit varies, but the average is 70.
- You will have to show your licence and passport or national ID card.
- Your rental agreement should include the following: unlimited mileage, comprehensive insurance cover, theft protection, 24-hour emergency roadside assistance, a replacement vehicle if the one you have rented becomes unusable.

- Some agencies include mileage in the cost but others may charge you extra above a certain distance, so check before you rent.
- Most international rental companies will let you return your car to other French cities, and even other countries, but there may be an extra charge for this. Always agree the drop-off point with the company first.
- Make sure you have adequate insurance and that you are aware of what you are covered for in the event of an accident.
- Bear in mind that low-cost operators may have an extremely high excess charge for damage to the vehicle.
- If your car breaks down on an *autoroute*, look for emergency telephones on the roadside. You can contact the breakdown services from here.

ROAD SIGNS

No entry except for buses and taxis

Road-toll pay station

A sign with the road number above

Speed limits for various road types, in kph

Give way to traffic

Parking 150m to the left

Parking only for those with disabilities

No left turn

A local directional sign

GENERAL DRIVING

Roads

- The *autoroute* is the French counterpart of the British motorway or American expressway and is marked by an 'A' on maps and road signs. A few sections around key cities or ports may be free of charge, but tolls are charged on the rest *(autoroutes à péage)*. Tolls are expensive but may well be worth the saving in time and energy. Always have some cash available as foreign credit cards may not be accepted at toll-booths. For information on *autoroute* conditions throughout France call 01 47 05 90 01 or look at www.autoroutes.fr.
- Brittany has hardly any official motorways except for a short stretch of the A84, which has now extended as far as Rennes from Caen in Normandy. Brittany has not yet introduced any road-charging schemes.
- Other roads in Brittany may be almost as fast and efficient as motorways, though major routes all tend to run east–west. The next level in France's road hierarchy is occupied by trunk roads or *routes nationales* (code-marked N). The fastest of these key routes are dual carriageways (divided highways) called *voies express*, notably Brittany's N12 (Rennes–Brest) and N165 (Brest–Nantes). The next grade of road is the *route départementale* (D), often surprisingly wide and fast. Minor rural lanes are labelled as C roads, ideal for leisurely jaunts in search of picturesque scenery or a picnic spot.
- Beware of traffic-calming measures, particularly as you approach built-up areas along a fast road. Road humps or ramps (signed *passage surélevé*) are much-used ways of making you slow down in Brittany.

The Law

- In France you drive on the right *(serrez à droite)*.
- The minimum age to drive is 18, although to rent a car you must be at least 20.
- In built-up areas vehicles should give way to traffic coming from the right *(Priorité à droite)*, unless signs advise otherwise. At roundabouts (traffic circles) with signs saying *Cédez le passage* or *Vous n'avez pas la priorité*, traffic already on the roundabout has priority. On roundabouts without signs, traffic entering has priority. A priority road can also be shown by a white diamond-shaped sign with a yellow diamond within it. A black line through the diamond indicates the end of priority. A red-bordered triangle with a black cross on a white background, with the words *passage protegé*, also shows priority.
- Holders of EU driver's licences who exceed the speed limit by more than 25kph (16mph) may have their licences confiscated by the police on the spot.
- You must wear a seatbelt.

Children under 10 must travel in the back, with a booster seat, except for babies under nine months with a specially adapted rear-facing front seat (but not in cars with airbags).
• Do not overtake where there is a solid single central line on the road.
• There are harsh penalties if the level of alcohol in the blood is 0.05 per cent or more. If you drink, don't drive.
• You must always stop completely at STOP signs, or you may be fined.

Road signs
• Road signs are split into three categories. Triangular signs with a red border are warnings, circular signs are mandatory (such as speed limits or No Entry) and square signs display text information. In rural Brittany, you may still find a few old-fashioned signs hewn from granite.
• Common signs include: *déviation* (diversion), *attention travaux* (roadworks), *sortie* (exit), *gravillons* (loose chippings), *chaussée déformée* (uneven road and temporary surface) and *nids de poules* (potholes).
• Before you take to the road, familiarize yourself with the French highway code on www.legifrance.gouv.fr .
• For more information on road signs see www.permisenligne.com.

Equipment
• Carry a red warning triangle in case you break down. Don't rely simply on hazard warning lights.
• Keep a spare-bulb kit in the car, as it is illegal to drive with faulty lights.
• It's worth stowing a parking 'clock' in your glove box; in certain areas you are allowed to park free of charge for a limited period, so you have to show what time you arrived.
• Take plenty of cloths or tissues (paper napkins or towels from cafés or service stations come in handy) to mop insects or mud off your lights and windscreen.

A parking meter (horodateur)

Fuel
• Fuel *(essence)* comes as unleaded (95 and 98 octane), lead replacement petrol (LRP or supercarburant), diesel (*gasoil* or *gazole*) and LPG.
• Many filling stations close on Sundays and at 6pm the rest of the week. You may find it difficult to locate a 24-hour station and some automatic dispensing machines may not accept foreign credit cards.
• Prices are highest at filling stations on *autoroutes*, and lowest at large chain supermarkets such as Leclerc or Intermarché. Fuel charges are very similar to those in the UK, so there is no great advantage in filling up on one side of the Channel rather than the other.

Parking
• Authorized parking spaces are indicated by road markings (white dotted lines). Blue markings, or those marked *Payant*, indicate a charge is due. Watch out for any signs indicating parking restrictions. Parking attendants are sometimes lenient with foreign vehicles in tourist areas, but don't push your luck!
• Charges usually apply from about 9am to 6.30pm, Monday to Saturday. Sometimes there's a free period at lunchtime (12.30–2). Sundays and holidays are generally free, but always check before parking your car. In certain popular holiday areas or tourist attractions, parking charges are imposed only in high season.
• To pay for parking, buy a timed ticket from a meter *(horodateur)* at the side of the road and display it in your car. Some towns operate on an honesty system and allow you some free time, but you must display a 'clock' showing when you arrived. You can get these in local shops or *tabacs*—or at the tourist office.

Car Breakdown
• If your car breaks down on an *autoroute*, look for an emergency telephone along the roadside that will connect you with the breakdown services.
• If you break down on the Paris *périphérique* or an *autoroute*, you must call the police or the official breakdown service operating in that area, rather than your own breakdown/insurance company.

Road Conditions
• To find out about traffic conditions, for example on the congested coastal routes in high season, visit www.bison-fute.equipement.gouv.fr (in French only). Queues can build up, particularly at weekends or towards the end of the day when people leave the beaches.
• For the National Road Information Centre (voice service in French) call 0836 682 000.
• For road conditions on *autoroutes* call 0892 681 077.
• For information on road conditions, call 0826 022 022.
• Autoroute FM provides useful and up-to-date traffic bulletins on the radio.

Maps
Good quality regional maps are invaluable in planning a trip. The AA (UK) publishes four France atlases as well as a series of France sheet maps. The AA website, www.theAA.com, has a helpful route planner. Most tourist offices can provide a local map free of charge.

Other ways to get around

Driving may be the most convenient way to tour Brittany, but if you are without a car there are other reliable ways to see at least the region's larger towns. Even if you have a car, you may sometimes wish to leave it at home and make a trip by train, bus or boat.

TRAINS

In general, France has excellent trains—fast, comfortable and usually on time. France's state railway, the Société Nationale des Chemins de Fer (SNCF), runs the services. These include Grandes Lignes (mainline routes) such as the ultra-modern, high-speed TGV (Train à Grande Vitesse) which can operate at speeds of up to 300kph/186mph, and Corail (fast intercity trains). TER trains (Trains Express Régionaux) operate on regional journeys. That said, the rail network in Brittany is not especially extensive, and while you can reach the main towns easily by train, many smaller places are served infrequently, if at all.

Tickets

- Fares are split into blue (normal) and red (peak). Reduced-rate fares are generally available for normal travel on mainline routes, excluding TGV and *couchette* services.
- Ticket prices vary according to the level of comfort (first or second class) and departure time. First class fares are roughly 50 per cent more expensive than second class.
- You can buy tickets in the stations, at SNCF offices or *boutiques*, which you'll find in major cities like Rennes or Brest, and through some travel agents. Tickets for TGV trains must be reserved. You can do this up to a few minutes before departure, although in peak season it is best to book well in advance. *Couchettes* must be booked at least 75 minutes before the train leaves its first station.
- Make sure you stamp your ticket *(composter)* in the orange machines on the platforms before you start your journey. You risk a fine if you forget.
- If you are under 26, you can get a 25 per cent discount (called Découverte 12–25) on train travel. Seniors also receive discounts (Découverte Senior).
- When you travel second class, there are lower rates for booking more than eight days in advance (ask for Découverte J8) and more than 30 days in advance (ask for Découverte J30).
- Ticket machines, with instructions in English, accept notes, coins and credit cards. They can also be used to collect tickets you have ordered on the internet, by telephone or Minitel.
- Once you are in France it may be difficult to change reservations made abroad.

Station Assistance

- If you need assistance or a porter, look for a member of the station staff, identifiable by their red waistcoats.
- You need a €1 coin deposit to use the luggage trolleys (carts).
- Some stations have a left-luggage office or coin-operated lockers, but security measures may mean this facility is not available. Electronic locks issue a printed ticket with a code number. You'll need to keep this ticket for when you return to collect your items.

Understanding Railway Timetables

- You can pick up free timetables *(horaires)* at stations, at tourist offices, or at SNCF offices or agencies.
- There are two styles of timetable: One for the Grandes Lignes, covering high-speed TGV and other mainline services, and another for the regional TER trains.
- Be prepared to decipher French railway terminology. On Grandes Lignes timetables, two rows of boxed numbers at the top refer to the *numéro de train* (train number) and to the *notes à consulter* (footnotes). In TER timetables, the train number is not listed.
- Footnotes at the bottom explain when a particular train runs *(circule)*. *Tous les jours* means it runs every day; *sauf dimanche et fêtes* means it doesn't run on Sundays and holidays. *Jusqu'au*, followed by a date, indicates the service runs only up until that date.

Other information

- Timetable, fare and service information is available from SNCF train stations, ticket outlets and travel agencies, by telephone (tel 08 91 67 68 69;

Brittany is an ideal destination for family cycling holidays

24 hours; 20.23c per minute), the internet or Minitel.

- A booklet called *Le Guide du Voyageur* gives you the A–Z (in French) of just about all you need to know on French railway travel (available at tourist offices, station booking offices).

BUSES

- Buses in Brittany cover a much wider network of destinations than the trains, but most individual routes are quite short. Buses are slightly less expensive than trains, and journey times are sometimes just as quick, but in rural parts of Brittany services may be infrequent, erratic or very seasonal.
- Réseau Penn-ar-Bed, which organizes all long-distance bus (coach) travel throughout Finistère, has recently introduced a flat-fare system of just €2 for any distance, with the exception of the Quimper–Brest route.
- A handy booklet called *Guide Envie*, available free from any tourist office, summarizes public transport systems throughout Brittany (road, rail and sea) with colour-coded maps indicating the main routes.
- Bus or coach stations *(gares routières)* are often located close to railway stations, and some attempt is made to co-ordinate train and bus services. Smaller towns without train stations are often linked by bus to the nearest railway station. These buses are sometimes operated by SNCF as a replacement for uneconomic rail services. Rail passes are valid on most SNCF buses, but check before you travel. For information on SNCF-run buses, telephone 0891 676 869 (24-hour service).
- Bus transport within cities is generally excellent and inexpensive (▷ 32–3), whereas rural areas are much less well served. Many routes operate largely for the benefit of schoolchildren or commuters rather than visitors, with long gaps during the day or complete breaks in holiday periods.

- You can generally buy tickets for short distances on board, but for longer journeys, buy tickets in advance at the bus station to reserve a seat.

TAXIS

- Taking a taxi is not the most cost-effective way of getting about but it may be the only convenient (or perhaps the only) option.
- The fare consists of an initial pick-up charge plus a charge per kilometre, (0.6 miles), and any extra charges for luggage and journeys during the evening or on Sundays. All taxis use a meter *(compteur)*.
- The best way to find a taxi is to head to a taxi stand, marked by a blue Taxis sign (often near railway stations, ferry terminals or main squares).
- Some taxis accept bank cards, but it is best to have cash available. It is usual to leave a tip of around 10 per cent.
- If you want a receipt, ask for *un reçu*.

BOATS

Boat travel is an important way of getting around in Brittany. Some island ferry links are maintained all year round, but pleasure excursions are mostly seasonal, between Easter and October.

BY BICYCLE

France is an exceptionally attractive destination for keen cyclists, and nowhere more so than Brittany, with plenty of glorious, diverse countryside, not too many mountains, and good facilities. Tourist offices supply maps and touring guides specifically for bicyclists, and there are lots of places to rent or repair a bicycle. Bicycles can be taken on most trains, generally free of charge (check the SNCF website for details).

BOAT RENTAL COMPANIES

Armor Excursions 02 98 61 79 66
trips from Roscoff around Morlaix Bay and to Île de Batz.

Batobus 02 97 21 28 29 **www.ctrl.fr**
Rade de Lorient to Port-Louis, Gâvres, Lorient, Locmiquélic and Larmor-Plage.

Vedettes de l'Odet 02 98 57 00 58
www.vedettes-odet.com
Excursions on the Odet from Bénodet, Concarneau, Loctudy, La Forêt-Fouesnant, Fouesnant, Quimper. Glass-bottomed boat trips to the Îles de Glénan.

Compagnie Finistérienne de Transports Maritimes (CFTM)
02 98 61 78 87
www.vedettes-ile-de-batz.com
Île de Batz, and the Morlaix bay from Morlaix and Roscoff.

Compagnie Corsaire 08 25 13 80 35
www.compagniecorsaire.com
Ferry link between St-Malo and Dinard. Excursions around the bay of St-Malo and the Îles Chausey.

Compagnie Penn Ar Bed 02 98 80 80 80 **www.pennarbed.fr**
The islands of Ouessant, Molène and Sein from Brest, Le Conquet and Audierne.

Navix 08 25 16 21 00
www.navix.fr
Golfe du Morbihan (Île aux Moines, Île d'Arz), Belle-Île, Houat from Vannes (Conleau), Port-Navalo, La Trinité-sur-Mer, Locmariaquer, Auray, Bono.

Société Morbihannaise de Navigation
0820 056 000 **www.smn-navigation.fr**
Belle-Île and the islands of Groix, Houat and Hoëdic from Quiberon and Lorient.

Getting around in Brittany's cities

Even Brittany's largest cities are modest in size compared with, say, Paris or Lyon, but they can still be confusing and harassing for motorists. However, most have excellent bus and train links to other bases in the region, along with exemplary networks of internal public transport. The areas most visitors want to see are generally quite compact, and manageable mainly on foot.

RENNES

A 20-minute stroll through the old town will take you to virtually all the city sights, largely on traffic-free streets. The main museums, however, lie on the noisier and more modern south bank, while the bus and railway stations are a lengthy trudge south. The tourist office just off quai Duguay can provide maps of the town and local transport, or you can pick one up at a Métro station. The modern buses and Métro (subway) system are both managed by the same company, called STAR. Tickets are valid on either system.

Métro Rennes is the only Breton town with a Métro system, known locally as Le VAL. Introduced in March 2002, it consists of just one line and 15 stations. Of these only three or so are likely to interest many visitors. These are Ste-Anne (at the north end of the old town, handy for Place des Lices), Place de la République (at the heart of the modern city), and Gares (near the bus and railway stations). Each station is designed by a different architect and reflects some aspect of local character. Tickets cost €1, and are valid for one hour on local STAR buses as well as Métro trains. You must validate your ticket in a machine at the start of your journey. A day ticket costs €3; a carnet of 10 tickets €9.20. The Rennes Métro is entirely non-smoking, and allegedly wheelchair-friendly (although the lifts were out of action on inspection). No pets are allowed.

Buses Buses operate every day on about 40 routes until late at night. You can buy tickets on board, or in one of the Métro stations. The STAR office is at 12 rue du Pré Botté (just south of the main post office on Place de la République; tel 02 99 79 37 37; www.star.fr). Bus No. 17 takes you to the railway and out-of-town bus stations from Place de la République; bus 57 goes to the airport from here. One sight you may want to reach by public transport is the Ecomusée du Pays de Rennes, some distance south of the city. Take the Métro (direction Poterie) as far as Triangle, then bus No. 61 to the stop called Le Hil Bintinais.

Taxis Taxi ranks can be found at the railway station, on Place de la République and by the town hall; tel 02 99 30 79 79 (Taxis Rennais).

Bicycles Rennes obligingly lets you borrow a bicycle free of charge for the day (though you have to leave a refundable deposit of €76). Contact Vélo Adshel, Pont de Nemours (a kiosk opposite Galeries Lafayette, parking de la Vilaine); tel 0820 808 808; open 9–7. Or you can rent one at Cycle Guédard, 13 boulevard Beaumont; tel 02 99 30 43 78.

BREST

This sprawling, reconstituted city has many industrial suburbs, but the bits most people want to see in Brest are mainly around the old port and the castle, easily walkable (if a bit hilly) towards the tourist office on Place de la Liberté at the top of rue de Siam. The commercial and naval docks spread a long way in both directions from the castle, and the waterfront is not easy to follow on foot because of access restrictions and juggernaut container lorries. Brest's splendid aquarium, Océanopolis, is best reached by bus.

Buses Brest has an excellent local bus network called Bibus Tickets cost €1, a carnet costs €8.30 and a day-pass €3. You can buy tickets on the buses. A ticket lasts an hour after you stamp it in the machine on the bus. Most bus routes stop at Place de la Liberté. To reach Océanopolis and the pleasure port, some way east of the city, take bus Nos. 3 or 15. The nearby Botanic Gardens (Conservatoire Botanique) can be reached by Nos. 25 or 27 (to Route de Quimper). Buses run from 6am until 10.40 pm (just after midnight on Friday, Saturday).
Bibus has an information kiosk at 33 avenue Georges-Clemenceau (Place de la Liberté); 02 98 80 30 30; www.bibus.fr.

Taxis You'll find taxi ranks at various convenient points around the city, such as at the station or on rue de Siam; call 02 98 80 43 43 (Radio Taxi Brestois) or 02 98 42 11 11 (Allo Taxi).

Bicycles Torch'VTT offers bicycle rental at 93 boulevard Montaigne; tel 02 98 46 06 07.

QUIMPER

Old Quimper is a pleasantly walkable place, though the riverbank thoroughfares take a lot of traffic, and there are some gradients. The historic old town lies just north of the River Odet. It's a 10-minute waterfront stroll on level ground past flower-decked bridges to Locmaria, where the ceramics museum and faïence factories are located.

Buses The local network is operated by QUB (Quimper Bus), which has an office at 2 quai de l'Odet; tel: 02 98 95 26 27. Route 32 goes near

Locmaria, though you still have a bit of a walk at the far end. All QUB's eight inner-city routes converge at Place de la Résistance near the tourist office, radiating out into the hilly suburbs on both sides of the river, which are not of great interest to most visitors. Buses 4 (direction Ty Bos) and 6 (direction Kerveguen) go past the out-of-town bus and railway stations.

Taxis Taxis generally congregate around the main bus terminal and parking area on the riverside, Place de la Résistance. To call one, tel 02 98 90 21 21 (Radio Taxi Quimperois), 02 98 52 07 72 (Allo Taxis), or 02 98 53 42 42 (Abassides).

Bicycles You can rent a bicycle from Torch'VTT at 5 rue de la Providence; tel 02 98 53 84 41 (about €15 per day).

VANNES

The old town of Vannes is only negotiable on foot, and it's unlikely you will make much use of public transport here. Other parts of the city you may wish to reach include Séné, Conleau and Port-Anna, on the Golfe du Morbihan, where boats take over from buses as the preferred mode of transport.

Buses Buses in and around Vannes are organized by TPV (Transports du Pays de Vannes), which has eight separate bus lines. Line 2 heads for Conleau via the port; Line 3 for the railway station to the north of the old town; Line 4 goes to Séné; Line 8 goes to the pleasant old village of Theix to the east. All buses terminate on Place de la République, just west of the walled town, and there are bus stops by the marina on Place Gambetta.
A more extensive network of TPV bus routes (*lignes périurbaines*) serves the greater Vannes area. Tickets lasting one hour cost €1.10, a mini-carnet of 4 tickets costs €4, and a carnet of 10

Le VAL in Rennes

costs €8.50 (children under 4 travel free). You can buy them from the driver, or in advance from local *tabacs*. A comprehensive timetable is available free at the tourist office, or from the bus information point Infobus TPV, on Place de la République; tel 02 97 01 22 23 (Monday–Friday 8.30–12.30, 1.30–6.30; Sat 8.30–12.30, 4–5); www.tpv.fr.

Boats Several companies operate from the Golfe du Parc or the Presqui'île de Conleau to various points around the Golfe du Morbihan, including the islands. (routes are summarized on page 31).

Taxis There are taxi ranks on Place Gambetta, Place de la République, and at Place de la Gare; tel 02 97 54 34 34 (GIE Radio Taxis Vannetais).

Bicycles Available from Cycles Le Mellac, 51 ter rue Jean Gougaud; tel 02 97 63 00 51 (about €14 per day).

LORIENT

If you are based here for any length of time, ask about the Passe-Partout inclusive tourist pass which gives you three days unlimited transport and a trip to the island of Groix. The area of most interest to visitors is by the pleasure port and submarine base of Kéroman. The best way to get about is by Batobus, a ferry system linking various points on either side of the Rade de Lorient (estuary). Services are summarized on page 31.

Buses, boats and bicycles Both Batobus (seven routes) and the local bus routes (22 lines) are organized by Compagnie des Transports de la Région Lorientaise (CTRL); a full bus/boat timetable, tickets and information are available by the port at the Boutique Transports, Gare d'Echanges, Cours de Chazelles; tel 02 97 21 28 29; www.ctrl.fr. The ticketing system is co-ordinated; tickets cost €1.15 and last an hour; a 10-ticket carnet costs €9.70 and a day pass €3.50. Buses run until 8pm; boats run every 30 minutes or so Mon–Sat 6.45–8, Sun/hols 10–7. CTRL routes cover the whole of the Blavet estuary area, including Port-Louis and Hennebont/Izinzac (Lines H, J, L), Larmor-Plage and Pont-Scorff (Line A).
CTRL also arranges bicycle rental at the same office at very cheap rates (€6.90 per day, plus a refundable deposit of €100). The office is open Tuesday–Friday 8–6.30, Monday, Saturday 9.30–12.30, 2.40–5.30).

Taxis Available down by the port; tel 02 97 21 29 29 (Radio Taxi Lorientais, 27 boulevard de Normandie).

ST-BRIEUC

This city is not much of a tourist attraction and it is unlikely you will base yourself here. Its historic heart is manageable on foot. St-Brieuc does, however, have an efficient bus service organized by TUB (Transport Urbains Briochins), so if you need to get about locally (for example to the port or local beaches), obtain a full timetable from the office on Place Duguesclin; tel 02 96 33 47 42, or ask at the tourist office.

Taxis Tel 02 96 94 70 70 (Armor Griffons); 02 96 78 39 24 (Daniel Houée) or 02 96 33 83 17 (Christian Le Potier)

VISITORS WITH A DISABILITY

Getting around France is gradually becoming easier, thanks to the improved design of buses and trains. Any recently constructed public building, including airports and stations, will have facilities for people with disabilities and mobility problems. But you'll still find challenges when getting around Brittany, especially in historic towns with narrow, cobbled streets.

Before you travel, check what facilities are available, for example, at your arrival airport (www.aeroport.fr) and your hotel; many older buildings do not have an elevator. If you have mobility problems and may require help during a flight, tell your airline when you reserve your ticket. You may also find useful information on individual airline websites. The easiest way for visitors with disabilities to reach France from Britain is by using Eurotunnel, where you can remain in a vehicle for the whole journey. If you are taking a ferry, make sure you arrive well in advance so that you can have help with boarding.

AIRPORTS

In Paris, both Roissy–Charles de Gaulle and Orly airports are well equipped for people with reduced mobility. Shuttle buses between terminals have ramps for wheelchairs, as well as voice announcements for people with visual impairments. The terminals have adapted toilets, low-level telephones and reserved parking spaces. For more information, ask for the leaflet Guide–Passager à Mobilité Réduite (fax requests to: 01 49 75 58 78 or email: DCCMP3@adp.fr). Various organizations offer specialist services from the airports into Paris, which you'll need to reserve in advance, such as Airhop (tel 01 41 29 01 29).

For information on facilities at airports in Brittany, contact Aeroguides (tel 01 46 55 93 43; www.aeroguide.fr).

TRAINS

Eurostar trains and terminals are wheelchair-friendly and wheelchair-users can also benefit from discounted tickets. France's long-distance trains are equipped for people with reduced mobility. On TGV and Corail trains, spaces for wheelchair-users are reserved in first class, although only a second-class fare is payable. Reserve at least 24 hours in advance. There are also adapted toilets. Most large stations have elevators or ramps to the platform. If you need assistance, request it when you reserve your ticket.

Facilities on regional trains tend to be more varied—check before you travel. For more information, call 0800 154 753, look up SNCF's website (www.sncf.com), or see the pamphlet Mémento du Voyageur à Mobilité Réduite.

USEFUL ORGANIZATIONS

Organization	Telephone	Website
Association des Paralysés de France	01 40 78 69 (Paris)	**www.apf.asso.fr**
This French organization for the disabled is represented in each *département*. See the website for more information on local facilities.		
Holiday Care Service	08451 249 971 (UK)	**www.holidaycare.org.uk**
Travel and holiday information for people with disabilities.		
Mobile en Ville		**www.mobile-en-ville.asso.fr**
A website packed with information on disability access and related issues.		
Mobility International USA		**www.miusa.org**
Promotes international travel and exchange schemes for people with disabilities.		
RADAR (Royal Association for Disability and Rehabilitation)	020 7250 3222	**www.radar.org.uk**
Literature on travelling with disabilities.		
Society for Accessible Travel and Hospitality (SATH)	212 447 7284 (fromUS)	**www.sath.org**
A US-based organization offering advice for visitors with disabilities and promoting awareness of their travel requirements.		
Tripscope	Tel 08457 585641 (UK)	**www.tripscope.org.uk**
Travel and transport information.		

Further information

See the website of the French tourist office for useful information on facilities for disabled visitors: www.franceguide.com. The French volume of a series called *Smooth Ride Guides* is available free of charge in English from the Maison de la France. This travel-planning handbook has been compiled with the co-operation of many disability organizations and tourist boards throughout France. Various venues, including airports, ferries, railways, museums, accommodation, are assessed for their user-friendliness for disabled visitors.

This chapter is divided into the four *départements* of Brittany, which are identified on the map on the inside front cover. Places of interest are listed alphabetically within each region, with the major sights listed on the opening page of each region. To locate all the sights, turn to the atlas on pages 197–211.

The Sights

MORBIHAN

The sandy beach resorts and islands of Brittany's Atlantic Coast are milder and sunnier than other parts of the region, which compensates for the less obviously photogenic coastal scenery. But Morbihan has no lack of physical drama. The *département* is named after its most startling geographical feature, the huge landlocked lagoon near Vannes (*mor-bihan* means 'little sea' in Breton), and the megalithic standing stones at Carnac and Locmariaquer attract visitors from far and wide.

MAJOR SIGHTS

The huge rock stacks of Aiguilles viewed from Port-Coton (above). The harbour in the busy fishing port of Sauzon (right)

BELLE-ÎLE-EN-MER

The largest of Brittany's islands lives up to its name, with glorious, varied scenery and many historic associations.

Belle-Île makes a perfect excursion from Quiberon, a 40-minute boat ride away (some 15km/9 miles due south). Its population rises to over 35,000 in summer, but never seems overcrowded. The western Côte Sauvage faces the full force of the Atlantic Ocean, and breakers pound its rugged cliffs. At one point Belle-Île was captured by British forces, but was exchanged for the island of Menorca in 1763. Towards the end of the 18th century a number of French Canadian families, reluctant to accept British rule, were resettled on Belle-Île. Many famous visitors, including actress Sarah Bernhardt, have since developed a lasting affection for this Breton outpost.

PORTS, MENHIRS AND BEACHES

The island's capital and main port, Le Palais, lies on the more sheltered eastern side. Excursion boats approach the harbour from the mainland beneath the ramparts of its star-shaped citadel, reinforced by Louis XIV's military strategist Vauban in 1682. The fortress, now privately owned and undergoing a lengthy restoration, contains the Musée Historique (tel 02 97 31 84 17; Jul, Aug daily 9–7; Apr–end Jun, Sep, Oct daily 9.30–6; Nov–end Mar daily 9.30–12, 2–5; adult €6.10, child 7–18 €3.05), tracing the island's past. Sauzon, Belle-Île's second port, is smaller but even prettier, a postcard scene of cottages painted in ice-cream hues, a toytown lighthouse and a harbour lined with fishing nets and crates of shellfish.

Interior landscapes range from treeless moorland to lush farmland, criss-crossed with footpaths and bicycle tracks. Here and there are prehistoric menhirs (standing stones); two in the northwest are known as Jean and Jeanne, lovers turned to stone as punishment for a pre-wedding night of passion. The coastline is pocked with caves and ringed with reef-strewn sandy beaches, some wild and exposed, others calm and sheltered. The 2km (1-mile) Plage des Grands Sables is one of the best for families. Port de Donnant on the west coast is popular with surfers, but is not for novice swimmers.

Don't miss The view of Les Aiguilles de Port-Coton, a series of sharp rocks off the western cliffs, was painted by Monet.

RATINGS

Historic interest	●●●
Outdoor pursuits	●●●●
Photo stops	●●●●

204 G14 Quai Bonnelle, BP30, 56360, tel 02 97 31 81 93; Mon–Sat 9–12.30, 2–6 Local buses run by Taol Mor (tel 02 97 31 32 32; Apr–end Sep, school hols); excursion coaches by Les Cars Bleus: tel 02 97 31 83 56 or Les Cars Verts: tel 02 97 31 81 88 Year-round ferry from Quiberon (tel 0820 056 000). Seasonal services from Lorient, Port-Navalo and La Turballe. Excursions from Belle-Île to the smaller islands of Houat and Hoëdic (Jul, Aug).

www.belle-ile.com

TIPS

- **You can get round Belle-Île by local bus (flat fare €2.50, child (4–12) €1.60; 10 ticket carnet €17, child €10), or rent a car, motor scooter or bicycle from Le Palais.**
- **Belle-Île's 100km (62 miles) of coastal footpaths are especially scenic, but some sections are risky (unstable cliffs and sea caves and paths are very slippery after rain). Escorted walks can be arranged with an experienced local guide. No bicycling is allowed on the coastal paths.**
- **Belle-Île has several riding stables, giving visitors another way to see the island.**

Carnac

Carnac shelters one of the most spectacular concentrations of prehistoric monuments in the world. Its seaside resort is purely for relaxation.

Carnac means 'the place where there are piles of stones'

A grand stone carving graces the entrance to Place de Église

The sandy seaside resort of Carnac-Plage

RATINGS

Good for kids	●●●●
Historic interest	●●●●●
Photo stops	●●●●
Beaches	●●●

BASICS

206 G13

The main office is in Carnac-Plage, 74 avenue des Druides, 56340, tel 02 97 52 13 52; Jul, Aug Mon–Sat 9–1, 2–7, Sun 2–7; Sep–end Jun Mon–Sat 9–12, 2–6. There's a seasonal office in Carnac-Ville, Place de l'Église; Apr–end Sep Mon–Sat 9–1, 2–7, Sun 2–7

TIM Line 1 runs from Vannes via Auray to Quiberon; Line 18 goes to Lorient. A local bus connects Carnac-Plage and Carnac town with the main *alignements* several times a day, Jun–end Sep

A *petit train* links Carnac-Plage with the *alignements* and La Trinité-sur-Mer in summer

www.carnac.fr
This is a sensible, informative site with an attractive, freeze-frame photo-montage; useful background on megaliths and resort facilities, an easy-to-follow calendar of events, tide tables and even the local weather forecast.

SEEING CARNAC

Carnac is a town of several parts. Its original core is an old village-like community known as Carnac-Ville. To the south, beyond a belt of saltmarsh lagoons, is Carnac-Plage, a modern seaside resort with five sandy beaches along the Baie de Quiberon. Facilities are excellent for families with children, and the resort is very busy in high season. But what most visitors want to see in Carnac are the *alignements* (long lines of standing stones), arrayed in three main groups just north of the town.

HIGHLIGHTS

MUSÉE DE PRÉHISTOIRE

10 Place de la Chapelle, 56340 Carnac-Ville 02 97 52 22 04 Mid-Jun to mid-Sep daily 10–12.30, 1.30–7; mid-Sep to mid-Jun Thu–Tue 10–12.30, 1.30–6, Wed 1.30–6; closed Jan Adult €5, child 6–18 €2.50 Tue, Thu at 11, 1.30, 3.30, 5 Jul-Aug; Sat/Sun at same times rest of year; adult €7.50, child €4.20; www.museedecarnac.com

A preliminary visit to this museum near the town church helps put Carnac's bewildering wealth of antiquities in context. Founded by a Scottish archaeologist, James Miln, in 1881, this two-floor building houses more than 6,000 prehistoric items (jewellery, tools, ceramics and human bones). Contents span many millennia, from the Paleolithic era (some 450,000 years ago) to the early Middle Ages, but most of the exhibits date from Neolithic times (4000–1000BC), when Carnac's monuments are thought to have been constructed. An explanatory booklet is available in English.

LES ALIGNEMENTS

Largest of the menhir complexes is the Alignements du Ménec, containing 1,099 stones. A short way east are the Alignements de Kermario (1,029 stones in 10 lines), and further on are the Alignements de Kerlescan, a smaller group of around 240 menhirs. Many of the stones have been removed or displaced over the years, and it is impossible to know exactly what the original formations looked like. Most can clearly be seen from the fenced roadside along the rue des Alignements, but conservation measures restrict visitors

from wandering at will among the stones. To get closer to the *alignements* you must join an hour-long guided tour (adult €4, child (12–20) €3); available in English Jul, Aug; reserve in advance (see below).

MAISON DES MEGALITHES

Route des Alignements 02 97 52 29 81 Jul, Aug daily 9–8; May, Jun daily 9–7; Sep–end Apr 10–5.15 Free; www.monum.fr

This information point near the Alignements de Ménec has a video presentation, topographic models and a selection of books about the sites. Sign up here for a guided tour around the megaliths. A terrace above the building provides a grandstand view of the *alignements*, enabling you to see the patterns more clearly than at ground level.

TUMULUS ST-MICHEL

Rue du Tumulus Freely accessible, but currently undergoing restoration

Some 300m (328 yards) east of the town, the tumulus of St-Michel is a prehistoric burial mound looking much like a natural hill. The mound, 12m (40ft) high, 125m (400ft) long and 60m (200ft) wide, is thought to date from around 4500BC. A low passage inside (no longer accessible for safety reasons) leads to two funerary chambers and stone compartments originally used for storing precious offerings. There's a fine view over the Baie de Quiberon from the top.

BACKGROUND

The scale of Carnac's fields of standing stones is impressive. More than 3,000 menhirs and other megalithic structures stand within a 4.5km (3-mile) radius. No one knows exactly who put them there or why. Theories abound, and estimates of the age and even the precise number of the stones vary widely. What most experts agree on is that the monuments—mostly long lines (*alignements*) of standing stones (menhirs) less than 2m (6ft) high—were erected sometime between 4500 and 1800BC and were used for some sort of religious or ritual activity. Some archaeologists believe the *alignements* are even older, far predating Stonehenge or the Pyramids.

There are more than 3,000 menhirs at Carnac

MORE TO SEE

ÉGLISE ST-CORNELY

Free guided tours in summer

The fine Renaissance-style 17th-century church on the town's main square is dedicated to the patron saint of horned beasts. Scenes from the saint's life decorate the ornate interior.

LA TRINITÉ-SUR-MER

Carnac's former fishing port on the Locmariaquer road (3km/1.5 miles) east of the town has an ultra-modern yacht marina. It is a leading sailing centre full of boutiques and restaurants.

TIPS

- The official English-language publication, *The Carnac Alignments*, gives a clear summary of the antiquities (€7; available in local bookshops and information points).
- Large expanses of brackish water near Carnac-Plage encourage mosquitoes, so bring some insect repellent.
- Combination tickets are available for the Musée de Préhistoire and the megaliths at Carnac and Locmariaquer; adult €7.

Golfe du Morbihan

This landlocked tidal lagoon is one of the most remarkable natural features of the Breton coastline. Meaning 'Little Sea' in Breton, its mild climate and picturesque islands make it an irresistible destination for water sports enthusiasts.

The harbour wall at Locmariaquer

The ruins of the 13th-century Suscinio castle

Lobster creels on the harbourside at Port Navalo

RATINGS

Good for kids	●●●●
Outdoor pursuits	●●●●●
Photo stops	●●●●

BASICS

207 H13

Maison des Associations, rue M J Coudrin, 56370 Sarzeau, tel 02 97 41 82 37; Jul, Aug Mon–Sat 9–12.30, 2–7, Sun 10–12; Sep–end Jun Mon–Sat 9–12, 2–6; rond-point du Crouesty, 56370 Port-Navalo, tel 02 97 53 69 69; Jul, Aug Mon–Sat 9–12.30, 2–7, Sun 10–1; Sep–end Jun Mon–Sat 9–12, 2–6; Tour Prison, Place Monseigneur Ropert, 56370 St-Gildas-de-Rhuys, tel 02 97 45 31 45; Jul, Aug only; Maison du Tourisme de Rhuys, BP 46, St-Colombier, 56370 Sarzeau, tel 02 97 26 45 26; Jul, Aug daily 9–7.30; Sep–end Jun Mon–Sat 9.15–12.15, 2–8, Sun 2–5.30.

TIM Lines 1, 6, 7 serve the gulf area; many more routes converge on Vannes

Vannes, Auray

Gulf tours start from Vannes (Conleau), Port-Navalo, La Trinité-sur-Mer, Auray, Locmariaquer, Bono, Port-Blanc and L'Armor-Baden

www.golfedumorbihan.com
Has some interesting features (in French) on the islands of the gulf, *sinagots* (oyster-fishing boats), plus a handy summary of local boat trips.

SEEING THE GOLFE DU MORBIHAN

The island-speckled gulf is virtually enclosed by the embrace of the Presqu'île de Rhuys apart from a narrow channel near Locmariaquer, through which constricted tides race furiously. The strong currents and muddy shores make swimming inadvisable, but despite this it's a very popular holiday area, well equipped with campsites, water sports and small, low-key resorts. Bono is one of the prettiest ports on the gulf, tucked away up the Auray estuary. Immediately south of the village is the megalithic site of Kernous, an impressive cluster of tumuli in a pine grove setting. The gulf has few good beaches, but the Plage des Sept-Îles is an idyllic pale, secluded sandbar accessible from the Pointe de Locmiquel on Île Berder (low-tide access on foot from L'Armor-Baden).

Boating is by far the best way to see the gulf. In summer, dozens of pleasure craft scoot across the shallow waters from many different starting points, threading a skilful course through the maze of islands. A few of the islands can be visited (foot passengers only), notably the Île aux Moines and Île de Gavrinis.

HIGHLIGHTS

ÎLE DE GAVRINIS

Ferries from L'Armor-Baden; tel 02 97 57 19 38; Easter–end Oct daily 10–12, 2–5 (closed Tue in Oct) Adult €10, child 8–17 €4

Gavrinis has one of Brittany's most impressive Neolithic monuments. An ornately decorated tomb buried beneath a grassy cairn displays a remarkable variety of carved patterns, including snakes and spirals, sunbursts and chevrons. Reached by a 15-minute ferry ride, it makes one of the most popular excursions anywhere on the gulf. The ferry fare includes the entrance charge to the site. Visitor numbers are limited, so reserve in advance in high season.

ÎLE AUX MOINES

At Port Blanc, tel 02 97 57 23 24; Jul, Aug daily 10–1, 2–6; Apr, May, Jun, Sep daily 10.30–12. 2.30–5 Izenah boats from Port-Blanc all year; Navix operates cruises from the *gare maritime* in Vannes (Apr–end Sep) Bicycles can be rented

The small sandy bay at Port Navolo on the Ruis Peninsula

Although called Monks' Isle, this, the largest and most varied of the gulf's islands, never actually had a religious community on it. The monks were absentee landlords, who merely collected taxes from the inhabitants. Apart from a couple of megalithic monuments, there isn't a great deal to see, but it's a pretty place of stone and thatched fishermen's cottages, creeks, palm groves and woodland.

PRESQU'ÎLE DU RHUYS

The mild microclimate of this straggling peninsula encourages lush, subtropical vegetation. Brittany's only vineyards grow here, as well as figs, pomegranates and camellias. Much of the waterfront on this part of the gulf is devoted to oyster-rearing, including the old salt pans at Le Tour du Parc. Arzon, at the far end of the peninsula, is one of the most attractive villages, while nearby Port Crouesty is home to a glitzy marina development offering health spa treatments.

CHÂTEAU DU SUSCINIO

207 H13 • 56370 Sarzeau 02 97 41 91 91 Apr–end Sep daily 10–7; Oct, Feb, Mar Thu–Tue 10–12, 2–6; Nov–end Jan Thu–Tue 10–12, 2–5 Adult €5, child 8–17 €2

This impressively moated 14th-century castle in the marshes southeast of Sarzeau was once a hunting lodge for the dukes of Brittany. Still partly roofless, but much restored, it has a medieval tiled floor in bright mosaic. Concerts are sometimes staged here in summer.

BACKGROUND

Several thousand years ago, sea levels rose to create the Little Sea (*Morbihan* in Breton) which gives its name to this part of Brittany. Now the waters are once again steadily creeping higher, drowning the myriad grassy islets that emerge at low tide. Measuring some 20km (12 miles) by 15km (9 miles), the gulf changes its appearance dramatically as the strong tides ebb and flow. A huge concentration of wildlife is attracted by the diverse range of habitats (dunes, saltmarshes, heath and pinewoods).

TIP

• For a more romantic way to appreciate the gulf, take a ride on an old-fashioned *sinagot*, a traditional oyster-fishing boat from Séné/Port Anna or Arradon (▷ 117).

MORE TO SEE

ST-GILDAS-DE-RHUYS

Jul–Sep guided tours Mon–Fri

This abbey church on the seaward side of the Rhuys peninsula is famed for its associations with Pierre Abelard, star-crossed lover of Héloïse, who became abbot here after his enforced exile from Paris in 1126.

LE BUTTE DE CÉSAR

From this Neolithic mound, sometimes known as the Tumulus de Tumiac, just outside Arzon on the D780, it is alleged that Julius Caesar witnessed the decisive victory of the Roman fleet over the Celtic Veneti in 56BC (▷ 16).

RÉSERVE NATURELLE DE SÉNÉ

Brouel-Kerbihan 02 97 66 92 76 Jul, Aug daily; Feb–end Jun Sun and hols (same hours) Guided field trips

This nature reserve, 6km (4 miles) southeast of Vannes, is one of the best places for birdwatching anywhere in Brittany.

Half-timbered buildings around the port at Auray

The 16th-century covered market at the Le Faouët

The calvary, dating from 1550, at the parish close in Guéhenno

AURAY

206 H12 · 20 rue du Lait, 56400 Auray, tel 02 97 24 09 75; Jul, Aug Mon–Sat 9–7, Sun 9–12; Sep–end Jun Mon–Fri 9–12, 2–6; Sat am only except in school hols. In Sainte-Anne-d'Auray, 26 rue de Vannes, tel 02 97 57 69 16; Jun–end Sep Mon–Sat 9.30–12.30, 1.30–6; Oct–end May Mon–Fri 9–12, 2–5 · Local buses operated by Auray-Bus (tel 02 97 47 29 64); TIM Line 1 to Vannes, Carnac, Quiberon; Line 16 to Ploërmel, Hennebont, Lorient; Line 6A to Bono, Larmor Baden, Port-Blanc · Auray TGV services to Quimper, Vannes, Lorient and Paris; 'Tire Bouchon' service to Quiberon (July, Aug only) · Pleasure cruises on River Auray and Golfe du Morbihan from St-Goustan · Guided tours of the town available from tourist office in summer (Jul, Aug Wed, Thu; adult €5, child over 10 €3). A *petit train* operates to St-Goustan in summer (30-min ride €3) www.auray-tourisme.com

A striking valley setting at the tidal limit of the River Auray makes the historic port of St-Goustan the most memorable part of Auray. Here, forced ashore by a storm, Benjamin Franklin spent a night in 1776. The object of his visit was to enlist Louis XVI's support in the American War of Independence. Quaint timbered inns and restaurants cluster around the cobbled quayside, and an old tuna-fishing schooner (now used as a souvenir shop) is permanently moored on the waterfront. The Promenade du Loc'h on the western bank gives fine views over the port. Auray's upper town focuses on the Place de la République, with its 18th-century Hôtel de Ville. In a nearby square, the church of St-Gildas deserves a glance for its Renaissance porch and marble altarpiece.

An even more famous church lies a short distance northeast of Auray. The basilica at Sainte-Anne-d'Auray hosts one of Brittany's most important *pardons*, on 25–26 July, when thousands converge to celebrate the feast day of the Virgin's mother, and a miraculous vision experienced by a local ploughman. Other shrines near Auray commemorate the unsuccessful counter-Revolutionary uprising by the Chouans, led by Georges Cadoudal (▷ 19).

Don't miss Near the basilica of Sainte-Anne-d'Auray stands a war memorial in the form of a huge wall enclosing a formal garden. The Monument aux Morts lists by name the quarter million or so Bretons killed in World War I (freely accessible).

The monument for Coretin Carre, the youngest soldier to enlist in the French army, at Le Faouët

LE FAOUËT

206 F10 · 3 rue des Cendres 56320 Le Faouët, tel 02 97 23 23 23; Jul–mid Sep, Mon–Sat 10–12.30, 2–6; mid Sep–end Jun Tue–Sat 10–12.30, 2–5.30 · TIM Line 15 to Lorient; Line 22 to Quimperlé www.paysroimorvan.com

The main feature of this appealing little backwater in the Montagnes Noires is its handsome covered market, which dominates the main square. The slate roof, topped with a clock tower, sweeps down almost to ground level; inside a forest of timbers propped on granite pillars shores it up. The market has been in use continuously since the 16th century. The nearby art museum, housed in a former Ursuline convent, contains a collection of works by Breton artists who settled here in the early 20th century (tel 02 97 23 15 27; mid Jun–end Sep daily 10–12, 2–6).

Many paintings depict local chapels, best-known of which is Sainte-Barbe, about 3km (2 miles) north of the town. This 15th-century building in Flamboyant Gothic style has a striking setting in a rocky gully overlooking the wooded Ellé valley. Legend has it that the chapel was built by a grateful knight caught in a terrible storm, which caused a rockslide. He prayed to Sainte Barbe, patron saint of lightning and artillery fire, and escaped unscathed. Visitors clamber down a steep flight of steps to see the chapel, which contains statues and stained-glass windows depicting the saint's life (Apr–end Oct daily; rest of year, hols only, Sat–Mon).

Don't miss Toll the bell at the top of the chapel steps to invoke Sainte Barbe's protection against thunderbolts—or attract the custodian's attention in the nearby house.

GUÉHENNO

207 J11 · Le Mairie, 56420 Guéhenno, tel 02 97 42 29 89 · TIM Line 11 from Vannes via St-Jean Brévalay

About 10km (6 miles) southwest of Josselin along the D778, the small, drowsy village of Guéhenno is worth a minor detour to see an unusual calvary, well outside the boundaries of Finistère, where most of Brittany's parish closes lie. This one dates from the mid-16th century. It suffered severe

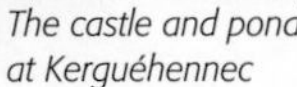

The castle and pond at Kerguéhennec

Boats moored in the clear waters at Port-Tudy on the Île de Groix

damage in the Revolution, but the local stonemasons demanded such high fees to restore it that the parish clergy decided to take on the work themselves. The amateurish results are unexpectedly delightful. The cock crows on a pillar in front of the cross to announce Peter's denial of Christ, who lies in the ossuary guarded by soldiers (free access all year).

HENNEBONT

206 G12 · 9 Place Maréchal Foch, 56700 Hennebont, tel 02 97 36 24 52; Jul, Aug daily 9–7; Sep–end Jun Mon–Sat 9–12.30, 2–6 · TIM Line 17 (Lorient–Pontivy); Line 16 (Lorient–Auray) · River trips on the Blavet to Port-Louis and Lorient, or to Île de Groix

Doughty fortifications indicate this town has quite a history, but Hennebont's metalworking industry and its unfortunate location just upstream from the submarine pens of Lorient were the cause of wholescale destruction in World War II. The massive towered gateway of Porte Broërec survives, and a wander round the ramparts gives fine views over the River Blavet. Most of the old walled city succumbed to incendiary bombs, but a few elegant old houses can be spotted here and there (as at 1 rue de la Paix), dwarfed by the huge basilica of Notre-Dame-du-Paradis at the top of the main street. The Parc de Kerbihan in the heart of the city contains some 400 species of trees and shrubs. Hennebont springs to life on Thursdays with one of the largest markets in Morbihan (no parking on main street). North of town at Inzinzac-Lochrist, ghosts of a once-great industrial scene linger on the waterfront. The Ecomusée Industriel traces the history of Hennebont's defunct iron-and-steel trade, and the Blavet canal that was its lifeline (tel 02 97 36 98 21; Jul, Aug Mon–Fri 10–6.30, Sat, Sun 2–6.30; Sep–end Jun Mon–Fri 10–12, 2–6, Sun 2–6; Sat 2–6 in Jun; guided tours Jul, Aug at 3pm).

Don't miss Vivid modern stained glass by Max Ingrand replaces the damage caused to the basilica in World War II.

ÎLE DE GROIX

205 F12 · Quai de Port-Tudy, 56590 Port-Tudy, tel 02 97 86 53 08; Jul, Aug daily 9.30–1, 2–7; Sep–end Jun Mon–Fri 9–12, 2–5 · From Lorient (all year), Larmor-Plage or Port-Louis (summer only) · You can rent bicycles, motor scooters or cars on quai de Port-Tudy, or take a taxi tour of the island

This island, a 50-minute ferry ride from Lorient, is a raised plateau fringed by steep cliffs. Most of the island's 3,000 residents live in the capital, Groix, just inland from Port-Tudy. The sheltered eastern coast has the best beaches, including the convex, almost tropical-looking Plage des Grands Sables, with fine, pale sand. The clear seas make it a popular spot for scuba-diving. The force of the Atlantic has left its mark on the western Côte Sauvage (wild coast), and the Trou d'Enfer blowhole on the southern coast is a memorable sight in rough weather. The island, 8km (5 miles) by 2km (1 mile), has little in the way of visitor facilities, but offers a welcome break from mainland bustle, with 25km (15 miles) of footpaths to explore. Rare minerals are found here, and there is a geological reserve near Locmaria (free access all year).

During the 1930s Groix had the largest tuna-fishing fleet in France. You can learn more about the history of the fleet at Port-Tudy's well-presented Écomusée, in a former canning factory (tel 02 97 86 84 60; Jul, Aug daily 9.30–12, 3–7; May, Jun, Sep daily 10–12.30, 2–5; Apr, Oct, Nov Tue–Sun 10–12.30, 2–5; Dec–end Mar Wed, Sat, Sun 10–12.30, 2–5).

Don't miss The tuna-fish weather vane on Groix church indicates the importance of the local industry.

Modern sculpture by Keith Sonnier at Kerguéhennec

KERGUÉHENNEC

207 J11 • 56500 Bignan · 02 97 60 44 44 · Mid-Jun to mid-Sep daily 10–7; mid-Sep to mid-Dec, mid-Jan to mid-Jun Tue–Sun 10–6 · Free · Light refreshments at the Café du Parc, served on the terrace in summer

www.art-kerguehennec.com

The classical parkland of an 18th-century château conceals a bizarre collection of surprises—a broken skiff dangling in the branches of a tree, a railway sleeper from which a sapling sprouts, a glasshouse filled with empty red plant pots. The Domaine de Kerguéhennec is an imaginative modern sculpture park (one of Europe's largest), run by Morbihan's departmental authorities. New pieces are constantly being installed, and the château's outbuildings are used as *ateliers* by visiting artists, or to stage exhibitions. There are tours of the interior in summer. A plan is available in English indicating the locations of the exhibits.

The magnificent château at Josselin (above), and operating the river lock on the canal (left)

RATINGS

Good for kids	●●●
Historic interest	●●●●●
Photo stops	●●●●

BASICS

207 J11

Place de la Congrégation, 56120 Josselin, tel 02 97 22 36 43; mid Jul–Aug daily 10–6; Apr–mid Jul and Sep Mon–Sat 9.30–12, 2–6, Sun 2–6; Oct–Mar Mon–Fri 9.30–12, 2–5.30, Sat 9.30–12

CTM Line 19 (Rennes–Pontivy via Ploërmel)

www.paysdejosselin-tourisme.com
No English translation yet, but quite useful on the main aspects of the town.

TIPS

- An important *pardon* is held each year on 8 September, in honour of the town's patron, Notre-Dame du Roncier.
- You'll get superb views of the castle from across the river in the Quartier Sainte-Croix.
- A joint ticket for the castle and the doll museum (adult €11.90, child 7–14 €8.20) is the best value, though each can be visited separately (castle €6.80, child €4.70; museum €6, child €4.30).
- A pleasant walk along the banks of the Oust leads to the Île de Beaufort, an idyllic spot for a picnic, watching boats pass through the lock.

JOSSELIN

Mirrored in the sparkling waters of the Oust, Josselin's turreted medieval castle is just as impressive inside as from the outside, and full of history from many periods.

You can learn more about Brittany's medieval history in this inland town than almost anywhere else. The town supposedly dates back to AD1000, when a ruling nobleman named it after his eldest son. Throughout the complex struggles of the Hundred Years War, the War of Succession and the Wars of Religion, Josselin stood in the thick of the fighting. The castle was built during the 14th century by Olivier de Clisson, one of the leading warlords of the Middle Ages, who succeeded Bertrand du Guesclin as Constable of France. He married into the powerful Rohan family, who at that time owned about a third of Brittany.

CHÂTEAU DE JOSSELIN

The castle (mid-Jul to end Aug daily 10–6; Jun to mid-Jul, Sep daily 2–6; Apr, May, Oct Sat, Sun and hols 2–6) was constructed on a bulwark of solid rock above the river. It was heavily restored in the 19th century after being dismantled on Cardinal Richelieu's orders in 1629, and damaged during the Revolution. A sober wall of stone guards the waterfront, with three circular towers topped by witch-hat turrets. A Renaissance screen was added between 1490 and 1510, its courtyard façade decorated with a riot of exquisitely carved detail. The interior is decorated in 17th- and 18th-century style. Remarkably, the castle is still inhabited by descendants of the Rohan family. In the converted stable block, the Musée des Poupées displays an absorbing collection of around 600 dolls, some dating from 1880.

OUR LADY OF THE BRAMBLES

A maze of cobbled alleyways links the courtyard to Josselin's main town square, where you'll find the 15th-century Notre-Dame-du-Roncier (Our Lady of the Brambles), allegedly built on the spot where a miraculous statue of the Virgin was found in a blackberry bush. Most of the church is in Flamboyant style, all gargoyles and lofty spires (guided tours in summer). Inside are the marble tombs of Olivier de Clisson and his second wife, Marguerite de Rohan. The belltower and the steeple date from the early 20th century.

Detail of a church ceiling painting in the village of Kernascléden

The Dolmen des Pierres Plates stands sentinel at Locmariaquer

KERNASCLÉDEN

206 G11 Information at the Mairie, 56540 Kernascléden, tel 02 97 51 61 16

This village's claim on the visitor's attention is its 15th-century chapel built by the influential Rohan family, who ruled the roost around Josselin and Pontivy in medieval times. The elaborately carved exterior has many interesting features, but it is the bright frescoes inside that really catch the eye. Most startling are the scenes in the south transept depicting hell, where hideous demons kebab the damned on sharp spikes, then stew them in cauldrons or roast them in barrels. Above the vaulted choir, the Virgin's life and the Passion are depicted. Christ rises from his tomb, and angelic musicians tune up for an everlasting concert in the north transept.

LOCMARIAQUER

206 H13 1 rue de la Victoire, 56740 Locmariaquer, tel 02 97 57 33 05; Apr–Sep daily; Oct–end Mar Mon–Sat Golfe du Morbihan excursions (including visits to Île aux Moines/Île d'Arz); ferry to Port-Navalo on the east side of the straits (Jul, Aug; foot passengers/bicyclists only) The *Fête de l'Huître* (oyster festival) celebrates the local *creuse de Locmariaquer* with tastings and exhibitions (third Sun in Aug)

Site Mégalithique de Locmariaquer

Route de Kerlogonan 02 97 57 37 59 Jul, Aug daily 10–7; May–end Jun daily 10–6; Sep–end Apr daily 10–12.30, 2–5.15 (last entry 45 min before closing time) Adult €4.60, child (18–24) €3.10

www.monum.fr

Megaliths are the chief attraction of this pretty little oyster port. The largest of them dwarf anything in nearby Carnac (▷ 38–9). The main monuments, on display at a fenced enclosure near the village entrance, are the Table des Marchands (a 30m/100ft dolmen), and the Grand Menhir Brise, shattered and recumbent, but still impressive at over 20m (66ft) long. Others include the Dolmen des Pierres Plates beside the sea, its 24m (80ft) chamber decorated with mysterious carvings (freely accessible; take a torch). Some tours are available in English—book well in advance. Admission is free on the first Sunday in the month (Oct–end May).

Locmariaquer is on the narrow straits at the entrance to the Golfe du Morbihan (▷ 40–1), where tides fizz in and out with all the force of agitated champagne. Sandy beaches line the seaward coast west of the Pointe de Kerpenhir.

LORIENT

206 F12 Maison de la Mer, quai de Rohan, 56100 Lorient, tel 02 97 21 07 84; Mon–Sat Lorient (trains to Quimper, Auray, Vannes and Rennes, plus TGV to Paris Gare Montparnasse) Batobus links across the estuary (Port-Louis/Sainte-Catherine/Larmor-Plage); Île de Groix excursions; river trips up the Blavet and around the harbour, including the submarine base Tours of the submarine base at Keroman arranged by the tourist office; mid-Jun to mid-Sep daily; adult €5, child €3 (free under 7)

www.lorient-tourisme.com

The name gives a clue to its colonial past. For Lorient, read Port de l'Orient, former HQ of the Compagnie des Indes, France's 17th-century trading company. An immense natural harbour was the source of Lorient's success as a commercial, naval and fishing port. But it was also the cause of its downfall in World War II, when Allied bombers pulverized the city in a frantic bid to destroy the German U-boat installations that presented such a threat to transatlantic shipping. Ironically, the concrete submarine pens in the port of Keroman mostly survived the raids, while the civilian quarters were smashed into rubble. Post-war reconstruction was rapid but mostly unimaginative.

Today little attracts visitors to Lorient except its August *Festival Interceltique*, the biggest musical event anywhere in France (▷ 121). Otherwise, Brittany's fourth-largest city is a lively commercial and university centre. The austerely modern church of Notre-Dame-de-Victoire is vividly lit by jagged stained-glass windows. *La Thalassa* is an oceanographic research vessel, now turned into a museum and maritime exhibition permanently moored at the Port de Plaisance (tel 02 97 35 13 00; Jul, Aug daily 9–7; Sep–Jun Mon–Fri 9–12.30, 2–6, Sat, Sun 2–6; closed Mon outside school hols).

The Grand Menhir at Locmariaquer

The church at Malestroit

A whitewashed crêperie by the parish church in Ploërmel

The riverside château at Pontivy

MALESTROIT

210 K12 17 Place du Bouffay, 56140 Malestroit, tel 02 97 75 14 57; Jul–Aug Mon–Sat 9–7, Sun 10–4; Sep to Jun Mon–Sat 9.30–12.30, 2.30–6.30
A *voie verte* bicycle trail begins at Malestroit; the tourist office supplies many suggested itineraries for walks and tours, some along the canal
www.malestroit.com

This quaint little baronial town on the River Oust (part of the Nantes-Brest Canal) has a long history, as the ancient buildings in its historic area suggest. In the now-ruinous Chapelle de la Madeleine, the kings of France and England signed a truce during the Hundred Years War. Slate-hung Gothic and Renaissance houses decked with turrets and droll carvings surround the Place du Bouffay and the church of St-Gilles. Here a hare plays the bagpipes, there a man in a nightshirt beats his wife.

At St-Marcel, 3km (2 miles) west of town, the Musée de la Résistance Bretonne (tel 02 97 75 16 90; mid-Jun to mid-Sep daily 10–7; mid-Sep to mid-Jun Wed–Mon 10–12, 2–6) recounts the contribution of the Morbihan Maquis (French Resistance) to the Allied effort in World War II. Ration cards, propaganda posters and the buckled engines of an American bomber are on display; an English translation of the guidebook is available. Local memorials commemorate the bloody battle fought here in 1944, when Maquis and Free French forces successfully diverted German troops from the Normandy landing beaches before D-Day.

PLOËRMEL

207 K11 5 rue du Val. BP 106, 56800 Ploërmel, tel 02 97 74 02 70, Jul, Aug Mon–Sat 9.30–7, Sun, hols 10–12.30; Sep–end Jun Mon–Sat 10–12.30, 2–6.30
www.ploermel.com

Located at a strategic junction of major roads, Ploërmel is now a thriving regional hub with a busy agricultural market. Visitors are reminded of its distinguished past in the patchy historic quarters that survived wartime damage. Curious carved figures adorn the 15th-century Maison des Marmousets at 7 rue Beaumanoir and the 16th-century church of St-Armel. A famous chivalric tournament known as The Battle of the Thirty was fought near Ploërmel in 1351. This gentlemanly attempt to determine the outcome of the War of Succession failed to prevent the debilitating struggle lasting a further 13 years.

Northeast of Ploërmel, the forest of Paimpont (▷ 98) extends over the boundaries of Ille-et-Vilaine, offering many legend-packed excursions. The local tourist office promotes attractions on the Morbihan side of the border under the Franco-Arthurian label of Brocéliande.

A large lake called the Lac au Duc, about 2km (1 mile) northwest of Ploërmel, is a great venue for outdoor pursuits such as fishing, canoeing, waterskiing and windsurfing. Paths lead around the shore, parts using a disused railway line. The lovely 3km (2 mile) lakeside Circuit des Hortensias leads through a magnificent collection of hydrangeas, which grow exceptionally well in Brittany (tel 02 97 74 02 70; open all year but best May–end Sep; free access).

A carving at Malestroit (left)

PONTIVY

206 H10 61 rue Général de Gaulle (by the castle), 56306 Pontivy, tel 02 97 25 04 10; Mon–Sat 10–12, 2–6
www.pays-pontivy.com

A former fiefdom of the Rohan family of Josselin (▷ 44), Pontivy's riverside château dates from around 1485 (tel 02 97 25 12 93; Jul, Aug daily 10.30–6.30; Feb–end Jun, Sep–Nov 10–12, 2–6; closed Mon, Tue off-season, and Dec, Jan), its twin turrets looming over a deep, dry moat. Events and exhibitions are sometimes held here in summer. A tangle of twisting streets, contemporary with the castle and now mostly pedestrianized, extends around the Place du Martray, where an animated market is held on Tuesdays. Much of the town's present appearance owes more to Napoleon than to the Rohans. His ambitious plan to link Nantes and Brest by a canal route safe from seaborne attack resulted in a neoclassical makeover of Pontivy's southwestern sector in a neat grid of stately boulevards and landscaped plazas. For a while, the town was known as Napoléonville.

The Blavet splits from the Nantes–Brest Canal at Pontivy, but both waterways are canalized, and the choice of routes makes it a major canal-boating hub. Downstream along the Blavet, about 12km (7 miles) southwest, many pleasure boats reach St-Nicholas-des-Eaux, many of whose thatched cottages are used as holiday homes. **Don't miss** The Site de Castennac just outside St-Nicholas gives a dramatic view over a bend in the river.

The citadel at Port-Louis

Point de Percho beach at the popular holiday resort of Presqu'île de Quiberon

PORT-LOUIS

206 F12 1 rue de la Citadelle, 56290 Port-Louis, tel 02 97 82 52 93; Jul, Aug Mon–Sat 9.30–12.30, 1.30–6.30, Sun 10–1; Apr, May Sep Mon 1.30–5.30, Tue–Fri 9.30–12.30, 1.30–5.30, Sat 9.30–12.30 Lorient Batobus ferry services connect Port-Louis with Lorient, Larmor-Plage and Gâvres, linking with local bus services www.ville-portlouis.fr

Port-Louis was the original headquarters of the Compagnie des Indes, a trading company set up by Cardinal Richelieu during Louis XIII's reign. After its initial failure it was relocated to the burgeoning port of Lorient (▷ 45), on the opposite side of the Blavet estuary. Despite this commercial setback, Port-Louis has retained a charm of scale and atmosphere conspicuously lacking in its upstart offspring across the roadstead. Its cobbled streets contain a number of elegant shipowners' houses dating from the 18th century. The imposing citadel overlooking the Rade de Lorient houses two excellent museums. One recounts France's 17th- and 18th-century colonial adventures, and the bitter rivalry with British and Dutch entrepreneurs; the other is the Musée National de la Marine. Both have the same entrance ticket and opening hours (tel 02 97 82 19 13 or 02 97 82 56 72; Apr to mid-Sep daily 10–6.30; mid-Sep to mid-Dec, Feb, Mar Wed–Mon 10–12, 2–6). From the fort's extensive southern ramparts you can see the village of Gâvres on a long sandspit across the virtually landlocked Mer de Gâvres. At Riantec, the Maison de l'Île de Kerner has an exhibition on local ecology, including oyster-farming (tel 02 97 84 51 49; Jul, Aug daily 10–7; Apr–end Jun, Sep Tue–Fri 10–12.30, 2–6, Sat, Sun 2–6; Oct–end Mar Sat, Sun 2–6). Beware of military firing ranges on local beaches.

PRESQU'ÎLE DE QUIBERON

206 G13 14 rue de Verdun, 56174 Quiberon, tel 02 97 50 07 84; Jun–Aug daily 9–1, 2–7; Sep–end May Mon–Sat 9–12.30, 2–6 TIM Line 1 to Vannes via Carnac and Auray Quiberon. In Jul and Aug the Tire-Bouchon (corkscrew) shuttle train operates between Quiberon and Auray, replaced by SNCF buses off-season Year-round connections to Belle-Île, and the smaller islands of Houat and Hoëdic Tourist office organizes walking tours in Jul and Aug (Wed 10.30) The Sémaphore park-and-ride on the main road, 1.5km (1 mile) north of town (free shuttle bus into town; Jul, Aug only) saves sitting in traffic jams Bathing is forbidden on the westerly Côte Sauvage (dangerous currents and sharp rocks), but the coastal footpath is a spectacular walk www.quiberon.com

Quiberon is one of Brittany's most popular holiday resorts, a long, slim peninsula in places scarcely wider than the single access road, fringed by sublime sandy beaches, and guarded by a 19th-century fort. The main town (also called Quiberon) lies at the southern tip of the peninsula, and from the *gare maritime* at Port-Maria ferries ply to and fro all year to Belle-Île (▷ 37). In high season the main road can be clogged with traffic as day-trippers head for the seaside. Grande Plage is the most popular family beach, while the windswept Plage de Penthièvre is a leading water sports base for all kinds of adventurous activities (kite-surfing, sand-yachting, windsurfing). The more sheltered eastern shores around St-Pierre-Quiberon and the pleasure port of Port Haliguen make a wonderful sailing venue. There's a large thalassotherapy institution on the south coast. Tourism has now replaced Quiberon's former dependence on sardine fishing, but the local fleet still lands its varied catch for the early morning *criée* (fish market). A well-known Breton fish-processing enterprise continues to thrive in Quiberon, and welcomes visitors for factory tours (▷ 119).

LA ROCHE-BERNARD

210 K13 14 rue du Docteur-Cornudet, 56130 La Roche-Bernard, tel 02 99 90 67 98; mid Jul–mid Sep daily 10–7; early–mid Jul daily 10–12.30, 2–6.30; Apr–Jun Mon–Sat 10–12.30, 2–6 and Sun in school hols; mid Sep–Mar Tue–Sat 10–12.30, 2–5.30 River trips to the Arzal dam in Jul–Aug

This *petite cité de charactère* makes a most appealing touring base for the Morbihan/Loire-Atlantique border country, its narrow streets clinging to a steep rocky bluff overlooking the Vilaine. An elegant modern suspension bridge carries the N165 *autoroute* across the river gorge, replacing one destroyed in World War II. The charming historic quarter has a fine selection of hotels and restaurants.

The fortunes of this inland port once flourished on riverine trade and boat-building. Barges laden with grain, salt, timber and wine sailed past to its quaysides on the River Vilaine. The Musée de la Vilaine Maritime (tel 02 99 90 83 47; mid-Jun to mid-Sep daily 10.30–12.30, 2.30–6.30; Easter hols, early Jun, late Sep 2.30–6.30; Apr, May, Oct Sat, Sun 2.30–6.30) shows how busy this waterway was in its heydey, when La Roche-Bernard served as the port for Rennes and Redon. It is housed in an elegant 16th-century building constructed into the cliffside. Since the construction of the Barrage d'Arzal 10km (6 miles)

Yachts moored in the Vilaine, at the old port of La Roche-Bernard

downstream, the river is no longer navigable to the sea. You can visit the dam by boat, and watch fish migrating up or downstream through a glass-walled observation room.

Don't miss There's a lovely beach at Pénestin, near the estuary mouth, called La Mine d'Or (gold mine). At sunset you can see how it got its name.

ST-FIACRE

206 F10 See La Faouët (▷ 42)
The *pardon* of St-Fiacre takes place third Sun in Aug

This little place, 2km (just over a mile) south of La Faouët, has one of Morbihan's most memorable churches. The unusual gable belfry, with its graceful spires, sets it apart, but the interior is even more remarkable. The brightly tinted rood screen dating from 1480 features a mass of delicate woodcarvings on biblical themes from both Old and New Testaments. Angels pirouette gracefully above a series of scenes representing the seven deadly sins in human form. Avarice is a peasant stealing apples; sloth a man playing the bagpipes; gluttony a man bizarrely vomiting a fox. Early 16th-century glass depicts the life of St. Fiacre.

The village church at St-Fiacre

16th- and 17th-century houses in Rochefort-en-Terre

ROCHEFORT-EN-TERRE

This enchanting place wins award after award in 'most beautiful village' competitions for its spectacular setting and historic charm.

RATINGS	
Historic interest	●●●
Photo stops	●●●●
Walkability	●●●●

210 K12 Place des Halles, 56220 Rochefort-en-Terre, tel 02 97 43 33 57; Mon–Fri 10–12.30, 2–6
Parking in the heart of the village is reserved for residents, but there is parking for visitors on the edge of town **www.rochefort-en-terre.com**

TIP

- **Circular waymarked walks lead round the town (blue signs; 6km/4 miles), and beyond into the scenic shale hills of the Grées plateau and the Malansac slate quarries to the east (yellow signs; 10km/6 miles).**

Perched on a high schist spur overlooking the Arz valley, Rochefort-en-Terre is a showpiece village surrounded by oak and chestnut woods. The Grande Rue (several streets linked by small squares) is lined with patrician-looking mansions sporting quirky details in every nook and cranny. Their individuality enhances rather than detracts from the essential harmony of Rochefort's architecture. Many of the sturdy granite buildings now house souvenir shops, art galleries, restaurants and *crêperies*. Flowers billow from dozens of tubs and window-boxes, and cameras snap at every turn.

The castle at the top of the town, a true 'rock fort'—the origin of the town's name—was originally built in the Middle Ages but destroyed in the Revolution and rebuilt piecemeal by two American brothers, Alfred and Trafford Klots, in the early 20th century. It is furnished in 16th- and 17th-century style. The grounds contain a folklore museum (tel 02 97 43 31 56; Jun–Sep daily; Apr, May Sat, Sun, hols).

The church of Notre-Dame-de-la-Tronchaye houses one of the most important religious relics in Brittany—a revered statue of Our Lady of Tronchaye, discovered in a tree in the 12th century.

A stained-glass window in the church of Notre-Dame-de-la-Tronchaye

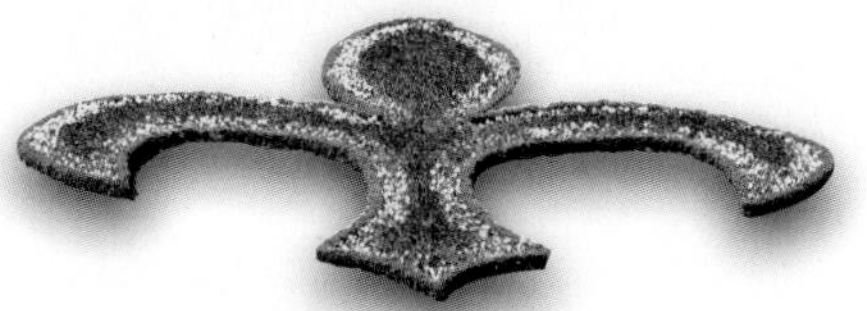

Vannes

This good-looking town has a livelier, more cosmopolitan feel than many Breton towns, and its well-preserved historic quarter is perfect for strolling.

Timber-framed architecture in the heart of Vannes

Vannes and his Wife

Yachts and pleasure boats in the marina area

SEEING VANNES

Vannes, at the northwestern end of the Golfe du Morbihan, is the most important tourist town in southern Brittany. The modern city is extensive and constantly busy with traffic, but its splendid walled old town is compact and mostly pedestrianized. The best starting point is the Porte St-Vincent in Place Gambetta. A web of narrow cobbled alleys full of timber-framed 15th- to 17th-century architecture surrounds the cathedral. The Place des Lices is a focal point, once the setting for medieval tournaments, while Place Henri-IV has another eye-catching assembly of overhanging, gabled houses. A produce market is held in the streets around the cathedral on Wednesdays and Saturdays, supplementing the covered market and the daily fish market on Place de la Poissonnerie. Today, the administrative heart of Vannes has shifted to Place de la République, outside the city walls. Beyond Porte St-Vincent, the Port de Plaisance bristles with yacht masts. The tree-lined Promenade de la Rabine runs along the waterfront to the *gare maritime* (commercial port) at Conleau, set on a trailing peninsula 4km (2.5 miles) to the south of town. Excursion boats bustle back and forth around the Golfe du Morbihan (▷ 40–1) all summer.

HIGHLIGHTS

CATHÉDRALE ST-PIERRE

☎ 02 97 47 10 88 🕑 Mon–Sat 8–7, Sun 9–7 (except during services) Jul, Aug

The much-restored Cathédrale St-Pierre is a mixture of architectural styles from the 13th to the 20th centuries. The main entrance on rue des Chanoines takes you through a fine Flamboyant Gothic doorway flanked by niches containing Renaissance statues of the Apostles. Modern stained glass admits some variegated light to the cathedral's sombre but airy interior. The Rotunda Chapel contains the remains of the city's patron, St. Vincent-Ferrier, a Spanish Dominican monk who achieved fame as a preacher and allegedly performed miraculous cures. When he died in Vannes in 1419, the townsfolk refused to return his body to Spain, and here it still lies in a black sarcophagus.

RATINGS	
Boat trips	●●●●
Good for kids	●●●
Historic interest	●●●●
Photo stops	●●●

BASICS

207 H13

1 rue Thiers, 56009 Vannes, tel 02 97 47 24 34; Jul, Aug daily 9–7; Sep–end Jun Mon–Sat 9.30–12.30, 2–6

Local city services are run by TPV; tel 02 97 01 22 23. Vannes is a major hub for many TIM services, including to Carnac, Auray, Quiberon (Line 1), Questembert, Rochefort-en-Terre (Line 9), La Roche-Bernard, Nantes (Line 8) and the Golfe du Morbihan. SNCF/TER bus service to St-Brieuc via Pontivy

Vannes is a major rail junction, with links to Auray, Quimper, Lorient, Brest, Redon, Rennes, Nantes, Paris

Boat trips around the Golfe du Morbihan and to Belle-Île from the port of Conleau

The Animation du Patrimoine department at the Hôtel du Roscanvec runs several guided walks throughout the summer

By the pleasure port (spaces furthest from Place Gambetta are free)

www.tourisme-vannes.com
Less comprehensive than a town of this importance deserves. No English version.

La Villa
Valencia
Restaurant
Moulerie

LA COHUE

02 97 01 63 00 Mid-Jun–Sep daily 10–6; Oct–mid-Jun daily 1.30–6 Adult €4, child €2.50, under 12 free A combined Pass'Musées ticket covers both municipal museums in La Cohue and Le Château Gaillard (see right); adult €5, child €3 Summer Mon–Sat at 2.30

Almost opposite the cathedral, this medieval covered market dates from the 16th century and is worth a visit in itself. Over the centuries it has served as a market building, a hall of justice and a general meeting place, but now houses the Musée des Beaux-Arts, containing permanent collections of paintings, silverware and engravings. There are a number of star exhibits, including the *Crucifixion* by Eugène Delacroix, and many works by Breton artists. Temporary exhibitions are regularly held on the ground floor, and guided tours are available.

MORE TO SEE

MUSÉE D'HISTOIRE DE D'ARCHÉOLOGIE

Château Gaillard, 2 rue Noé, 56000 02 97 01 63 00 Mid-Jun–Sep daily 10–6 Adult €3.50, child €2.60, under 12 free (combined entrance ticket with Musée des Beaux Arts €5/€3)

The austere 15th-century Château Gaillard houses a collection of prehistoric items, including funerary axeheads and items of jewellery.

Busy cafés at Place Gambetta

A flower-filled window box in a 16th-century house

Promenade de la Garenne

RAMPARTS

Whatever else you do in Vannes, don't miss the chance to walk past the fortifications along the Promenade de la Garenne, a raised walk along a stream past the most photogenic bits of the old city walls, carpeted with immaculate formal gardens. The Porte Prison is the oldest surviving city gate, dating from the 13th century. Near the Porte Poterne, look out for the well-preserved 19th-century *lavoirs* (wash-houses), and the distinctively turreted Tour de Connetable. (▷ 137, town walk.)

BACKGROUND

With access to the sea from the perfectly sheltered waters of the Golfe du Morbihan, Vannes made an obvious power-base for the Veneti, the seafaring Gaulish tribe defeated by Caesar in 56BC. In the 9th century it became the focus of Breton unity under Nominoë, first Duke of Brittany, and shared the honour of being the Breton capital with Nantes before Brittany was formally signed over to the French crown in 1532. Its superbly protected port played an important trading role, but today it caters only for pleasure traffic from the peninsula of Conleau, south of the city, and the canalized harbour that links the old town with the Golfe du Morbihan.

Equine statue of Richemond, constable of France, in front of the Hotel de Ville

VANNES AND HIS WIFE

Corner rue du Rogues and rue de Noé

A famous carved corbel peers out from an old house (now an Italian restaurant) on the corner of rue du Rogues. These humorous, ruddy-faced figures are known as *Vannes et sa Femme* (Vannes and his Wife).

PARC DU GOLFE

The Parc du Golfe, on the Conleau waterfront near the *gare maritime*, has several family-oriented attractions, including an imaginative exhibition on the Golfe du Morbihan, a butterfly garden, a tropical aquarium, funfair and picnic site.

TIPS

- **La Huche à Pains, at 23 Place des Lices, is a superb bakery selling mouth-watering Breton cakes, pastries and savoury snacks.**
- **Rusty-sailed sloops ply the waters of the Golfe du Morbihan from Port Anna. These are *sinagots* (traditional shellfish-gathering craft), now restored for use as summer excursion vessels. Contact Les Amis du Sinagot; tel 06 14 93 04 69.**

FINISTÈRE

Brittany's western extremities are the most culturally distinctive. This is where you are most likely to hear the Breton language spoken and see traditional dress worn. Typically Finisterian too is its rich heritage of church architecture, most idiosyncratic in the ornate parish closes. The wild capes of Crozon and Sizun make spectacular touring, but the placid idylls of the Odet and Aven estuaries in southern Cornouaille are no less rewarding.

MAJOR SIGHTS

Sailing boats pulled up onto the shore at Audierne

The waters of the wooded estuary at Beg-Meil

The sandy beach at Bénodet, at the mouth of the Odet estuary

AUDIERNE

204 C10 8 rue Victor-Hugo, 29770 Audierne, tel 02 98 70 12 20; Jul, Aug Mon–Sat 9–12.30, 2–7; Sep–end Jun Mon–Sat 9–12, 2–6 Penn-ar-Bed trips from Sainte-Evette pier to the Île de Sein take about an hour (tel 02 98 70 02 37)
www.audierne-tourisme.com

This remote corner of Brittany is less crowded in summer than some areas, but Audierne stays active all year round. Its former prosperity is derived from tuna-fishing, and it still has a sizeable seine-netting fleet (bream, sea-bass, monkfish), but its main source of revenue comes from shellfish. Traditional Breton houses line the waterfront and rise in tiers to an upper town of narrow streets and quaint shops. The baroque belfry of 17th-century Église St-Raymond-Nonnat dominates the upper town, its exterior decorated with ship carvings. The large beach at Sainte-Evette southwest of town is one of Audierne's main assets, with a marina, water sports and the pier from which excursion boats shuttle to the Île de Sein in summer. An unexpectedly engrossing maritime attraction called Aquashow (Apr–end Sep daily; Oct–end Mar, school hols; closed Jan; adult €10.50, child 4–14 €7.50) overlooks the estuary at the north end of town, showcasing the marine and freshwater sealife of Brittany. It has an appealing café with a waterfront terrace.

BEG-MEIL

205 D11 La Cale (by the port), tel 02 98 94 97 47; mid-Jun to mid-Sep only Mon–Sat 9.30–12.30, 3–7, Sun 10.30–12.30 Boat excursions to the Îles de Glénan, up the Odet estuary, and a summer ferry service to Concarneau
www.ot-fouesnant.fr
www.fouesnant-tourisme.com

Unspoiled pine-fringed beaches are the chief appeal of this sleepy little seaside resort: Its huge expanses of pale soft sand are ideal for families with small children. Beg-Meil's setting on a headland jutting into Concarneau bay gives it tranquil views across shimmering seas towards the Îles de Glénan and the Baie de la Forêt. Not much happens apart from fishing and a few water-sports. The catch of the day is sold from a kiosk by the tourist office every evening, but you can try your luck at *pêche-à-pied* for crabs and prawns at low tide. Footpaths follow the coastline in both directions along undeveloped dune-belts. Cap Coz to the north has more idyllic sheltered beaches, while the more remote south-facing beaches beyond the Pointe du Mousterlin are popular with naturists. Other paths meander inland through cider orchards and a host of wild flowers.

BÉLON

205 E11 2 rue des Gentilshommes, 29340 Riec-sur-Belon, tel 02 98 06 97 65; Jul, Aug Mon–Sat 9.30–12.30, 2.30–7, Sun, hols 10–12.30; Sep–end Jun, Mon, Tue, Thu, Fri 9.30–12, 1–5; or Place de l'Église, 29350 Moëlan-sur-Mer, tel 02 98 39 67 28; Jul, Aug Mon–Sat 9–12, 2–6, Sun 10–12; reduced hours rest of year Vedettes Aven-Bélon river trips Jul and Aug (from east bank; summer ferry service across the river at Port de Bélon)

Bélon is all about oysters, raised here in prodigious quantities on the tidal mud-flats. This complex, unbridged estuary of labyrinthine creeks and lanes is tricky to explore by road. The best way to get an idea of these scattered villages and minuscule harbours half concealed in low-lying, wooded banks is to take a boat trip from Port de Bélon or Pont-Aven. The main communities are Riec-sur-Bélon and Moëlan-sur-Mer, both some distance from the waterfront, but most of the oyster-beds (some can be visited for guided tours and tastings) lie around the Port de Bélon, which spans both banks. A small, ruined fort guards the estuary where it meets the River Aven at the Pointe de Penquernéo. Smart hotels and restaurants in rural backwaters (all proffering oysters, needless to say) cater for sophisticated tastes. Excellent walks follow both banks of the river.

BÉNODET

205 D11 Avenue de la Mer, 29950 Bénodet, tel 02 98 57 00 14; mid-Jun to mid-Sep Mon–Sat 9–7, Sun 10–6; mid-Sep to mid-Jun Mon–Sat 9.30–12, 2–5 Boat trips up the Odet estuary to Quimper, and to Loctudy and the Îles de Glénan Bicycle rental from Cycletty, 5 avenue de la Mer, tel 02 98 57 12 49
www.benodet.fr

The Odet estuary is one of the most beautiful in Brittany, and Bénodet takes full advantage of its fine natural setting near the mouth of the sparkling river. Half-hidden châteaux peep from steep, thickly wooded banks, where herons and kingfishers search for prey. Though still quite small, Bénodet is one of the region's leading beach resorts, always packed with families and sailing enthusiasts in summer. Amenities are excellent, from water sports and seaside activities for children, to a wide choice of boat cruises on the estuary or out to the Îles de Glénan (▷ 64). La Mer Blanche, a large lagoon enclosed by a long sand-bar stretching west of the Pointe de Mousterlin, provides an additional water playground. The seafront casino has low minimum stakes and an unstuffy dress code.

Brest

Brest's colossal natural harbour is its greatest asset, and a significant commercial port. The huge Océanopolis aquarium by the Port de Plaisance is one of the best in Europe.

Inside the Océanopolis aquarium

Detail of a statue on the promenade at Brest

The bridge at Pont de Recouvrance

RATINGS

Boat trips	●●●●
Good for kids (Océanopolis)	●●●●
Historic interest	●●●
Photo stops	●●●

BASICS

199 C8

Place de la Liberté, 29210 Brest, tel 02 98 44 24 96; Jul, Aug Mon–Sat 9.30–7, Sun/hols 10–12;Sep–end Jun Mon–Sat 9.30–12.30, 2–6

The inner-city bus system (Bibus) is well organized with flat-fare tickets; out-of-town routes serve many west Breton destinations (Crozon, Roscoff, Le Conquet, Brignogan-Plage); regular CAT service to Quimper

Brest is a major Breton rail terminal, linked to Paris by a high-speed TGV service (4hr 20min), and to many other Breton towns (Landerneau, Morlaix, Lannion, St-Brieuc, Quimper)

Ferry links to the Crozon peninsula (Le Fret/Camaret); harbour trips from the Port du Commerce (near castle), or Port de Plaisance du Moulin Blanc (near Océanopolis)

Brest-Guipavas airport, tel 02 98 32 01 00, is 11km (7 miles) east of town

www.marie-brest.fr
Designed for residents rather than visitors, but some useful material that can be a little difficult to track down.

SEEING BREST

At first sight, Brest isn't one of Brittany's most obvious tourist attractions. Its massive and costly post-war refit has left much of it tidy but unenticing in the way of many modern cities, and little beyond the waterfront repays exploration. But if you brave its relentless traffic and dispiriting industrial suburbs, you'll find some lively nightlife, good shops and worthwhile sights, notably the impressive aquarium. The port is the heart of the city, always throbbing with life. Its setting on one of the most beautiful bays in France gives views across the busy natural harbour of a constantly changing panorama of passing shipping—a harbour cruise is highly recommended. One of the liveliest central streets is the rue de Siam, named after a delegation of Siamese ambassadors bearing gifts to the court of Louis XIV in 1686. It has many shops and restaurants, and seven modern fountains in sleek black granite. The outlying St-Martin quarter to the northeast of the city survived most of the bombing and gives some idea of Brest's pre-war appearance. It is now a raffish, studenty quarter of pubs and clubs.

HIGHLIGHTS

OCÉANOPOLIS

56 C2• Port de Plaisance du Moulin Blanc 02 98 34 40 40 Apr–end Aug daily 9–6; Sep–end Mar Tue–Sat 10–5, Sun, hols 10–6 (also open Mon during French school holidays). Closed 2 weeks in Jan Adult €15, child 4–17 €10.50, family tickets available; free access to shops and restaurant No. 7 from Place de la Liberté

www.oceanopolis.com

Brest's most high-profile visitor attraction lies on the waterfront some way east of the commercial docks. Océanopolis is a vast and ambitiously presented aquarium with a serious engagement in scientific research and conservation, based on all aspects of life in the oceans. You could easily spend all day here; arrive early to beat the crowds and make the most of it. More than 10,000 marine creatures live in aquariums as large as 1 million litres (220,000 gallons). The park is divided into three sections—Polar, Tropical and Temperate—and

contents cover everything from seaweeds and ocean currents to marine pollution and global warming.

Attractive gardens in the grounds of the château (above)

CHÂTEAU DE BREST

56 A3 • Le Port (between Pont de Recouvrance and cours Dajot) 02 98 22 12 39 Apr to mid-Sep daily 10–6.30, mid-Sep to mid-Dec, Feb, Mar Wed–Mon 10–12, 2–6 (closed mid-Dec to end Jan) Adult €5, student €3.50, under 18 free Guided tours available for groups on request
www.musee-marine.fr

At the mouth of the River Penfeld right by the docks, the castle miraculously escaped the bombs. Its foundations are ancient, and the 14th-century chronicler Froissart declared it one of the largest fortresses in the world. The castle houses the naval headquarters and the Musée de la Marine (Maritime Museum). One memorable exhibit is a German pocket submarine from World War II.

MUSÉE DES BEAUX ARTS

56 B2 • 24 rue Traverse 02 98 00 87 96 Wed–Sat and Mon 10–12, 2–6, Sun 2–6 Adult €4, under 18 free (free entrance first Sun of month)

Brest's Fine Arts Museum is noted for its extensive collection of works from the Pont-Aven Symbolist school, including works by Paul Sérusier and Emile Bernard. One of the most eye-catching paintings is Kneipp's trompe l'oeil cow, whose real horns protrude in 3D from the canvas.

CONSERVATOIRE BOTANIQUE

56 C2 • 52 Allée du Bot 02 98 41 88 95 Garden daily 9–6 (8 in summer), free; information point Jul to mid-Sep Sun–Thu 2–5.30; mid-Sep to end Jun Sun, Wed 2–4.30; greenhouses Jul to mid-Sep Sun–Thu 2–5.30; mid-Sep to end Jun by guided tour every Sun at 4.30 Bibus No. 3, 17, 25, 27 (Palaren stop) Head towards the airport from city centre (D712), take D233 towards Quimper at Place de Strasbourg, and watch for signs on your left

Conservation is the watchword at this fine botanical garden not far from Océanopolis. In beautifully kept grounds covering more than 20 hectares (54 acres) of a deep valley, rare and endangered species abound. A stream runs through it, feeding a chain of ponds and water features.

TIPS

- From the Port de Commerce or Moulin Blanc near Océanopolis, take a boat trip and get some idea of the scale of this magnificent natural harbour.
- EU/NATO state citizens can take a guided tour of the naval base by the castle (Jun–end Sep; you'll need some ID).
- Free shows and concerts are held at the port on Thursday evenings in July and August (Les Jeudis du Port), and the waterfront is always lively with bars and restaurants.
- A walk along the cours Dajot promenade near the castle gives an excellent overview of the dockyards and the Rade de Brest.
- Brest hosts a huge world-wide gathering of traditional sailing vessels such as tall ships every four years—the next will be in mid-July 2008; plans are already under way.
- Brest is easy to reach by public transport if you don't want the strain of driving.

MORE TO SEE

PONT DE RECOUVRANCE AND TOUR TANGUY

56 A2 ☎ 02 98 45 05 31

Jun–end Sep daily 10–12, 2–7; Oct–end May Wed, Thu 2–5, Sat, Sun 2–6; daily 2–6 during school hols

This huge lift-bridge is said to be the highest in Europe. The small history museum inside contains photographs, paintings and vivid dioramas showing what Brest looked like before the bombs fell.

BACKGROUND

Brest is one of France's largest cities and has been a significant settlement since Roman times. Its natural deep-water port, protected by the Presqu'île de Crozon, has long been home to a large naval base, now second in France after Toulon. As its role was primarily defensive, Brest missed out on the boom years of privateering and colonial trading that enriched many other Breton ports, and its economy remains troubled even today, especially since the decline of the shipbuilding industry. It is still a world-class marine repair base, and is gradually establishing a new wave of high-tech and service industries. Much of Brest's older architecture was destroyed during World War II, when it was an important German U-boat base. It suffered ferocious attacks both from the Allies attempting to forestall submarine assaults on transatlantic convoys, and from the retreating Germans, who blew up as many of the port installations as they could. The city was hastily rebuilt in a bleak, functional grid of angular boulevards and draughty plazas lined with high-rise slabs, although efforts have been made to soften the buildings with parks and gardens.

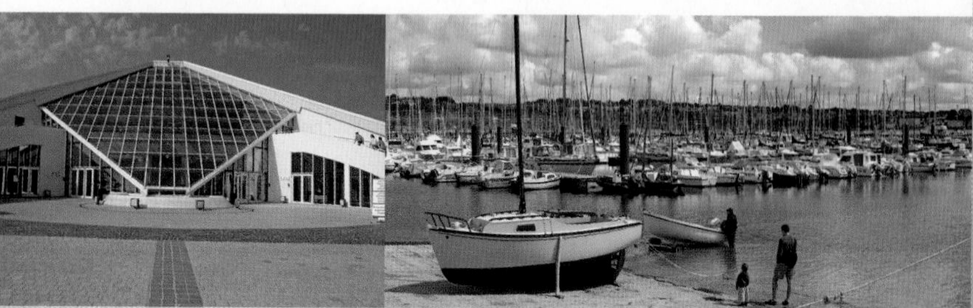

Océanopolis is a concrete-and-glass structure built in the form of a crab (above left).
A view of the harbour at Brest (above right)

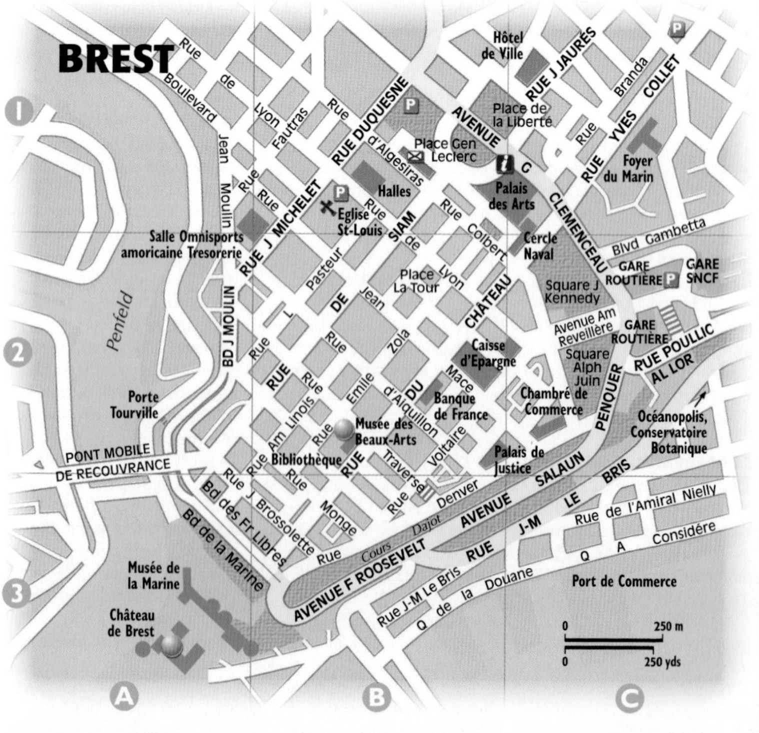
BREST
1
2
3
A
B
C
Rue de Lyon
Boulevard Jean Moulin
Fautras
Rue Duquesne
Rue d'Algesiras
Hôtel de Ville
Place de la Liberté
Avenue
Rue J Jaurès
Branda
Rue Yves Collet
Place Gen Leclerc
Palais des Arts
Foyer du Marin
Halles
Eglise St-Louis
Rue J Michelet
Rue Siam
Rue de Lyon
Rue Colbert
Cercle Naval
Clemenceau
Blvd Gambetta
Gare Routière
Gare SNCF
Salle Omnisports amoricaine
Tresorerie
Penfeld
BD J Moulin
Pasteur
Place La Tour
Château
Square J Kennedy
Avenue Am Reveillère
Gare Routière
Rue Poullic al Lor
Square Alph Juin
Penquer
Caisse d'Epargne
Zola
Emile
Rue de Jean
Rue Am Linois
Banque de France
Chambré de Commerce
Porte Tourville
Musée des Beaux-Arts
d'Aiguillon
Océanopolis, Conservatoire Botanique
Pont Mobile de Recouvrance
Bibliothèque
Traverse
Voltaire
Palais de Justice
Rue J Brossolette
Rue Monge
Denver
Avenue Salaun
Bd des Fr Libres
Bd de la Marine
Cours Dajot
Avenue F Roosevelt
Rue J-M Le Bris
Rue de l'Amiral Nielly
Q A Considére
Musée de la Marine
Château de Brest
Rue J-M Le Bris
Q de la Douane
Port de Commerce
0 250 m
0 250 yds

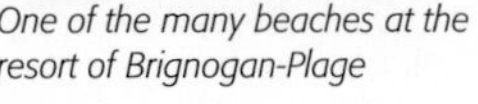

One of the many beaches at the resort of Brignogan-Plage

The Alignements de Lagatjar on the Crozon Peninsula

Dinghies sailing past the Château du Taureau at Carantec

BRIGNOGAN-PLAGE

199 D7 Le Bourg, 29890 Brignogan-Plage, tel 02 98 83 41 08; Jul, Aug Mon 10–1, 4–7, Tue–Sat 9.30–1.30, 4–7, Sun, hols 10–1; Sep–end Jun Tue–Sat 10–12, 2.30–4
www.ot-brignogan-plage.fr

This popular resort on a horseshoe bay occupies a particularly attractive port of Brittany's northern coastline. Its eight linked coves of lovely golden sand are scattered with eroded granite boulders in curious shapes, rather like those on the Côte du Granit Rose (Pink Granite Coast, ▷ 81) but less brilliantly tinted. The plage de Ménéham is one of the most enticing beaches, 2km (1 mile) west of the village. Nearby is the Menhir Marz, an 8m (25ft) standing stone topped by a small stone cross denoting the transition from pagan to Christian times. The church of Goulven to the southeast is a fine example of Finistère's Flamboyant Gothic architecture, dating from the 15th century. A small visitor facility called La Maison des Dunes on the Plouescat road reveals the rich flora and fauna of the Keremma shoreline, now a protected site (tel 02 98 61 69 69; Jul, Aug daily 10.30–6; Sep–end Jun Mon–Fri 2.30–5.30; escorted bird watching and nature walks on Sun, horse-riding Jul, Aug).

CAMARET-SUR-MER

198 B9 15 quai Kléber, 29570 Camaret-sur-Mer, tel 02 98 27 93 60; Jul, Aug Mon–Sat 9–7, Sun 10–1; Jun, Sep Mon–Fri 9–12, 2–6; (5 off-season); seasonal information point by the fort (Mon–Sat 9.15–12, 2–5 summer only)
Seasonal ferries from Camaret to the islands of Sein and Ouessant, and also to Brest
www.camaret-sur-mer.com

Once a leading fishing port specializing in sardines and crayfish, Camaret has reinvented itself with some success as a sailing and beach resort. The forlorn wrecks of abandoned fishing vessels decaying picturesquely in the harbour bear witness to the decline of its prime industry, but visitors throng its unassuming quaysides all summer long, where cafés and seafood bistros make an excuse to linger. It's an attractive little place, a popular haunt of the Impressionist painter Eugène Boudin in the mid-19th century, and still something of an artists' enclave with many galleries and craft studios. The Maison du Patrimoine (tel 02 98 27 82 60; mid-Jun to mid-Sep daily 2–5; mid-Sep to mid-Jun Mon–Fri 2–5), a small maritime museum sharing premises with the tourist office, contains displays on boatbuilding and photographs of Camaret's old *sardiniers* (sardine boats). Beaches flank both sides of the harbour, which is protected by a natural shingle jetty called Le Sillon.

At the far end of Le Sillon stands the quaint 17th-century chapel of Notre-Dame-de-Rocamadour, a pilgrim site dedicated to the seafarers of Camaret. Votive models of ships and oars dangle from its hull-shaped ceiling. Part of the belfry, still unrepaired, was destroyed by an English cannonball in 1694. Next to the chapel is a diminutive, salmon-tinted fort, Tour Vauban, dating from 1689. It contains a modest museum (tel 02 98 27 91 12; mid-Jun to mid-Sep daily 2–5; joint entrance ticket with Maison du Patrimoine) dedicated to its brilliant military architect. Summer boat trips take visitors on fishing expeditions, or to the Tas de Pois (Pile of Peas) sea stacks off the Pointe de Pen-Hir. Camaret makes a fine base from which to explore some of the sensational coastal scenery of the Crozon peninsula (▷ 140–2).

Don't miss Just west of town beyond the striking Pointe du Toulinguet are about 40 stumpy megaliths known as the Alignements de Lagatjar (freely accessible).

CARANTEC

200 E7 4 rue Pasteur, 29660 Carantec, tel 02 98 67 00 43; Jul, Aug Mon–Sat 9.30–7, Sun 9.30–12; reduced hours rest of year
www.ville-carantec.com

This exclusive little resort stands on a headland jutting into Morlaix bay, and is best enjoyed from coastal vantage points such as the Chaise du Curé (Priest's Chair)—a clifftop rock formation. It became fashionable at the turn of the 20th century, and still retains a certain celebrity glamour. It has a delightful setting amid pines and lush, bright vegetation, and lovely beaches studded like jewels in secluded coves; the plage du Kelenn is one of the best. A tidal causeway connects Carantec with the Île Callot, reachable on foot at low water. A *pardon* and Blessing of the Sea take place in the Notre-Dame chapel here on the Sunday after 15 August. The Musée Maritime contains a modest exhibition of vintage sailing boats and displays on oyster-farming and corsairs, plus some interesting material on local Resistance activity during World War II (Jul, Aug Fri–Wed 10–12, 3–6; Easter hols, late Jun 2.30–6).

Don't miss The island fortress in the bay is the Château de Taureau, built to guard Morlaix from incursions by English raiders, and used as a prison during the reign of Louis XIV. It can be seen from the promontory of Penn-al-Lann, east of the resort.

Wild flowers growing on the grassy shores of Cap Sizun (above), and a canoe surfer on the crest of one of the foaming waves (left)

RATINGS

Outdoor pursuits	●●●
Photo stops	●●●●●
Walkability	●●●●

BASICS

204 B10

Pointe du Raz (▷ 71). There's a small office at 64 rue des Bruyères, Beuzec, tel 02 98 70 55 51; Jul, Aug Mon–Sat 9–12.30, 2–6.30; Sep–end Jun Mon–Fri 9–12, 2–5 (closed Wed in winter) and also one at Plouhinec, 2 rue du Général de Gaulle, tel 02 98 70 74 55; Jul, Aug Mon–Sat 9.30–12.30, 2–7, Sun 9.30–12.30; Sep–end Jun Mon–Fri 9–12, 2–6, plus several small information points

CAT Lines 7 and 8 from Quimper to the Pointe du Raz via Douarnenez/Audierne

www.beuzec-cap-sizun.com
www.plouhinec-tourisme.com
A simple but effective site (French only)

TIPS

- Wear sensible footwear if you plan any walking (the rocks can be slippery).
- Take binoculars if you're keen on bird watching (you may be able to borrow some at the Reserve du Cap Sizun).
- The *Fête des Bruyères* (Heather Festival) takes place at Beuzec-Cap-Sizun in mid-August, celebrating Breton culture and music.

CAP SIZUN

Wreathed in legends, Cap Sizun is by any standards a spectacular and formidable section of coastline, culminating in the dramatic Pointe du Raz.

This rugged peninsula of southeastern Finistère forges due west into the Atlantic surf that crashes on its headlands. It ends in a tumble of boulders at Pointe du Raz (▷ 71), an unforgettable sight in a gale. Though this falls short of being Brittany's most westerly point by a narrow margin, it makes a fitting candidate for France's true *finis terra*—the end of the world—as indeed it was for the early Celts who believed that from here lay the route to the afterlife. Other coastal highlights on the western cape include the Baie des Trépassés (Bay of the Dead), where currents wash up the corpses of shipwrecked mariners on its exposed beach. On a clear day, you can usually see the Île de Sein from here, just above the waterline. North of the bay lies the desolate, treeless Pointe du Van, less crowded in high season in the Pointe du Raz, and reachable only on foot across heathland. From these cliffs, magnificent views extend all around the cape.

EXPLORING THE NORTH COAST

The most impressive scenery lies to the north, and the best way to appreciate it is to walk along the coastal path west of Douarnenez. But you can get some idea of it by car, ducking off the D7 to various exhilarating viewpoints at intervals. A lighthouse warns shipping off the rocks of the Pointe du Millier. The Cap Sizun bird sanctuary (tel 02 98 70 13 53; Jul, Aug daily 10–6; Apr–end Jun 10–12, 2–6; guided tours) near Goulien is reached along a clifftop path, and best visited in the nesting season between April and mid-June. The turbines of a nearby wind-farm look ready to mince any local birdlife into pâté, but a visitor outlet called the Maison du Vent (tel 02 98 70 04 09; Jun–end Aug) explains the advantages of this renewable resource.

HEADING SOUTHWARDS

The quieter southern coastal road passes through Plogoff, scene of a fierce protest against a proposed nuclear power station during the 1970s, and Plimelin, with its charming 16th-century chapel of St-Tugen. A beautiful sandy beach graces the Anse du Cabestan near Audierne (▷ 53).

The château at Kerjean: half-castle, half-Renaissance manor

Stone-fronted buildings by the River Aulne at Châteaulin

Frescoes at the Châteauneuf-du-Faou

CHÂTEAU DE KERJEAN

199 D7 • 29440 St-Vougay 02 98 69 93 69 Jul, Aug daily 10–7; Jun, Sep Wed–Mon 10–6; reduced hours rest of year Adult €4, child (7–17) €1 Signposted off the D30 between Plouescat and Landivisiau www.chateau-de-kerjean.com

This fortified manor was built in the 16th century, when Louis Barbier decided to commission a home that would outdo that of his rival and one-time overlord at nearby Lanhouarneau. It is one of the grandest of Brittany's Renaissance manors, and unlike some Finisterian châteaux, relatively easy to find. In summer, it hosts various exhibitions and open-air theatrical performances. The building was damaged by fire in 1710 and suffered again during the Revolution, when its last owner was guillotined. In 1911 it passed into state ownership and was restored and filled with appropriate antique furnishings from the Léon region. Though not original to the house, these authentic country pieces, such as box beds and linen presses, were once staple items in every respectable Breton household. The huge kitchen and cellars can also be visited, and so can the ornate chapel decorated with angels and dragons. The moated building sits in 20ha (50 acres) of parkland lined with stately avenues of beech trees. The grounds also contain a gallows tree where local malefactors met their end.

Don't miss The lovely Renaissance well in the second courtyard has a canopy supported on Corinthian columns.

CHÂTEAULIN

199 D9 Quai Cosmao, 29150 Châteaulin, tel 02 98 86 02 11; Jun–end Aug Mon–Sat 9.30–12.30, 2–7, Sep Tue–Sat 9.30–12.30, 2–7; in winter Wed 2.30–6.30, Sat 9.30–12.30 Châteaulin (Brest–Quimper via Landerneau) The huge Leclerc hypermarket (the biggest in central Finistère) signed off the Crozon road is a useful stop for any essential supplies, a tank of fuel, or a decent coffee (Mon–Sat 9–7.30; closed Sun).

A tranquil setting on the meandering River Aulne, surrounded by water meadows and wooded cliffs, makes this untouristy little town a pleasant stopover. Keen fisherfolk head to Châteaulin to intercept the salmon and trout that leap upriver through its *passe à poissons* (fish ladder) in the spring (a salmon forms part of the town's coat-of-arms). Another draw is its annual grand prix cycle race, held in September. If neither of these pastimes appeals, simply enjoy a wander through the town, whose unpretentious but dignified buildings span both banks of a looping bend in the river. Thursday is the liveliest day, when the market is held in the Quartier des Halles. 2km (1 mile) downstream on the next meander is Port-Launay, Châteaulin's former port on the tidal section of the river. The Aulne forms the western section of the Nantes–Brest Canal, and recent improvements make it navigable for leisure boats along the whole of its course.

Don't miss The hillside 15th- to 16th-century Chapelle de Notre-Dame stands below the ruined château on the left bank. Outside is an early calvary bearing a carving of the Last Judgement.

CHÂTEAUNEUF-DU-FAOU

205 E9 Place Ar-Segal, 29520 Châteauneuf-du-Faou, tel 02 98 81 83 90; Apr–end Sep, Tue–Sat 10–12.30, 2–7, Sun 10.30–12; reduced hours rest of year (closed Wed am, Sun, Mon) Canal-boat rental and excursions in summer from Aulnes Loisirs Plaisance, tel 02 98 73 28 63

Châteauneuf is one of the main touring hubs of the Montagnes Noires (Black Mountains), a sparsely populated region of rounded escarpments along the leafy Nantes–Brest Canal, scattered with wayside chapels and quiet rural villages of dark slate. Châteauneuf is typical, set on a wooded ridge overlooking the locks and weirs of the canalized Aulne.

About 8km (5 miles) east of Châteauneuf is Spezet, right in the heart of the Montagnes Noires and the middle of a strongly Breton-speaking region. Every Whitsuntide (May/June), it holds a festival of the Breton language. If you can follow the signposts (all in Breton) it's a great area for walking, criss-crossed with dozens of footpaths leading through unspoiled, varied countryside of woods, streams and moorland. On the way, you will encounter many minor curiosities—fountains, menhirs and calvaries. About a kilometre (half a mile) south of the village is the chapel of Notre-Dame-du-Crann, dating from 1535, which contains a remarkable set of stained-glass windows relating scenes from the lives of Christ, the Virgin Mary and the saints. To the south of Châteauneuf (signed off the D36 near St-Goazec) lies the country park and château of Trévarez (tel 02 98 26 82 79; Jul, Aug daily 11–6.30; Apr–end Jun, Sep daily 1–6; Mar Wed, Sat, Sun, hols 2–5.30), built around the turn of the 20th century. The château grounds contain a splendid collection of roses and flowering shrubs.

Don't miss The chapel containing the font in Châteauneuf's church is decorated with frescoes painted by the renowned artist Paul Sérusier, a member of the Pont-Aven school, who lived here for over 20 years.

A tranquil beach scene along the coast of Concarneau (above), and a section of the ramparts which surround the town (left)

RATINGS

Boat trips	●●●●
Cultural interest	●●●●
Historic interest	●●●
Photo stops	●●●●

BASICS

205 E11

Quai d'Aiguillon, 29185 Concarneau, tel 02 98 97 01 44; Jul, Aug Mon–Sat 9–7, Sun 10–4; Sep–end Jun Mon–Sat 9–12.30, 2–5.30

Line 20 to the main train line at Rosporden; 21 to Port Manech; 14 to Pont-Aven/Quimperlé and Quimper via La Forêt-Fouesnant

To the Îles Glénan or along the Odet estuary

Tours of the Ville-Close and the Port de Pêche; contact tourist office

The Blue Nets Festival is held in late Aug (folk events)

www.tourismeconcarneau.fr
A bright, attractive site making good use of photos; clear, well-organized menu; an English version is on its way

TIPS

- **Parts of the ramparts are accessible on foot, and give splendid views of the town and harbour (daily 9–5; small charge in high season—adult €0.80, child €0.40).**
- **Good walks around Concarneau include the Boucle de Moros, following the banks of the River Moros upstream.**

CONCARNEAU

The picturesque Ville-Close (walled town) is Concarneau's pride and joy, along with the fishing industry on which much of its prosperity hinges.

Guarding the eastern approaches to a deep and sheltered bay, Concarneau combines the attractions of a beautifully restored historic quarter with the purposeful bustle of a working fishing port. Its dynamic fish auctions (*criées*) animate the quaysides every weekday morning. The town has excellent shops and restaurants, and is also a popular seaside resort, with good beaches and plenty of boat trips.

THE VILLE-CLOSE

Concarneau's historic walled town (Ville-Close) sits on a rocky island within the port, completely surrounded by granite ramparts. Measuring little over a kilometre (half a mile) from end to end, it can easily be explored on foot in a couple of hours. The town was first fortified in the 11th century and was at its most formidable in the 14th. It was subsequently reinforced by the military strategist Vauban during Louis XIV's reign, and has changed little since. Visitors approach the Ville-Close via a fortified bridge and gateway from Place Jean Jaurès. The main street, rue Vauban, is flanked by 16th- to 18th-century buildings, now mostly occupied by flower-decked shops and cafés.

ALL ABOUT FISHING

For an illuminating overview of the fishing industry, visit the excellent Musée de la Pêche (Fishing Museum, Jul, Aug daily 9.30–8; Sep–end Jun daily 10–12, 2–6, adult €6, child €4) near the entrance to the Ville-Close (video show, live aquarium). You can go aboard one of its exhibits, the disused trawler *Hemerica*, to experience a glimpse of life at sea. Concarneau's seine-netting fleet of over 160 deep-sea trawlers ventures well beyond home waters as far as Africa and the Indian Ocean, mainly for tropical tuna. The fish auction held at quai de la Criée (guided visits in French only Easter–end Nov through Vidéo-Mer, tel 06 80 26 34 25) is the largest in Brittany; catches are offloaded throughout the night and dispatched across France. If you prefer live fish, visit the Marinarium, on the seafront at the Place de la Croix (tel 02 98 50 81 64; Feb–end Dec daily), the world's oldest institute of marine biology.

Boats moored in the bay in front of the port of Le Conquet

LE CONQUET

This seductive coastal village is a springboard for trips to the islands of Ouessant and Molène and Armorique marine nature reserve.

198 B8 Parc de Beauséjour, 29217 Le Conquet, tel 02 98 89 11 31; Jul, Aug Mon–Sat 9–12.30, 3–7, Sun, hols 9–12.30; Sep–end Jun Tue–Sat 9–12.30 Line 31 to Brest To Molène and Ouessant www.leconquet.fr

RATINGS	
Boat trips	●●●●
Outdoor pursuits	●●●
Photo stops	●●●
Walkability	●●●●

TIPS

- Ferries depart from the Sainte-Barbe *embarcadère* (landing stage) in the outer harbour.
- Choose a calm day for a boat trip to Ouessant or Molène; it is a notoriously bouncy ride.

Le Conquet is a lively fishing port, whose quaysides are always bustling with boats and full of lobsterpots and piles of netting. This ancient port is the most attractive of any of the coastal resorts in this part of Brittany. Casting a protective eye over the port entrance is La Maison des Seigneurs, part of a larger fortress dating from the 15th century and now a private home. The tiny hilltop chapel of Notre-Dame-de-Bon-Secours makes an interesting contrast to Brittany's larger, more ornate, churches.

AROUND LE CONQUET

From Le Conquet, you can tour the *abers* (fjordlike sea inlets) of northwestern Finistère, or take a ferry to Île d'Ouessant (▷ 65) and Île Molène. A glass-bottomed boat trip reveals the rich marine life in the crystal waters of the Parc Naturel Régional d'Armorique (Armorique Regional Nature Park), now classed as a Biosphere Reserve by UNESCO. Le Conquet has some excellent walks. Take a short stroll to the Kermorvan lighthouse across the estuary, or a longer 5km (3-mile) hike down the low-lying coastal watch-path (*sentier des douaniers*) to Pointe St-Mathieu, where another lighthouse guards a wild stretch of rocky coastline by the ruins of an ancient Benedictine abbey. An exhibition inside explains its history (tel 02 98 89 10 52; Jul, Aug daily; Wed, Sat, Sun in low season; closed Nov–Feb). As dusk falls, 15 local lighthouses flash their warnings off Finistère's deadly reefs. The Pointe de Corsen, 8km (5 miles) north of Le Conquet, is the most westerly point of Finistère. Signposts say it's 5,080km (3,200 miles) to New York.

Statuettes each occupying a niche at Daoulas Abbey

DAOULAS

199 D8 **Abbey** 21 rue de l'Église, Daoulas 02 98 25 84 39 Jul, Aug daily 11–7; Sep–end Jun 10–5 during exhibitions only Adult €6, child €3 (10–18), park only: adult €4, child €2 www.abbaye-daoulas.com

The old linen-weaving centre of Daoulas is famed principally for its abbey, an evocative Romanesque cloister in serene gardens. It stands just a short walk above the town of honey stone at the head of a creek flowing into the Rade de Brest. The abbey now serves as a cultural base, staging exhibitions all summer long. It was badly damaged during the Revolution, but has now been restored and is in the care of the local authority. A medieval herb garden contains an extensive collection of medicinal plants. Excavations steadily reveal more of the abbey's secrets.

DOMAINE DE MENEZ-MEUR

199 D9 • 29460 Hanvec 02 98 68 81 71 Jul, Aug daily 10–7; May, Jun, Sep daily 10–6; Mar, Apr, Oct, Nov Wed, Sun, school hols 1.30–5.30; Dec–end Feb school hols only 1–5 Adult €3.30, child €2.10 (8–14) Various guided tours www.parc-naturel-armorique.fr

Laid out around a renovated farm, this animal park in the heart of the Monts d'Arrée extends over some 400ha (1,000 acres) of undulating countryside, conserving many aspects of traditional land management. Visitors may encounter a variety of endangered Breton fauna, such as rare breeds of cattle and deer. Waymarked walks, play areas, a bar-restaurant and picnic site makes this an all-purpose family day trip, enjoyable as well as educational.

Sunset on the bay at Douarnenez

DOUARNENEZ

Once a leading light of the sardine industry, this fishing port is now a guardian of Brittany's maritime heritage and its associated expertise.

199 C10 2 rue du Dr Mével, 29172 Douarnenez, tel 02 98 92 13 35; Jul, Aug Mon–Sat 10–7; Sep–end Jun Mon–Sat 10–12, 2–6 Line 7 and 9 to Quimper; Line 7 to Pont-Croix, Audierne and the Pointe du Raz Harbour and sea-fishing trips with Vedettes Rosmeur

RATINGS	
Beaches	●●●
Cultural interest	●●●●
Good for kids	●●●
Photo stops	●●●

TIPS

- **Douarnenez is rather a disorienting place, so the first thing to do is get hold of the tourist office's excellent town map.**
- **Douarnenez is a good place to try the Breton cake *kouign amann*, which was invented here.**

Douarnenez is Brittany's second fishing town after Concarneau, and was once France's largest sardine port. Its workmanlike bars and restaurants have a real salty air, cheek-by-jowl with warehouses and marine businesses of many kinds. The town has three sheltered harbours—the main reason for its long success as a fishing port. A *criée* (fish auction) takes place in the early mornings. Hilly streets zigzag down to the narrow estuary harbour of Port-Rhu, which accommodates Douarnenez's maritime museum.

MARITIME MUSEUMS

The splendid Port-Musée (mid-Jun to mid-Sep daily 9–7; combined entrance with Musée du Bateau adult €6.20, child €3.85), approached from Place de l'Enfer, occupies the entire harbour area. Part of it consists of an impressive assembly of traditional working vessels afloat at the quayside, the other section is the covered Musée du Bateau, containing some 40 or so smaller vessels from all over the world. Demonstrations of traditional nautical skills such as sail-making and net-repairing take place in summer.

HISTORY AND LEGEND

The town's history pre-dates Roman times when it specialized in making *garum*, a pungent fish sauce much prized in Roman cuisine. In the 16th century, residents were plagued by the notorious pirate La Fontenelle, who ransacked houses and stole the stone to build his own château on the Île d'Tristan, just offshore.

The annual pardon *at Le Folgoët*

LE FOLGOËT

199 C7 14 Place du Général-Le-Flo, 29260 Lesvenen, tel 02 98 83 01 47; Jul, Aug Mon–Fri 9.30–12.15, 2–6.30, Sat 9.30–12.15, 2–5, Sun 10.30–12; Sep–end Jun Mon–Fri 9.30–12, 2–6, Sat 9.30–12. Information also available at the Musée de Folgoët (€2, free under 14), near the church at Le Folgoët, tel 02 98 21 11 18; mid-Jun to mid-Sep Mon–Sat 10–12.30, 2.30–6.30, Sun 2.30–6.30 Lines 38 (Brignogan–Brest) and 40 (Brest–Roscoff) pass through Le Folgoët

A spectacular *pardon* takes place every September in this little village on the southwest side of Lesneven, when locals dress up in traditional Breton costumes and pilgrims converge from far and wide to pay homage to the resplendently enshrined 15th-century Black Virgin of Folgoët. Le Folgoët means 'Fool's Wood', a reference to the miraculous legend of Salaün (Solomon), a 14th-century simpleton who lived in nearby oak woods. Salaün could speak only the Breton version of 'Hail Lady Virgin Mary', which he reiterated constantly throughout his life. He begged for food and drank water from a local spring (now a fountain by the east wall of the church). When he died, a lily sprang from his grave bearing the words 'Ave Maria' in Latin, and word spread that he was a saint. The Breton nobility financed the outsized Gothic basilica of Notre-Dame which dominates the village. Restored after the Revolution, it contains a fine rood screen and altars of Kersanton granite. In late July, motorists gather in Le Folgoët to have their cars blessed at another religious ceremony, the *pardon* of St. Christophe, patron saint of travellers. Given France's appalling road accident statistics, this may not be such a crazy idea.

The beautiful carving of the parish close at Guimiliau (above), and inside the church (right)

GUIMILIAU

The parish close at Guimiliau is one of Brittany's best—the decorated calvary is a brilliant example of religious art.

Guimiliau's *enclos paroissial* dates from 1588, and is one of the most complex and interesting anywhere in Finistère. The term 'parish close' refers to the walled enclave of consecrated ground beside a church, generally used as a graveyard. Most of the parish closes were created during the 16th and 17th centuries, when vast sums were expended on amassing the finest examples of the mason's art. Generous patrons outdid each other in their efforts to build the most impressive monuments. Parish closes typically consist of a triumphal archway through which funerary processions pass, a carved calvary depicting the passion of Christ, and an ossuary or funerary chapel in which bones were once interred (these are now sometimes used as information points, gift shops, museums).

THE CALVARY

Over 200 carved figures crowd the supporting plinth of this ornate granite structure, all sculpted in contemporary 16th-century dress, and beautifully detailed (notice the braided rope on the donkey). On the cross, Christ and the Virgin are accompanied by St. Peter, St. John and local hero St. Yves. Among the busy tableau of figures below, the four evangelists stand guard at the corner buttresses, while the disciples size up the roast lamb at the Last Supper with keen anticipation. Elsewhere is a grisly scene of a young girl being indecently assaulted and dragged into hell by sadistic demons. Catell Gollet was a careless pleasure-seeker who fell from grace when she stole consecrated wafers at Mass for her lover (the Devil in disguise).

THE CHURCH

The church, in Flamboyant Renaissance style, is just as interesting as its surrounding parish close. From the ornately carved south porch, where a cat and dog chase each other among the 12 apostles, you step into an interior encrusted with vivid carved woodwork. Highlights include a 17th-century organ loft built by Thomas Dallam and a baptismal font with elegant spiral columns.

RATINGS

Cultural interest	●●●●●
Historic interest	●●●●
Photo stops	●●●

BASICS

199 E8

Information available at the Mairie, rue de l'Église, tel 02 98 68 75 06

Free parking on the main street

TIPS

- **There is no convenient public transport to the village, so you will need your own wheels. Occasional escorted summer tours can be arranged around the parish closes.**
- **Avoid sightseeing inside the church during Mass.**
- **Guimiliau has no local tourist office; leaflets about the parish closes and suggested self-guided itineraries are available from other regional offices such as Landerneau or Morlaix.**
- **A short explanatory summary is available in English inside the church.**

A sculpture of Joan of Arc, in the south porch of the church

Pleasure-craft moored at the marina in La Forêt-Fouesnant

Giant boulders by the Rivière d'Argent at Huelgoat

Bagpipe players at a festival in Landerneau

FOUESNANT AND LA FORÊT-FOUESNANT

205 D11 Espace Kernévéleck, 29170 Fouesnant, tel 02 98 51 18 88; Jul, Aug daily; Sep–end Jun Mon–Sat; or 2 rue du Vieux Port, 29940 La Forêt-Fouesnant, tel 02 98 51 42 07; Jul, Aug Mon–Sat 9.30–1, 2–7.30, Sun 10–1; Sep–end Jun Mon–Sat 9.30–12, 2–5 Boat trips to the Îles de Glénan and up the Odet estuary Both tourist offices, though they operate quite separately, are extremely efficient and a mine of useful information about the local area
www.fouesnant-tourisme.com
www.ot-fouesnant.fr

The Fouesnant (pronounced fway-non) region incorporates several scattered communities amid the fertile apple-growing country at the head of the Baie de la Forêt, where twin wooded creeks create a glassy mirror at high tide, and views extend towards the Îles de Glénan. Brittany's best cider is alleged to come from here, and the annual *Fête du Cidre* (July) involves traditional *coiffes* and Breton costumes. The smaller village of La Forêt-Fouesnant, is in a separate commune on the verdant easterly inlet of the St-Laurent estuary. Port-la-Forêt, its modern marina, bristles with the masts of some 800 pleasure-craft in high season. The tidal fishing port, in contrast, is a much sleepier place, though shellfish, especially oysters, are an important source of revenue; *viviers* sell live wares down by the waterfront.

HUELGOAT

200 E9 Moulin du Chaos, 29690 Huelgoat, tel 02 98 99 72 32; Jul, Aug daily 10–12.30, 2–5; Sep–end Jun information at the Mairie Parking and picnic sites around the shoreline

One of the last vestiges of Brittany's great central forest, Huelgoat (High Wood) is a prime location for a host of outdoor activities, especially walking. This waterfront site has attracted settlers since earliest times; the fortified Camp d'Artus dates from Gallo-Roman days, and various canals were dug in the 19th century, when mineral deposits of lead and silver were extracted. Now part of the Parc Naturel Régional d'Armorique, Huelgoat stands on the edge of a lake surrounded by hilly woodland where waymarked paths radiate in all directions. The 1,000ha (2,470-acre) forest extends over the southern slopes of the Monts d'Arrée, gashed by deep valleys. Huelgoat's woodland was much denser and more extensive until quite recently; much was destroyed in about a quarter of an hour during the hurricane of October 1987. Replacement plantings are steadily taking over from the many veteran trees that fell at the height of the storm. The Jardin de l'Argoat and Arboretum du Poerup (tel 02 98 99 95 90; Easter to mid-Sep daily 10–6; mid-Sep to Easter daily 10–5) contains a fine collection of exotic trees and plants, many in danger of extinction. The resort is a low-key cluster of slatey grey-and-white Breton houses well interspersed with vegetation. The Rivière d'Argent (Silver River) carves its tortuous, foam-flecked passage through a jumble of mossy trees and giant, strangely eroded boulders (▷ 143 for a detailed walk in the Huelgoat area.)

ÎLES DE GLÉNAN

205 D12 Municipal tourist office at Fouesnant; information is also available from local offices at excursion ports Boat trips from Bénodet, Concarneau, Quimper, La Forêt-Fouesnant, Loctudy, Beg-Meil

This archipelago of a couple of dozen islets and reefs just 20km (13 miles) offshore is famed for its shell-strewn white-sand beaches and calm, limpid waters, which provide perfect conditions for scuba-diving and sailing. The École des Glénan sailing school on Penfret island is world renowned for dinghy and catamaran training courses. Pleasure-boats dock only on Île de St-Nicolas, which has a scattering of houses, a scuba-diving school and a shellfish farm. Île Guiautec is a wildlife sanctuary (allegedly the smallest in the world), home to many seabirds and a unique species of narcissus, which flowers in mid-April.

LANDERNEAU

199 D8 Pont de Rohan, 29800 Landerneau, tel 02 98 85 13 09; Jul, Aug daily Mon–Sat 9–12.30, 1.30–7, Sun 10–1; Easter–Jun, Sep Mon–Sat 9–12.30, 1.30–5; closed Sat, Sun in winter Landerneau (on TGV Paris-Brest route); connections to Quimper
www.tourisme-landerneau-daoulas.fr

The former capital of the Léon region was once an important inland port at the tidal limit of the River Elorn, and grew rich on the cloth trade. Occasional freight vessels from Brest still unload bulk cargoes at its quaysides, then hastily depart to catch the tide. Its star asset is the Pont de Rohan, a superb, rare example of an inhabited bridge, dating from 1510. The wobbly slate-hung houses are still lived in. Other turreted buildings can be seen near the waterfront. Most date from the late 17th and early 18th centuries, when Landerneau enjoyed its commercial heyday. Landerneau is a popular angling centre (the river abounds with trout and salmon), and also good for shopping—the Comptoir des Produits Bretons on quai Cornouaille may solve any present-buying requirements (▷ 123).

The rugged cliffs of Île d'Ouessant (above), and a remote hillside crêperie *(right)*

ÎLE D'OUESSANT

The largest of Finistère's westerly islands gives a fascinating insight into the bygone lifestyle of Breton seafarers.

Its Breton name (anglicized as Ushant) means 'Isle of Terror', but this refers more to the notoriously hazardous shipping lanes offshore, with their razor-sharp reefs, sea fogs and powerful currents. Many shipwrecks have occurred on this coast despite the lighthouses and warning systems, most notoriously the *Amoco Cadiz*, which went aground off Portsall in 1978, spilling some 220,000 tonnes of toxic crude oil into the sea. But despite the buffetings of the Atlantic gales, the winter climate is exceptionally mild and frost-free.

AROUND THE ISLAND

Ouessant is the largest of several islands off the northwest coast of Finistère, measuring about 7km (5 miles) at its longest. Both the archipelago and its surrounding waters, which are rich in marine life, form part of the Parc Naturel Régional d'Armorique (Armorique Regional Nature Park). Large numbers of migrant birds visit the island, attracted by the lighthouse beams. Most of the islanders subsist on a traditional mix of fishing, farming and tourism. Seaweed- and mussel-farming are newer enterprises. Much of the treeless terrain consists of heathland or sparse unfenced sheep pasture. Ferry passengers arrive at the Baie du Stiff on the east coast of Ouessant. Lampaul is the only real village; it has a few modest hotels, shops and cafés. At the ferry terminal you can rent a bicycle, or arrange a minibus, taxi or horse-drawn carriage tour around the island, or even a horse. An Ecomusée at Niou Uhella (Apr–end Sep, school hols daily 10.30–6.30; Oct–end Mar Tue–Sun 2–4), set in a couple of brightly painted fisherman's cottages, reveals the traditional way of life on Ouessant and its largely matriarchal society (women ran the island economy while the men went off to sea), which persisted well into the 20th century. The Phare du Creac'h (tel 02 98 48 80 70; same hours as Ecomusée), on the west coast, has a museum of lighthouses and coastal warning systems. Otherwise, best things to do on Ouessant are to explore the island and enjoy some fresh air, perhaps with a picnic. A footpath circuits the island's rocky coastline, but there are shorter walks from Lampaul, in fact 45km (28 miles) of paths altogether.

RATINGS	
Cultural interest	●●●●●
Photo stops	●●●
Walking/bicycling	●●●●●

198 A8 · Place de l'Église, 29242 Lampaul · There is no scheduled land transport on the island, but taxis and minibuses are on standby in the holiday season · Boat trips from Le Conquet and Brest; some also call at Molène · You can fly to Ouessant from Brest Airport in summer

www.ot-ouessant.fr
A fairly simple but quickly accessible and easy-to-follow site, with a basic outline of island services and places of interest
See also **www.**ouessant.fr (the site of the local Mairie)

TIPS

- **The easiest beach to reach from the ferry terminal is the Plage du Corz near Lampaul, but you'll find quieter ones if you walk a bit further.**
- **A bicycle is the most convenient way of getting around Ouessant if you have limited time, though you may find bicycling more strenuous than expected into a headwind. Rates from around €10 per day. Bicycling is not permitted on the coastal paths (some of the most scenic).**

A terrace of creeper-covered houses in the old village

The ruins of the Romanesque Abbey of St-Guénolé

LAMPAUL-GUIMILIAU

Often listed as one of the great parish closes of Finistère, the church is more remarkable for its vivid interior than its calvary.

RATINGS	
Cultural interest	●●●●●
Historic interest	●●●●

199 D8 No tourist office, but information available at the Maison du Patrimoine (opposite the church), tel 02 98 68 64 47; mid-Jun to mid-Sep Mon–Fri 10–1, 2.30–6, Sun 10–12.30 Landivisiau The ossuary is now a souvenir shop, as at Guimiliau

TIPS

- **Pick up an explanatory leaflet inside the church, available in English (€0.35).**
- **There is no public transport to the village itself, but Landivisiau station is a short taxi-ride away, and within feasible walking distance.**

Lampaul-Guimiliau, near Landivisiau in the Elorn Valley, vies with nearby Guimiliau (▷ 63) and St-Thégonnec (▷ 78) for the distinction of best parish close. The calvary itself, which is older than the rest of the close, is relatively plain compared with those of its rivals, but its other features are magnificent. The *porte trimphale* (triumphal arch) is surmounted by three crosses, while the adjoining *chapelle funéraire* (ossuary) has turreted buttresses and grapevine decorations.

INSIDE THE CHURCH

The church, its tower foreshortened by a lightning strike in 1809, seems modest from outside (notice the porch of Kersanton stone), but its lavish baroque interior of polychrome timbers and riotous carvings is astonishing. In pride of place across the nave stretches a 16th-century rood beam (*poutre de gloire*), carved with scenes from Christ's passion and crowned with a large, brightly painted crucifix. The robbers look particularly malevolent. The six high-relief 17th-century altarpieces are especially noteworthy, all crowded with detail and decorated with vines and barley-sugar columns. One of the most accomplished recounts the life of John the Baptist; others depict the Birth of the Virgin and the Breton legend of St. Miliau, beheaded by his jealous brother. Fountaining arterial blood, he calmly holds his severed head in his hands. On the north wall, the virginal Sainte Marguerite triumphs over an extremely grumpy devil (represented as a dragon).

LANDÉVENNEC

199 D9 **Abbey** 29560 Landevennec 02 98 27 35 90 Jul to mid-Sep daily 10–7; May, Jun, mid–end Sep Sun–Fri 2–6; Oct–end Apr Sun 2–6 (Sun–Fri 2–6 in school hols) Adult €4; child 8–18 €2.50; new abbey free of charge. A guide is available in English (€1.50) Abbey shop selling regional products, some made by the monks

On a hook-nosed peninsula where the final bend of the Aulne estuary meets the Rade de Brest, Landévennec enjoys an exceptionally mild microclimate, as the lush, Mediterranean-style vegetation billowing all around local gardens amply testifies. It is a most picturesque spot (a *site naturel protégé*), with views over the Rade de Brest, and upstream to the modern Térénez suspension bridge. Visitors come here to see the ruins of its ancient abbey, founded by St. Guénolé in the 5th century. King Gradlon, who ruled the legendary island city of Ys before it flooded in the 6th century, is allegedly buried here. Over the centuries, the abbey has undergone many vicissitudes, but retains some beautifully carved capitals and columns in Romanesque style. A museum presents the history of the abbey and displays archaeological finds. A modern wing still houses a Benedictine community, who welcome visitors to join in their services. There is also an on-site shop selling a number of regional products, including the monks' delicious homemade fruit preserves.

Don't miss The Corniche de Térénez, following the D791 from Le Faou to the Pont de Térénez, gives marvellous views over the estuary, and the shipyard where decommissioned naval vessels are stripped down for scrap.

The renaissance houses in the main cobbled square in the heart of the town (above) and a wood carver at work (right)

LOCRONAN

This glamorous little town is one of the prettiest in Brittany, its patrician architectural heritage exceptionally harmonious and virtually unaltered since the 17th century.

Locronan was a sacred site for the Druids, then a place of Christian pilgrimage after the death of the Irish missionary St. Ronan in the 5th century. The town's golden age in the 17th century was based on the production of sailcloth, but when Louis XIV abolished its monopoly in hemp, Locronan's economy quickly collapsed. In the ensuing centuries, money was never available to update the buildings, leaving the architecture much as it was in the town's heyday. Today, the lovely old Renaissance houses of warm granite and silvery slate are perfectly preserved, and decked in flowers all summer long. Many have been converted into restaurants, shops or galleries, and tourist revenue has revived the town's fortunes.

EXPLORING THE OLD TOWN

At the heart is the old town square, Place de l'Église, where the 15th-century church of St. Ronan (summer daily 9–12, 2–6; reduced hours rest of year) is a masterly example of a style known as Ogival Flamboyant. The pulpit is carved with scenes from the patron saint's life. The square contains an old well, and is surrounded by superbly preserved 17th- and 18th-century buildings; some are the former homes of rich cloth merchants, or administrative offices of the East India Company. It was used as a backdrop during the filming of Roman Polanski's *Tess* (1979). Rue Moal, with more humble weavers' homes, leads to the 15th- and 16th-century church of Notre-Dame-de-Bonne-Nouvelle (Our Lady of Good News; daily 9–6), with stained glass by Alfred Manessier (1911–93). The Musée Municipal, in Place de la Mairie, houses historic items and exhibits relating to the local area (same hours as tourist office).

ARTS AND CRAFTS

The Surrealist painter Yves Tanguy (1900–55) had a home on rue Lann; today various potters, painters and sculptors have studio and gallery space in the town. The Maison des Artisans, on Place de l'Église, displays high-quality craft products in a splendid dormered building.

RATINGS

Cultural interest	●●●
Historic interest	●●●
Photo stops	●●●
Shopping	●●●●

BASICS

204 D10

Place de la Mairie, 29180 Locronan, tel 02 98 91 70 14; Mon–Sat 10–12, 2–7 Jul, Aug; Mon–Fri 10–12, 2–6 Apr–Jun, Sep; Mon–Fri 2–6 Oct, mid Dec–end Mar; closed Nov–mid Dec

Line 10 (Quimper–Camaret) runs through Locronan

Several outlying parking areas, all crowded in high season (€3 mid-Jun to mid-Sep)

www.locronan.org
An appropriately quaint presentation for this historic town, good on heritage and arts and crafts shops, but short on practical details such as opening times and parking

TIP

- Every year in mid-July a procession called *La Petite Troménie* re-enacts St. Ronan's penitential daily climb up the hill behind the town. Every sixth year, a longer pilgrimage (*Grande Troménie*) takes place through the countryside—the next is due in 2007. These ancient rituals are major religious events and a great visitor attraction.

The 19th-century viaduct (above), and an old shingled house nestled between timber-framed houses in the old town (left)

MORLAIX

A handsome old town, a striking setting and lots of attractive shops make this historic port an enjoyable visit.

RATINGS	
Historic interest	●●●●
Photo stops	●●●
Shopping	●●●●
Walkability	●●●●

BASICS

200 E8

Place des Otages, 29600 Morlaix, tel 02 98 62 14 94; Jul, Aug Mon–Sat 10–12.30, 1.30–7, Sun 10.30–12.30; Sep–end Jun Mon–Sat 10–12, 2–6

CAT 16 (Lannion); 51 (Locquirec); 52 and 61 (Huelgoat); 53 (Roscoff, St-Pol-de-Léon via Carantec); 55 (Plougasnou, le Diben) SNCF (Roscoff)

Morlaix is on the main Paris–Brest route, with frequent services to St-Brieuc, Brest and Roscoff

River trips from the port

www.morlaix.fr
www.morlaixtourisme.fr
Both of these sites require additional facilities such as macromedia Flash, Acrobat; some useful links, for example to museum site, but generally poor on detailed factual information. Limited sections in English

TIPS

- Morlaix has lots of enticing food shops and wine-merchants, as well as an excellent market (Saturday).
- The wooded banks of the Morlaix river make fine routes for walking and bicycling, past boatyards, oyster-beds and artichoke fields.

Morlaix sits in a ravine at the head of a large estuary, in the shadow of a monumental 58m (190ft) viaduct, built in the 1860s to carry the Paris–Brest railway. Below it, the old town rises up the steep valley sides in a series of narrow lanes, known locally as *venelles*. It's a rewarding place to explore on foot, though the best views involve some steep gradients. Despite being some 12km (7.5 miles) from the open sea, the town still serves as a significant port, though most of the present traffic in the canalized marina just north of the viaduct consists of pleasure-craft rather than cargo vessels. A handsome if shabby old cigar factory (now decommissioned) makes an impressive waterfront landmark.

REVENGE IS SWEET

Morlaix was once Brittany's third city, prospering on fishing, ship-building, linen, tobacco, paper and more than a little piracy, which made it a target for reprisals. In 1522 the English fleet attacked after Breton corsairs ransacked Bristol. Morlaix's citizens took their revenge when they found the English sleeping off hangovers after helping themselves to the town's wine. The town's coat of arms reflects this incident, showing an English leopard fighting a French lion, with the motto *S'ils te mordent, mords-les* (If they bite you, bite them back).

THE PAST PRESERVED

In the old town, several of Morlaix's idiosyncratic timbered *maisons à lanterne* (lantern houses) survive, characterized by a central hall and a fireplace that carries through to the top of the house. The Maison de la Reine Anne, in the rue du Mur, is where Anne of Brittany stayed in 1505 (tel 02 98 88 23 26; Jul, Aug Mon–Sat 10–6.30; closes at 6 May–end Jun; at 5 in Sep). The recently restored Maison à Pondalez is at 9 Grand Rue (tel 02 98 88 68 88; Jul, Aug Tue–Sat 10.30–12.30, 2–6.30; Apr, May, Sep Mon, Wed–Sat 10–12. 2–6, Sun 2–6; Oct–end Mar, Jun Mon, Wed–Sat 10–12. 2–5), and now forms the reception building for the reconfigured Musée de Morlaix. Léon furniture and Breton paintings are on display inside, but the building itself is the main focus of interest.

Small boats in the bay at Morgat

Mill wheels at Kérouat in the Monts-d'Arrée Économuséum

The fantastically detailed calvary at Pleyben

MONTS D'ARRÉE

199 E8 The head office for the Armorique Regional Nature Park is at 15 Place aux Foires, 29590 Le Faou, tel 02 98 81 90 08. Local tourist offices include 10 rue du Général-de-Gaulle, Le Faou tel 02 98 81 09 84; 3 rue Argoat, 29450 Sizun, tel 02 98 68 88 40 (Apr–end Sep). You can pick up information in many local villages and *ecomusées*, such as at Domaine de Menez-Meur (▷ 61). See also Huelgoat, Moulins de Kerouat
www.parc-naturel-armorique.fr

This sparsely populated belt of ancient hills stretches in a long, narrow ridge across some 60,000ha (148,000 acres) of central Finistère, through a variety of landscapes, including bogland, gorse and heather moors, and granite plateaux. Once these hills towered higher than the Alps, but present altitudes rarely exceed 350m (1,148ft). The summits themselves range from saw-toothed crests to softly contoured dumplings. It's an area imbued with legends and full of wildlife, including wild boar and even some reintroduced beavers. It is now a protected zone, part of the Parc Naturel Régional d'Armorique, but certain areas are used as military training grounds. The most memorable way to experience these hills is on foot; otherwise car-touring is the only practical method. A climb up Roc'h Trévézel, the highest summit (384m/1,260ft), gives extensive views, while the eerie peat bog of Yeun Elez makes an unusual walk—stick to the marked paths.

MORGAT

198 C9 Place d'Ys, 29160 Morgat, tel 02 98 27 29 49; mid-Jun to mid-Sep daily (an all-year office is just up the road in Crozon, ▷ 000) Boat trips to the sea caves (Apr–end Sep); summer ferry to Douarnenez

A popular holiday spot on the Crozon peninsula, Morgat has a sheltered sandy beach in an alluring pine-backed setting. It became fashionable at the end of the 19th century, when Belle-Époque hotels were built by the Peugeot family. It has a large yacht marina, and various other water sports (windsurfing, kayaking, catamaran sailing) are catered to at the *centre nautique*. One popular boat tour goes to the sea caves beyond the headland of Beg-ar-Gador, noted for their strange mineral tints. A breezy clifftop walk leads around the coast to the wild Cap de la Chèvre. Large areas of coastal marshland near Morgat are a great magnet for birdlife, and are now nature reserves.
Don't miss La Grotte de l'Autel (Altar Cave) is the largest and most impressive of the local caves, whose cathedral-like dimensions give it its name. It is reachable only by boat.

MOULINS DE KÉROUAT

199 E8 • 29450 Commana 02 98 68 87 76 Jul, Aug daily 11–7, Jun Mon–Fri 10–6, Sat–Sun 2–6; mid-Mar to end May, Sep, Oct Mon–Fri 10–6, Sun, hols 2–6; in winter school hols Mon–Fri 10–5 Adult €4.50, child (8–18) €2.10; last tickets sold one hour before closing time Guided visits and demonstrations You can buy stone-ground flour and bakery products made from it
www.pnr-armorique.fr

This mill complex in an abandoned Monts d'Arrée village east of Sizun has been restored, and now forms one of the Armorique Regional Nature Park's small educational *écomusées*, showing how this typical rural community would have functioned during the 19th century. Besides the two mills, you can see the furnished mill-owner's house, and the associated bread-ovens, tannery, stables and barns. The earliest parts of the Moulins de Kérouat date from 1610, and were once owned by a mayor of Commana. The domestic quarters belonged to a well-to-do family. One of the mills is in working order, and you can watch the grinding mechanisms in action. Buckwheat flour (still used in classic Breton pancakes called *galettes*) ground at the mills is on sale in the shop. An English guide leaflet is available.

PLEYBEN

199 E9 Place Charles de Gaulle, 29190 Pleyben, tel 02 98 26 71 05; Mon–Fri 10–12, 2.30–6.30, Sat 10–12, 2.30– 5.30 At Pont Coblant you can rent a houseboat or kayak to explore the canalized River Aulne.

Pleyben is famed for its parish close, particularly its unusual calvary, which is one of Finistère's finest and well worth a detour. South of the Monts d'Arrée, Pleyben lies some way from the majority of the parish closes up in the Elorn valley. The calvary base is taller than in most parish closes, with two tiers of carvings. Scenes from Christ's life enliven the structure, which is full of quirky details (a pie ready for the Last Supper, and Christ washing the disciples' feet). These graphic carvings served to spread the good word to illiterate congregations. The church of St-Germain d'Auxerre has a mix of styles: a Renaissance tower flanked by a Gothic spire. The interior has many interesting features: panelled vaulting, coloured statuary, painted beams and a stained-glass window in the choir depicting the Passion of Christ. The ossuary, one of Brittany's oldest, dating from the mid-16th century, now contains a little history exhibition.

Men and women in traditional Breton costume link hands as they parade down a street in the town of Pont l'Abbé

A vendor selling lace products at a stall in Pont l'Abbé

PLOUGUERNEAU

199 C7 Place de l'Europe, 29880 Plouguerneau, tel 02 98 04 70 93; Jul, Aug Mon–Sat 9.30–12.30, 2–7, Sun, hols 10.30–12.30; Easter–end Jun Mon–Sat 9.30–12, 2–5 (closed Wed pm); Sep–Easter Mon, Tue 9.30–12, Thu–Sat 9.30–12, 2–5 (the office in nearby Lannilis may be open if Plouguerneau is closed: Place de l'Église 29870, tel 02 98 04 05 43) Visits to Île Vierge lighthouse (from Lilia); glass-bottomed boat trips (from Perros) www.abers-tourisme.com

The main attraction of this low-key resort village is the lovely beaches scattered around the coast to the northwest. Disparate communities of grey-and-white holiday homes lie around Lilia, where summer boat trips ply to the Phare de la Vierge, tallest lighthouse in France (82.5m/274ft) set amid a chaos of low-tide rocks. A stumpier predecessor stands alongside. Plouguerneau itself has a small museum devoted to the local trade of seaweed-gathering—the Écomusée de Plouguerneau (tel 02 98 04 60 30; Jul, Aug Wed–Mon 2–6; Apr–end Jun, Sep Wed–Mon 2.30–5), which explains the techniques and uses (all in French). The village church contains a collection of quaint wooden statuettes of saints, placed here by grateful parishioners who had escaped the plague.

Children dressed in Breton costume

The church of Notre-Dame du Grouanec just southeast of Plouguerneau has a restored parish close. Grouanec also has a display in the Chappelle St-Michel dedicated to the zealous 17th-century missionary Michel Le Nobletz, who used maps and paintings on wood or sheepskins to illustrate the Christian message to his often-illiterate flock (Jul–end Sep).

Plouguerneau is a useful base for exploring the scenic *abers* (fjord-like sea inlets) that characterize the far northwest coast of Finistère. These are drowned river valleys flooded after the last Ice Age. Tides alternately turn them into brimming mirrors or straggling mud-slicks. Heading southwest over the bridge at Lannilis, you reach Aber-Wrac'h, one of the most picturesque stretches of the Finistère coast, a popular sailing resort with dune-backed sandy beaches and boat trips. The island-scattered Baie des Anges (Angel Bay) is a magical scene, best viewed from the breakfast room of the hotel that bears its name (▷ 169). Sunset views are also stunning on this coast. Nearby Aber-Benoît is a scuba-diving and shellfish-rearing resort.

PONT L'ABBÉ

204 C11 10 Place de la République, 29120 Pont l'Abbé, tel 02 98 82 37 99; Jun–end Aug Mon–Sat 9.30–12.30, 2–7, Sun 10–12.30; Mar–end May Mon–Sat 9.30–12.30, 2–5.30. There's a useful regional office, Maison de Tourisme, rond-point de Kermaria (spot the beached trawler at the roundabout just north of town); tel 02 98 82 30 30; Mon–Fri 9–12, 2–6 and also a *Point Accueil* at Le Sémaphore, Lesconil, 29740 Plobannalec-Lesconil, tel 02 98 87 86 99; Jul, Aug Tue–Sat 9.30–12.30, 2–7; Sep–end Jun Tue–Fri 9.30–12.30 Boat trips from Loctudy to Îles de Glénan, Bénodet, Odet estuary The *Fête des Brodeuses* is a major folk festival in mid-July www.pontlabbe-lesconil.com

The former port and self-styled capital of the Penmarc'h peninsula commands the bridgehead on a complicated estuary which forms a sheltered lagoon just south of the town. Pont-l'Abbé has a long and eventful history dating from medieval times. Attractive granite houses line its main streets. A museum of Bigouden culture rambles over three floors of its 14th-century château (tel 02 98 66 09 03; Jun–end Sep daily 10–12.30, 2–6.30; Easter–end May Mon–Sat 10–12, 2–5). Unmissable exhibits are the distinctive costumes of the Bigouden region, including the gravity-defying *coiffes* (headdresses) measuring up to 30cm (1ft) high, which were habitually worn well into the 20th century. Costumes, lace and hand-embroidered dolls are on sale in local shops, and a large regional market is held on the two main squares on Thursdays.

About 2km (1 mile) south of town, the richly furnished Manoir de Kérazan once belonged to the Astor family; the estate and interior museum can be visited (tel 02 98 87 50 10; mid-Jun to mid-Sep daily 10.30–7; Apr to mid-Jun, mid–late Sep Tue–Sun 2–6; adult €5.55, child (7–15) €3). A passenger ferry connects the quiet seaport of Loctudy with its opposite number Île-Tudy, on a trailing sandspit virtually blocking the estuary mouth. A magnificent beach stretches to Sainte-Marine, on the nearby Odet estuary.

A distant view of the lighthouse at Pointe du Raz

A cobbled street in Pont-Croix

POINTE DU RAZ

204 B10 Maison de la Pointe du Raz, tel 02 98 70 67 18; Jul, Aug daily 9.30–7.30; Apr–end Jun, Sep daily 10.30–6; Oct–end Mar Sun only 2.30–5.30 (daily 10.30–6 in school hols) CAT or Le Coeur Lines 7, 8 (Quimper via Douarnenez/Audierne); free shuttle bus to point from parking area (summer only) Huge parking area by visitor centre, chargeable Apr–end Sep and during school hols) Guided nature rambles www.pointeduraz.com

If not quite Brittany's most westerly extremity, the 70m (230ft)-high Pointe du Raz is certainly one of the most dramatic of its wild headlands, at the western tip of Cap Sizun (▷ 58). Here the land meets the Atlantic Ocean in a crescendo of breaking waves, charging wind and screeching gulls. The views plunging to the sea through rugged chasms in the rocks and across to the Île-de-Sein are awe-inspiring, and quite different from those of the Pointe du Van to the northeast. You can't drive out to the point, but must park some distance inland at an unobtrusively landscaped reception complex containing exhibition space, cafés and shops. A video presentation relays the legend of the Lost City of Ys, submerged as a punishment for the evil ways of Dahut, daughter of King Gradlon, whose murdered lovers were thrown into the Gouffre de Plogoff, a pothole where the sea boils amid rocks far below.

The statue of Notre-Dame des Naufragés at Pointe du Raz

In July and August a shuttle-bus service operates to the lighthouse; otherwise it is a walk of about a kilometre (half a mile) along a paved footpath. Over a million visitors come here annually and in high season the whole area gets very crowded, hence the stringent conservation measures. You can walk out to the last rocky ridge, where there are safety ropes and cables, but the rocks can be very slippery. A powerful tidal race pours back and forth through the straits between Raz and Sein at up to 7 knots, but a few adventurous line fishermen brave the churning currents to catch sea bass.

Don't miss The statue of Notre-Dame des Naufragés (Our Lady of the Shipwrecked) by the signal station gazes towards the reefs and rocks of the Île-de-Sein, a sentimental but poignant reminder of the perils of this coastline.

PONT-CROIX

204 C10 Rue Laennec, 29790 Pont-Croix, tel 02 98 70 40 38; Jul–end Sep Mon–Sat 10–12.30, 2–7, Sun 10–12.30, 3–5; Oct–end Jun Mon–Sat 10–12.30, 2–5

This historic little hilltown at the gateway to Cap Sizun is an obvious defensive site, and was the seat of a powerful medieval family. Pont-Croix stands at the River Goyen's tidal limit and was once a significant inland port, its imposing architecture an indication of its amassed wealth. The town rises up in terraces through a maze of narrow streets flanked by houses of mellow stone. One impressive 16th-century residence on rue de la Prison contains the Musée du Marquisat, a local history exhibition of traditional Breton costumes and furnishings (tel 02 98 70 51 86; mid-Jun to mid-Sep daily 10.30–12.30, 3.30–6.30; rest of year Sun, hols 3–6). However, the town's most interesting building is the church of Notre-Dame de Roscudon, founded in the 13th century and constructed in a distinctive English-influenced style. It has a striking Flamboyant Gothic porch with three delicate gables and a fine belfry with a tall spire. Romanesque arches prop up the nave, superseded by Gothic ones in the choir. There is a superb woodcarving of the Last Supper in the chapel behind the altar.

The entrance to the Notre-Dame de Roscudon in Pont-Croix

THE SIGHTS

Pleasure-boats moored in the harbour at Pont-Aven (above), and a painting on display in the window of the art gallery (left)

RATINGS	
Cultural interest	● ● ● ●
Photo stops	● ● ● ●
Shopping	● ● ● ●
Walkability	● ● ● ●

BASICS

205 E11

5 Place de l'Hôtel-de-Ville, 29930 Pont-Aven, tel 02 98 06 04 70; Jul, Aug Mon–Sat 9.30–7.30, Sun, hols 10–1, 3–6.30; Apr–end Jun, Sep Mon–Sat 9.30–12.30, 2–7, Sun 10–1; Oct–end Mar Mon–Sat 10–12.30, 2–6

Cadoual bus 14a (Quimper–Quimperlé via Concarneau

Boat trips explore the estuary in summer

www.pontaven.com
A bit slow and cumbersome to navigate.

TIPS

- Pont-Aven is a good place for souvenir shopping, with more than 70 art galleries of all kinds. Food products (especially biscuits) and Quimper *faïence* are also widely available. Note that the *galettes* sold here are biscuits, not pancakes.
- A boat trip or drive down the estuary to Port-Manec'h takes you past glorious scenery and photogenic waterfront settlements such as Kerdruc and Rosbras.

PONT-AVEN

Visitors flock here to recapture the scenes that inspired so many artists in the 19th century, and find the town and its setting as picturesque as ever.

It's hard to imagine that this little place was once a busy cargo port and a water-powered industrial base with over a dozen racing mills. The tightly packed granite houses that line its hilly streets were built during its prosperous heyday in the 17th and 18th centuries. Today Pont-Aven's main sources of revenue are the visitors who come to discover more about its famous school of painters, supplemented by a successful line in biscuit-manufacturing.

Many artists still live and work in Pont-Aven, but you don't have to be an art connoisseur (or a biscuit fan) to enjoy this town. Most visitors discover its charms during a quiet stroll beside the rock-strewn River Aven past old mills and waterfalls. The Promenade Xavier Grall is a landscaped garden walkway leading from the bridge that gives the town its name. Dense woods cloak the riverbanks, most famously the painterly haunt of the Bois d'Amour to the north.

The town occupies the final bridging point before the tumbling river leaves its rock-bound valley and broadens into a dazzlingly beautiful ria (drowned estuary), some 12km (7.5km) north of the open sea. On a fine day towards sunset, the quality of the light is unforgettable.

THE PONT-AVEN SCHOOL

The town's principal sight, just off the main square by the tourist office, is the Musée de Pont-Aven (Tel 02 98 06 14 43, Jul, Aug daily 10–7; Apr–end Jun, Sep, Oct 10–12.30, 2–6.30; Feb, Mar, Nov, Dec 10–12.30, 2–6; closed Jan; adult €4, child 12–20 €2.50). This houses both permanent collections of the Pont-Aven school, and temporary exhibitions of past and present art. Here you'll find historic photographs of Pont-Aven, and works by leading artists such as Paul Serusier and Emile Bernard. There are even one or two minor pieces by Paul Gauguin, most renowned of all the painters associated with Pont-Aven.

A statue of Paul Gaugin

Pleasure-boats tied up in the harbour at Port Manec'h

The wide sandy beach at the popular resort of Le Pouldu

A carving at Penmarc'h church

PORT MANEC'H

205 E11 18 Place de l'Église, 29920 Névez, tel 02 98 06 87 90; Mon–Sat 9.30–12, 2–6 (tickets for boat excursions, guided walks, exchange facilities in summer, maps and guides)
www.nevez.com

This little resort presides over the mouth of the Aven–Belon estuary, where the two rivers converge in a V-shape. Its chief asset is a fine sandy beach, which became popular at the turn of the 20th century; the beach huts date from this period. A hillside path links the port and the beach, giving fine views of the pine-strewn coast. The sheltered waters provide an ideal water sports venue; good facilities for boat rental and sailing tuition are available at the prestigious Centre Nautique de Cornouaille. Nearby Raguenez-Plage, with its solitary little hotel, is another gorgeous bit of coastline overlooking a tidal island. Inviting walks follow the banks and cliffs. Inland, distinctive houses built of 2m (6.5ft) standing stones and thatch are unique to this region. Signed near Port-Manec'h, the English-style Jardins de Rospico contain lush plantings of over 2,000 species (tel 02 98 06 71 29; mid-Jun to mid-Sep daily; Apr to mid-Jun Tue–Sun).

LE POULDU

205 F12 Boulevard Charles Filiger, 29360 Clohars-Carnoët, tel 02 98 39 93 42; Jul, Aug Mon–Sat 9.30–12.30, 1.30–6.30, Sun 10–12; Sep–end Jun Mon–Sat 9.30–12.30, 1.30–5.30
www.cloharscarnoet.com

In 1889, a splinter group of prominent Pont-Aven painters, led by Gauguin, broke away from their less talented fellow artists and moved to the quieter coastal community of Le Pouldu at the mouth of the River Laïta further east. Close to the Morbihan border, this resort is now much expanded with holiday homes, and the long, enticing beaches that made it a fashionable watering hole in the late 19th century attract summer crowds. The mural paintings at La Maison de Marie Henri, where Gauguin lodged (now the Café de la Plage), are copies of works the artist left behind in lieu of rent (tel 02 98 39 98 51; guided tours Jul, Aug daily; Jun, Sep Wed–Sun; Apr, May, Oct, Nov Thu–Sun).

PRESQU'ÎLE DE CROZON

198 C9 Boulevard Pralognan-la-Vanoise, 29160 Crozon, tel 02 98 27 07 92; Jun–end Sep Mon–Sat 9.30–1, 2–7, Sun 10–1; Oct–end May Mon–Sat 9.30–12, 2–5.30 Summer ferry from Le Fret to Brest; boat trips from Camaret and Morgat
www.pnr-armorique.fr

This spectacular peninsula forms part of the Armorique regional park, culminating in a three-pronged cape of irresistible wave-lashed drama. Scenic highlights of its cliff-lined westerly coast are the Pointe des Espagnols, the Pointe de Pen-Hir, the Château de Dinan and Cap de la Chèvre. The main resorts are Camaret-sur-Mer (▷ 142) and Morgat (▷ 69). Other sightseeing includes the evocative abbey of Landévennec (▷ 66), plus a handful of little museums operated by the regional park authorities. The rounded heathery summit of Ménez-Hom at its eastern end gives a vast panorama of the area, while the north coast offers fine glimpses of the Rade de Brest through wooded inlets. Exquisite beaches of pale sand lapped by turquoise seas line its southern shores around Douarnenez Bay. Crozon, the largest community on the peninsula, has a fascinating altarpiece in its church of St-Pierre, whose wonderfully crowded panels relate the story of the Ten Thousand Martyrs, slaughtered for their Christian faith by the Emperor Hadrian in the second century AD.
(▷ 140–1 for a drive around the Crozon peninsula.)

PRESQU'ÎLE DE PENMARC'H

204 C11 Place Maréchal-Davout, St-Pierre, 29760, tel 02 98 58 81 44; Jul, Aug daily 9.30–7.30, Sep–end Jun Mon–Fri 9.30–12.30, 2–6, Sat 2–6. Other small offices at Lesconil, Guilvinec, St-Guénolé, Pouldreuzic, or call in at the regional Maison de Tourisme on the northern outskirts of Pont-l'Abbé
www.penmarch.fr

Traditional culture is kept alive in this remote southwesterly peninsula, sometimes known as the Pays Bigouden. Breton costumes are still eagerly fetched out of the closet for *pardons* and festivals, and Celtic dancing and music can be enjoyed at local *festou-noz* (night parties) in summer. At one time, this region enjoyed great prosperity, but pirate raids led by the brutal La Fontanelle and the vagaries of the fishing industry caused economic hardship.

Guilvinec, France's fourth fishing port, showcases its leading industry in an interactive discovery centre with a panoramic terrace overlooking the *criée* called Haliotika (tel 02 98 58 28 38; mid-Mar to mid-Oct, school hols Mon–Fri; also Sat, Sun in summer). St–Guénolé, on Finistère's southwestern tip, has a fine lighthouse of Kersanton granite. The 65m (214ft) Phare d'Eckmühl beams its rays over 50km (30 miles). It is open to visitors for a small charge (tel 02 98 58 60 19; Apr–end Sep daily; Oct–end Mar weekends).

Quimper

The spiritual heart of lower Brittany, Quimper, is a lively reservoir of Breton culture with a well-preserved old quarter and shops filled with local ceramics.

A flower stall at the indoor market in Quimper

A typical Breton motif, used in traditional faïence *decoration*

Selling traditional lace and dresses

RATINGS	
Cultural interest	●●●●
Historic interest	●●●●
Shopping	●●●●●
Good for food	●●●●

BASICS

205 D10

Place de la Résistance, 29000 Quimper, tel 02 98 53 04 05; Jul, Aug Mon–Sat 9–7, Sun 10–1, 3–5.45; Apr to end Jun, Sep Mon–Sat 9.30–12.30, 1.30–6.30 (and Sun 10–12.45 in Jun, early Sep only); Oct to Mar Mon–Sat 9.30–12.30, 1.30–6

A major hub for west Finistère with CAT and Caoudal services in all directions, including 1 (Brest via Le Faou, Plougastel-Daoulas); 2 (Pont-l'Abbé, Île-Tudy); 4 (Pont-l'Abbé, Guilvinec, Penmarc'h); 7 and 8 (Pointe du Raz via Audierne); 9 (Douarnenez); 10 (Camaret-sur-Mer via Locronan, Crozon, Le Fret); 14 (Concarneau, Pont-Aven, Quimperlé); 15 (Beg-Meil); 16 (Bénodet)

Quimper. Frequent services to Brest, Lorient, Vannes, Rennes, Paris

Boat trips down the Odet to Bénodet; kayak rental at Locmaria

The tourist office organizes guided tours of the cathedral and the old town

The *Festival de Cornouaille* (Jul) attracts Celts from across Europe

Most obvious parking is near the tourist office on the banks of the Odet

SEEING QUIMPER

The name comes from the Breton word *kemper*, meaning a confluence of rivers. The Steir meets the Odet in the middle of the city, crossed by numerous flower-lined footbridges. The *vieille ville* extends on either side of the Steir, mainly to the west of the cathedral, whose soaring spires help you keep your bearings. Narrow, cobbled alleys wind past tottering, dormered houses. Parisian-style outdoor cafés and waterfront brasseries make Quimper an inviting place to watch the world go by. It's also an excellent place to shop for classy Breton souvenirs, particularly knitwear and ceramics.

HIGHLIGHTS

CATHÉDRALE ST-CORENTIN

Place St-Corentin May–end Oct Mon–Sat 9.30–12, 1.30–6.30, Sun pm only; open from 9am in winter

The magnificent cathedral was founded in the 13th century, but not completed until the 19th, when the twin spires were added. Its renovated interior gives an air of light and space, but the nave is oddly skewed in relation to the chancel. Stained glass depicts local Cornouaille nobility along with their patron saints—a veritable *Who's Who* of Breton feudal luminaries.

MUSÉE DÉPARTEMENTAL BRETON

1 rue du Roi Gradlon 02 98 95 21 60 Jun–end Sep daily 9–6; Oct–end May Tue–Sat 9–12, 2–5. Sun 2–5; closed Mon, hols Adult €3.80, under 18 free

A splendid array of furniture, crafts and archaeology illustrates the history and culture of south Finistère. A highlight is the collection of Breton costumes. Prehistoric and medieval items are displayed on the ground floor, with embroidery and ceramics on upper floors. It is housed in the former Bishop's Palace, dating from the 16th century. Adjoining the museum is the palace garden (Jardin de l'Évêque), used for summer concerts.

MUSÉE DES BEAUX-ARTS

40 Place St-Corentin 02 98 95 45 20 Jul, Aug daily 10–7; Wed–Mon

Enjoying coffee outside a half-timbered café (above)

The bridge at Quimper (left), and a carved statue on the front of a house (above)

10–12, 2–6, Sun 2–6, rest of year; Adult €4, youth 12–26 €2.50 Access for people with disabilities
www.musee-beauxarts.quimper.fr
This is one of the largest and best art galleries in Brittany, containing over 400 French, Dutch, Flemish and Italian old masters and 19th-century Breton works. The Pont-Aven school is well represented (look out for Gauguin's goose, originally painted on the door of his lodging house). One room is devoted to the drawings and watercolours of Max Jacob, a poet and artist from Quimper.

MUSÉE DE LA FAÏENCE

14 rue J. B. Bousquet 02 98 90 12 72 Mid-Apr to mid-Oct Mon–Sat 10–6 Adult €4, child (7–17) €2.30 Guided tours (some in English)
www.quimper-faiences.com
Quimper has been connected with the production of ceramics (*faïence*) for three centuries. The industry developed in Locmaria, on the site of the Roman settlement of Aquilonia, and the first *faïencerie* was set up in 1690, producing a tin-glazed earthenware that became immensely popular. True Quimper-ware, with its blue-and-yellow flower and bird pattern, is handmade, with a potter's or decorator's signature. The Musée de la Faïence gives an excellent summary of the industry's history, and has a superb display of examples. One of Quimper's biggest and oldest ceramics producers, H. B. Henriot, is next door to the museum in rue Haute. It gives regular guided tours, and has a huge factory showroom (▷ 124).

BACKGROUND

Quimper stands on ancient foundations; evidence of settlements dates back to the Iron Age. In Roman times the city was known as Aquilonia, and served as an inland port. During the Dark Ages, Quimper became associated with the legendary King Gradlon of Cornouaille, whose equestrian statue rides high on the cathedral's west façade. He appointed the saintly hermit Corentin Bishop of Quimper. Quimper was an influential city throughout Brittany's independence but lost its power after the union with France in 1532.

www.quimper-tourisme.com
A good clear site, with well-organized menus and links; interesting material on the faïence industry, surrounding region, and practical information on transport, passport tickets, guided visits and so on

TIPS

- Quimper is easily reached by public transport from many towns in Brittany, which saves you the trouble of finding somewhere to park.
- Mount Frugy, the wooded hill on the south bank of the Odet (70m/230ft), gives a wonderful view of the town—good for walks and picnics.
- Traditional Breton music sessions are held on summer Thursday evenings in the Jardin de l'Évêque.
- The modern Halles (covered market) on quai du Steir is a great place to stock up on provisions. Look out for its delicatessen stalls and bakeries.

A band performing in the port at Roscoff (above), and a statue of a corsair (left)

ROSCOFF

This *petite cité de caractère* is arguably the most attractive of any of the French Channel ferry ports. Small, compact and unspoiled, it deserves more exploration than many of its transient visitors give it.

For a place of such modest dimensions, Roscoff certainly sings for its supper. Besides being a major ferry terminal, it is also a seaside resort specializing in thalassotherapy and seaweed products, and a busy commercial port, mainly for the export of locally reared shellfish and *primeurs* (early vegetables). In earlier centuries, Roscovite privateers took a lively interest in plundering foreign shipping (mainly British), but they also assisted in smuggling huge quantities of contraband to English shores. In 1973 the construction of the deepwater Port de Bloscon for car ferries and container shipping to the east of the town revitalized Roscoff's economy, while leaving the delightful old town behind its original fishing port undisturbed.

EXPLORING THE TOWN

Roscoff occupies a twin-pronged promontory west of Morlaix Bay. The old quarters splay behind the seafront around the Vieux Port. Many handsome granite buildings hint at its lucrative privateering past. A significant landmark is the church of Notre-Dame-de-Croaz-Batz, a Gothic church originally funded by the merchants and corsairs of the town. In new, expanded premises near the railway station, La Maison des Johnnies tells the story of the itinerant salesmen who took their prized *onions rosés* to Britain in the early part of the 20th century (tel 02 98 61 25 48; Jul, Aug daily 3–7; Feb–end Jun, Sep–end Dec by arrangement). Near the ferry terminal is an exotic subtropical garden, with more than 3,000 species (tel 02 98 61 29 19; Mar–Nov daily).

ÎLE DE BATZ

The boat ride to this little outpost (pronounced 'Ba') of sandy beaches just offshore takes 15 minutes, but ferries depart from two different landing stages, depending on the state of the tide. The island itself is just 4km (2.5 miles) long, and easily walkable in half a day. The main sight on Batz is another exotic garden, the Jardin Georges Delaselle (tel 02 98 61 75 65; Jul, Aug daily; Apr–end Jun, Sep Wed–Mon, Oct weekends; guided tours on Sun at 3pm).

RATINGS	
Historic interest	●●●
Photo stops	●●●
Shopping	●●●
Good food	●●●●

BASICS

199 E7

46 rue Gambetta, 29681 Roscoff, tel 02 98 61 12 13; Mon–Sat 9–12, 2–6; (also Sun am in Jul and Aug)

Lines 40 (Brest), 52 (Quimper via St-Pol-de-Léon, Morlaix, Huelgoat, Pleyben), 53 (Morlaix via Carantec)

Roscoff; regular services to Morlaix for connections with Brest, Quimper, St-Brieuc

Brittany Ferries to Plymouth (all year) and Cork (summer only); year-round trips to Batz

www.roscoff-tourisme.com
Admirably clear, elegant and well-organized site with lots of interesting features (for example on seaweed, onions) as well as plenty of hard facts. English version. Some files available only in PDF format

TIPS

- Roscoff has some attractive shops. It's a good place to look for presents, such as stripy Breton knitwear and unusual seaweed beauty products.
- Every August, Roscoff holds a festival dedicated to its most famous vegetable, the *Fête de l'Onion Rosé* (Breton dancing and music, and lots of onions).

Turbulent waters beneath an old arched bridge at Quimperlé

The rooftops of St-Pol-de-Léon, viewed from the Kreisker chapel

Sainte–Croix church at Quimperle

QUIMPERLÉ

205 F11 Main office, open all year, is in the upper town at 45 Place St-Michel, 29300 Quimperlé, tel 02 98 96 04 32; Jul, Aug daily; Sep–end Jun Mon–Sat. A seasonal *point d'information* can be found by the bridge in the lower town, Le Bourgneuf, same tel; Jul, Aug Mon–Sat Quimperlé (TVG Quimper–Paris line) Summer cruises and kayak rental along the Laïta Guided tours of the town, and through the national forest of Carnoët www.quimperletourisme.com

As the preponderance of religious architecture in the town suggests, Quimperlé began life as a monastic community. It was founded by Benedictines in the 11th century, and later joined by Ursuline and Capuchin houses, but despite its pious origins, Quimperlé has no shortage of convivial pubs and bars. The name of the town, like Quimper, indicates a meeting place of rivers, in this case the Ellé and the Isole, which converge here to form the Laïta estuary, once navigable by sizeable vessels as far as Quimperlé. The town is built on two levels. The old town clusters around the Église Sainte-Croix on an island where the two rivers meet, while the newer *haute ville* lies uphill, focused on the Gothic church of Notre-Dame de l'Assomption, generally known as St-Michel.

Sainte-Croix is one of Brittany's most refined examples of Romanesque architecture, designed to a circular Greek Cross plan echoing the Church of the Holy Sepulchre in Jerusalem. The original belltower collapsed in 1862, causing considerable damage to the rest of the church. Its replacement stands separate from the main building.

A number of quaint, half-timbered buildings are scattered around the town. The Maison des Archers on rue Dom-Morice is one of the best examples (used for temporary exhibitions); other fine houses can be seen on rue Bremond-d'Ars.

South of the town, the 750ha (1,800-acre) Forêt de Carnoët extends through the Laita valley, a popular area for walks and picnics.

ST-HERBOT

200 E9 Nearest is at Huelgoat (▷ 64)

This Monts d'Arrée village 7km (4 miles) southwest of Huelgoat has a gem of a church in Flamboyant Gothic style. Set in a glade of trees, it seems quite disproportionate in size and grandeur to the modest scale of the community it serves. Its formidable 30m (97ft) tower is encrusted with delicate pinnacles and openwork arches. Outside stands an unusual calvary dating from 1571, sculpted in Kersanton stone in a curiously modern, almost cartoon-like style. St. Herbot, patron saint of cattle, presides at one of the elegant porch entrances to the church, framed by angels. The church interior contains some fine glass and woodwork and a granite floor, but its most striking feature is the carved oak screen around the chancel. In times gone by, local farmers would leave pats of butter or tufts of hair from the tails of their cattle on the stone tables by the screen as an offering to St. Herbot, in hopes of a blessing for their livestock.

ST-POL-DE-LÉON

199 E7 Place de l'Evéché, 29250, tel 02 98 69 05 69; Jul, Aug Mon–Sat 9–12, 2–7, Sun, hols 10–12; Sep–end Jun Mon–Sat 9–12, 2–5.30 St-Pol-de-Léon (on Morlaix–Roscoff line)

At the heart of a busy market-gardening region, St-Pol's primary role is that of agricultural hub. Huge container lorries and tractors laden with cauliflowers, artichokes and onions thunder through the town for most of the year, especially for its Tuesday market, which takes place in the main square. The tourist office arranges summer tours round some of the highly productive farms in the area to show how the top-quality vegetables of the *Ceinture d'Orée* (Gold Belt) are grown and packed for market. Historically, St-Pol served as one of Lower Brittany's leading religious areas, and was the seat of its first bishop, St. Paul (Pol) the Aurelian, a Welsh monk. The town is no longer a bishopric, but the cathedral (Mon–Fri 10–12, 2–6, Sun 2–6; guided tours Jul, Aug), built between the 13th and 16th centuries, still looms over the marketplace. Unusually, it is constructed in Norman limestone rather than the ubiquitous granite of most Breton churches.

The weighty Gothic towers of the cathedral are overshadowed by St-Pol's most dominant building, the soaring belltower of La Chapelle Notre-Dame-du-Kreisker (Jul, Aug daily 10–12, 2–6; reduced hours in low season). Topped by Brittany's highest spire, it rises to 78m (256ft), pierced by flower-like shapes to reduce wind resistance. You can climb the tower for magnificent views extending as far as the Monts d'Arrée (Jul, Aug only). Several historic buildings can be seen in St-Pol's older streets, particularly in rue Général-Leclerc. The 16th-century Maison Prébendale, distinguished by its emblazoned façade, was a former canon's residence.

St-Pol has one or two reasonable beaches and good water sports facilities, so attracts some conventional seaside tourism.

Stained-glass windows in the church in the parish close of St-Thégonnec (above), and the calvary (left)

RATINGS

Cultural interest	●●●●●
Historic interest	●●●●
Photo stops	●●●●

BASICS

199 E8

A small information point operates in summer at Park an Illis, 29410 St-Thégonnec, tel 02 98 79 67 80; mid-Jun to mid-Sep Mon–Sat 10–1, 2–6; otherwise contact the local Mairie, tel 02 98 79 61 06

The calvary and close are freely accessible at all times; the church is open at conventional hours all year round

TIPS

- An organization called SPREV (Sauvegarde du Patrimoine Religieux en Vie) arranges free guided tours of the parish closes in July and August (ask the local tourist office for details, tel 02 98 79 67 80).
- There's no convenient public transport to St-Thégonnec, but it does have a little railway station on a line from Morlaix; alternatively catch a coach from Morlaix railway station.
- Keen walkers can find their way to St-Thégonnec on the GR380 (long-distance footpath), which runs from Morlaix to Lampaul-Guimiliau (another fine parish close, ▷ 66).

ST-THÉGONNEC

This star parish close was one of the last to be built in Finistère, and no expense was spared. Its magnificent calvary vividly encapsulates the torment of Christ.

The parish of St-Thégonnec was one of the richest in Léon by the end of the 16th century. Its wealthy merchants dug deep into their pockets to outdo all their rivals in this idiosyncratic Finistèrian art form. From the outset, this church clearly aims to impress its earthly visitors as well as God. The patron saint of this village is little known outside Brittany, but the story goes that St. Thégonnec tamed one of the wolves that had eaten his donkey, and harnessed it to his cart to carry him around. Depictions of him in his wolf-cart are clearly recognizable throughout the region.

THE CLOSE

The archway at the entrance to the parish close is suitably triumphal, constructed in 1587 in Renaissance style with niches and scrolls, surmounted by lantern turrets. The exuberantly decorated ossuary crypt contains a masterly oak Entombment sculpture dating from 1702. It was carved by the Morlaix sculptor Jacques Lespaignol.

THE CALVARY

The calvary was constructed in 1610. Scenes from the Passion on this multi-branched calvary are especially graphic. Notice the Roman soldiers, and the faces of the Christ's revilers, grimacing monstrously in Renaissance dress. One of these figures is alleged to have been modelled on the Protestant king Henry IV, who expediently converted to Catholicism in 1592 before signing the Edict of Nantes. St. Thégonnec puts in an appearance in his trademark wolf-cart on a low niche.

THE CHURCH

The church suffered a serious fire in 1998 and is still undergoing restoration. The chapels on the north side were severely damaged when the roof collapsed, but the valiant efforts of parishioners and dozens of firefighters managed to keep the flames from destroying its most precious treasures, including its splendid carved pulpit, dating from 1683. The figures depicted on its crowded surfaces include the four Cardinal Virtues, the Evangelists, and the Angel of Judgement.

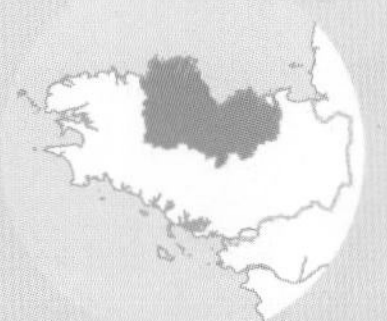

CÔTES-D'ARMOR

The great glory of this *département* is its coastline. Besides the magnificent natural scenery of the Emerald and Pink Granite coasts, several of its towns (Dinan, Tréguier, Paimpol) are among the most popular in Brittany. On the borders of Upper and Lower Brittany, Côtes-d'Armor is a transitional zone, subtly shifting from the French-speaking 'Gallo' culture of Haute-Bretagne to the region's more distinctive Celtic character further west.

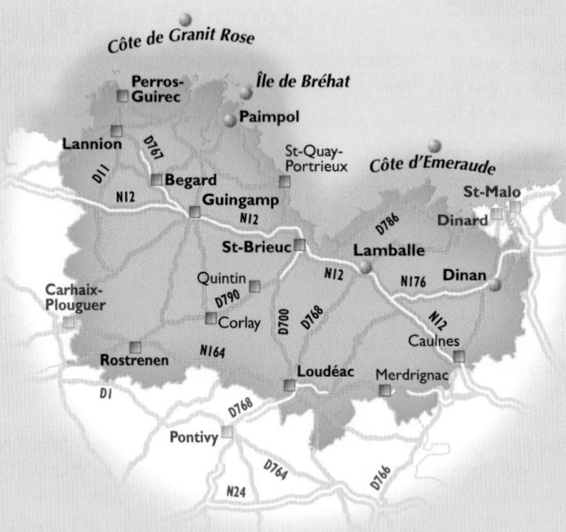

MAJOR SIGHTS

The dramatic Breton coastline at Cap Frehel (above), and playing boules in the sunshine in Erquy (left)

RATINGS	
Boat trips	●●●●●
Photo stops	●●●●●
Walkability	●●●●●
Beaches	●●●●●

BASICS

202 L7

Main offices in St-Malo, Dinard, St-Briac-sur-Mer, St-Cast-le-Guildo and Le Val-André (see separate entries). Additional offices are at rue du Châtelet, 22750 St-Jacut-de-la-Mer, tel 02 96 27 71 91, Mon 1.30–5.30, Tue–Fri 9–12, 1.30–5.30, Sat 9–12; Le Bourg, 22240 Fréhel, tel 02 96 41 53 81, Tue-Sat 9–12.30, 2.30–6; and 29 boulevard de la Mer, 22430 Erquy, tel 02 96 72 30 12, Jul, Aug Mon–Sat 9.30–1, 2–7, Sun 10–12.30, 3.30–6.30; Sep–end Jun Mon–Sat 9.30–12.30; 2–5. See also Sables-d'Or-les-Pins

CAT Line 2 (Fréhel–St-Brieuc) and Line 14 (St–Malo–St-Cast-le-Guildo)

St-Malo

Boat trips from all the larger resorts

www.erquy-tourisme.com
www.pays-de-frehel.com
Mainly for locals, but easy to navigate and full of information

TIP

- **Colour-coded, numbered marker posts along the Cap Fréhel coastal footpath make things easier for emergency rescue services. Note details of the nearest one if you need to call for help.**

CÔTE D'EMERAUDE

Verdant cliffs and headlands give this rugged stretch of coastline its name, as well as the sparkling waters. Views are truly spectacular both from land and sea.

The 19th-century artists who immortalized scenes along the Emerald Coast represent just a handful of many thousands of visitors captivated by its stunning natural beauty. The most beautiful and least built-up stretches lie immediately southwest of the Pointe de Grouin and around Cap Fréhel. Roads hug the coast closely here, making it possible to see something of this panoramic scenery by car. The best ways to experience the Emerald Coast, however, are on foot or by boat. Most of its larger resorts are described separately in this chapter; see also the driving tours on pages 144–5 and 148–9.

CAP FRÉHEL

This headland, 70m (230ft) above the sea, is one of the most dramatic vantage points along the Emerald Coast. Gnarled cliffs of distinctive reddish-grey sandstone plunge to the frothing waves, providing nesting places for countless seabirds (guided nature tours Jun–end Sep daily through the Syndicat des Caps; tel 02 96 41 50 83). You can visit and climb Fréhel's square-towered lighthouse (tel 02 96 41 40 03; Apr–end Sep daily at the keeper's discretion), and on a clear day see as far as the Channel Islands. The headland east of Fréhel is memorable for the romantic, irresistibly photogenic fortress of La Latte (tel 02 96 41 40 31, guided tours Jun–Sep daily; Oct–Apr Sat, Sun, school hols 2–6). West of Fréhel lie some of Brittany's most beautiful beaches, notably at Sables-d'Or-les-Pins (▷ 89) and Le Val-André (▷ 92). Between these two lies Erquy, one of France's leading scallop-fishing ports.

THE CENTRAL RESORTS

Deep inlets and estuaries gouge into the coast between Cap Fréhel and St-Malo (▷ 106–8). Most striking is the great Rance estuary, biting inland between Dinard (▷ 95) and St-Malo. A host of small, pleasantly traditional family seaside resorts capitalize on the glorious sandy beaches. Seabirds search through the oyster beds of the Baie de la Fresnaye, and hundreds of mussel-posts emerge from the inshore mudflats of the Baie d'Arguenon.

The pink-tinged old stone oratory at St-Guirec, near Ploumanac'h (above), and the lighthouse along the coastline (right)

CÔTE DE GRANIT ROSE

The extraordinary outcrops of eroded russet granite that characterize this part of Brittany make this stretch of coastline unforgettable.

The Pink Granite Coast, between Trébeurden and Paimpol, is one of the most dramatic stretches of Brittany's northern shoreline. The coastline gets its name from the local granite's startling hues: pinkish-brown in harsh sunlight, warming to a vivid coppery glow at sunset. Pink granite is a popular building material all along this coast, a sharp contrast to the grey stone or white-painted cement in other areas of Brittany.

AROUND PLOUMANAC'H

The most remarkable and easily accessible scenery lies around Ploumanac'h, just west of Perros-Guirec (▷ 146–7 for a walk along this stretch of coastline). Resort facilities are excellent for active holidays, but this coast gets very crowded in high season. Both Perros-Guirec and Trébeurden have large, well-equipped marinas. Offshore lies the bird sanctuary archipelago of Les Sept Îles, where puffins and petrels breed. The islands are easily accessible by boat.

PRESQU'ÎLE DE PLOUGRESCANT

East of Perros-Guirec a maze of narrow lanes carries you through the tiny settlements of the remote Plougrescant peninsula. While the rocks are less brightly tinted here, colour is provided by vivid gorse on the heathy hinterland, earning this area the name Côte des Ajoncs—Gorse Coast. The fishing village of Port-Blanc has a quaint chapel whose eaves swoop almost to the ground. Further north lie wind-blown promontories such as Pointe du Château or Le Gouffre, and a picturesque little house sandwiched between huge boulders.

PRESQU'ÎLE SAUVAGE

The next of these ragged coastal tatters culminates in a strange sandspit called the Sillon de Talbert, which straggles 3km (2 miles) seawards, a haunt of nesting terns. The Phare des Héaux stands some way offshore, one of the highest in France. Find out about seaweed-gathering at the seaweed research centre (Centre d'Etude et de Valorisation des Algues (CEVA), near the main village of Pleubian.

RATINGS

Beaches	●●●●
Good for kids	●●●●
Outdoor pursuits	●●●●●
Photo stops	●●●●●

BASICS

201 G6

Offices at Lannion, Perros-Guirec, Tréguier and Paimpol (see separate entries); also at Place de Crec'h Hery, 22560 Trébeurden, tel 02 96 23 51 64, Jul, Aug Mon–Sat 9–7, Sun, hols 10–1; Sep–end Jun Mon–Sat 9–12, 2–6; Maison de la Presqu'île, carrefour de Kerantour, 22740 Pleudaniel, tel 02 96 22 16 45, Jul, Aug daily 9.30–12.30, 2–7; seasonal information points at Ploumanac'h, Port-Blanc, Plougrescant and Trégastel

CAT Lines 7 and 15 serve this coast, with more limited routes around Plougrescant for schools

Lannion, Paimpol

Trips to Les Sept Îles from Perros-Guirec, Ploumanac'h, Trégastel, and to l'Île de Bréhat from Paimpol

TIPS

- **The Sillon de Talbert makes a fine walk, but be very cautious of tidal cut-off points at the far end; access is restricted in spring when the terns are nesting.**
- **Take a flight from Lannion airport for an overview of this spectacular coastline; tel 02 96 46 41 00 (15–30 minute trips from €35 per person).**

Dinan

This gorgeous fortified town at the head of the Rance is one of Brittany's best-preserved medieval towns, with some of the region's most characterful buildings and stunning views.

The waterfront buildings overlooking the River Rance

The castle keep at Dinan

Five-floor residences overlooking Place de Guesclin

SEEING DINAN

Dinan clings to a steep wooded bluff high above the Rance valley, encased in sturdy walls. The best way to see the compact old town is on foot, though the gradients are steep in places. Parts of the 600-year-old ramparts are walkable, giving magnificent views. From the old quarter, cobbled streets clamber down the hillside to an exceptionally attractive port. But the true heart of Dinan beats within its ancient walls, around picturesque lopsided buildings. The grand set pieces are the castle, the clock-tower and several churches and convents, but the humbler merchants' houses are every bit as delightful with their drunken timbering and jettied façades propped on stone pillars. Many now house hotels, restaurants, art galleries and craft shops.

HIGHLIGHTS

CHÂTEAU-MUSÉE AND RAMPARTS

Rue du Château · 02 96 39 45 20 · Jun–end Sep daily 10–6.30; Oct–end May daily 1.30–5.30 (closed Jan) · Adult €4.10, child €1.60, under 12 free

The museum in the ruined 14th-century castle keep has displays ranging from prehistoric times to the early 20th century, including local crafts. From the rampart sentry path, magnificent panoramic views extend over the town and valley. Highlights are the 15th-century Tour de Coëtquen (the castle's old artillery tower) and the Promenade de la Duchesse-Anne, which brings you into the terraced gardens of the Jardin Anglais.

OLD TOWN

In the 12th century, Dinan crusader Rivallon le Roux pledged that, if he survived, he would return to his home town and pay for a church dedicated to Christ. The resulting Gothic and Romanesque St. Sauveur basilica was built between the 12th and 18th centuries. Relics include the heart of Bertrand du Guesclin, whose equestrian statue stands in the market square of Place du Guesclin.

RATINGS	
Historic interest	●●●●
Good for food	●●●●
Photo stops	●●●●●
Shopping	●●●●

BASICS

202 L9

9 rue du Château, 22105 Dinan, tel 02 96 87 69 76; Jun to Sep Mon–Sat 9–7, Sun 10–12.30, 2.30–6; mid-Sep to mid-Jun Mon–Sat 9–12.30, 2–6

CAT to St-Malo, St-Cast-le-Guildo; TAE to Dinard and Rennes

Dinan; services to St-Malo via Dol-de-Bretagne

St-Malo and Dinard along the Rance

The biennial *Fête des Remparts* takes place in even years (next in late July 2006)

Place du Guesclin (Fri–Wed only; check signs carefully to see which spaces are free of charge)

www.dinan-tourisme.com
Interesting historical information, two virtual tours and places to visit in the Rance valley.

Equestrian statue of Bertrand du Guesclin (left), and the scenic port of Dinan (facing page)

TIPS

- Climb the Tour de l'Horloge for wonderful views of the old town and the Rance valley (Jun–end Sep daily 10–6.30; Apr, May daily 2–6.30).
- You can take boat trips along the Rance between St-Malo and Dinan from April to September. Tidal conditions make it tricky to go both ways within a day, but you can easily do one journey by boat and return by bus or train.

The Gothic Église St-Malo has a superb English organ, dating from the Romantic period, and beautiful stained-glass windows illustrating great moments in the town's history (guided tours in both churches Jun–end Aug). Other buildings to look out for are the old monastery of the Ancien Couvent des Cordeliers with its 15th-century cloisters and pepperpot roof turrets, and the 17th-century Maison du Gisant, with its recumbent statue.

PORT

Narrow, cobbled rue de Jerzual and its continuation, rue du Petit-Fort, wind down to the river from the heart of the old town. The Maison du Gouverneur (tel 02 96 39 29 97; Jun–end Sep daily) is a spectacular half-timbered house containing a display of regional furniture.

An old lady tends flowers in a window in Jerzual Street

A tourist boat in serene waters at the Dinan port

- A petit train will save you a steep climb up from the port if you time it right (Easter to mid-Oct 10–6; adult €5, child (3–12) €3.50). Dinan bus No. 4 is cheaper, but infrequent.
- On Thursdays (market day), no cars are allowed to park in Place du Guesclin.

Waterfront warehouses bear witness to the former success of Dinan's riverine trade, and the harbour now makes a pleasing scene of restaurants and cafés. The waterfront Maison d'Artiste de la Grande Vigne is the former home of artist Yvonne Jean-Haffen (1895–1993), now a museum displaying her works (tel 02 96 87 58 72; late May–Sep daily). On the opposite (Lanvallay) bank of the river, the Maison de la Rance contains an exhibition about the river's history, economy and wildlife (tel 02 96 87 00 40; Apr–Oct daily; Sun only in winter).

MORE TO SEE

LÉHON

This pretty hamlet is a pleasant 2km (1-mile) walk across the river from Dinan. Visitors come to see the 12th-century priory of St-Magloire (Jul, Aug 10–12, 2.30–6.30; adult €3, child (12–18) €2, free under 12).

The Post Bridge and viaduct at Dinan (above), and an aerial view of the town (right)

BACKGROUND

Dinan dates back well over a thousand years, but it didn't achieve great prominence until it acquired a Benedictine monastery in the 10th century. It played a major role in the Hundred Years War, when it was defended by local hero Bertrand du Guesclin. Under the ownership of the Dukes of Brittany, Dinan prospered as a trading port, mainly from the proceeds of sail-cloth and leather, and multifarious cargoes floated to and from its tidal quaysides.

Taking a boat trip around the Île de Brehat (above), and relaxing on a café terrace (right)

ÎLE DE BRÉHAT

This tiny rural idyll makes a seductive day-trip from the mainland. It has no must-see sights, but is a picturesque, traffic-free retreat for walking or bicycling.

According to legend, Christopher Columbus learned of a sea route to the New World from the intrepid fishermen of Bréhat. In summer, thousands of visitors, mostly day-trippers from Pointe de l'Arcouest north of Paimpol, boost the island's resident population tenfold. It isn't hard to discover why this island paradise deserves investigation.

Just 2km (1 mile) offshore, Bréhat consists of two tiny islands like tattered butterfly wings pinned together by a 16th-century bridge called the Pont-ar-Prat. A ring of copper-coloured reefs protects its coves of pink shingle from Atlantic breakers. Each of these low-lying islands, measures less than a kilometre (half a mile) in length.

ÎLE SUD

Most of Bréhat's 470 or so residents live in the south island, where the mild Gulf Stream climate has encouraged a profusion of Mediterranean plants in the gardens of prettily painted villas. Ferries dock at the tiny Port Clos, on the south coast. The hilltop fortress here houses a glass-blowing studio, the Verreries de Bréhat (tel 02 96 20 09 09; Apr–end Sep daily ; Oct–Mar Mon–Fri). The Grève de Guerzido, the island's best beach, faces the mainland on Bréhat's southeast corner. From Port Clos it is a 500m (550yd) walk north to the main village, Le Bourg. West of here is the Chapelle St-Michel, highest point on Bréhat, whose 39 steps lead to a splendid view. Nearby, the Moulin à Marée du Birlot is a restored 17th-century tidal mill (which is occasionally open to the public, depending on the tide).

ÎLE NORD

Beyond Vauban's bridge spanning the sheltered port known as La Corderie, the northern island is quieter and more windswept, but smothered in wild flowers and full of birds. The billowing hydrangeas, mimosa and geraniums give way to wilder, turf-covered moorland flecked with gorse, bracken and occasional pines. Two lighthouses and a semaphore signal station make focal points for walks. The pink-granite Phare du Paon, off Bréhat's northeastern tip, has marvellous coastal views. Inland, the Rosedo lighthouse dates from 1862.

RATINGS

Photo stops	●●●●
Walking and bicycling	●●●●●

BASICS

201 H6

Le Bourg, 22870, tel 02 96 20 04 15; Tue–Sat 10–12.30, 2–4.30

Vedettes de Bréhat (tel 02 96 55 79 50) operate year-round services from Pointe de l'Arcouest, just north of Paimpol (summer crossings also run from Binic, Erquy, Perros-Guirec, Le Val-André and St-Quay-Portrieux). Round-the-island trips from Port-Clos in summer

TIPS

- No visitors' cars are allowed on the island, but you can rent bicycles at the ferry terminal to get around.
- Bréhat's maritime microclimate is surprisingly dry and sunny; these low-lying landmasses interrupt few Atlantic rain clouds.
- In summer, it can be hard to find a table at local cafés or restaurants, so take a picnic and find a quiet spot well away from the main port and village.

One of the well-preserved timbered buildings in Lamballe

The church of Brélévenez, with its granite 15th-century spire

THE SIGHTS

LAMBALLE

A handsome old quarter and several interesting sights make this inland town worth a visit, while France's second-largest national stud will delight any horse-lover.

RATINGS	
Historic interest	●●●
Photo stops	●●●

202 K8 Maison du Bourreau, Place du Martray, 22402 Lamballe, tel 02 96 31 05 38; Jul, Aug Mon–Sat 9.30–6.30, Sun, hols 10–12; Sep–end Jun Mon–Sat 10–12.30 , 2–5/6 (closed Mon am, Wed pm, Sat pm off-season) CAT to St-Cast, Erquy, St-Brieuc, Le Val-André Lamballe

TIPS

- Guided walking tours are organized through the tourist office on Wed and Fri in high season.
- In July and August, *Les Jeudis Lamballais* (Lamballe Thursdays) enliven the town (free concerts, carriage rides, horse shows and more).

Lamballe's *raison d'être* is its role as administrative and market hub for the prosperous Penthièvre agricultural region. Large cattle markets are held here, and related industrial enterprises such as animal feed preparation and leather-processing occupy its spreading suburbs. The area most visitors want to see is the old town, compactly knotted around the Place du Martray, where picturesque timbered buildings stand in an excellent state of preservation. The tourist office occupies the eye-catching Maison du Bourreau (Hangman's House), along with a couple of worthwhile little museums. One devoted to the folk history of Lamballe contains costumes, ceramics, tools and prehistoric items (Jul, Aug Mon–Sat 9.30–6.30; variable hours rest of year). The other showcases the varied work of the local artist Mathurin Méheut, born in the town in 1882 (tel 02 96 31 19 99; Apr, Jun–end Sep Mon–Sat; May, Oct–end Dec Wed, Fri, Sat). An early exponent of art nouveau, Méheut designed jewellery and wallpaper as well as painting Breton daily life and fishing scenes. One of his specialist interests was shipping, and after World War II he became official painter to the French Navy.

THE NATIONAL STUD

The Haras National (national stud) was originally set up in 1825. Its palatial stables house some 70 stallions, many of which are hefty Breton draught horses. Visitors are welcome to look round on guided tours (tel 02 96 50 06 98; mid-Jul to late Aug daily 10.30–5.30; restricted hours rest of year).

LANNION

200 G7 Quai d'Aiguillon 22300 Lannion, tel 02 96 46 41 00; Jul, Aug Mon–Sat 9–7, Sun, hols 10–1; Sep–end Jun Mon–Sat 9.30–12.30, 2–6
Lannion Lannion is a great base for kayaking and canoeing; the *stade d'eau vive* is an artificial white-water course near Pont Sainte-Anne where national championships and training sessions are held By the tourist office on quai d'Aiguillon
www.ot-lannion.fr

This old port spread over the hilly banks of the Léguer is Côtes-d'Armor's second-largest town, a major route-hub and now a prosperous business centre. Despite the modern bustle, this former capital of the Trégor region has managed to retain its traditional Breton character in an old-town core of timber-framed or slate-hung buildings with overhanging façades and quaint corbels carved with strange beasts or human faces. These 16th- and 17th-century buildings are mainly concentrated around the cobbled Place du Général Leclerc and the church of St-Jean-du-Baly.

Lannion's most interesting church is the Église de Brélévenez (guided tours Jul, Aug) in the upper town, reached by a long flight of steps. Founded in the 12th century by the Knights Templar, its elaborate interior is adorned with carved capitals and a Romanesque apse and crypt containing an accomplished *Entombment* sculpture. The views are well worth the 142-step climb (or you can drive to it if you prefer).

Down on the waterfront, long quaysides and wooded towpaths extend along the estuary towards the picturesque hillside hamlet of Le Yaudet. Upstream, ancient chapels and châteaux litter the sinuous Léguer valley, followed along most of its course by a long-distance footpath (GR34A).

Lac de Guerledan at Mûr-de-Bretagne

The lighthouse at Perros-Guirec, on the Pink Granite Coast

MÛR-DE-BRETAGNE

206 H10 Place de l'Église, 22530 Mûr de Bretagne, tel 02 96 28 51 41; Jul, Aug Mon–Sat 10–12.30, 2–6.30, Sun 10.30–12.30; reduced hours in winter; seasonal lakeshore information points, at Bon-Repos, tel 02 96 24 82 20; Gouarec (old station), tel 02 96 24 98 73; St-Aignan (Maison de Pays), tel 02 97 27 51 39 Lac de Guerledan and Nantes–Brest Canal

Far inland on the borders of Côtes-d'Armor and Morbihan, this resort presides over the artificial Lac de Guerledan, a serpentine reservoir that now marks the navigable limits of the Nantes–Brest Canal. The massive concrete dam across the Blavet was constructed in the 1920s and now creates the largest lake in Brittany; hydroelectric power installations and an impressive array of recreational facilities supplement its primary function of conserving a controllable water supply. All summer long, the lake is a flurry of sails as pleasure-craft and windsurfers tack in all directions. Beau Rivage is a popular shoreside leisure centre (tel 02 96 26 02 18 or 06 09 38 03 26) where you can rent boats and arrange waterskiing.

There's little of interest in Mûr-de-Bretagne itself, but the surrounding countryside of woodland and gorges reveals many hidden surprises: calvaries and chapels, sacred fountains and disappearing rivers. St-Aignan has a charming 12th-century church containing a carving of the Tree of Jesse. An exhibition about the Guerledan dam can be seen in the nearby Musée de l'Electricité (tel 02 97 27 51 39; mid-Jun to mid-Sep daily 10–12.30, 2.30–6.30); guided visits of the barrage are also available.

Don't miss The evocative 18th-century ruins of the Abbaye de Bon Repos, on the western side of the lake, are gradually being restored. It has a pleasant restaurant and a permanent exhibition. Various summer happenings are staged here, including exuberant sound-and-light shows in August (tel 02 96 24 85 28).

PERROS-GUIREC

200 G6 21 Place de l'Hôtel de Ville, 22700 Perros-Guirec, tel 02 96 23 21 15; Jul, Aug Mon–Sat 9–7.30, Sun, hols 10–12.30, 4–7; Sep–end Jun Mon–Sat 9–12.30, 2–6; small seasonal annexe in Ploumanac'h Les Sept Îles from the Gare Maritime at Plage de Trestraou or Port de Ploumanac'h; also to Bréhat and along the coast The *Festival des Hortensias* is a costume-packed parade in early August www.perros-guirec.com

Summer visitors crowd to this large resort on Brittany's Pink Granite Coast, whose fine sandy shores are littered with strangely eroded, exotically tinted outcrops of granite. The *sentier des douaniers* coastal watchpath from Perros-Guirec to Ploumanac'h leads past the best of the pink granite scenery (▷ 146–7). Many houses are built in the local stone, giving the town a mellow pink hue, especially at sunset. Just offshore lies the seabird sanctuary of Les Sept Îles, seasonal home to over a dozen nesting species, including puffins, guillemots and gannets. Several companies run boat trips in season.

With its casino (tel 02 96 49 80 80; daily 10am–3am/4am Jun–Sep; gaming tables from 9.30pm; reduced hours in low season), smart marina and seawater spa, Perros-Guirec has an air of leisured sophistication and celebrity chic. It attracts a fashionable clientele of bright, active young things as well as families with children and retired folk, who have colonized the villas in its leafy suburbs. It is one of the biggest sailing resorts on the north Breton coast, and has some lively nightlife, good shops and lots of beach activities. Parts of the waterfront are rather spoiled by the busy coastal road, but the central beaches—Plage de Trestraou and Plage de Trestrignel—are absolutely stunning. The resort sprawls rather confusingly over a hilly headland circuited by serpentine roads, where elegant private villas and hotels hog magnificent views from wooded cliffs.

Apart from its spectacular natural scenery, Perros-Guirec has no unmissable sights. In the heart of town, crowning the hilly promontory, the church of St-Jacques-la-Majeur has a curious spiky belfry and an elaborate trefoil porch (Mon–Sat 9.30–12, 2.30–6, Sun am outside services only).

Don't miss The 15th-century Chapelle Notre-Dame de la Clarté (daily 9.30–12, 2–6), west of town, was built as a commemorative seamark by a fogbound mariner saved from imminent shipwreck by a heavenly shaft of light.

Breton musicians on the quayside at Perros-Guirec

Ruins of the Abbey de Beauport at Paimpol

The Château de Quintin on the River Gouet

PAIMPOL

The traditional home port of the Icelandic fishermen still reverberates with sea shanties and gritty nautical atmosphere.

201 H7 Place de la République 22504 Paimpol, tel 02 96 20 83 16; mid-Jun to mid-Sep Mon–Sat 9.30–7.30, Sun, hols 10–6; mid-Sep to mid-Jun Mon–Sat 9.30–12.30, 1.30–6.30 CAT Line 9 runs to Pointe de l'Arcouest (Bréhat ferry terminal) and St-Brieuc; Line 7 to Treguier and Lannion Paimpol. Trains or SNCF buses to Guingamp for connections to Brest, St-Brieuc, Rennes Ferries to Île de Bréhat from Pointe de l'Arcouest **www.**paimpol-goelo.com

RATINGS	
Boat trips	●●●●
Cultural interest	●●●●
Shopping	●●●

TIP

• Combined tickets (adult €5.50, child €2.65) allow access both to the Musée de la Mer and the Musée du Costume Breton, in a nearby building on rue Raymond-Pellier (tel 02 96 22 02 19; Jul, Aug daily 10.30–12.30, 2.30–6).

Paimpol is very much a working port, and its two crowded harbours are full of activity. In centuries gone by, the town's fishermen would set sail from here to search for cod for months at a time in the perilous waters around Iceland. This deep-sea heritage is vividly recounted at the Musée de la Mer in an old cod-drying factory on rue Labenne (tel 02 96 22 02 19; Easter to Sep daily). Today, Paimpol has replaced cod-fishing and whaling with inshore coastal fishing and oyster-farming in the Trieux estuary. The August *Fête du Chant des Marins* revives the seafaring traditions of Paimpol in songs and shanties, and an annual *pardon* in the church of Notre-Dame-de-Bonne-Nouvelle continues a long tradition of blessing the fishing fleet.

Although it is not conventionally pretty, Paimpol's port is never short of visitors. It makes an enjoyable excursion base for the Île de Bréhat, the Trieux estuary and the Goëlo coast. Every Tuesday, a lively market takes place in the central streets, which have some handsome old buildings and shopfronts.

Just southeast of Paimpol, the Anglo-Norman Abbaye de Beauport first welcomed pilgrims on their way to Santiago de Compostela in the 13th century. Its graceful Gothic ruins have been restored and can be visited (tel 02 96 55 18 58).

Don't miss A steam locomotive train follows the scenic Trieux Valley, and is a terrific excursion for children of all ages (▷ 150).

PLEUMEUR-BODOU

200 F7 Les Chardons, 22560 Pleumeur-Bodou, tel 02 96 23 91 47; Jul, Aug Mon–Sat 10–12.30, 2.30–6, Sun 10–1; Sep–end Jun Mon–Fri 9.30–12.30, 2.30–5, Sat 10–12.30 From nearby resorts **www.**pleumeur-bodou.com

Unmistakably identified by what looks like a giant golf ball, the heathland village of Pleumeur-Bodou plays host to an ambitious complex of family attractions marketed under the name of Cosmopolis. The huge Radôme (radar dome; Jul, Aug daily 11–7; reduced variable hours off season), measuring some 50m (160ft) high and more than 200m (650ft) in circumference, is made of a Dacron shell just 2mm (0.8in) thick. Raised air pressure inside protects it from high winds. Formerly the Centre National d'Etudes des Telecommunications (CNET), this hit the headlines in July 1962 when the first transatlantic signals arrived from the US satellite *Telstar*. It now houses the fascinating Musée des Telecoms (tel 02 96 46 63 80; Jul–Aug daily 11–7; reduced variable hours off season). These multimedia, interactive exhibits encompass over 200 years of long-distance message-relay history, from earliest semaphore to the latest video and internet technology. It's a wonderful way of keeping the kids quiet on a wet day, and a genuinely enlightening experience. Nearby is the Planétarium de Bretagne (tel 02 96 15 80 30; daily programme in summer; closed Wed, Sat in winter, and all Jan; some shows in English). Also on the Cosmopolis site is the incongruous Village Gaulois (tel 02 96 91 83 95; Easter to Sep), a re-creation of a Gaullish village from Roman times Proceeds go to a Third World educational charity.

Weathered tree stumps and pink rocks bound the grassy dunes that line the stretch of sandy beach at Sables-d'Or-les-Pins

A pink half-timbered house on a central street in St-Brieuc

QUINTIN

201 H9 6 Place 1830 Quintin, tel 02 96 74 01 51; Jul, Aug Mon–Sat 9.30–1, 2.30–6, Sun 10.30–1, 2.30–5; mid-Jun and early Sep Mon–Sat 9.30–12.30, 2–6; mid-Sep to mid-Jun Tue–Sat 9.30–12, 2–7 Quintin (connections to St-Brieuc and Loudéac) Guided tours in summer, Thu 3 **www.**quintin.fr

Renowned for its fine linen in the 17th and 18th centuries, this *petite cité de caractère* prospered on supplying materials for the elaborate headdresses (*coiffes*) and collars traditionally worn by Breton women. Before the Revolution, the town's economy depended almost entirely on weaving. Today, the handsome old houses rise in tiers on the hillside overlooking the River Gouët, a natural defensive site. Corbelled and timber-framed buildings dating from the 16th and 17th centuries line the streets and squares of the old quarter, particularly the Grande Rue, Place 1830, and the Place du Martray. The imposing neo-Gothic basilica contains the relics of St. Thuriau and a piece of the Virgin's girdle said to have been brought back from Jerusalem during the Crusades. Notre-Dame-de-Délivrance (Our Lady of Safe Delivery) is naturally venerated by expectant mothers. At the east end of the church, the Porte-Neuve is the last remaining section of the old town walls. The unfinished Château de Quintin, its earliest wing dating from 1640, houses a fine collection of porcelain (tel 02 96 74 94 79; mid-Jun to mid-Sep daily 10.30–12.30, 1.30–6.30; Easter to mid-Jun, mid–end Sep Wed–Mon 2–5; Nov–Easter Sun 2–5). The Musée-Atelier des Toiles de Quintin, on historic rue des Degrés, recounts the local linen industry (tel 02 96 74 84 01; Jun–end Sep Tue–Sun 1.30–6.30; weaving demonstrations).

Don't miss The holy water stoups in the basilica of Notre-Dame-de-Délivrance are made from giant shells from Java.

SABLES-D'OR-LES-PINS

202 K8 The main office is at Plurien, 2km (1 mile) inland, tel 02 96 72 18 52; Jul, Aug Mon–Sat 9.30–12.30, 2–7, Sun 10–12; restricted hours off-season. In Sables-d'Or-les-Pins itself there's a wooden kiosk on the main street, allée des Acacias, tel 02 96 41 51 97; Jul, Aug Mon–Sat 9–7, Sun 10–12, 4–6 Swimming in the sea can be dangerous because of strong currents

The long stretches of golden sand and verdant pines that give this resort its name are the main attractions. You can rent a beach buggy or take in a round of golf, but most people come here simply to enjoy an exceptionally photogenic stretch of seaside.

Sables-d'Or-les-Pins is essentially an artificial resort—even the beach is a bottle blonde created from imported sand. Work began in the early 1920s but the project was abandoned before completion after the financial crash of 1929. A wide but oddly makeshift central boulevard flanked by ornate parades of shops and cafés hints at the grand design originally envisaged, though it has the insubstantial air of a film studio backlot. Swimming on some local beaches can be dangerous because of the strong currents that swirl around the sandbanks.

Just south of Sables-d'Or-les-Pins, the older village of Plurien adds some historical gravitas, with a Templar church and the remains of a Gallo-Roman villa.

ST-BRIEUC

201 J8 7 rue St-Gouéno, 22044 St-Brieuc, tel 02 96 33 32 50; Jul, Aug Mon–Sat 9–7, Sun 10–1; Sep–end Jun Mon–Fri 9–12, 1.30–6, Sat 9–12.30, 2–6 Main TGV line between Paris, Rennes and Brest Plenty of large central parking areas, but take change for the meters; Place de la Resistance is handy for shops, sights and tourist office **www.**baiedesaintbrieuc.com

This sprawling town at the head of a huge bay is the administrative capital of Côtes-d'Armor. It's a thriving business hub and a rendezvous of regional transportation networks, though frankly not much of a tourist attraction. Its geography is complicated by deep river valleys, over which roads stride on stilted viaducts. Within a carapace of drab industrial suburbs, the old town occupies the fork of high ground between the converging rivers Gouédic and Gouët. The fortified cathedral of St-Etienne on Place Général de Gaulle (daily 8–7) is its most prominent landmark, and the surrounding streets contain a few agreeable medieval buildings. The Musée d'Art et d'Histoire provides some well-presented background on the Côtes-d'Armor region free of charge (tel 02 96 62 55 20; Tue–Sat 9.30–11.45, 1.30–5.45, Sun 1.30–5.45).

St-Brieuc has no shortage of decent shops and restaurants (particularly around the pedestrianized rue St-Guillaume), and a lively range of performing arts and events generated by its student population. The port of Le Legué occupies an unexpectedly secluded enclave of wharves and warehouses beside the steeply wooded Gouët estuary. Yachts, fishing boats and bulk cargo vessels share this waterway, which is one of the busiest ports in Brittany, currently undergoing expansion. Several small beach resorts extend along the seafront near Plérin, enjoying fine views over the bay.

A local fisherman unloading his catch at St-Cast-le-Guildo

An old cannon guards the clifftops overlooking the port and bay at St-Cast-le-Guildo

ST-CAST-LE-GUILDO

202 L8 Place Charles de Gaulle, BP 9, 22380 St-Cast-le-Guildo, tel 02 96 41 81 52; Jul–Sep daily 9–7.30; Mon–Sat 9–12, 2–6 rest of year 1 to Lamballe (nearest rail station); 2 to St-Brieuc via Erquy and Le Val-André (Jul, Aug only); 13 to Dinan; 14 to St-Malo. A local service called Big Bus shuttles around this spread-out resort for a flat fare At the port *Fête de l'Huître* (oyster festival) is at the end of Jun www.ot-st-cast-le-guildo.fr

'Sanka' (as it's pronounced) is one of the liveliest bucket-and-spade resorts on Brittany's Emerald Coast (▷ 80), popular with families for its seven sandy beaches. It is ideally situated for excursions to Dinard, Dinan and St-Malo or for walks along the wild footpaths of Cap Fréhel. The resort became a popular watering hole in the 19th century, when prosperous villas sprang up to take advantage of Emerald Coast views. In its Belle-Époque heyday it had an exclusive reputation rivalling Dinard, but today it is a little too suburban to be truly chic.

The resort has several separate districts and its geography takes some fathoming. Le-Guildo is an old seaport on the Arguenon river. Its associated market town is called Notre-Dame. Here you'll find humble stone cottages set near the ocean, and the ruined château of Gilles de Bretagne overlooking the bay. St-Cast consists of L'Isle (the port), Les Mielles (the resort area, with a beautiful wide sandy beach) and Le Bourg (the administrative hub). L'Isle is a popular port of call for yachts in summer, but it is a tidal harbour and offshore islets make navigation a challenge.

The Grand Plage (Large Beach) at Les Mielles is a stunner, stretching over 2km (1 mile) south of the port. It has excellent water sports facilities, a summer fairground, and an attractive square of shops, bars and restaurants at its northern end. The southern tip of the beach is marked by the small chapel of Notre-Dame-de-la-Garde, on a headland of the same name. Between St-Cast and Le-Guildo is the tiny settlement of Pen-Guen, with its own fine beach. It is renowned in French golfing circles for its links course, one of the oldest in the country.

A rocky promontory on the coast by St-Cast-le-Guildo

ST-QUAY-PORTRIEUX

201 J7 17 bis rue Jeanne d'Arc, 22410 St-Quay-Portrieux, tel 02 96 70 40 64; Jul, Aug Mon–Sat 9–7, Sun, hols 10.30–12.30, 5.30–6; Sep–end Jun Mon–Sat 9–12.30, 2–6.30 CAT Line 9 (Paimpol–St-Brieuc, both on rail routes) Trips to Bréhat Jun–end Sep; pleasure and fishing trips round Goëlo coast from Port d'Armor www.saintquayportrieux.com

This former cod-fishing port is now a glitzy, well-equipped beach and sailing resort besieged by Parisian families in August. Its five wide, sheltered beaches are safe and good for children. It has a seafront casino (tel 02 96 70 40 36; daily 10am–4am; musical soirées Fri, Sat from 10pm) and summer activities galore. Its older, prettier quarters have become somewhat eclipsed by amorphous modern suburbs. The massive marina of Port d'Armor bolted on to its old fishing harbour holds up to a thousand boats, and is certainly an economic asset if not a thing of beauty. Inshore fishing still continues, ranking St-Quay ninth among France's fishing ports; scallops and lobster are among the main catches.

The settlement is very old, tracing its origins back to a Celtic hermit (St. Quay or Ké), who landed here in the Dark Ages, but it was only in the 19th century that it gained popularity, as a health spa. St-Quay-Portrieux stands on the border zone between French-speaking Upper Brittany (Haute Bretagne) and the Breton-speaking Lower Brittany (Basse Bretagne), and Celtic cultural traditions and Breton place-names gradually become more prominent as you head westwards. The little fishing village of Binic 8km (5 miles) south somehow manages to retain a sense of its own identity.

A castle on one of the many offshore islets close to the resort of Trégastel-Plage

Inside the cathedral at Tréguier

TRÉGASTEL

200 F6 Place Sainte-Anne, 22730 Trégastel, tel 02 96 15 38 38; Jul, Aug Mon–Sat 9.30–1, 2–7, Sun, hols 10–12.30; Sep–end Jun Mon–Sat 9.30–12, 2–6 Boat trips to Les Sept Îles in summer
www.ville-tregastel.fr

This popular beach resort attracts a loyal following for its beautiful beaches of white sand amid a glorious jumble of bizarrely rounded rocks and offshore reefs of pink granite. The coastal footpath (*sentier des douaniers*) and a scenic road called the Corniche Bretonne make splendid promenades from which to enjoy the scenery. One of the best vantage points is the *table d'orientation* between the beaches of Coz-Pors and Grève-Blanche. Île-Grande, further down the coast towards Trébeurden, can be reached by a bridge from the D788. On the island, the Maison LPO (tel 02 96 91 91 40; Jul, Aug daily 10–1, 2.30–7; Jun, Sep, school hols daily 2–6; Oct–end May Sat, Sun 2–6) is an ornithological centre explaining the flora and fauna of Les Sept Îles north of Perros-Guirec (▷ 87).

The Aquarium Marin (tel 02 96 23 48 58; Jul, Aug daily 10–7; Apr–end Jun, Sep daily 10–12, 2–6; Oct, school hols daily 2–5), ingeniously shoehorned into crevices between startling granite boulders, showcases the sea-life around this coast, complete with a tidal model. The Forum de Trégastel is an ugly shed of a building housing a splendid covered swimming pool complex (tel 02 96 15 30 44; Mon 4–7.30, Tue, Thu 10.30–1.30, 3–9; Wed, Fri 10.30–1.30, 5–7.30; Sat 10.30–6.30; Sun, hols 10–6.30) with slides, flumes and fountains, accessible directly from the plage de Coz-Pors. If the sea is too cold for comfort, these pools are maintained at a comfortable 30°C (86°F).

On the Trébeurden road, 2km (1 mile) south, Kerguntuil has a Neolithic passage grave and dolmen. Other megaliths can be seen along the coastal road.

TRÉGUIER

201 G7 67 rue Ernest Renan, 22220 Tréguier, tel 02 96 92 22 33; Jul, Aug Mon–Sat 9–12.30, 2–6, Sun 10–1, 2–6; Sep–end Jun Mon–Sat 9–12.30, 2–6 Bicycles and kayaks can be rented from the Bar Les Plaisanciers down by the port; tel 02 96 92 49 69
www.paysdetreguier.com

High on a commanding site overlooking the Jaudy estuary, Tréguier is an obvious defensive site. Its sheltered tidal port is now supplemented by an attractive yacht marina. Its administrative role as the principal community of the Trégor region has now been superseded by Lannion, but it is still a diocesan capital and an important market town for a fertile vegetable-growing area. The handsome granite and half-timbered buildings in the old town confirm its pre-Revolutionary prosperity from the flax trade, but these days it seems a sleepy place, catering more for tourism than industry.

Tréguier was founded in the 6th century by an obscure Celtic monk (St. Tugdual), but another saint has become more memorably associated with the town. Yves Helori, born near Tréguier in 1253, is the patron saint of lawyers. Famously incorruptible, St. Yves became a champion of the poor, and is often depicted in Breton churches flanked by a wealthy man and a poor client in rags. His tomb (a 19th-century copy after damage caused in the Revolution) lies in Tréguier cathedral, surrounded by votive candles and plaques of thanks—some from law students who managed to pass their exams.

The pink granite cathedral (Jun–end Sep 9–7; Oct–end May 9–12, 2–6; free guided tours Jul, Aug Sun–Fri; separate access to treasury and cloisters, by chargeable tour only in summer, free off-season) is mostly Gothic with a few surviving bits of Romanesque in the Hastings tower. Most striking is its spire, pierced with geometric shapes, like those from a pack of cards. Immediately around the cathedral lies a spacious square and ancient streets filled with attractive old buildings, many containing restaurants and shops. The house belonging to the writer and rationalist philosopher Ernest Renan, born here in 1823, is now a museum to his memory (tel 02 96 92 45 63; Jul, Aug daily 10–12, 2–6; Apr–end Jun, Sep Wed–Fri 10–12, 2–6, Sat, Sun 2–6); his statue presides over the main square.

On summer Wednesdays (market day), Tréguier springs into life with a series of fun-packed *Mercredis en Fête*, held in the town's main square (concerts, hog-roasts, street entertainment). A huge *pardon* (one of Brittany's largest and most celebrated) takes place in Tréguier on the anniversary of the death of St Yves (third Sunday in May).

Eternal Father, *set on top of the rocks of the Corniche Bretonne, near Trégastel-Plage*

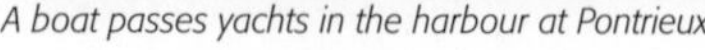
A boat passes yachts in the harbour at Pontrieux

The long sweep of the beach at Le Val-André

TRIEUX ESTUARY

201 H7 Main offices at Tréguier or Paimpol. Also Maison de la Presqu'île, carrefour de Kerantour, 22740 Pleudaniel, tel 02 96 22 16 45; Jul, Aug daily 9.30–12.30, 2–7; Maison d'Eiffel, 22260 Pontrieux, tel 02 96 95 14 03; Jul, Aug daily 10.30–6.30; reduced hours off-season; and Place du Centre, 22740 Lézardrieux, tel 02 96 22 16 45 Pontrieux Barge trips from Pontrieux (some at night); kayak rental at Loguivy or Pontrieux In August, Pontrieux holds the *Fête des Lavandières*, in celebration of its former washerwomen
www.pontrieux.com
www.cc-lezardrieux.com

Up on the east bank of the river mouth, the pretty little village of Loguivy-de-la-Mer is a leading Côtes-d'Armor fishing port, though its harbour dries out at low tide. Lenin once holidayed here, relaxing from revolutionary notions. The Trieux estuary is an immensely popular sailing playground; Lézardrieux's huge state-of-the-art yacht marina dwarfs the rest of the tiny *ville fleurie*, with its distinctive 18th-century church. A graceful suspension bridge spans the estuary at this point, carrying the busy D786 between Paimpol and Lannion, and providing grandstand river views.

More amazing vistas can be seen from the formidable Château de la Roche-Jagu 14km (9 miles) upstream from Lézardrieux, built in the 15th century on a wooded bluff guarding a sharp meander in the river. Restored after the 1987 hurricane, it is now open to the public (tel 02 96 95 62 35; Jul, Aug daily 10–7; Feb–end Jun, Sep, Oct 10.30–12.30, 2–6); tours include some of its ornate Renaissance-style rooms. Exhibitions and events are held here in summer, including an August jazz festival. The castle gateway contains a pleasant restaurant.

Straddling the head of the river between wooded banks, Pontrieux is a delightful surprise, a small, likeable town well stocked with handsome flower-strewn buildings and a strong sense of civic pride. Art galleries and craft studios fringe Pontrieux's streets, and down on the waterfront sleek yachts berth alongside homey houseboats. Many old public wash-houses, preceding the days of the laundromat, have been carefully restored by local enthusiasts. The most striking local landmark is the Maison d'Eiffel (now the tourist office), a 16th-century timbered tower once used by the port authorities to survey river traffic.

Don't miss A steam train runs along the Trieux Valley between Paimpol and Pontrieux (La Vapeur du Trieux, ▷ 150). You can book a one-way trip from Pontrieux, but returns are available only from Paimpol.

LE VAL-ANDRÉ

202 K8 Rue Winston Churchill (by the Casino), 22370 Le Val-André, tel 02 96 72 20 55; Apr–end Sep daily 9–1, 2–7; Oct–end Mar Mon–Sat 9–12.30, 2–5.30 CAT 2 to St-Brieuc and Erquy/Fréhel Cruises and fishing trips around Cap Fréhel, to Île de Bréhat from Dahouët; excursions in a traditional sailing lugger (*La Pauline*).
www.val-andre.org

Established in the 1880s, Le Val-André still has a Belle-Époque feel to its elegant, bow-fronted villas set in spacious seafront plots. The resort occupies a grid-like strip of streets behind a dazzlingly beautiful beach stretching almost 2km (1 mile) between the wooded headlands of Pléneuf and La Guette. The seafront promenade provides direct, traffic-free access to the sands. Just off the Pointe de Pléneuf lies the bird sanctuary islet of Le Verdelet, which can be reached on foot at exceptionally low tides (bird-watching trips organized every Wed in Jul and Aug by Vivarmor Nature; tel 02 96 33 10 57). Cliff paths lead round the headland, offering marvellous views over St-Brieuc Bay, and further beaches to the northeast. West of the resort is the picturesque old fishing port of Dahouët, squeezed behind a narrow rock-lined channel. It is now used mainly as a yacht marina, its granite quays fringed with attractive waterfront bars and restaurants.

Le Val-André is excellent for water sports; sailing dinghies, catamarans, windsurfers and kayaks can all be rented from the main beaches. The northerly beach of Plage de la Ville Berneuf is a popular destination for sand-yachting (*char à voile*). There's a fine golf course behind the beach too; Golf Blue Green has twice hosted the French Open in recent years. The seafront Rotonde Casino with its art deco ocean-liner architecture contains a panoramic café-restaurant, and a cinema and theatre, as well as the usual range of gaming tables and slot machines (tel 02 96 72 85 06; daily 10am–3am, 4am Fri–Sun). Beachfront bars keep things humming until the small hours. During July and August, jazz sessions are held in a park behind rue Amiral Charner.

Le Val-André is ideal for young children, with its wide expanses of soft, clean, gently shelving sand and lots of beach activities. A *petit train* plies around the seafront in summer.

Don't miss Pipapo is a wonderful ice-cream shop on rue Winston Churchill (near the tourist office).

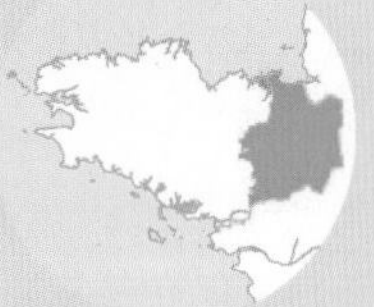

ILLE-ET-VILAINE

This easterly region is named for its strategic waterways linking the Channel with the Atlantic Ocean. First landfall for many seaborne visitors is the lively ferry port of St-Malo. Car-drivers spot the unforgettable image of Mont-St-Michel's island abbey piercing the haunting mudflats of the bay on the Normandy border, while grand medieval fortresses (Fougères, Vitré, Combourg) guard the Breton borderlands.

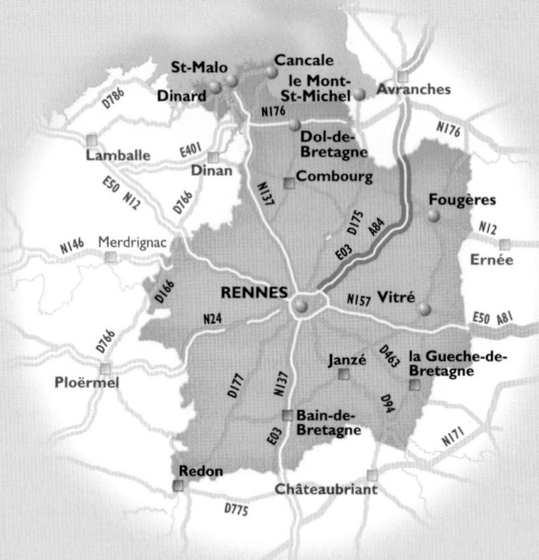

MAJOR SIGHTS

The long drive to the Château de Caraduec, near Bécherel

The buildings of Cancale looking down at its port

THE SIGHTS

BÉCHEREL

208 L10 9 Place Alexandre Jehanin, 35190 Bécherel; tel 02 99 66 75 23; daily 10–12, 2–5.30
www.becherel.com

Once an important linen-weaving town, Becherel is now renowned throughout Brittany (and indeed Europe) for its wealth of antiquarian and second-hand bookstores. Bibliophiles converge from all over the region, especially during its monthly book fairs, held on the first Sunday of the month, and its Easter book festival. Stock includes material written in the Breton language.

Becherel's medieval castle, dating from 1124, also deserves a visit, and the town has an especially well-stocked and obliging tourist office .

Just 1km (half a mile) west of Bécherel, the elegant 18th-century Château de Caradeuc features classical sculpture reminiscent of the style of Versailles (tel 02 99 66 77 76; Jul, Aug daily 12–6; Easter–end Jun, Sep, Oct Sat, Sun and hols 2–6).

CHÂTEAU DE COMBOURG

203 M9 • 23 rue des Princes, 35270 Combourg 02 99 73 22 95 Jul, Aug daily; Apr–end Jun, Sep, Oct Sun–Fri Adult €5.50 , child (10–18) €4.50
www.combourg.net

The château at lakeside Combourg is where the French Romantic writer François-René de Chateaubriand (1768–1848) spent a period of his youth. Founded in the 11th century by the archbishop of Dol, it underwent many changes throughout the Middle Ages before coming into the hands of the Comte de Chateaubriand, father of the writer. The author's experiences here are recalled in his book *Memoires d'Outre-Tombe*.

CANCALE

Brittany's charming oyster capital is the place to sample the perfect *plateau de fruits de mer*, or begin an exploration of the Emerald Coast.

RATINGS	
Cultural interest	●●●
Good for food	●●●●
Walking	●●●●

203 M8 44 rue du Port, 35260 Cancale, tel 02 99 89 63 72; Jul, Aug Mon–Sat 9–7; Sep–end Jun Mon–Sat 9–12.30, 2–6. Seasonal information point at the Halle-à-Marée, port de la Houle, tel 02 99 89 74 80; summer holidays only TIV and Les Courriers Bretons services from St-Malo and Dol-de-Bretagne Sea-trips in *La Cancalaise*, a splendid replica of one of the elegantly rigged oyster-boats (*bisquines*) that once trawled for wild oysters in the bay (▷ 130)
www.ville-cancale.fr

TIP

- **It isn't true that you can eat oysters only when there's an 'r' in the month, but seafood poisoning is generally more prevalent in the summer, when temperatures are higher. Always eat oysters on the day you buy them, and check that the shells are tightly closed, or close when tapped.**

The muddy shores of Cancale may not look very inviting for a beach holiday, but they are ideal for rearing oysters. Oyster-farming developed after the collapse of the cod-fishing industry, and today some 5,000 tonnes are harvested annually. You can sample the shellfish either from the market stalls by the lighthouse (daily all year) or at the restaurants that line the waterfront in the old fishing port of La Houle. There are two main kinds of oyster: the saucer-shaped *huîtres plats*, which are native to the bay, and *huîtres creuses* (hollow oysters), which have crinkled shells and are imported at a juvenile stage from other parts of Brittany.

To find out more about oysters, visit La Ferme Marine, an oyster farm on the southern outskirts of the resort (guided visits mid-Jun to end Oct, daily in English at 2, in French at 11, 3 and 5; mid-Feb to mid-Jun, mid-Sep to end Oct Mon–Fri at 3 in French only). Here you can visit the oyster beds and see how oysters are prepared for market, and you can also taste and buy them.

In the upper town, the Musée des Arts et Traditions Populaires, in the 18th-century deconsecrated church of St-Méen, recounts the history of oyster-farming in Cancale (tel 02 99 89 71 26; Jun–Sep). For a small fee (adult €1, child €0.50; keys available at the tourist office) you can climb the church tower (189 steps) for panoramic views over Mont-St-Michel bay.

The charming port at Dinard (above), and the view over the tops of waterfront houses of the Rance Estuary (right)

DINARD

This exclusive resort rivals the Riviera in the seaside glamour stakes. If the sea temperatures are a little cooler, the setting, cafés and beaches are no less alluring.

Dinard occupies a rocky outcrop at the mouth of the Rance estuary, just west of St-Malo (▷ 106–8). Until the mid-19th century, Dinard was just a typical Breton fishing port, but it was then discovered by the American and British moneyed classes, who colonized palatial seaside villas overlooking the glorious bay scenery. During the Belle-Époque years of the early 20th century, Dinard became the resort of choice for yachting, gambling and other well-heeled leisure activities. Dinard remains a chic and expensive resort, and still has strong Anglo-Saxon connections, including an air link to London.

SEAFRONT STROLLS

Dinard has several very beautiful sandy beaches. The Plage de l'Écluse (or Grande Plage) is the largest and most fashionable, while Prieuré and St-Enogat are quieter and have more of a family atmosphere. A public footpath, the Chemin de Ronde, leads along the coast past a profusion of exotic vegetation. The central section, from Plage du Prieuré in the south to the Pointe du Moulinet, is the Promenade du Clair de Lune (Moonlight Promenade)—a wonderful place for an afternoon or evening stroll, with a magical view across the estuary.

HIGH ROLLERS

Mid-stage behind the main beach stands the Casino Barrière de Dinard, in boulevard Wilson (tel 02 99 16 30 30; gambling daily 9pm–4am; dining daily 12–2.30, 7.30–10.30, 11 at weekends). Nearby is an Olympic-sized, covered, heated seawater swimming pool (tel 02 99 46 22 77; daily 10–12.30, 3–7.30). Huge tides and constant sea breezes provide magnificent conditions for sailing all season. France's first tennis club was opened at Dinard in 1879, and its spectacular coastal golf links near St-Briac is one of the country's oldest and most revered courses.

Don't miss A festival of British cinema attracts many celebrity visitors every October. A statue of Alfred Hitchcock balances on a giant egg near the Plage de l'Écluse, with fierce-looking birds on his shoulders.

RATINGS

Beaches	●●●●
Boat trips	●●●●
Outdoor pursuits	●●●●●
Photo stops	●●●●

BASICS

202 L8

2 boulevard Féart, 35802 Dinard, tel 02 99 46 94 12; Jul, Aug daily 9.30–7.30; Sep–end Jun Mon–Sat 9–12.30, 2–6, Sun 2–6

Regular TIV, CAT and TAE services to St-Malo, La Richardais, St-Lunaire, St-Briac-sur-Mer and Lancieux; to Cancale, Dol and Mont-St-Michel; and to Dinan and Rennes

Compagnie Corsaire runs the all-year Bus-de-Mer link with St-Malo; summer cruises to Cancale bay, Cap Fréhel, and up the Rance to Dinan

Dinard-Pleurtuit airport, tel 02 99 46 18 46 is 6km (4 miles) south of the town (direct Ryanair flights from London Stansted; helicopter joyrides round the Emerald Coast)

www.ville-dinard.fr
Adequate but could do with updating.

TIP

- **Dinard's casino, bars and café terraces keep things humming until the small hours. On summer evenings the Promenade du Clair de Lune is floodlit, with concerts and *son-et-lumière* shows in the gardens.**

The distinctive outline of Mont-St-Michel, viewed across misty fields from Mont-Dol (above), and inside the cathedral of St-Samson (left)

DOL-DE-BRETAGNE

Dol's imposing cathedral dominates the marshy hinterland of the Baie de Mont-St-Michel.

Centuries ago, the sea covered the low-lying Marais de Dol, leaving the Capital of the Marshes stranded on its rocky dais above the waves. Gradually the sea retreated into the bay, and the saltmarshes or *polders* (a Dutch term) turned into fertile pasture protected by dykes. Sheep raised on this reclaimed land are much prized for their delicately flavoured meat, and are often described on local menus as *'gigot d'agneau pré-salé'* (salt-meadow lamb). The old town of Dol has some fine historic buildings along the Grande-Rue des Stuarts.

DOL CATHEDRAL

A religious community was first established in Dol by St. Samson, one of the seven founding saints, in AD548. The massive cathedral (daily 9–12, 2–6) was begun in the 12th century and constructed piecemeal over several hundred years, though it suffered repeated attacks and had to be rebuilt. Funds eventually ran out and one of its towers was never completed. The great doorway in the south wall is one of its finest features; inside, its colossal dimensions and Gothic vaulting impress—the nave is almost 100m (300ft) long and 20m (65ft) high at the domed crossing. The medallion panes in the chancel window are said to be the oldest stained glass in Brittany (13th century).

The rambling premises of the adjacent bishop's palace house an ambitious exhibition called Cathédraloscope (Easter–end Oct daily 10–7), devoted to the history of medieval cathedrals.

ANCIENT STONES

Le Mont-Dol, 2km (1 mile) to the north, is a curious outcrop of granite erupting 65m (213ft) from the surrounding polders. Despite its modest height, the grandstand views are remarkable. It shows signs of very early settlement and has religious associations: A supposed footprint in the rocks is alleged to belong to the Archangel Michael, left behind as he sprang across the bay to the rock of Mont-St-Michel after subduing the Devil.

About 2km (1 mile) south of Dol just off the D795 is the tallest of Brittany's standing stones, the Menhir du Champ-Dolent. It stands 9.5m (31ft) high, and is freely accessible in a small picnic site.

RATINGS

Historic interest	● ● ● ●
Photo stops	● ● ●

203 M8 3 Grande-Rue-des-Stuarts, 35120 Dol-de-Bretagne, tel 02 99 48 15 37; Jul, Aug daily 10–7; Sep–end Jun Mon 2.30–6.30, Tue–Sat 10–12.30, 2.30–6.30 Routes to St-Malo, Rennes, Cancale Dol-de-Bretagne

www.pays-de-dol.com
A useful site with some English.

TIPS

- **The vocabulary used in the labelling for the Cathédraloscope exhibition is rather technical. Ask if you can borrow an English translation at reception.**
- **The Promenades des Douves, accessed from Place Chateaubriand, leads along the old ramparts, giving a fine overview of the town and surrounding countryside.**
- **The parking area by the harbour is prone to flooding at certain high tides, so check before you leave your vehicle here for any length of time.**

The clustered towers crowning the walls of the feudal castle at Fougères (above), and the north facade of Église St-Leonard (right)

FOUGÈRES

The picturesque fortifications guarding this border hilltown made a formidable bastion against attack from the east.

A goose-necked bend in the River Nançon provided a temptingly defensible site to the great castle-builders of medieval times. When Brittany was an independent duchy, its eastern marches were always vulnerable to attack from the rapacious kings of France. Fougères' magnificent fortress (mid-Jun to mid-Sep daily 9–7; Apr to mid-Jun, mid–end Sep 9.30–12, 2–6; Feb, Mar, Oct–end Dec daily 10–12, 2–5) is a series of concentric enclosures protected by massive curtain walls. Some of the inner structures and the high keep have vanished over the centuries, but the ramparts are virtually complete. The castle towers, bright with geraniums in summer, make a postcard scene reflected in the river, which acts as a natural moat.

The design of the fortress followed tried-and-tested medieval norms, but its location *below* rather than above the town it was intended to protect is unusual. The castle was captured several times during the Hundred Years War, and played a backdrop role in the Catholic anti-Republican revolt described in Balzac's novel *Les Chouans* (1821). A drawbridge over the Nançon leads to the ramparts from the picturesque old Marchix quarter, once a place of mills and tanneries for Fougères' thriving leather and shoe-making trades.

THE HAUTE VILLE

A steep climb leads to the mostly pedestrianized upper town, perched on the rocky spurs above the winding river. Exceptional views of the lower town and castle can be seen from the public gardens near the church of St-Léonard. Many of the houses in the *haute ville* date from the 18th century, but one quaint 16th-century building on the main street contains a museum dedicated to the local Impressionist artist Emmanuel de la Villéon (1858–1944; tel 02 99 99 19 98; mid-Jun to mid-Sep daily 10.30–12.30; 2–6; mid-Sep to mid-Jun Wed–Sun 10–12, 2–5). The octagonal granite belltower in a little square off rue Nationale is Brittany's oldest, dating from 1397.

Don't miss A fascinating little clock museum can be visited above the shop of one of Brittany's last master watchmakers at 37 rue Nationale (tel 02 99 99 40 98).

RATINGS	
Good for food	●●●
Historic interest	●●●●●
Photo stops	●●●●

209 P9 · 2 rue Nationale (*Haute Ville*), 35300 Fougères, tel 02 99 94 12 20, Jul, Aug Mon–Sat 9–7, Sun 10–12, 2–4; Sep–end Jun Mon 2–6, Tue–Sat 10–12.30, 2–6 · TIV to Rennes; Courriers Bretons to St-Malo; SNCF connections to Vitré (nearest station)

www.ot-fougeres.fr
Easy to navigate; good English content

TIPS

- **A *petit train* called the Oriental Express (May–end Sep daily 10–7) takes you up the hill from the château, with a commentated tour.**
- **Ask the tourist office about inclusive 'passport' tickets for the château, clock museum and a *petit train* ride.**
- **Fougères holds one of the largest and liveliest cattle markets in France. You can visit on Thursdays from 3 (route d'Alençon, on the Aumayllerie ring road towards Vitré).**

The water source of Merlin's Fountain at Forêt de Paimpont

The square lanterned tower at the church in Hédé

An old tidal mill overhanging the waters of the Rance Estuary

FORÊT DE PAIMPONT

208 K11 By the abbey, 35380 Paimpont, 02 99 07 84 23, Jul, Aug daily; Feb–end Jun, Sep to mid-Dec Tue–Sun. Pedalos can be rented on the lake Bicycle rental from Bar Le Brécilien beside Paimpont's tourist office; rue Général de Gaulle, tel 02 99 07 81 13 (rates from about €9 for half a day to €23 for a weekend); also from Pays de Merlin, tel 02 99 07 80 23 **www.**broceliande-tourisme.info **www.**oust-broceliande-vacances.com

The medieval troubadour poet Chrétien de Troyes had much to do with the transformation of this ancient forest into the mystical Brocéliande, the Breton equivalent of Camelot, land of King Arthur, Merlin and the Knights of the Round Table. Wreathed in legends, the Forest of Paimpont, or Brocéliande, is a diffuse area now extending some 7,000ha (17,500 acres) across the borders of Morbihan and Ille-et-Vilaine southwest of Rennes. It is believed to be one of the last remaining bits of the primeval forest that once covered much of Brittany's *argoat*, or interior. The countryside consists mainly of sandy heathland and scattered lakes as well as trees.

Local tourist offices arrange escorted visits to Arthurian sites, such as the sacred Fontaine de Barenton, where Merlin was enthralled by the sorceress Viviane (the Lady in the Lake) in a circle of air. They can also provide walking maps and guides (ask for detailed directions to places of interest, which can be tricky to find). Access to certain areas may be restricted during the hunting season (Nov–end Mar).

The lakeside village of Paimpont is the main touring base at the heart of the forest, an unusual settlement of purplish granite with a single main street beside a 13th-century abbey. The church has interesting woodcarving and a venerable rose window. The sacristy contains the reliquary of St. Judicaël in the form of a silver arm. At Tréhorenteuc the stained-glass windows in the church intertwine Arthurian legends with Christianity, while the mostly 19th-century Château de Comper contains the Centre de l'Imaginaire Arthurien, an exhibition of Celtic legends (tel 02 97 22 79 96; Apr–early Oct).

HÉDÉ

208 M10 Maison du Canal d'Ille et Rance, by locks at La Madeleine, 35630 Bazouges-sous-Hédé, tel 02 99 45 48 90; Jul, Aug daily; Apr–end Jun, Sep, Oct Wed–Mon; Nov–Mar Wed, Sun

The most noteworthy feature of this mill village on the Ille-et-Rance Canal is a staircase flight of eleven locks (*onze écluses*) in the hamlet of La Madeleine just north of Hédé. The total drop is nearly 27m (90ft). A small exhibition and film show at the Maison du Canal visitor centre (in the old lock-keeper's cottage) tell the story of this costly 19th-century project, undertaken to connect the Atlantic and Channel coasts of Brittany by canalized waterways (adult €2.50, child €1.70).

Nearby Hédé is a pretty place full of streams and ponds, with old houses of grey stone in beautifully kept gardens, and castle ruins crowning an outcrop of rock.

Tinténiac, to the northwest, is another attractive canal village with a handsomely turreted church. Its waterfront museum of rural trades, Le Musée de l'Outil et des Métiers (tel 02 99 68 09 62; Jul–end Sep), contains a collection of about 2,000 tools and equipment used by the cobblers and coopers of yesteryear.

RANCE ESTUARY

203 L8 See Dinard, Dinan, St-Malo St-Malo or Dinan River cruises from the *gare maritime* on the Dinard side of the barrage with Croisières Chateaubriand; tel 02 99 46 44 40; also from St-Malo and Dinan

Huge tides surge twice daily up the Rance, rising to the height of a four-floor building and changing the river scenery almost beyond recognition. The Rance valley is one of the most prominent geographical features of the north Breton coastline, carving a deep tidal trench inland as far south as Dinan, where it links with canalized waterways spanning Brittany. It's a stunningly beautiful river, meandering into hidden creeks past cider orchards and harbour villages. The best way to see the estuary is to take a boat trip upstream to Dinan, where you can visit the Maison de la Rance to find out more about the river's complex ecosystem (▷ 82–4).

The great bridge near the mouth of the river between Dinard and St-Malo carries a four-lane highway. Alongside it stands the extraordinary tidal barrage known as the Usine Marémotrice de la Rance, built during the 1960s and now supplying around 3 per cent of Brittany's energy needs. This ambitiously 'green' contribution towards the challenge of replacing fossil fuels with renewable energy is not without environmental costs: The expense of silt-dredging and the impact on bird and fish habitats are considerable. The Espace Découverte visitor centre at the Dinard end of the barrage road gives some fascinating background on the dam and its effects on the river (tel 02 99 16 37 14; Tue–Sun 1–7; free self-guided tour). Access to this site may be restricted during security alerts.

Mont-St-Michel

Mont St-Michel is more than a church on a rock in a bay. The silhouette of the walled abbey rising from the mists was the very symbol of France and French ingenuity long before the Eiffel Tower was even a stack of rivets and girders.

A tranquil scene of the Baie du Mont-St-Michel

The sunlight-bathed buildings of Mont-St-Michel

There is no shortage of souvenir stalls at this popular destination

SEEING MONT-ST-MICHEL

This fortified religious community, separated from the mainland by quicksands and tides, is a surreal sight, especially through the early morning sea mists. Reached via a causeway, just north of Pontorson, the Mount was originally an island in the sea between Normandy and Brittany. Officially not within Brittany's borders, it is now a UNESCO World Heritage Site.

Although, in peak season, the Mount is one of the most crowded visitor attractions in the country, it is well worth making the effort to cross the causeway from the mainland. Don't venture onto the mudflats unless you are part of a guided walk, as tides can sweep in quickly. If you're visiting during the peak summer months, arrive at around 8am or after 5pm to miss the crowds. Never mind your aching calf muscles—continue climbing the steps of the abbey once you have reached the summit of the Mount itself. Views of the protected Baie de Mont St-Michel from the very top of the Abbey are stunning.

HIGHLIGHTS

THE ABBEY

☎ 02 33 89 80 00 🕓 May–end Aug daily 9–7 (last entry 6); Sep–end Apr daily 9.30–6 (last entry 5) 💶 Adult €8, under 18 free
www.monum.fr

You can join a guided tour around the abbey and discover the huge treadmill in which prisoners once trudged to work a system of pulleys to haul building materials up the side of the Mount. The abbey is often referred to as *La Merveille* (the wonder), but this epithet actually applies to a Gothic extension commissioned by King Philippe Auguste of France in the 13th century to celebrate his conquest of Normandy. The name reflected the amazing feat of the architects and builders who created it in just 20 years. The *Merveille*, with its three

RATINGS	
Good for kids	●●●
Historic interest	●●●●
Photo stops	●●●●●

BASICS

203 N8

50170 Le Mont St-Michel, tel 02 33 60 14 30; Jul–end Aug daily 9–7; Apr–end Jun, Sep Mon–Sat 9–12.30, 2–6.30, Sun 9–12, 2–6; Oct–end Mar 9–12, 2–6, Sun 10–12, 2–5;

From Rennes, St-Malo

You could take the TGV to Rennes, which connects with a morning bus-link to the Mount. There is also a station at Pontorson, 9km (6 miles) from the Mount, from where you can take a bus

The visitors' parking area alongside the present causeway is to be replaced with parking for 4,200 cars 2km (1 mile) south of the coast road, on the mainland. Parking will cost €4, but a free shuttle-bus service (eventually to be replaced by a dedicated railway line) will take visitors from their vehicles to the Mount

€0.35

www.ot-montsaintmichel.com
Excellent factual site with information on tides.

carte
Le Mont - Saint - Michel
Le Mont Saint-Michel
LE MONT
ST-MICHEL
LE MONT SAINT-MICHEL
Le Mont Saint-Michel
LE MONT SAINT-MICHEL

The road leading to Mont-St-Michel (left), and a statue of St-Michael in the abbey (above)

Purbeck Marble arches in the cloisters of the Abbey

The picturesque Mount is hugely popular with artists

An open Bible in a side chapel in the abbey complex

floors of dining rooms for pilgrims, nobles and monks, is topped by a tranquil cloister garden, with a window looking out to sea.

MAISONS DE LA BAIE

☎ Courtils 02 33 89 66 00; Le-Vivier-sur-Mer 02 99 48 84 38; St-Léonard 02 33 89 06 06 Jul–end Aug daily 10–7; Apr–Jun, Sep, school hols daily 2–6; www.maison-baie.com

Back on the mainland, you can enjoy wonderful views of the Mount from the Maison de la Baie vantage points at Le-Vivier-sur-Mer, Courtils and St-Léonard. These individually themed mini-museums offer a perspective on the daily life of the abbey in past times, along with excellent displays of local wildlife. They also organize escorted treks across the sands to the Mount, on foot and horseback.

BACKGROUND

The Mount has drawn pilgrims since AD708, when St. Aubert, Bishop of Avranches, built a modest chapel on the 79m (260ft) granite Mont Tombe, after seeing a vision of the Archangel Michael. Benedictine monks settled here and a village soon formed around them. A Romanesque church was constructed on the site in the 11th century, and work continued on other buildings over the following years. The Mount was fortified against the English during the Hundred Years War (mid-14th to mid-15th centuries) and managed to resist attack. Work continued on the abbey from the 15th to the 17th centuries, and the site spent time as a prison after the Revolution. It opened to visitors as a national monument in 1874, and in 1897 Emmanuel Frémlet's gilded statue of St. Michael was placed on top of a new steeple, 157m (515ft) high. A monastic community returned to the site in 1969, and monks and nuns continue to provide a spiritual anchor within what might otherwise be merely a hub of tourism and history. Although 3.5 million visitors come to Mont St-Michel each year, the resident population is just 35.

A project (due to finish in 2007) is under way to surround the Mount with the sea at high tide to combat generations of silting, now 5m (16ft) deep. A footbridge will replace the causeway.

TIPS

- When the main street is packed with people, climb the steps to the less crowded ramparts to look down on the village and across the sea.
- Rather than pay the €8 admission charge to visit the abbey, you could time your visit to coincide with the midday mass, when tickets are free. You can take your time walking through the monument after the service.
- At La Mère Poulard, world-famous omelettes, beaten in age-old copper bowls, have fortified pilgrims and visitors alike for years.

A typically busy street scene

Rennes

Brittany's cosmopolitan capital city is a modern metropolis with a lively medieval heart. In previous centuries, the city played an important role in the region's political struggles.

The Palais St-Georges, a former Benedictine abbey

A brightly coloured town house in Place Ste-Anne

Outdoor cafés in a central square in the old town

RATINGS

Cultural interest	●●●●
Historic interest	●●●●
Photo stops	●●●
Shopping	●●●

BASICS

208 M11

11 rue St-Yves, 35064 Rennes, tel 02 99 67 11 11; Jun–end Sep Mon–Sat 9–7, Sun 11–6; Oct–end May Mon–Sat 10–6, Sun 11–6

Lots of bars surround Place Sainte-Anne; most close Sat lunch

Efficient local network operated by STAR (who also operate the Métro; tickets valid on both)

Rennes; direct links to St-Malo, Dinan, Vitré, Vannes, Quimper, Brest, Nantes and many other towns

UrbaVag electric boats cruise the waterways around Rennes Apr–end Oct

Aéroport de Rennes, St-Jacques-de-la-Lande; tel 02 99 29 60 00 (Air France internal connections, and a direct Flybe service from Southampton)

Free parking is available on boulevard Sébastopol, off quai de la Prévaleye on the River Vilaine, just a 10-minute walk southwest of the tourist office and central sights

www.tourisme-rennes.com
A lively site with lots of useful links

The altar at St-Pierre church in Rennes (right)

SEEING RENNES

Inside the city's modern, industrial shell is an old town of fascinating medieval streets, along with excellent museums and grand civic architecture. The rue du Champ-Jacquet has some of the city's oldest and most beautiful half-timbered buildings. The tourist office is a good place to start a visit, as you can pick up a map marked with a walking route covering the main sights (French only), and a leaflet on the city's history (English). After exploring the old town on the north bank of the Vilaine, wander through the Jardin du Thabor for a change of pace. These beautiful gardens were once the grounds of a Benedictine abbey.

Rennes hosts several major festivals, which attract many visitors. Biggest is *Les Tombées de la Nuit*, a cultural jamboree that takes over the whole of central Rennes at the beginning of July. Organ concerts take place in the main churches in summer, and jazz concerts in October. The party spirit doesn't end with the tourist season: Yaouank is a *fest-noz* (night festival) held on the third Saturday in November, while the huge rock festival of Transmusicales takes place in early December.

HIGHLIGHTS

MUSÉE DES BEAUX-ARTS

104 C3 • 20 quai Émile Zola 02 99 28 55 85 Tue–Sun 10–12, 2–6
République Adult €4.05, under 18 free
www.mbar.org

This art gallery has paintings ranging from 14th-century Primitives to Impressionists and members of the Pont-Aven school. Artists represented include Leonardo da Vinci, Rubens, Paul Gauguin and Pablo Picasso. Look out for a powerful canvas by the 19th-century artist Luminais, depicting the legend of Ys (▷ 5). Archaeological collections include Egyptian and classical items.

CATHÉDRALE ST-PIERRE

104 A2 • Rue de la Monnaie Jul, Aug Tue–Sat 9.30–12, 3–6, Sun 9.30–12; Sep–end Jun daily 9.30–12, 3–6

Rennes' cavernous cathedral dates from the 19th century, but it has a

TIBI·DABO·CLAVES·REGNI·CŒLORUM

TIPS

- Place Railier du Baty, a pleasant square near the cathedral, is a good place to sit and enjoy a coffee.
- Beware of traffic, even in streets or squares that appear to be pedestrian-only.
- The Musée de Bretagne (www.musee-bretagne.fr), dedicated to Breton history and culture, is currently closed awaiting relocation to the city's futuristic Champs Libres in 2006. This ambitious new complex will include the Espace des Sciences, an interactive science museum (www.espace-sciences.org).

The modern complex of the airport at Rennes

wonderful 16th-century Flemish retable in the fifth chapel on the right. Its 10 panels, depict scenes including the birth of Mary and the marriage of Mary and Joseph. The delightful rue de la Psalette, curving behind the cathedral, is a medley of beautiful half-timbered 15th-century houses. Psalette was the local word for the cathedral choir; the street once resounded with their singing.

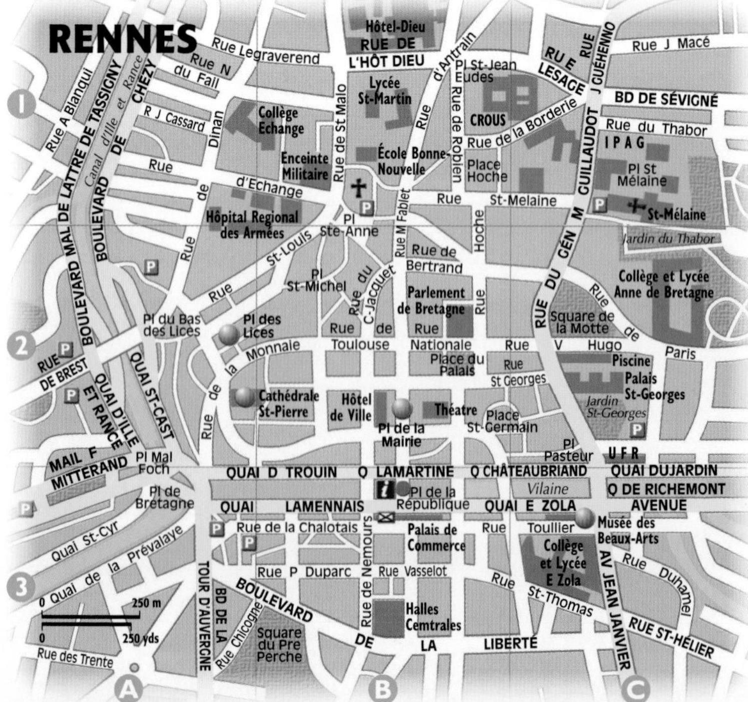

Place de la Mairie (left)

MORE TO SEE

CHAPELLE ST-YVES

The converted Chapelle St-Yves now houses the tourist office, where you'll find a permanent exhibition on the history of Rennes. The building is worth seeing for its impressive beams and the restored carvings in the chapel.

The Vilaine River in the heart of the city (above)

PLACE DES LICES

104 A2

This fine square of stone and timbered mansions once hosted jousts, although since the 17th century it has served as a market place. Today, one of Brittany's most animated markets is held here every Saturday (ends 1pm). Bars and restaurants keep it lively in the evenings. Near here is Porte Mordelaise, a fine gateway with a restored drawbridge, intended as a ceremonial entrance to the city. It dates from 1440, when the city walls were enlarged.

PLACE DE LA MAIRIE

104 B2

In the spacious Place de la Mairie you can admire the magnificent Hôtel de Ville (town hall), designed by Jacques Gabriel in the 18th century (free guided visits mid-Jul to mid-Aug Mon–Fri at 11, 2 and 5). The huge clock tower, known as Le Gros, links two curving side wings. From here, look down towards the elegant Palais de Commerce in Place de la République.

BACKGROUND

Rennes shared parliamentary power with Nantes and Vannes during the Middle Ages, becoming the undisputed Breton capital during the time of Anne de Bretagne (1477–1514). From then on it played a key role in Brittany's political struggles, including rebellions against the heavy taxation imposed during Louis XIV's reign, the Revolutionary Terror and the German occupation in World War II. The city was almost entirely demolished by fire in 1720—only the area between the market square (Place des Lices) and the city's two waterways escaped. It was subsequently rebuilt in severe Classical style. The city's population has doubled since World War II to nearly 250,000, this figure boosted by students at the two universities and the prestigious medical school, who keep the city's cultural activities and nightlife humming. Commerce and industry flourish, and the headquarters of the car manufacturer Citroën lie just outside. The city feels more French than other Breton towns.

ÉCOMUSÉE DU PAYS DE RENNES

Ferme de la Bintinais, route de Châtillon-sur-Seiche 02 99 51 38 15 Apr–end Sep Tue–Fri 9–12, 2–6, Sat 2–6, Sun 2–7; Oct–end Mar Tue–Fri 9–12, 2–6, Sat 2–6, Sun 2–7 Adult €4.60, child 6–14 €2.30 Triangle, then bus 61 to Hil-Bintinais Picnic site

www.ecomusee-rennes-metropole.fr

On the southern outskirts of Rennes, this folk museum is set in an old cider farm. Farming equipment, reconstructed interiors, and rare livestock breeds re-create a picture of rural life from the 16th century onwards.

PALAIS DU PARLEMENT DE BRETAGNE

104 B2 • Place de la Mairie

Guided tours can be arranged daily all year round (reservations strictly through the tourist office); adult €6.10, child 7–15 €3.05

The former seat of the Breton parliament (now housing the Court of Appeal) occupies the north side of Place de la Mairie. Ironically, having survived the fire of 1720, it was almost totally destroyed in a fire in 1994. Restoration is now complete and its intricate timber-framed roof and beautiful coffered ceilings look as impressive as before.

LE MAJESTIC
Fish & Chips
7/7
"LE MAJESTIC"
HAMBURGER
BAR
COFFEE SHOP
CAFE
FAST-FOOD
Sandwiches

St-Malo

Brittany's largest ferry port has a proud maritime past and a magnificent walled citadel. Besides the attractions of good beaches and plenty to see and do, its wide choice of hotels and excellent transport links make it a fine touring base.

Walking along the walled citadel of St-Malo-Intra-Muros

A crest on the wall of a building in Porte St-Vincent

The buildings and old city area of St-Malo

SEEING ST-MALO

If possible, come to St-Malo by sea. First impressions can be disappointing for motorists, because the port has a bewildering road system and becomes very congested in high season, while the railway station is a drab and inconvenient distance from the historic quarter. But an approach from the waterfront is truly majestic, revealing the stately citadel apparently afloat on its rocky plinth, attached by slender moorings to the rest of the town. Most of the main sights and beaches lie within walking distance of the port's multiple ferry terminals and yacht marinas. The helpful tourist office just outside the city walls can quickly orientate you with an excellent range of maps and guides.

HIGHLIGHTS

CITADEL

St-Malo's main attraction is its walled city, known as Intra Muros ('within the walls'), faithfully restored from Vauban's original design after large-scale devastation in 1944. The arched gateways at intervals frame inviting glimpses of cobbled shopping streets and elegant outdoor cafés. The towering ramparts (which mostly survived the bombardments) provide wonderful views of the old town and a fascinating seascape. Offshore to the north lie the remains of the Fort National, another Vauban fortification, long used as a prison (tel 02 99 85 34 33; Jun–end Sep, depending on the tides). Sights within the walls include the Cathédrale St-Vincent on Place J. de Châtillon (daily 9.45–12, 2–6), with its modern stained glass and diamond-shaped mosaic commemorating Jacques Cartier's exploration of Canada in 1535. The aquarium concealed in the ramparts has an extraordinary range of tropical fish (tel 02 99 56 94 77; daily Jul, Aug 9.30am–10pm; Apr–end Jun, Sep, Oct daily 10–7, Nov–end Mar 10–6).

RATINGS

RATINGS	
Boat trips	●●●●●
Historic interest	●●●●
Photo stops	●●●●

BASICS

203 L8 • Esplanade St-Vincent, 35400, tel 02 99 56 64 43; Jul–Aug Mon–Sat 9–7.30, Sun, hols 10–6; Apr–end Jun, Sep Mon–Sat 9–12.30, 1.30–6.30, Sun, hols 10–12.30, 2.30–6; Oct–end Mar Mon–Sat 9–12.30, 1.30–6

Local services run by St-Malo Bus; TIV, TAE, Les Courriers Bretons services all over the Emerald Coast, and to Mont-St-Michel, Cancale (via Paramé/St-Servan), Dol-de-Bretagne, Dinan, Fougères, Rennes

St-Malo

Emerald Coast cruises and river trips up the Rance to Dinan with Compagnie Corsaire, Etoile Marine Croisières (▷ What to do); Bus de Mer to Dinard; ferry connections to UK and Channel Islands with Brittany Ferries, Condor Ferries and Emeraude Jersey Ferries

P Try along the Chaussée du Sillon (main beach road) if there's no space near the walls

www.saint-malo-tourisme.com Admirably clear, in French and English.

The nautical explorer Robert Surcouf

TIPS

- A rampart walk gives a splendid 360-degree panorama of the old coastline. The complete circuit is about 2km (1 mile) long. There is free access at several points, including all the main gates to the citadel (unsuitable for wheelchair users).
- Hotels and cafés within the walled city tend to be more expensive than those on the outside.

Fort National (above), and the ramparts surrounding the walled city (right)

MORE TO SEE

ST-SERVAN

In this oldest part of the town, the imposing Tour Solidor houses the Musée International du Long Cours Cap-Hornier (tel 02 99 40 71 58; Apr–end Oct daily 10–12, 2–6; closed Mon in winter), an exhibition about the mariners who braved the perilous sea route around Cape Horn.

GRAND AQUARIUM

✉ Avenue de Général Patton BP27, 35402 ☎ 02 99 21 19 00 🕐 Daily, hours variable in high season, 10–6 in winter; closed part of Nov and Jan 🖐 Adult €13.50 , child (4–14) €9.80 www.aquarium-st-malo.com

This huge modern aquarium is excellent for children and makes a good wet-weather destination.

ROTHÉNEUF

This pleasant coastal village beyond the long beaches of Paramé was the home of Jacques Cartier, who pioneered France's colonization of eastern Canada. His family *malouinière*, the Manoir de Limoëlou, contains the Musée Jacques Cartier (tel 02 99 40 97 73; Jul, Aug daily; Jun, Sep Mon–Sat; Oct–end May tours Mon–Sat.

MUSÉE D'HISTOIRE DE LA VILLE

✉ Château de St-Malo, Esplanade Félicité Lamennais, Intra Muros ☎ 02 99 40 71 57 🕐 Apr–end Oct daily 10–12.30, 2–6; Nov–end Mar Tue–Sun 10–12, 2–6 🖐 Adult €5, child (8–16) €2.50, under 8 free

The town's history museum within St-Malo's old castle recalls the port's seafaring past. On the second floor, look out for the carved figurehead destined for the prow of a corsair vessel, depicting a 17th-century sailor. One room describes the life of St-Malo fishermen in Newfoundland. Another floor deals with great men of St-Malo, including the brilliant naval commander and privateer Robert Surcouf (1773–1827).

ÎLE DU GRAND BÉ

At low tide you can cross the causeway to the rocky island of Grand Bé to see the tomb of the writer Chateaubriand (1768–1848) and splendid views of the walled city and the surrounding coastline. Children will enjoy this walk as there are rocks to clamber on and pools to explore. Don't get stranded by the tide: If you do, there's a six-hour wait before you can walk back!

BACKGROUND

St-Malo has a long and fascinating history, dating from the 6th century, when a Welsh monk (St. Maclow) gave his name to a religious settlement on the rugged headland of Aleth (now the suburb of St-Servan). In later centuries, the inhabitants moved to the more easily defensible site of St-Malo-en-l'Isle and walled themselves in to escape Viking raiders. From then on, the isolated Malouins developed a strongly individualistic streak, and even declared their city an independent republic at one stage. Fortified by Vauban in the 17th century, St-Malo prospered as a fishing and trading port, while also growing rich on the proceeds of piracy and the slave trade. Its entrepreneurial mariners (explorers, merchants, fishermen, corsairs) built beautiful mansions (*malouinières*) all over the town. Some Malouins achieved lasting fame, notably Jacques Cartier, discoverer of Canada.

Boats moored in the town of Redon

The portico entrance to La Roche aux Fées

One of several sandy beaches in St-Briac-sur-Mer

REDON

210 L13 Place de la République, 35600 Redon, tel 02 99 71 06 04; Jul, Aug daily; Sep–end Jun Mon–Sat Redon; connections to Vannes, Rennes and Nantes Boat trips at the port Autumn chestnut festival, *Foire aux Marrons* (gourmet recipes in local restaurants)
www.tourisme-pays-redon.com

This *ville fleurie* is a popular boating hub; you can rent canoes or barges, or take an organized boat trip along the River Vilaine or the Nantes–Brest Canal. Redon was first settled in AD832, and developed as a river port for Rennes, growing prosperous on the proceeds.

Don't be put off by the charmless station area; the old town (around the Grande Rue) and the quaysides of the port have some fine old buildings and much more character. The Musée de la Batellerie (Waterways Museum), at quai Jean-Bart, concentrates on daily life on the canals at the height of their importance (tel 02 99 72 30 95; mid-Jun to mid-Sep daily 10–12, 3–6; mid-Sep to mid-Jun Sat–Mon, Wed 2–6). The Benedictine abbey of St-Sauveur displays a mix of Romanesque and Gothic styles, and has a separate belltower.

In high season, *Les Vendredis du Port* (Port Fridays) cheer up the town with *moules-frites* and sea shanties, and in autumn (chestnut time), it puts on a series of concerts called *La Bogue d'Or*, incorporating traditional Haute-Breton music.

LA ROCHE AUX FÉES

209 N11 A small hut with external storyboards provides some interpretative information

This impressive megalithic dolmen, or *allée couverte*, lies in remote countryside near Essé, some 34km (21 miles) southeast of Rennes (signed off the D41 between Janzé and Retiers). It consists of about 40 slabs of purple schist, some weighing as much as 45 tonnes. Experts differ on the precise purpose of the 'Fairies' Rock', but it is thought to date from around the 3rd millennium BC. According to an old custom, betrothed couples would walk around the monument in different directions and count the stones. If their calculations differed, the prospect of a successful union was deemed unlikely.

ST-BRIAC-SUR-MER

202 L8 49 Grande Rue, 35800 St-Briac-sur-Mer, tel 02 99 88 32 47; Jul–Aug daily 10–12.30, 2.30–6.30 mid Apr–Jun, Sep Tue, Thu–Sat 10–12, 2–5, Wed 2–5; Tue, Fri 10–12, 2–5, Sat 10–12 rest of year
www.saint-briac.com

This delightful little fishing resort guards the mouth of the pine-clad Frémur estuary, the boundary between Ille-et-Vilaine and Côtes-d'Armor. It has glorious islet-speckled coastal views, and was painted by many artists in the late 19th century, including Renoir, Signac and Emile Bernard. It is now a popular sailing venue and the harbour office is in the impressive premises of a 19th-century château on the Presqu'île du Nessey. A knot of older streets around the harbour adds character to its scattered modern holiday homes. The stained-glass windows in its church show scenes from the life of St. Briac, who arrived here from Ireland in the Dark Ages. Notice the carved mackerel on the north façade.

ST-LUNAIRE

202 L8 Boulevard Général de Gaulle, 35800 St-Lunaire, tel 02 99 46 31 09; Jul, Aug daily 9–7; Sep–Jun Mon, Thu, Fri 2.30–5
www.saint-lunaire.com

This beach resort's profile is raised by its proximity to classy Dinard, of which it is now virtually a suburb. It has similarly grand marine architecture: stately Belle-Époque villas command fine vantage points along the Emerald Coast. Its beaches are separated by a scenic headland called the Pointe du Décollé, which juts into the bay. Best resort beach is La Grande Plage.

St. Lunaire was an Irish monk who settled here in the 6th century. The attractively simple 11th-century church of St-Lunaire stands in a glade of trees. It contains the tomb of the founding saint, resting on a Gallo-Roman sarcophagus.

LE VIVIER-SUR-MER

203 M8 Maison de la Baie, Port-Est, 35960 Le Vivier/Cherrueix, tel 02 99 48 84 38; Jul, Aug daily; Sep–end Jun Mon–Sat
www.maison-baie.com

There's little sign of the bustle of sea-trade that once took place on these shores. Now the shallow, sheltered seas of Mont-St-Michel bay retreat far beyond mud-flats at low tide, creating ideal homes for mussels, raised here in their millions, strung on ropes attached to tall *bouchots* (posts). *Mytiliculture* (mussel farming) is serious business at Le Vivier, accounting for some 25 per cent of France's total production. Huge processing sheds can be seen by the port. Nearby, a visitor centre gives an excellent introduction to this unusual industry (exhibition, film show) and organizes escorted field trips and tours of the mussel beds on a tractor-drawn *petit train*. The immense beaches of flat sand along this coast are popular for sand-yachting, especially in the resort of Cherrueix.

The towers of the castle piercing the summer sky at Vitré (above), and cobbled streets in the town (left)

RATINGS

Historic interest	●●●●
Photo stops	●●●●

BASICS

209 P11

Place Général de Gaulle, 35500 Vitré, tel 02 99 75 04 46; Jul, Aug daily 10–12.30, 2–7; Sep–end Jun Mon 2.30–6, Tue–Fri 9.30–12.30, 2.30–6, Sat 10–12.30, 3–5

SNCF bus links to Fougères, and regular services to Rennes

Vitré; regular services to Rennes. Vitré is on the TGV Paris–Brest route, though few express trains actually stop here

Night tours of the old town are organized by the tourist office

A large, convenient parking area lies beside the station and tourist office just beyond the ramparts

www.ot-vitre.fr
A welcoming and very useful little site, with an English version and sensible practical details as well as historical material.

TIPS

- Vitré can easily be visited on a day-trip by public transport from Rennes. The railway station is conveniently near the heart of the town.
- A 'passport' ticket gives access to Vitré's two châteaux and several small museums, which have standard opening hours (adult €4, child €2.50).

VITRÉ

A splendidly preserved medieval survival crammed with picturesque half-timbered houses around a formidable castle.

King Henry IV once paid the town a famous compliment, declaring 'Were I not King of France, I would be a citizen of Vitré.' Today the handsome, compact old town remains as attractive as it was in its medieval heyday, and is easy to explore on foot. Timber-framed, slate-hung houses lurch in all directions on its hilly, cobbled streets, guarded by a turreted castle. Best seen from a belvedere by the River Vilaine called the Tertres Noires, Vitré's magnificent fortifications appear as a silhouette of bristling turrets, drum towers and ramparts. One of its most atmospheric residential quarters is called the Faubourg du Rachapt (meaning 'repurchased'), referring to a ransom paid to English forces besieging the town during the Hundred Years War. In earlier centuries Vitré grew wealthy on the textile trade (hemp, wool, sailcloth and leather). Some of the most interesting and best-preserved merchants' houses are in rue de la Baudrairie, the street of the leather-workers. The 17th-century author and shrewd political observer Madame de Sévigné (famed for her letters about life at the French court) lived at 9 rue Sévigné, and also at a palatial country retreat southeast of the town, the Château des Rochers-Sévigné (tel 02 99 96 76 51; same hours as Château de Vitré).

CASTLE AND CHURCH

The medieval castle on its rocky riverside bluff played a vital role in the borderland defences between Brittany and France, and was a constant target of attack (tel 02 99 75 04 54; Jul–end Sep daily 10–6; Apr–end Jun daily 10–12, 2–5.30; Oct, mid-Feb to end Mar Mon–Fri 10–12, 2–5.30, Sat, Sun 2–5.30; Nov to mid-Feb Wed–Fri 10–12, 2–5.30, Sat, Sun, Mon 2–5.30). A twin-turreted gateway leads into its triangular inner ward, where small museum displays can be visited in the Tour de l'Argenterie and the Tour St-Laurent.

The church of Notre-Dame within the ramparts dates from the 15th and 16th centuries. An unusual feature is an exterior pulpit, from which virulent Catholic sermons were preached at the Protestant Huguenot families who lived in the houses opposite. Vitré became a Huguenot stronghold during the Wars of Religion, which caused much local tension.

This chapter gives information on things to do in Brittany other than sightseeing. It is divided into four *départements*, which are indentified on the map on the inside front cover.
Within each region, towns are listed alphabetically.

What to Do

SHOPPING

Throughout France shopping is an enormous pleasure, and Brittany is no exception. In this productive agricultural and fishing region, the best and freshest harvests from *terre* and *mer* are stacked in lavish profusion on every food counter and market stall—a feast for the eye as well as the palate. Packed and processed edibles (cider, biscuits, caramels, canned fish) make appetizing and easily portable buys, while specialist crafts like pottery, linen and knitwear effortlessly fill the gift-and-souvenir gaps on your shopping list. For information on opening times and reclaiming VAT, see Planning (pages 183, 188).

MARKET FORCES

Only major business cities such as Rennes or Brest have large department stores or multinational branded chains. City-centre stores like Monoprix and Prisunic usually have a supermarket section. Chain mini-markets include 8 à Huit, Shopi and Marché Plus.

Outside Boutique Bretonne in Quimper

In smaller neighbourhoods, the specialist family-run businesses which have disappeared from many places in Britain remind us how well the French balance their way of life despite commercial pressures. Every town and village has its selection of *boulangeries-pâtisseries* (bakery/cake shops), *boucheries* (butchers), and probably one or two *charcuteries-traiteurs* (delicatessens) or *poissonneries* (fishmongers) as well. Small grocery stores selling general food supplies are called *épiceries* or *alimentations*.

These are the backbone of the food-shopping experience in Brittany, underpinned by the weekly markets that spill so vividly on to the streets and squares of larger towns, and the covered produce markets or *halles*, which display enticing wares most weekdays in regional centres. Farmers' markets are a growing phenomenon, selling items like goats' cheese, buttermilk, or home-cured *charcuterie* from independent producers once or twice a month in summer. In the countryside, farm shops and roadside stalls offer surplus produce to passers-by, especially at harvest time. Pick your own soft fruit at St-Meloir-des-Ondes, or stock up on early vegetables *(primeurs)* and artichokes in the fertile Golden Belt near St-Pol-de-Léon.

CATCH OF THE DAY

Some of Brittany's larger fishing ports, including Roscoff, Concarneau, Douarnenez, Quiberon and Le Guilvinec, hold a *criée* or fish auction, generally very early on weekday mornings. These are aimed primarily at professional wholesale buyers who distribute the catch to shops and restaurants throughout northern France in refrigerated containers, but it is often possible to buy superb fresh fish and seafood at quayside stalls.

Look out too, for shoreside *viviers* (fish farms), where live shellfish await in large tanks. Just point out which lobster or langoustine takes your fancy, and it's yours. Le Forêt-Fouesnant, Primel-Trégastel (near Morlaix), Camaret and Aber-Benoît have *viviers* offering direct sales to the general public. At Cancale and along the River Bélon you can buy oysters inexpensively from producers' stalls, while the commercial mussel-rearing ports of Le Vivier-sur-Mer and St-Jacut-de-la-Mer are the places to look for fresh *moules*.

The busy Halles fish market in Douarnanez

Processed seafood is an important Breton export. The days of the great sardine fleets are long gone, but firms like La Belle-Iloise (with outlets all over Brittany) and Gonidec (based in Concarneau) still produce a superb range of gourmet fish products (mackerel rillettes, marinaded tuna, smoked salmon, cured sprats), all

enticingly packaged in tins and jars.

Seaweed is an increasingly important marine industry. Finistère's north coast supports some 800 different varieties, some of which are used in pharmaceutical, cosmetic and culinary products. The Roscoff firms of Thalado and Algoplus make an interesting range of seaweed soaps, skincare lotions and nutritional supplements, on sale locally.

HEADY BREWS

Since the *département* of Loire-Atlantique was transferred to the Pays de la Loire region in 1973, Brittany no longer produces significant

Local crockery on sale in Locronan

quantities of wine. The crisp, dry Muscadet wines from Nantes are widely available, but the more typical local drink is cider, produced from the lush orchards of the Rance and Odet valleys and sold directly by many producers. Beer is another traditional Breton tipple. A resurgence of independent microbreweries has resulted in an interesting range of real ales such as Coreff, Dremmwell and Telenn Du. Chouchen is a kind of mead, made with honey and strongly alcoholic, while Pommeau is an aperitif made with apple juice and Calvados. Lambig is a powerful cider brandy, good for flambéed dishes. Brittany even distills its own whisky (Warenghem) near Lannion. You'll see all sorts of fruit-flavoured liqueurs and digestifs on sale too.

SAILOR GEAR

The signs Coopérative Maritime or Comptoir de la Mer in any Breton harbour town indicate a hybrid chandlery store for visiting holidaymakers as well as amateur and professional seafarers. Among the anti-fouling paints and outboard motors you'll find a selection of fashionably rugged weatherproof clothes (brightly coloured sailing jackets, sou'westers and kabigs—a heavy outdoor cape with scallop fastenings), along with classy Breton knitwear in jaunty red or navy stripes, just as wearable ashore as on board. Reputable designer labels include Armor Lux, Guy Cotten and Saint-James. Maritime souvenirs (barometers, sextants, knot pictures, ship models) are also on sale, but if you're looking for a genuine nautical antique, visit a specialist dealer, or watch out for marine markets held occasionally, for instance at Douarnenez or La Trinité-sur-Mer.

ARTS AND CRAFTS

Quimper *faïence* (tin-glazed earthenware) with its classic designs of flowers, birds and costumed figures is perhaps the most recognizable Breton handicraft, available in countless stores throughout the region, but most prominently in its home town at the factory showroom of H. B. Henriot (▷ 124). Glassware, woodcarvings, paintings, household linen and recordings of Breton music are other popular buys. Many handicraft shops and galleries can be found in the historic quarters of popular tourist destinations such as Vannes, Quimper and St-Malo. Craft workshops and artists' studios are concentrated in villages such as Locronan, Brasparts, St-Meloir-des-Ondes, Camaret-sur-Mer, Rochefort-en-Terre, La Gacilly and Pont-Scorff. Antique and bric-à-brac shops are places to look for traditional Breton furniture or smaller keepsakes like wooden spoons, butter-moulds and decorated biscuit tins.

MODERN STORES

Supermarkets and hypermarkets have sprung up in and around most Breton towns, undeniably convenient for car-borne travellers wanting a one-stop shopping fix.

Navy-and-white Breton T-shirts outside a shop in Concarneau

Branches of Champion, Intermarché or Casino supermarkets are easily spotted along many urban highways. Best of the big hypermarkets is the Breton-based chain Leclerc, which originated in Edouard Leclerc's home town of Landerneau. At these large undercover malls you can buy everything from wet fish to dishwashers. Besides a classy selection of fresh and processed food, you'll find a wide choice of books, magazines, stationery, clothing, electronics and housewares. Leclerc can also oblige with well-maintained, free toilets, a coffee shop and a cheaper-than-average fuel top-up.

SPORTS AND ACTIVITIES

Brittany is a splendid outdoor pursuits destination. The tourism authorities produce a number of specialist brochures on most of the activities listed below; for some ideas on activity holidays, see www.formulesbretagne.com. Many activities focus on the waterfront, and if you are keen on water sports, look out for the 36 nautical bases belonging to the Point Passion Plage group, which offer high-quality facilities, safety surveillance and common tariffs.

BICYCLING

Brittany isn't the most challenging terrain for serious bikers, but perfectly suits recreational cyclists who don't want too many gradients. Several bicycling routes are recommended by the bicycling federation, including VTT (mountain bike) ones. Accommodation and luggage transportation can be arranged. The UK operator Cycling for Softies organizes undemanding holidays staying in small family hotels (tel 0161 248 8282; www.cycling-for-softies.co.uk). Breton Bikes is another British-owned operator, based in Plelauff, Côtes d'Armor (tel 02 96 24 86 72; www.bretonbikes.com).

Boating on the lake at Mûr-de-Bretagne

BIRDWATCHING

Brittany is one of the best places in Europe to spot birds. It lies on transatlantic migration routes, and has a huge diversity of habitats. Over 20 areas are designated as bird sanctuaries, including several islands.

BOATING

Cruising Brittany's estuary rivers and inland waterways is immensely popular. Rent a canal cruiser from one of the many boating centres (such as Dinan, Redon, Pontivy, Carhaix) on the Ille-et-Rance or Nantes–Brest canals, and take life in the slow lane for a while.

CANOEING AND KAYAKING

The calm bays and estuaries around the Breton coast make ideal playgrounds for these popular sports, which can be easily mastered.

DIVING

The clear waters off the Breton coast are ideal for scuba diving. Sub-aqua activities are especially popular on the Crozon peninsula (wreck diving off Finistère), St-Malo and Concarneau. Look for PADI-accredited clubs.

FISHING

Sea-fishing has been a way of life for centuries in Brittany. Many local boat-owners will take visitors out for a day or two in search of mackerel and sea-bass. Over 20,000km (12,500 miles) of rivers and inland waterways make an angling paradise too, mainly for trout and salmon. *Pêche à pied*, or low-tide shell-fishing with nets, hoes and rakes, is another favourite pastime for Breton families. Strict regulations apply to all types of fishing for environmental and conservation reasons, and fines levied for transgressions can be hefty.

GOLF

Brittany has more than 30 golf courses. There are many choices available, ranging from a single round to a full week's play on several courses. Golf is a more sociable, family-oriented game in France than in other countries, and course etiquette is generally unstuffy, though fees can be high.

There are many places to rent bicycles throughout Brittany

Tailor-made golfing packages are available from a number of specialist operators.

HORSE-RIDING

Lots of horsy activities can be pursued in Brittany, where most resorts lie within easy reach of riding stables. Riding along the quieter beaches, or across the Baie de St-Brieuc, is particularly popular. Equibreizh is a 2,000km (1,250-mile) network of signposted bridleways traversing Brittany (ask for the Topo-Guide describing the routes). The two national stud farms at Lamballe and Hennebont organize many equine events in summer. Horse-racing is very popular in

France, and Brittany has numerous race-courses (*hippodromes*), of which Loudéac is one of the most renowned.

SAILING

Brittany's glorious coastline and long-established seafaring traditions give it a head start in the water sports world. Breton yachtsmen like Eric Tarberly have become legends in their own lifetime. Numerous sailing schools and marinas offer splendid facilities, and many have strong links with British yacht clubs (hundreds of yachts cross the Channel in both directions each year).

SAND-YACHTING

This sport, also called sand-karting or land-sailing (*char à voile*), is almost as exhilarating for spectators as for participants. The Baie de Mont-St-Michel and the Baie de Quiberon are two of the best venues, but there are over a dozen other schools.

SURFING

The wilder shores of Brittany, such as Plage de la Torche near Audierne, attract adventurous, experienced surfers, but there are also less challenging places to have a go, such as Dinard and Larmor-Plage.

THALASSOTHERAPY

Seawater health cures are big news in Brittany, and thalassotherapy centres specializing in this form of treatment have sprung up in a dozen or so resorts all around the coastline, including St-Malo, Dinard, Roscoff, Bénodet, Quiberon and Carnac. In these luxurious spas, you can be bombarded with high-pressure jets, massaged with seaweed creams and assailed with aerosol vapours in the pricey pursuit of health and beauty—or just relax in the jacuzzi.

WALKING

Brittany has one of the longest coastal footpaths anywhere in France. The GR34 (waymarked in red-and-white) runs all the way from Mont-St-Michel on the Normandy border to the Golfe du Morbihan. Much of it follows the old watchpaths (*sentiers des douaniers*) used by armed coastguards against smugglers in the 18th century. There are also many beautiful walks to be discovered in inland Brittany, particularly the trails striking through the scenic Monts d'Arrée. You can also follow canal towpaths and ancient pilgrim routes, or circuit offshore islands.

A golf course overlooking the sea in St-Cast-le-Guildo

Walkers following one of the many hiking trails in Brittany

FOR CHILDREN

Just about everywhere in this family holiday destination is child-friendly. Hotels provide family rooms, restaurants offer child menus, visitor attractions and transport companies give reductions on admission charges and fares. Lots of animal and amusement parks, aquariums, discovery centres and museums appeal to children of all ages.

BEACHES AND WATER SPORTS

Brittany's beaches are the greatest attraction for young families. Here children can build sandcastles and explore rock pools to their heart's content. Remember, though, that the Breton coast can be dangerous, and observe warning signs. Virtually all the seaside resorts make special efforts in the holiday season with beach clubs, festivals and activities designed with children in mind. Some hold a *Fête aux Mômes*, which includes lots of clowns, bands, acrobats, rides and parades. Water sports clubs involve children from an early age, and it is not uncommon to see tiny tots barely past the nappy stage setting fearlessly off into the Big Blue in some sailing craft or other, albeit carefully supervised.

Children playing on trampolines on the beach at Bénodet

ENTERTAINMENT AND NIGHTLIFE

Bretons are of Celtic ancestry and are great communicators. Strong oral and musical traditions encourage live performance art throughout the year, and many events are staged during the summer, when most visitors are around. The language barrier may discourage foreign visitors from attending French-speaking classical theatre productions, and even more from ones performed in Breton, but dance, opera and concerts of all types attract many holidaymakers as well as locals.

WHAT TO DO

INFORMATION AND BOOKING

The mainstream cultural venues, predictably enough, are in the larger cities, especially those with a sizeable student population, such as Rennes and Brest. To find out what's going on, call in at any tourist office, or look out for listings in local papers and magazines. Tickets for shows and events can sometimes be purchased at tourist offices too.

MUSIC

Music is one of the strongest social bonds in Brittany, and the clearest expression of the region's cultural distinctiveness. Some of the biggest folk festivals in Europe are staged here, including Lorient's Festival Interceltique. Some half million visitors are drawn here annually to hear traditional instruments like the Celtic harp, the *bombarde* (a kind of oboe) and the *biniou* (Breton bagpipes), played by Breton bands known as *bagadou*. Other styles of music are also celebrated, including jazz, classical and rock. Concerts are held in major arts venues, particularly Ubu in Rennes, or the Quartz in Brest. Al fresco musical events take place at summer festivals.

CINEMA

The overwhelming majority of films shown in Brittany are dubbed into French, but a few places show some foreign films in the original version *(version originale)* with French subtitles. Several film festivals have raised Brittany's cinematic profile in the past decade, notably at Dinard, Rennes, Brest and Douarnenez.

NIGHTLIFE

University towns and the more glamorous seaside resorts are the places to find most going on after dark, though in winter most places are very quiet indeed. In summer, however, you'll find clubs and pubs, piano bars, café-theatre and casinos humming until the small hours. There isn't a particularly overt gay scene in Brittany, though you will obviously find gay bars and clubs in the larger cities like Rennes and Brest.

FESTIVALS AND EVENTS

Events take place all year round in Brittany, though the vast majority are held during the holiday season between Easter and October. Any tourist office can provide a full list of local events, and most publish their social calendar on official websites. Some are internationally famous and attract huge gatherings.

PARDONS AND PILGRIMAGES

Many Breton communities celebrate the feast day of their patron saint with a ceremony called a *pardon*, beginning with a solemn mass and followed by a procession behind the saint's relics. The day then proceeds more merrily with music, dancing and feasting. On these occasions you can see traditional costumes worn, and hear Breton spoken or sung. Other religious events are annual pilgrimages to a religious site, such as Locronan or Ste-Anne-d'Auray.

FESTOU-NOZ

The *fest-noz*, or night festival, is a more secular Breton tradition involving Celtic music and dancing in much the same style as an Irish or Scottish *ceilidh*. Its original purpose was to inject a little impetus into the important business of stamping down the earthen floors of the villagers' houses.

FOOD, MARITIME AND FOLK FESTIVALS

Many coastal ports celebrate the source of their livelihood, the sea, with an annual festival. This may have its roots in a service of thanksgiving, or be a purely secular jamboree, as at Côtes d'Armor's Fête de la Coquille St-Jacques (scallop festival), or Binic's Fête de la Morue (cod festival). Some commemorate former fishing communities, such as Concarneau's Fête des Filets Bleus (Blue Nets) or Paimpol's Fête des Terres-Neuvas (Newfoundland Fishermen). Many include parades, fireworks and regattas down by the port. Events involving traditional working boats are especially popular.

MORBIHAN

Dark-red sails set, an old gaff-rigged sailing boat approaches the coast

The warm, sunny climate and south-facing coastline of Morbihan inevitably places a strong emphasis on resort activities, and here, as in most parts of Brittany, boat trips and water sports are widely available, particularly in the sheltered waters of the Golfe du Morbihan and the Baie de Quiberon. Inland lakes and waterways provide alternative playgrounds for boat-lovers. Morbihan has some particularly good family attractions, with excellent discovery centres, industrial showrooms and interesting animal parks. Old Vannes has good shopping, and there's no shortage of nightlife and summer entertainment in the larger resorts.

KEY TO SYMBOLS
- Shopping
- Entertainment
- Nightlife
- Sports
- Activities
- Health and Beauty
- For Children

ARRADON

BELLE PLAISANCE

Nicolas Bourdy, 24 chemin de Gravellic, 56610 Arradon
Tel 02 97 44 80 91
www.belleplaisance.com

On the Golfe du Morbihan you can rent old-fashioned and beautifully restored sailing boats with a professional sailor to navigate and give instruction. Decide where you want to go and for how long, or leave it to the experts. Book at least one week in advance and note that credit cards are not accepted. You can also rent kayaks and motor boats.

Mar–end Oct, by appointment €45 per person (whole day); €25 per person (half day), €15 6.30pm–8pm with aperitif; €15 8.30pm–10pm to watch sunset, all departing from Arradon port.

ARZAL

LES VEDETTES JAUNES

Barrage d'Arzal, 56190 Arzal
Tel 02 97 45 02 81

Book an excursion upstream on the Vilaine from the Arzal dam (departures also from Redon and La Roche-Bernard in summer). Easily identifiable in vivid sunshine yellow, these sleek, double-decker motor-launches give excellent visibility. Lunch and candlelit dinner cruises are available. Boats have sun-decks, air-conditioning and commentary.

Year-round, but most choice in Jul, Aug From adult €8.50, child (4–11) €5 for a basic cruise, or from €35–€48 (adult), including an on-board meal (reduced prices and special menus for children under 8); drinks extra

BELLE-ÎLE

LES CALÈCHES DE LOCMARIA

Chemin du Petit-Houx, 56360 Locmaria
Tel 02 97 31 76 67
www.lescaleches.com

Horse-drawn carriage rides lasting one hour, half a day or a whole day (with a picnic if you like) can be arranged every day of the year at this village on the southeastern side of the island. Carriages hold up to five passengers each; parties of 10 can be catered for on a single tour.

BILLIERS

DOMAINE DE ROCHEVILAINE

Pointe de Pen-Lan, 56190 Billiers
Tel 02 97 41 61 61
www.domainerochevilaine.com

The Aqua Phénicia spa at this gorgeously located luxury hotel (▷ 166) has an impressive range of health and beauty treatments, including hydro-massage, seaweed masks and anti-cellulite sessions. Ladies can have their moustaches removed for as little as €9, while a five-day well-being course costs €462, excluding board and lodging.

BRANDÉRION

LA TISSERIE

56700 Brandérion (7km/4 miles from Hennebont in the direction of Auray; signed off N165)
Tel 02 97 32 90 27

Another of the well-organized *espaces découvertes* near Lorient, this weaving discovery centre shows how the skill developed through history. You can watch weavers at work, using a variety of techniques, and have a go yourself in summer workshops aimed especially at children.

Daily 10–12.30, 2–6; phone for hours rest of year · Adult €3.50, child €2.60

CARNAC

EXPLORASUB

12 boulevard de la Plage (Hôtel Le Plancton), 56340 Carnac
Tel 02 97 52 62 80
www.explorasub56.com

Explorasub runs PADI-approved sub-aqua courses at all levels for exploration in the Baie de Quiberon. They also arrange themed expeditions in a semi-rigid boat. Beginners' trials are available from eight years old.

All year

LE FAOUËT

L'ABEILLE VIVANTE ET LA CITÉ DES FOURMIS

Kercadoret, 56320 Le Faouët
Tel 02 97 23 08 05
www.abeilles-et-fourmis.com

Welcome to the sociable world of the bees and the ants, revealed in transparent display cases, including a glass sweet-jar and an old television set. You can try the honey and buy honey products in the shop. There's a picnic site, bar and wheelchair access.

Apr–end Sep daily 10–12.30, 1.30–6 (10–7 in Jul, Aug) · Adult €6, child (4–15) €4

LA GACILLY

YVES ROCHER

La Croix des Archers, 56200 La Gacilly
Tel 02 99 08 35 84
www.yves-rocher.fr
www.paysdelagacilly.com

A ferry full of people arriving at Le Palais, Belle-île

Beauty magnate Yves Rocher has turned his home village and production headquarters into a high-profile tourist attraction. Imaginative botanical gardens contain a fascinating collection of plants used for culinary, pharmaceutical, cosmetic and industrial purposes. The Végétarium is a multimedia exhibition space devoted to the plant kingdom. Guided tours of the production site show how the plants are used in Yves Rocher's eco-friendly beauty products. There are also many ancillary arts and crafts shops.

Gardens open all year free of charge; Végétarium end May–early Oct; closes lunchtimes; telephone for precise dates and times. Guided tours of the entire complex daily mid June–early Oct · Adult €6.50, child €4.50, under 10 free

GUIDEL

LABYRINTHE DU CORSAIRE

Kerdrien, 56520 Guidel
Tel 02 99 81 17 23
www.labyrintheducorsaire.com

One of Europe's largest maize mazes, covering some 11ha (4.5 acres) with 10km (6 miles) of pathways, picnic sites, and lots of fun things to do while you're getting lost, such as strategy games, bouncy castles and puzzles. There's a similar attraction near St-Malo.

Jul, Aug · €6.80, under 3 free

MALANSAC

PARC DE PRÉHISTOIRE

56220 Malansac
Tel 02 97 43 34 17
www.prehistoire-bretagne.com

Dinosaurs roam the forests of a disused slate quarry not far from Rochefort-en-Terre. This is a multi-language introduction to the evolution of man in Brittany. The site is enhanced by a shop, bar, picnic site and disabled access.

Apr to mid-Oct daily 10–7.30 (last entry 5.30); mid-Oct to mid-Nov Sun only 1.30–6 · Adult €9, child (5–11) €5

MALESTROIT

CLUB DE CANOË KAYAK

la Daufresne, 56140 Malestroit
Tel 02 97 75 29 86

This club has kayaks and two- or three-seater canoes for rental, and will suggest circular routes on the River Oust and Nantes–Brest Canal. It also provides tuition and hosts events.

Jul, Aug daily 9–7; off-season telephone to make a reservation · Kayak rental from about €6 per hour, €17 per day; two-seater canoes from €7.60 per hour, €22 per day

MONTERBLANC

AÉRO GOLFE EVASION

Aérodrome de Vannes-Meucon, 56250 Monterblanc
Tel 02 97 61 89 37

For an aerial perspective of the Golfe du Morbihan, take a joy ride from Vannes' little aerodrome north of the city. Four different circuits are suggested. Payments must be made in advance by cheque or cash only, but are completely refundable if flights have to be cancelled in bad weather.

From €35 per person, assuming a full payload of three passengers; half price for children under 12

PLOËRMEL

CLUB NAUTIQUE PLOËRMEL–TAUPONT

Base Nautique, Lac du Duc, 56800 Ploërmel
Tel 02 97 74 14 51
www.cnp.asso.fr

The huge reservoir lake north of Ploërmel makes a great playground for waterbabies of all ages. There are optimist dinghies suitable for four–six-year-olds, waterskis from six years old, canoe-kayaks, rowing boats, catamarans, windsurfers, sailboats and RIBs for adults. You can also have private tuition or join a course.

Jul, Aug Mon–Fri 9–7, Sat, Sun 2–7; rest of year Mon–Fri 9–12, 2–6, Sat 2–6

PONT-SCORFF

L'ODYSSAUM

Moulin des Princes, 56620 Pont-Scorff
Tel 02 97 32 42 00
www.sellor.com

Follow the complex lifestyle of wild salmon as they travel up to 14,000 km (8,750 miles) across the Atlantic from Greenland to their birthplace to spawn and die. This excellent interactive discovery outlet in a verdant setting on the River Scorff enables you to learn about migration research, fishing techniques and conservation measures. Afterwards, taste some of the fish in the riverside Bistrot Saumon with its panoramic terrace. Summer events, field trips.

Jul, Aug Tue–Fri 9–7, Sat–Mon 2–7; rest of year Tue–Fri 9–12.30, 2–6, Sat–Mon 2–6 Adult €5.30, child (5–17) €4

PORT-LOUIS

LE TEMPS D'UNE ESCALE

11 rue de la Marine, 56290 Port-Louis
Tel 02 97 82 41 13

Here you'll find decorative objects, art and sculptures made from wood, clay and other materials in the form of animals and ships. There are also ceramic vases and lamps. Everything is made locally. Credit cards are not accepted.

May–end Sep daily 9–12, 2–7, rest of year Mon–Wed, Fri, Sat 9–12, 2–7, Thu and Sun 9–12; Closed 2 weeks in Sep Batobus from Lorient

Water sports are hugely popular: Kayaking on a river in Brittany

QUIBERON

HOUAT AND HOËDIC

Gare Maritime, Port-Maria, 56170 Quiberon
Tel 02 97 35 02 00
www.smn-navigation.fr

Besides serving the major islands of Belle-Île and Groix, the Société Morbihannaise de Navigation (SMN) also plies to the smaller, quieter islands of Houat and Hoëdic (Duck and Duckling) all year round. With a combined population of around 500, these tiny islands derive their income from a mix of fishing and tourism. Summer departures also leave from Vannes, La Trinité-sur-Mer and Port-Navalo (Navix, Compagnie des Iles). Cars are not allowed, but you can take a bicycle.

Sailings range from just one per day in winter to about six in high season; journey time around 45 minutes
Adult return €26 approx (seasonal variations)

LA MAISON D'ARMORINE

Zone d'Activités Plein Ouest, 56170 Quiberon
Tel 02 97 50 24 24
www.maison-armorine.com

Find out how the traditional Breton sweet called a *niniche* (a long, thin lollipop) has been made since 1946 by visiting the factory at Quiberon, on the same site as the Conserverie La Belle-Iloise and the Maison Lucas. The four branches of this sweetshop (candy store) in Carnac Plage, Quiberon, Belle-Île and La Trinité-sur-Mer sell about 50 different varieties of *niniche*. Other typical sweets include Salidou (toffee with butter).

Guided tours Jul, Aug at 10, 11, 2.30 and 3.30; rest of year at 11 and 3 only (closed Dec–Jan) Free

MAISON LUCAS

Zone d'Activités Plein Ouest, 56170 Quiberon
Tel 02 97 50 59 50

Michel Lucas welcomes visitors to have a look around his smoke-house, where top-quality fish straight from the fishmarket just down the road are expertly filleted, oak-smoked and vacuum packed. Try smoked salmon or mackerel, tuna sausage, eel, haddock, kippers or marinated sardines. Naturally you can also buy on site, and there's even a refrigerated mail-order service within France. Check out the wet-fish *poissonnerie* down on the seafront, too, next to M Lucas's superb fish restaurant, La Criée (▷ 155).

Closed Jan Free

RHUMERIE LE NELSON
20 Place Hoche, 56170 Quiberon
Tel 02 97 50 31 37
This lively rum pub down near the port is not to be missed. It serves about 50 different types of rum from all over the world and plays music dating from the 1960s onwards. Live concerts (mostly rock) are held about twice a week. Internet access is also laid on.
Mon–Sat 12pm–2am (also Sun in high season); closed Jan

VENT DE SABLE
Isthme de Penthièvre, l avenue de St-Malo, 56510 St-Pierre Quiberon
Tel 02 97 52 39 90
www.char-a-voile.bretagne.com
The glorious smooth expanses of gleaming sand at Penthièvre on the breezy northwest shores of the Quiberon peninsula are ideal to watch or learn sand-yachting (*char à voile*). Safety helmets are supplied; eye protection and gloves advised. Keep your distance if you are spectating, as the speeds attained by these fragile craft are awesome. The minimum age is 10.
All year, depending on tides
From about €32 for a 2-hour session

QUISTINIC

VILLAGE DE POUL-FÉTAN
56310 Quistinic
Tel 02 97 39 51 74
www.poul-fetan.com
This 'living history' attraction re-creates a typical Breton village of the 16th century. Costumed staff show how everyday domestic tasks such as spinning, laundry and butter-making were carried out, and there's a film show and demonstrations and events every afternoon.
Jul, Aug daily guided tours 10–1, unguided access 1–7; Jun, Sep daily 2–7; Apr, May Wed, Sat, Sun 2–7
Adult €6 (€7 Jun–end Sep), child (6–12) €3

RIANTEC

LA MAISON DE L'ILE KERNER
56670 Riantec
Tel 02 97 84 51 49
www.riantec.com
This interesting *espace découverte* (discovery centre) run by the Pays de Lorient tourist authorities is located on a small islet in the tidal lagoon of Gâvres near Port-Louis. Guided bird-watching and flower-spotting expeditions are organized all year round to introduce visitors to some of the flora and fauna of this rich conservation zone. There's also an on-site shop.
Jul, Aug daily 10–7; Apr–end Jun, Sep Tue–Fri 10–12.30, 2–6, Sat–Mon 2–6; Oct–end Mar Sun 2–6 Adult €3.80; child €2.90; family €11.30 (ticket sales end one hour before closing time)

Locally made wicker baskets for sale

ROCHEFORT-EN-TERRE

VANNERIE TY AR MAN
Rue des Douves, 56220 Rochefort-en-Terre
Tel 02 97 43 41 64
A quaint little shop in one of Rochefort's charming old timbered houses near the castle, crammed to the ceiling with rustic caneware—mainly baskets of all shapes and sizes, but also mats, furnishings, ornaments and similar items.
All year, though erratic off-season

ST-GILDAS-DE-RHUYS

GOLF DE RHUYS-KERVER
Domaine de Kerver, 56730 St-Gildas-de-Rhuys
Tel 02 97 45 30 09
www.formule-golf.com
This standard 18-hole, par-72 golf course has a great location at the heart of a bird sanctuary on the Golfe du Morbihan. It also has 30 practice holes and a putting green.
Jul, Aug daily 8–8; rest of year daily 9–dusk Apr–end Sep €48, rest of year €34

SAINT-PHILIBERT

LA TRINITAINE
Kerluesse, 56470 Saint-Philibert
Tel 02 97 55 02 04
www.latrinitaine.com
There are over a dozen outlets of this huge food-processing company in Brittany, but this one on the road between Auray and Locmariaquer is one of the biggest, and, being well supplied with parking spaces; is a good place to stock up with provisions or presents. The extensive modern premises stock a vast array of Breton produce, including fresh fruit and vegetables, charcuterie and bakery goods, as well as the trademark biscuits. When you need a break from shopping, there are play and picnic areas and an on-site café. The store also has wheelchair access.
Daily 9–12.30, 2–7

VANNES

LE COMPTOIR CELTE
8 rue Saint-Vincent, 56000 Vannes
Tel 02 97 01 05 04
An attractive shop in the old town, this is a good place to look for a wide range of typical Breton products, including woodcarvings and ceramics, kitchen utensils, boat models, gourmet fish specialities and music recordings.
Mon–Sat 10–12.30, 2–7 (from 9am Wed and Sat; no lunchtime closing in summer)

LA HUCHE À PAINS

23 Place des Lices, 56000 Vannes
Tel 02 97 47 23 76

A magnificent bakery and cake shop on the market place, established for over 20 years, selling lots of delicious Breton specialities, including the house *pain d'épices* at €16 per kilo. It also does a fine range of sandwiches, quiches, pizzas, salads, home-made soup and other snacks, ideal for picnics while you're exploring the old town. Specials include *tulipe des îles* (an almond and chocolate fruit tart).

Mon–Sat 7am–8pm

PALAIS DES ARTS

Place de Bretagne, 56019 Vannes
Tel 02 97 01 62 00
www.mairie-vannes.fr/palaisdesarts

This large theatre with varied productions has something to please everyone, with plays, circus acts, ballet, dance, jazz, *chansons*, classical music and opera. Family tickets are available.

Mon–Sat 8.30pm Adult €18–€21, child (under 26) €12

VANOCÉA

20 rue Emile Jourdan/Boulevard de Pontivy (N of N165), 56000 Vannes
Tel 02 97 62 68 00
www.mairie-vannes.fr

This freeform municipal swimming pool measures some 650sq m (7,000sq ft) and has a huge waterslide, geysers, bubble beds, a diving section and pools for children. The complex also includes a weights room, a fitness studio, solarium and sauna. There's wheelchair access with a submersible chair.

Daily, late opening Tue, Fri 5.30pm–10pm Complex tariff structure with lots of special deals

FESTIVALS AND EVENTS

JULY, AUGUST

FESTIVAL PLACE AUX MÔMES CARNAC

In common with many popular Breton resorts, Carnac makes special efforts for children during the summer holidays. Free open-air entertainment involving puppets, clowns, acrobats, storytellers and singers takes place every Tuesday in high season at 6pm behind the tourist office in Carnac Plage.

Jul, Aug

FESTIVAL SAUMON PONT-SCORFF

Music, fireworks and salmon-fishing demonstrations dedicated to the king of the River Scorff. Instructive as well as fun.

Three days in mid-Jul

Enjoying the fun of the medieval festival in Moncontour

FÊTES MÉDIÉVALES HENNEBONT

Hennebont regresses into medieval pageantry at the end of the month with tournaments, troubadours, jugglers and a medieval market.

Last weekend in July

JAZZ À VANNES VANNES

Tel 02 97 01 62 44
www.mairie-vannes.fr/jazzavannes

Jazz artists converge on Vannes for a series of open-air concerts in mid-summer.

Late Jul to early Aug

FESTIVAL INTERCELTIQUE LORIENT

2 rue Paul-Bert
Tel 02 97 21 24 29
www.festival-interceltique.com

This is one of the biggest bashes in Brittany, indeed throughout France, attracting crowds of well over half a million people from all over the Celtic fringes of Europe. More than 4,500 performers liven up the port area in time-honoured style with traditional music, dancing, folklore, feasting and fun. Night parties (*festou-noz*) keep things humming until the small hours. Book well ahead for accommodation.

Early to mid-Aug

NUITS MUSICALES DU GOLFE VANNES

A series of classical concerts arranged in the fine churches around the Golfe du Morbihan, including Elven, Arradon, Theix, Saint-Avé. Get information on bookings at Vannes tourist office.

2–3 weeks early to mid-Aug

SEPTEMBER

PARDON DES ABOYEUSES JOSSELIN

The so-called 'Barking Pardon' of Our Lady of the Brambles (Notre-Dame-du-Roncier) in Josselin refers to the curious tale of a beggar woman who came to ask for a drink of water at the well. The village women drove her roughly away with dogs and curses, but immediately their cries turned to dog-like howls as a punishment, for the beggar woman was the Virgin in disguise. Each year at the annual *pardon*, the women of Josselin ask ritual forgiveness for their lack of charity, lest the barking curse take hold again.

8 Sep

FINISTÈRE

A secluded sandy beach near the tiny resort of Brignogan-Plage in Finistère

Finistère is the most fiercely Celtic and fervently Catholic part of Brittany, and the region's cultural and religious festivals are a major attraction for visitors. Its long and varied coastline with sheltered estuaries and offshore islands gives ample scope for boat trips and *nautisme* of all kinds. Inland, outdoor pursuits like walking, riding and bicycling are popular, especially in the Armorique regional park. Quimper and Brest have big-city nightlife, including lively arts venues and many bars and clubs. Shopping is very good in Finistère too, with lots of speciality products on sale, and a host of interesting markets and craft fairs. Note that some of the best attractions for children (Domaine de Menez Meur, Aquashow, Océanopolis, Douarnenez Port-Musée) are described in the Sights section.

KEY TO SYMBOLS

- Shopping
- Entertainment
- Nightlife
- Sports
- Activities
- Health and Beauty
- For Children

L'ABER WRAC'H

CENTRE DE VOILE DE L'ABER-WRAC'H

4 port de l'Aber Wrac'h, 29870 Landéda
Tel 02 98 04 90 64
www.cvl-aberwrach.fr

Sailboat rental and tuition are offered in the scenic, sheltered waters of the Baie des Anges on Finistère's northwestern coast. The fully accredited sailing school supplies catamarans, sea-kayaks, sailboards and dinghies. There are events, courses and a children's club.

Apr–end Sep reception Mon–Sat 9.30–12.30, 2.30–5.30 Sample prices: half-day family outings on a 6m (20ft) Blue Djinn €95 (max 5); kayak €10 (half-day), sailboard €31 (half-day)

BREST

LE QUARTZ

2/4, avenue Georges Clémenceau, 29210 Brest
Tel 02 98 33 70 70
www.lequartz.com

Inject a shot of culture into your visit to Brest. This major avant-garde arts venue near the tourist office off Place de la Liberté has two performance halls, hosting experimental and popular theatre, ballet and dance, classical music, jazz, world music, opera, operetta and arthouse films. The Cinémathèque de Bretagne (film library) is also housed here.

Box office Tue–Fri 1–7, Sat 2–7 (until 9pm whenever there's a performance). Closed Mon, hols and Jul, Aug Ticket prices start at around €6, averaging about €25 for a major concert or drama performance

PATINOIRE DE BREST RÏNKLA STADIUM

Place Napoleon III, quartier Bellevue, 29210 Brest
Tel 02 98 03 01 30
www.rinkla-stadium.com

This ice rink is home to the Albatross professional ice hockey team. Watch a live game or highlights on one of two huge TV screens, or go skating yourself. There is a café-bar, shop and children's play area on site. You can take bus line 5 or 6 to Bellevue or Patinoire.

Sep–end May public skating Sun 10–12.30, 2.30–5.30 Wed, Sat,

2.30–5.30; Tue, Thu, Fri 8.30pm–11.30pm, longer hours in school hols incl 2.30–5.30 daily
Adult incl skate rental €7.20, child under 18 €6.30

LE CONQUET

AQUAFAUNE

26 rue Sainte-Barbe, 29217 Le Conquet
Tel 02 98 89 14 13

Take a trip on a glass-bottomed boat out to the clear waters of the Molène archipelago to watch grey seals, dolphins and a host of other sea life in this marine nature reserve, which forms part of the Armorique Regional Nature Park. Trips last two and a half hours, with commentary.

Feb–Oct (timetable depends on the tide) Adult €23, child (4–16) €14, child under 4 €2

FOUESNANT

LES BALNÉIDES

Allé de Loc'hilaire, 29170 Fouesnant
Tel 02 98 56 18 19
www.balneides.com

This massive indoor waterpark is a useful family bolthole on a wet day. It claims the longest waterslide in Brittany (75m/248ft), and a range of waterjets, as well as a sauna.

Daily but very variable hours, longer in school hols Adult €5.65, child (2–18) €4.80

GUIMAËC

DOMAINE DE KERVEGUEN

29620 Guimaëc (northeast of Morlaix near Locquirec)
Tel 02 98 67 50 02

Here the Cidre de l'Elysée (as served at the Elysée Palace, apparently) is carefully made by natural methods and traditionally matured in oak casks, giving a high-quality, award-winning product well worth bringing home. The premises are ancient and mellow, with a fine dovecote in among the orchards.

Jul, Aug Mon–Sat 10.30–6.30; Apr–end Jun, Sep and in school hols pm only, or by appointment Free

ÎLE D'OUESSANT

TY CRENN ÉQUITATION

Stang Ar Glann, 29242 Ouessant
Tel 02 98 48 83 58

Discover this island, France's westernmost point, on a horse or Shetland pony. There are several different routes passing many beautiful spots, and trek lengths vary from an hour to three days. Call ahead to book your place but note that credit cards are not accepted.

Daily 9–6 1 hour €16, 2 hours €31, half-day €36 (min 3 people)

LANDERNEAU

COMPTOIR DES PRODUITS BRETONS

3 quai de Cornouaille, 29800 Landerneau
Tel 02 98 21 35 93
www.comptoir-produits-bretons.com

This enticing shop is one of the best places to look for presents and souvenirs. On display is a huge range of Breton crafts and regional products—foods, music recordings, maritime mementoes such as boat models or seascapes, nautical outdoor gear, Breton beers, cider and whisky, Celtic-style jewellery, Quimper *faïence* and glassware.

Mon–Fri 9.30–12, 2–7, Sat 9.30–12.30, 2–7, Sun 2–6.30

Checking directions on one of Brittany's footpaths

MORLAIX

SONOTHÈQUE

9 rue d'Aiguillon, 29600 Morlaix
Tel 02 98 15 21 75

This barn-like shop is a great place to buy music, DVDs, books and even guides and maps. There's also a branch in Brest.

Tue–Sat 10–12.30, 2–7

LE THÉÂTRE DU PAYS DE MORLAIX

20 rue Gambetta, 29600 Morlaix
Tel 02 98 15 22 77
www.ville.morlaix.fr

Recently renovated, this is now a superb venue for plays, local and world music, films and ballet. There are street performances every Wednesday from mid-July to mid-August.

Performances daily 8pm (ticket office open daily 1.30–5pm) Adult €15, child (under 12) €4

PLOMODIERN

CELTIC VOL LIBRE

Breugnou, 29550 Plomodiern
Tel 02 98 81 50 27
www.vol-libre-menez-hom.com

The modest heights of Ménez-Hom, last of the hills in the Monts d'Arrée range, give extensive views over the Crozon peninsula, and provide sufficient elevation for hang-gliding (*parapente*). You can take a trial flight with a qualified pilot, or hone existing skills. Check your insurance cover.

Flights depend on weather conditions 10-minute trial flight in a two-man apparatus €50; a morning's introduction €70

PONT-AVEN

VEDETTES AVEN–BÉLON

Port du Pont-Aven, quai Théodore Botrel (Easter–end Sep)
Port du Bélon, 29340 Moëlan-sur-Mer (Jul, Aug)
Tel 02 98 71 14 59

Drift past manor houses, castles, tidal mills and oyster beds in a comfortable, panoramic motor-launch, accompanied by the calls of sea-birds and the occasional vivid flash of a

kingfisher. Three different excursions take in the scenic wooded estuaries of the Aven and Bélon, departing from Pont-Aven or Port-Bélon. The commentary is available in English.
Daily Apr–end Sep, depending on tides Adults €8–€13, child (4–12) €5–€8, child (1–3) €1

QUIMPER

ARMOR LUX

60 bis rue Guy Autret, 29556 Quimper
Tel 02 98 90 05 29
www.armor-lux.com
This store specializes in marine clothing and has been making the classic Breton striped sweaters here for more than 60 years. Reserve ahead to take a tour of the factory. In the shop, you'll find the latest designs as well as discontinued lines.
Daily 9.30–7, shorter hours in winter

WHAT TO DO

BISCUITERIE DE QUIMPER STYVELL

8 rue du Chanoine Moreau, Locmaria, 29000 Quimper
Tel 02 98 53 10 13
This venerable firm based in the pottery quarter makes a traditional speciality called *crêpes dentelles* according to the *l'hermine d'or* recipe over a century old. The name means 'lace pancakes' but these buttery confections are light, crisp biscuits rather like folded wafers, perfect to eat with ice cream or puddings, or nibble with drinks. Vanilla-flavoured batter is laid out in flat blocks, cut into thin strips and rolled up on a knife. Each pancake is made separately by hand.
Shop: daily 9–7; crêpe making: 10.30–12, 3.30–5

LA FAÏENCERIE H. B. HENRIOT

Rue Haute, Locmaria, 29337 Quimper
Tel 02 98 90 09 36 or 0800 626 510 (for guided tour timetable)
www.hb-henriot.com
The largest and most high-profile of the pottery firms in Quimper, still using the traditional method of hand-decoration. Each piece is personally signed by the artist. Regular, well-advertised tours of the factory (some in English) show visitors the manufacturing process. A huge on-site showroom offers Quimper ware at a range of prices, with substantial discounts for slightly imperfect stock.
35-minute tours all year, varying seasonally according to demand (Jul, Aug Mon–Sat, off-season Mon–Fri); showroom Mon–Sat 9.30–7 Adult €3.50, child (8–14) €2

Fine lace mats on display in the town of Pont-l'Abbé

KELTIA MUSIQUE

1 Place au Beurre, 29000 Quimper
Tel 02 98 95 45 82
Come here to browse through the wide selection of Breton and Celtic music recordings and books. There are also musical instrument manuals and similar items.
Tue–Sat 10–12, 2–7

LES MACARONS DE PHILOMÈNE

13 rue Kéréon, 29000 Quimper
Tel 02 98 95 21 40
Eye-catching displays of beautifully coloured macaroons fill the windows of this quaint old shopfront in the heart of the old town. All are made on the premises by France's premier *macaronier* Rolland Padou. Sandwiched with tasty fillings like a sort of bourbon biscuit, these feather-light confections are irresistible for children, or indeed anyone with a sweet tooth. The house special is a *macaron au caramel au beurre salé*, but you might try the bright green pistachio or sugar-pink varieties.
Tue–Fri 9–7.15, Sat 9–7.30, also Mon in July, Aug (same hours)

LE QUARTIER

10 esplanade François-Mitterand, 29107 Quimper
Tel 02 98 55 55 77
www.le-quartier.net
Opposite the Théâtre de Cornouaille, this contemporary art gallery puts on four temporary exhibitions of modern art each year. It has disabled access and a library. Free escorted visits are held on Saturday afternoons.
Daily 10–12.30, 1.30–6, (closed for three weeks between exhibitions)
Adult €1.50; admission free on Sun, and for students (under 26), children (under 16), senior citizens (over 65)

THÉÂTRE DE CORNOUAILLE

1 esplanade François Mitterand, 29337 Quimper
Tel 02 98 55 98 98
www.theatrequimper.asso.fr
A mixed schedule of concerts, plays, films and other presentations take place at the main auditorium of this leading arts venue, Quimper's regional theatre. Other shows are held in Quimper's Max-Jacob theatre, or l'Auditorium, with outposts in Le Guilvinec, Pont-l'Abbé and Châteaulin.
Performances Sep–end Jun
€16–€28

QUIMPERLÉ

LA MAISON DES ARCHERS

5 rue Dom-Morice, 29300 Quimperlé
Tel 02 98 39 06 63
One of the most beautifully preserved houses in the old town, dating from around

1570, is now used as a venue for temporary summer exhibitions. In summer 2005, for example, there was a fascinating display of traditional Breton musical instruments. It's worth going in just to see the building, but details of what's on are available at the tourist office.
Wed–Mon 10–12, 2.30–7
Variable—combined tickets €1.60–€2.40 (adult), €0.80–€1.20 (child) are valid for two local exhibitions

ROSCOFF

LA MAISON DU KOUIGN-AMANN

18 rue Armand Rousseau, 29680 Roscoff
Tel 02 98 69 71 61
This tiny shop prides itself on a Breton speciality called *kouign-amann*, a sweet cake made with best butter and wheat flour. It originated in Douarnenez, but is now sold all over the region. This place serves it warm—the best way to eat it.
Daily 8.30–12.30, 2.30–7 (8.30–7 or 8pm in summer)

THALADO

5 rue Victor-Hugo, 29680 Roscoff
Tel 02 98 69 77 05
Not far from the thermal spa, this discovery facility is the place to learn all about seaweed and its uses. Besides a small permanent exhibition on the history and harvesting of seaweed, it holds enthusiastic talks and lectures, and organizes guided beachcombing walks. Seaweed products are on sale for culinary, pharmaceutical and cosmetic uses.
Mon–Sat 9–12, 2–7 Free admission to centre; guided walks €5 (adult), €3.50 (child 10–16), under 10 free

SAINT-NIC-PENTREZ

CLUB DE CHAR À VOILE DE PENTREZ

5 rue du Ménez-Hom, Pentrez Plage, 29550 St-Nic
Tel 06 11 80 09 79
www.charavoilepentrez.com
Try sand-yachting and kite-surfing on this superb beach north of Douarnenez, which, at low tide, is 3km (2 miles) long and 5km (3 miles) wide, giving you plenty of space. The minimum age for these activities is seven, and it's a good idea to reserve in advance. Credit cards are not accepted.
Summer daily 9–12, 1.30–6; most of rest of year Fri–Sun 1.30–6 From about €15 per hour

FESTIVALS AND EVENTS

JULY, AUGUST

BREST 2008
Tel 02 98 32 20 08
Every four years, Brest hosts a massive gathering of traditional sailing vessels and working boats from all over the world.
Mid-Jul; next due 12–20 Jul 2008

LES MERCREDIS MUSICAUX/LE CINÉMA DANS LA PRAIRIE QUIMPERLÉ
For several Wednesdays during the summer holidays, free open-air concerts are held on place St-Michel in the upper town at 9pm.
Jul–Aug

LES MERCREDIS EN FÊTE MORLAIX
Entertainers (musicians, comedians, acrobats) take to the streets on Wednesday afternoons in summer around the main square by the viaduct.
Mid-Jul to mid-Aug

FESTIVAL DE CORNOUAILLE QUIMPER
www.festival-cornouaille.com
This is one of Brittany's most important cultural events, held annually for about nine days in midsummer for over 80 years. Some 4,500 artists arrive from all over Europe and put on concerts, exhibitions, shows and entertainments.
Mid to late Jul

FESTIVAL DES FILETS BLEUS CONCARNEAU
Tel 02 98 97 09 09
http://filetsbleus.free.fr
The three-day Blue Nets Festival recalls harsh times in the early 20th century, when the sardine shoals disappeared and Concarneau's fishing-based economy collapsed. Today it is one of Finistère's liveliest folk festivals.
Third week in Aug

NOVEMBER

FESTIVAL EUROPÉEN DU FILM COURT DE BREST BREST
Tel 02 98 44 03 94
www.filmcourt.fr
Brest's prestigious short-film festival attracts many cinema-goers and film buffs in late autumn. About 50 films compete from countries throughout Europe, all of course, in *version originale*.
About 10 days in early to mid-Nov

PARDONS

Some of the most celebrated religious processions in Finistère are held at Locronan (mid-July), Sainte-Anne-la-Palud (last Sunday in August) and Le Folgoët (late July, ▷ 62). But the smaller ones encountered by chance in local villages can be just as moving and interesting.

ST-POL-DE-LÉON

TIFFANY

1 bis Rue de Batz, 29250 St-Pol-de-Léon
Tel 02 98 19 11 25
Everything is made on site in this unusual stained-glass studio, which sells lightshades, mirrors, windows and all sorts of gifts in coloured glass. Commissions and repairs are undertaken.
Tue–Sat 9.30–12, 2–7

CÔTES D'ARMOR

The lighthouse at Perros-Guirec on the Cotes d'Armor

As elsewhere in Brittany, the interest for most visitors lies on or near the coastline. The Côtes d'Armor enjoy the twin assets of the Côte de Granit Rose (Pink Granite Coast), and the most beautiful sections of the Côte d'Eméraude (Emerald Coast). The area has several of Brittany's most popular and glamorous seaside resorts offering sports, activities, festivals and excursions galore. The main towns of St-Brieuc and Guingamp have little to attract holidaymakers, though their resident populations support good shops and some nightlife and entertainment. But Dinan is a delightful experience for visitors at any time of year, with a lively social calendar and lots of enticing shops.

KEY TO SYMBOLS

- **Shopping**
- **Entertainment**
- **Nightlife**
- **Sports**
- **Activities**
- **Health and Beauty**
- **For Children**

BÉGARD

ARMORIPARK

22140 Bégard (NW of Guingamp)
02 96 45 36 36
www.tregorgoelo.com/armoripark

This popular theme park has plenty to amuse, including animals, trampolines, pedalos, bouncy castles, mini-golf, waterslides, bumper boats, heated outdoor pool and lots more. There's a picnic area inside the park, and on-site catering.

Mid-Jun to end Aug daily 11–7; Apr to end-Jun, Sep Wed, Sat 1–6, Sun, hols 11–6 Seasonal tariff €9.50 in summer €8.50 children, free for children under 1m (3ft 3in) tall; family tickets €31

CAP FRÉHEL

PÂTISSIER-CHOCOLATIER R JOUAULT

Place de Chamblis, 22240 Bourg de Fréhel
Tel 02 96 41 41 31

In this cottage-style building in the middle of the village you can buy typical pastries such as *far breton*. The bakery has won the European Lauriers d'Or trophy for its superb *kouignamann* (cake made with sugar, butter and almonds). Another speciality is *palet de Fréhel* (nougatine, almond and chocolate).

Jun, Sep daily 8–8; rest of year 8–1, 3–6.30; closed Oct

DINAN

L'ART DU VERRE

66 rue du Petit Fort, 22100 Dinan
Tel 02 96 39 93 31

Stylish square-cut modern glassware created by Maurice and Evelyne Roinel is on sale at this charming atelier on the quaint old street leading down to the harbour. These handsome pieces in glowing primary colours would grace any contemporary home.

Daily 10–12.30, 2–7; closed Jan

COMPTOIR DE LA RANCE

23A rue du Quai, 22100 Dinan
Tel 02 96 39 89 51

An attractively stocked version of the well-known marine co-operative found in many Breton harbour towns. Here you'll find a stylish range of nautical clothing and some enticing souvenirs, including Breton linen, glass and china, bird carvings, seashell pictures, and mobiles for children.

Summer daily 10.30–7; rest of year daily 11–1, 2–7 (6pm Sun)

ITOHA

Bateau Donata, Le Port, 22100 Dinan
Tel 02 96 87 05 92
www.itoha.com

This enterprising business is based on a boat called Donata moored down at the port. On board, insulated fleecy clothing for sailing and other outdoor pursuits is designed and sewn up from a microfibre textile developed for polar expeditions. There's a rapid made-to-measure service.

Mon–Sat 10–12.30, 2.30–7

BOWLING LE BELEM

8 rue de la Tramontane, ZAC des Alleux, 22100 Taden
Tel 02 96 87 03 08

For an energetic, fun-packed time, head for the ten bowling lanes of this attractively located entertainment centre just north of Dinan. Other than bowling, there are karaoke sessions and themed soirées, snooker, video games, and a snack restaurant and a bar.

Daily 3pm–3am in Jul, Aug; Tue–Thu noon–1am, Fri noon–3am, Sat 3pm–3am, Sun 3pm–1am rest of year
Prices vary depending on the time of day (the earlier you go, the cheaper, from €6 per session, including shoes)

CLUB CANOË-KAYAK DE LA RANCE

18 quai du Tallard, 22100 Lanvallay
Tel 02 96 39 01 50
www.nautismebretagne.fr

Down by the port, just across the river, this club rents out canoes and kayaks for trips on the River Rance lasting from one hour to one day. Credit cards are not accepted. Weekend rentals and courses are available all year round.

Jul, Aug daily 9–7; rest of year Wed 2–4.30, Sat 2–5, Sun 10–12 or by appointment
Kayak €10 per hour for single, €15 per hour for double

DANFLEURENN NAUTIC

Port de Dinan, 22100 Dinan
Tel 06 07 45 89 97

Rent a self-drive motor-launch from this quayside kiosk to explore the glorious River Rance at leisure. Boats hold four to eight passengers, and you don't need a licence.

Easter–end Oct daily 10–7
From €25–€30 per hour; €114–€129 for a whole day (7 hours)

LAMBALLE

GP KARTING

Zone Sports-Méchanique, Saint-Aaron, 22400 Lamballe
Tel 02 96 50 09 09
www.gp-circuit.com

This open-air karting track measures 800m (2,600ft), with 70 karts in a range of engine sizes. You can have lessons if you wish or simply rent a kart in blocks of 10 minutes. The bar, snack bar and terrace all have great views. The minimum age is seven.

Bottles of wine on display at a sunny street market

Jul, Aug daily 10–dusk; rest of year Wed, Sat 2–dusk, Sun 10am–dusk; other times by appointment
€10 for 10 minutes

LANNION

STADE D'EAU VIVE

8 rue de Kermaria, 22300 Lannion
Tel 02 96 37 43 90

Lannion is famed for its white-water rafting experience on a section of the River Léguer, where Olympic teams are trained. Here you can practise kayaking or rafting all year round in the middle of town. Several supervised basins allow visitors of all ages and stages of proficiency to perfect their skills in complete safety. Rafts holding up to six people, inflatable canoes, or kayaks can be rented. Safety helmets and lifejackets are provided.

Jul, Aug daily 9–5.30, or by reservation

PAIMPOL

LE PUB

3 rue des Islandais, 22500 Paimpol
Tel 02 96 20 82 31

This piano bar and pub near the harbour puts on a varied range of music and appeals to a wide age range. It has a bar on the ground floor (which serves meals) and a dance floor upstairs.

Thu–Sun 9pm–5am, Mon–Wed 9.30pm–4am

VOILIERS TRADITIONNELS

22500 Paimpol

Paimpol's maritime past is recalled in the elegant rigging of several traditional sailboats *(vieux gréements)*, which make a fine sight around the Bréhat archipelago and along the Goëlo coast. In summer fishing trips and pleasure cruises are advertised from Paimpol harbour. Look out for the replica sardine fishing boat called *Eulalie*, or the tuna boats *La Nébuleuse* and *Vieux Copain*.

Jul, Aug daily cruises; Apr–end Jun, Sep to mid-Nov weekends

PERROS-GUIREC

LES GALERIES DE KER-ILIZ

8 rue du Général de Gaulle, 22700 Perros-Guirec
Tel 02 96 91 00 96

This large mall not far from the tourist office, formerly the home of architect James Boullié, sells products made or crafted in Brittany, such as Quimper porcelain, Celtic jewellery, dolls, linen, cards, music, pottery, wooden items, biscuits and nautical clothing.

Jul, Aug daily 10–12.30, 2.30–7.30; shorter hours off-season (closed Sun pm and Mon am)

WHAT TO DO

PORT MINIATURE
Boulevard du Linkin, Port de Plaisance, 22700 Perros-Guirec
Tel 02 96 91 06 11
Scale-model electric replicas of ferries, trawlers, tug boats, lifeboats and so on make an entertaining way to spend a quarter of an hour on an enclosed basin at the pleasure port. Learn a bit about navigation and marine signalling too.
Jul, Aug daily 10.45–7.30; Apr–end Jun, hols and long weekends 2.30–6
€4 per person (3–103!) for a 15-minute session (free for under 3s)

PLÉDÉLIAC

CHÂTEAU DE LA HUNAUDAYE
Le Chêne au Loup, 22270 Plédéliac
Tel 02 96 34 82 10
www.la-hunaudaye.com
Revisit the Middle Ages at this majestic moated castle dating from the 13th–15th centuries. Exhibitions, 'living history' events and family activities take place all summer, so there's lots for children to do. There are also guided tours.
Mid-Jun to mid-Sep daily 10.30–6.30; school hols Sun–Fri 2.30–6; Apr to mid-Jun, mid-Sep to end Oct Sun 2.30–6; closed Nov–end Mar Adult €3 (€3.80 mid Jun–mid Sep), child €2 (€2.75)

ST-BRIEUC

MAISON DE LA BAIE
Site de l'Etoile, 22120 Hillion
Tel 02 96 32 27 98
A varied schedule of activities and events is organized throughout the year by this energetic visitor facility in the coastal nature reserve of the Baie de St-Brieuc. Find out about the effects of the huge tides on the local ecosystem through talks and shoreline field trips for birdwatching (over 200 species), beach-combing and visiting mussel beds. Book outings in advance; sensible footwear and clothing are advised.
Oct–May Wed, Fri, Sun 2–6; Jun and Sep Wed-Fri, Sun 2–6; Jul–Aug Mon–Fri 10.30–6.30, Sat, Sun 1.30–6.30
Visitor centre exhibitions adult €3, child (6–12) €2.50; outings/activities, telephone for details

LA BRIQUETERIE
22360 Langueux, Les Grèves
Tel 02 96 63 36 66
www.baiedesaintbrieuc.com
The site of an old tile factory and brickworks makes an unusual family attraction on the Baie de Saint-Brieuc. You can visit the old kiln where the tiles and bricks were fired in 1864. Pottery workshops and a miniature railway are ancillary activities.
Jul, Aug Wed–Mon 11–6.30; Jun, Sep Wed, Fri–Sun 11–6.30, Oct–end May Wed, Fri–Sun 2–6; closed mid-Dec to end Jan Adult €4, child (6–12) €2.50

A golf course at St-Cast-le-Guildo, on the Côtes d'Armor

ST-CAST-LE-GUILDO

LA FERME DES LANDES
Notre Dame du Guildo, 22380 St-Cast-le-Guildo
Tel 02 96 41 12 48
A cider lover's heaven with cider from different apple varieties, plus cider vinegar and apple juice, all home-brewed by the enthusiastic owner. Taste, buy and tour the farm (by appointment only). Every Friday afternoon in summer a farmers' market is held here.
Jun–end Aug daily 10–8; reduced hours off-season

GOLF CLUB DE PEN-GUEN
Route du Golfe, 22380 St-Cast-le-Guildo
Tel 02 96 41 91 20
www.golf-st-cast.com
This superbly situated 18-hole, par-68 golf course lies on the east side of town, with direct access to the lovely beach of Pen-Guen. Though quite short, the course is technically challenging and interesting for all standards. There's a driving range and putting green to keep the keenest golfer busy.
Apr–end Sep daily 7.30am–8pm; rest of year daily 9–5.30 Green fees €49 in summer, €38 off-season, €29 in winter (reduced rates for couples)

TRÉBEURDEN

TI AL LANNEC
14 allée de Mezo Guen, 22560 Trébeurden
Tel 02 96 15 01 01
www.tiallannec.com
Mini-cures and beauty treatments of many kinds are on offer at one of Côtes d'Armor's most attractive and relaxing hotels. Choose an anti-ageing seaweed facial, a synergetic massage or a reflexology session at the Espace Bleu Marine spa. The minimum age is 16.
Daily 9–12, 2.30–8 Entrance charge €10 (free for hotel clients); treatments start from €23

TRÉGASTEL

ÉCOLE D'ÉQUITATION FOSSEY
13 rue du Calvaire, 22730 Trégastel
Tel 02 96 23 86 14
Go horse-riding through the Breton countryside, in a forest or along the seashore of the Côtes d'Armor region. You can also take lessons at the school to improve your riding skills. Telephone in advance to reserve your place.
Tue–Sat 9–7, Sun–Mon 9–12; closed 2 weeks in Sep €19 per hour

LE VAL-ANDRÉ

COMPTOIRS DE L'OUEST
10 quai des Terres-Nuevas, port de Dahouët, 22370 Pléneuf-Val-André
Tel 02 96 63 18 84

The old port and yacht marina of Dahouët, west of the resort, is a good place to search for antiques. In one or two of the old sail-lofts down on the quayside you'll find an Aladdin's Cave of miscellaneous bric-à-brac and Breton bygones—great fun for browsing even if you don't want to buy anything.
Daily 10.30–12.30, 3–7 in summer hols, Fri–Sun (same hours) in low season. Closed mid Sep–mid Oct and Jan

CASINO LA ROTONDE
1 cours Winston Churchill, 22370 Pléneuf-Val-André
Tel 02 96 72 85 06
This handsome art deco-style casino looks rather like an ocean liner berthed on the seafront esplanade. It is small and civilized but not at all snobbish. Minimum stakes are modest, so you needn't lose your shirt here. Besides slot-machines, roulette and blackjack tables, it has a restaurant, a terrace café, and a cinema and a theatre. Minimum age 18.
Daily 10am–3am (4am Sat) all year (4am Fri–Sun in Jul–Aug)

LES SUCETTES DU VAL-ANDRÉ
Cours Winston Churchill, 22370 Pléneuf-Val-André
Tel 02 96 32 93 93
If you have children to amuse (or even if you don't!) this lollipop kiosk which sets up shop in the holiday season near the tourist office and casino is not to be missed. It sells around 60 varieties of heavenly stickiness, all made using natural ingredients. Flavours range from eucalyptus to pear and chocolate. Try the seaweed toffee *(craquant aux algues)* too. It's a local enterprise; tours and tastings at the factory in nearby St-Alban can be arranged.
Summer only

FESTIVALS AND EVENTS

APRIL

FÊTE DE LA COQUILLE ST-JACQUES
ERQUY/ST-QUAY-PORTRIEUX/ LOGUIVY-SUR-MER
Three resorts take it in turns to host this annual homage to the revered scallop, dredged in huge quantities from the seabed each year. There are exhibitions, processions and fireworks.
2 days in Apr (Loguivy's turn comes round in 2007)

MAY

PARDON DE SAINT-YVES
TRÉGUIER
This event is one of the most important and spectacular religious festivals in Brittany, marking the anniversary of the death of Yves Hélori, patron saint of lawyers, born near Tréguier in1253.
Third Sun in May

JULY, AUGUST

FESTIVAL INTERNATIONAL DE HARPE CELTIQUE
DINAN
Tel 02 96 87 36 69
www.harpe-celtique.com
A prestigious music festival dedicated to the Celtic harp, with concerts and master-classes.
6 days in Jul · Ticket prices from €5 (inclusive passes available)

FÊTE DES REMPARTS
DINAN
This biennial festival held in even-numbered years draws large crowds for an ebullient medieval romp with jousting and jollity around the old fortifications.
Every second year, a weekend in late July

MERCREDIS EN FÊTE
TRÉGUIER
For six consecutive Wednesdays in summer, the main streets and squares of the town bustle with life. After the weekly market held in the morning, concerts, barbecues and general entertainment go on well into the evenings.
Jul, Aug · Free

JAZZ À L'AMIRAUTÉ
LE VAL-ANDRÉ
On summer Tuesdays a series of jazz concerts is staged in the Parc de l'Amirauté near the seafront.
Jul, Aug Tue 9pm · Free

BON-REPOS, PIERRES DE LÉGENDES
SAINT-GELVEN
Tel 02 96 24 82 20
www.bon-repos.com
Enterprising use is made of the evocative remains of the Abbaye de Bon-Repos, an ancient abbey near the shores of the Lac de Guerledan. In high season it hosts an elaborate *son-et-lumière* historical spectacle with music and special effects. Local people take part, and all profits go towards the restoration of the abbey.
Aug · Adult €18, child (10–16) €9 (tickets are less expensive if you book in advance)

FESTIVAL DE LA DANSE BRETONNE ET DE LA ST-LOUP
GUINGAMP
Nine days of merriment involving concerts, traditional Breton dancing contests, street entertainment and exhibitions. Information from the tourist office.
Mid-Aug

FÊTE DU CHANT DE MARIN
PAIMPOL
Tel 02 96 55 12 77
An immensely popular folk festival recalling the times and traditions of this seafaring community, and the songs sung by its fishermen.
3 days in early Aug · €14 per day (adult), €28 for the whole festival; child €4–€8 (free under 6)

ILLE-ET-VILAINE

The island of Mont-St-Michel, with the tower of the abbey church piercing the sky above

WHAT TO DO

This part of Brittany is generally marketed as Haute Bretagne. It's quite a mixture, encompassing the regional capital of Rennes with its big-city shops and nightlife, as well as Brittany's largest ferry port of St-Malo, which caters for its transient visitors in many ways. Nearby lies the exclusive resort of Dinard and the magnificent Rance estuary, providing plenty of opportunities for boat excursions and water sports. There's plenty for families with children in this *département*, and cultural activities for grown-ups too.

KEY TO SYMBOLS

- Shopping
- Entertainment
- Nightlife
- Sports
- Activities
- Health and Beauty
- For Children

BAZOUGES-LA-PÉROUSE

LE VILLAGE

2 Place de l'Hôtel de Ville, 35560 Bazouges-la-Pérouse
Tel 02 99 97 43 60
www.levillage-bazouges.com

Throughout the year, this village is the scene of an innovative artistic experiment, playing host to many artists who present visual and performing arts in several local venues. In the summer you can see open-air exhibitions, café-theatre and street entertainment.

Jul, Aug daily 2.30–6.30; Apr–end Dec weekends 2–6 Free

CANCALE

MARCHÉ AUX HUÎTRES

Quai St-Thomas, Port de la Houle, 35260 Cancale

Whether or not there's an 'R' in the month, you can buy oysters from the little stalls by the waterfront parcs (oysterbeds) at the old port of La Houle. Prices start at around €3.50 per dozen for *creuses* (hollow oysters). The flat ones *(huîtres plates)*, which can be as big as dinner-plates, are more expensive, and wild oysters trawled from further offshore *(huîtres sauvages)* are priciest of all.

All day, every day, all year

LA CANCALAISE

La Halle à Marée, quai Gambetta, La Houle, 35260 Cancale
Tel 02 99 89 77 87
www.lacancalaise.com

This lovely replica of one of Cancale's traditional oysterboats *(bisquines)*, built by a local association of enthusiasts in 1985, offers summer trips in the Baie de Mont-St-Michel. Its 350sq m (3,700sq ft) of rigging are a fine sight under full sail. Book in advance.

Sailings Apr–end Oct daily 9–6; office hours 2–5 (closed Wed, Sun) Around €42 per person per day

DINARD

LES 2 ALIZÉS

2 boulevard Albert 1er, 35800 Dinard
Tel 02 99 88 17 93
www.emeraude-cinema.fr

Dinard is a great place for film-buffs. This cinema, just behind the main beach, sometimes puts on undubbed or *version originale* films (VO).

All year Adult €5.50–€7, child (under 12) €5; the cheaper rate during daytime

CASINO BARRIÈRE DE DINARD

4 boulevard Wilson, 35802 Dinard
Tel 02 99 16 30 30
www.lucienbarriere.com

This casino is one of Brittany's more exclusive venues,

overlooking the superb main beach of La Nice du Nord. Here you'll find roulette, blackjack, stud poker and more than 100 one-armed bandits. There's a smart dress code and over-18 age limit.
Sun–Thu 10am–3am, Fri–Sat 10am–4am; gaming tables open from 9pm; closed Mon, Tue off-season
€11 charge to play at the tables

PISCINE MUNICIPAL
2 boulevard Wilson, 35800 Dinard
Tel 02 99 46 22 77
This Olympic-sized pool, 50m by 25m (164ft by 82ft), is filled with heated seawater, an enticing alternative to the glamorous but often chilly waves on Dinard's lovely main beach, where there are many activities for children.
Jul, Aug daily 10–12.30, 3–7.30; telephone for times rest of year Adult €4, child (5–18) €3.20

HÉLISTAR
Aérodrome de Dinard-Pleurtuit, 35800 Dinard
Tel 0820 200 225
Get a whole new perspective on the Emerald Coast with a helicopter joy-ride from Dinard's airfield southwest of town.
All year €135 for a 30-minute spin

FOUGÈRES

LE COQUELICOT
18 rue de Vitré, 35300 Fougères
Tel 02 99 99 82 11
On a hilly street a short walk from the old town, this popular bar is a well-known pub-concert offering live music (jazz, folk, rock, blues) and café-theatre. Some 70 different beers are on sale.
Tue–Sat 4pm–3am; concerts usually Thu–Sat at 9; closed Sun, Mon and part of Jul, Aug €5 (variable)

PETIT TRAIN DE FOUGÈRES
35300 Fougères
Tel 02 99 99 71 72
This *petit train* (known as L'Oriental Express) gives you a good excuse to avoid climbing the steep hill to the old town. The 45-minute tour starts from the castle forecourt and finishes at the tourist office, passing through the public gardens. Your journey is enlivened by a multilingual commentary. Passport inclusive tickets include entrance to the castle and a guided tour—ask at the tourist office.
May–end Sep daily 10–7 Adult €5, child (under 12) €4

LANHÉLIN

COBAC PARC
35720 Lanhélin
Tel 02 99 73 80 16
www.cobac-parc.fr

Oysters on sale at one of Brittany's criées *(fish auctions)*

This theme park on a large wooded site near Combourg between Rennes and St-Malo promises lots of fun for all the family, with animals, rides, a heated boating and leisure pool, miniature railway, video games, mini-golf, magic mirrors and lots more.
Variable schedule Apr–end Sep (open most days Jul, Aug) €11 (3–14), €13 (15+) with all rides etc included in the entry price

PLERGUER

LA CHÈVRERIE DU DÉSERT
Le Desert, 35540 Plerguer
Tel 02 99 58 92 14
Children will enjoy this goat farm with lots of different animals, where cheese products are on sale (you can taste the cheese first), along with other regional food products.
Jul, Aug daily 11–6.30; Apr–end Jun, Sep Wed–Mon 2.30–6.30, Sun, hols 11–6.30; closed Oct–end Mar Adult €5, child €4

PLEUGUENEUC

LA BOURBANSAIS
Domaine de la Bourbansais, 35720 Pleugueneuc
Tel 02 99 69 40 07
www.300-labourbansais.com
You'll find this zoo, with many protected species, in the grounds of the impressive Château de Bourbansais (worth a visit in its own right) just off the N137 east of Dinan. It has a playground with a bouncy castle for children, a snack bar, a tea room and a gift shop.
Apr–end Sep daily 10–7; Oct–end Mar 2–6 Zoo, gardens and shows: adult €14, child (4–14) €10; supplement for château interior: adult €4, child €2

REDON

CINE MANIVEL
12 quai Jean Bart, 35600 Redon
Tel 02 99 72 28 20
www.cinemanivel.fr
Staffed by bright young volunteers, this sleek new avant-garde cinema next to the maritime museum down on the waterfront is a breath of fresh air. It puts on independent arthouse films, some in *version originale*. There's a foyer café, open half an hour before the first screening, with modern art and occasional live music. All in all, it's a very 'happening' place—*ça bouge*!
Sun–Thu 2–8.30pm (start of last film); Fri, Sat last showing 10.30pm
Adult €6.70, child/student €5.40

RENNES

HARMONIA MUNDI
3 rue Jean-Jaurès, 35000 Rennes
Tel 02 99 78 33 64
This high-quality chain of music stores has just a couple of branches in Brittany, but is

one of the best places to look for recordings of all types, including classical, Celtic, jazz and modern music.
Mon 2.30–7 (except Aug), Tue–Sat 10–7

THÉÂTRE NATIONAL DE BRETAGNE (TNB)
1 rue St-Hélier, 35040 Rennes
Tel 02 99 31 12 31
www.t-n-b.fr
This theatre has three separate performance halls for drama, dance, jazz and classical music. There's also a cinema screening independent and experimental films in their original language. You can have lunch or dinner in the restaurant and bar.
Mon, Tue, Thu, Fri 8.30; Wed, Sat 7.30; Sun 4 Theatre tickets start at around €21 Gare SNCF

WHAT TO DO

LA RICHARDAIS

L'ATELIER MANOLI
9 rue du Suet, 35780 La Richardais
Tel 02 99 88 55 53
www.manoli.org
Over 400 sculptures representing the innovative life work of the artist Manoli, whose varied creations can be seen in public places all over France, are on display in this museum and sculpture garden.
Jul, Aug daily 10.30–12, 3–7, Apr–end Jun, Sep–end Nov Sat, Sun hols 3–7 Adult €4, child €3, under 12 free

ST-MALO

THÉÂTRE DE ST-MALO
6 Place Bouvet, 35400 St-Malo
Tel 02 99 81 62 61 (box office)
www.theatresaintmalo.com
The leading theatre in the region hosts major touring productions, concerts, opera, big band shows, plays, musicals, one-man shows and children's performances.
The bar is open pre-show and in the interval, and there is good access for visitors with disabilities.
Booking office Tue–Fri 10–12, 2–6.30, Sat 10–12, 2–6 (up until 9pm on performance nights); shows start at 8.30 (4.30 on Sun); children's shows once a month on Wed at 2.30 and 4.30 Adult €26–€33, child (under 18) €10

BAR DE L'UNIVERS
Place Chateaubriand, 35400 St-Malo
Tel 02 99 40 89 52
www.hotel-univers-saintmalo.com
This hugely popular old hotel bar is smothered with historic photos, and models of sailing ships dangle from the beams. In the evenings, it throbs with life, smoothly supervised by the efficient, friendly, English-speaking staff serving up lots of bottled Belgian beers, interesting cocktails, Irish whiskeys and excellent wines.
Daily 7am–1.30am (until 2am in summer)

ST-MELOIR-DES-ONDES

LES PETITS FRUITS DE LA BAIE
5 rue des Clossets, 35350 St-Méloir-des-Ondes
Tel 02 99 89 10 06
Pick-your-own fresh soft fruit (strawberries, raspberries and other summer fruit) at this farm. The on-site shop sells jams and preserves, and a farmers' market takes place once a week in high season.
Jan–end May (kiwi fruit); May–end Oct (red berries) Mon–Sat 8–12, 3.30–6.30; farmers' market Jul, Aug Mon 5–8

FESTIVALS AND EVENTS

MARCH

FESTIVAL DU JAZZ
VITRÉ
Artists and bands delight locals and visitors with free performances in the town's streets, bars, squares and restaurants.
A week in early Mar

JULY

PROMENADE AU CLAIR DE LUNE
DINARD
This panoramic coastal walk through luxuriant vegetation is enjoyable at any time of year, but in summer the gardens are enhanced by a *son-et-lumière* show, and romantically illuminated with different music playing every evening.
Jul–end Sep

TOMBÉES DE LA NUIT
RENNES
Tel 02 99 32 56 56
www.tdn.rennes.fr
A huge pan-Celtic celebration with modern rock music, dance and theatrical performances in the old streets of the city.
First week in Jul

AUGUST

JUMPING INTERNATIONAL DE DINARD
DINARD
This major show-jumping event attracts competitors from all over the world.
Four days in early Aug

OCTOBER

FESTIVAL DU FILM BRITANNIQUE
DINARD
The British film festival is a highlight of Dinard's social calendar and a place for celebrity-spotting in autumn, originally sparked off by Alfred Hitchcock's use of Dinard as a film-set for *The Birds*.
3 days in early Oct

DECEMBER

LES TRANSMUSICALES
RENNES
Tel 02 99 31 12 10
www.lestrans.com
The bars and clubs of Rennes take on a new lease of life when this international rock-and-roll festival hits town. Some gigs are held in the Théâtre National de Bretagne.
Second week in Dec

Out and About

This chapter describes three walks and four drives that explore all four *départements* of Brittany. The locations of the tours are marked on the map on page 134.

LOCATION OF WALKS AND TOURS

KEY TO THIS MAP

2 Drive
■ City / Town
4 Walk

1. Walk
The Old Town of Vannes
(▷ 135–137)

2. Drive
Vannes to the Landes de Lanvaux (▷ 138–139)

3. Drive
The Crozon Peninsula
(▷ 140–142)

4. Walk
Around Huelgoat (▷ 143)

5. Drive
The Emerald Coast
(▷ 144–145)

6. Walk
Ploumanac'h Walk
(▷ 146–147)

7. Drive
St-Malo and Dinan
(▷ 148–149)

An aerial view of Dinan (above), the castle at Rochefort-en-Terre (left), and pink granite rocks at Ploumanac'h (below)

KEY TO ROUTE MAPS IN THIS CHAPTER

- Start point
- Route
- Alternative route
- Route direction
- Walk start point on drive
- Featured sight along route
- Place of interest in Sights section
- Other place of interest
- Viewpoint
- Height in metres

1. WALK

THE OLD TOWN OF VANNES

Vannes now extends far beyond its original walls, a thoroughly modern city with varied commercial and industrial interests. But the historic quarter is miraculously well preserved inside its fortifications. Most motorized traffic is banned from its confines, so exploring Old Vannes on foot is a positive pleasure—a great relief from its noisy and confusing outlying road systems.

Busy café terraces at Place Gambetta in Vannes

THE WALK

Length: 2km (1.25 miles)
Allow: 2 hours
Start/end: Place Gambetta

HOW TO GET THERE

Follow signs to the Port de Plaisance, where plenty of parking is available along the waterfront.

★ Crescent-shaped Place Gambetta, laid out in the 19th century, presides at the head of the pleasure port, its lively bars and brasseries within sight and earshot of bristling masts and clanking halyards. The marina occupies the canalized, partly culverted River Marie, a mere trickle as it flows past the ramparts, but a vital link between the old city and the Golfe du Morbihan, Vannes' gateway to the Atlantic.

Follow signs to the tourist office immediately west of Place Gambetta, in a fine 17th-century building on rue Thiers. Pick up a plan of the old town, then return to Place Gambetta and enter the old town via Porte St-Vincent.

1 Porte St-Vincent is the city's finest surviving gateway. It was first built in 1624, but underwent a neoclassical makeover in the mid-18th century, when its defensive machicolations were replaced with ornamental shell niches, columns and capitals.

Walk up rue St-Vincent Ferrier to the Place des Lices.

2 Place des Lices, a large, sloping space of several interlinked squares, was used as a tilt-yard in the 16th century, but these days it's a marketplace. On it stand the bright, airy premises of Les Halles (covered food market), opened in 2001. A produce market is held in the square on Wednesdays and Saturdays.

Take rue Rogue, leading off the square to the left, and walk just a few paces to the first junction (rue Noé). On this corner, you'll see a quaint red-timbered building that is now an Italian restaurant. From its upper floor lean the carved granite figures of a jolly 16th-century couple known as Vannes and his Wife, as if greeting passers-by. On the other side of rue Noé stands the Château Gaillard, a 15th-century mansion now housing the archaeology museum.

3 The Musée d'Histoire et d'Archéologie contains finds from various sites in Morbihan, ranging from Neolithic axeheads of smooth, polished jadeite to coins and scraps of glass and pottery. The building itself is worth seeing; it was formerly used as an assembly hall for Brittany's parliament.

Crossing Place Valencia, you will pass the stone and timber-framed house (No. 17) where the Spanish mystic and city patron St. Vincent-Ferrier died in 1419. Wind through the narrow, shop-filled lane called rue des Orfèvres into hilly Place St-Pierre, where the huge cathedral dwarfs the buildings around it.

4 The Cathédrale St-Pierre displays elements from many

Tourist shops in a square in the heart of the city

The 13th-century ramparts at Vannes

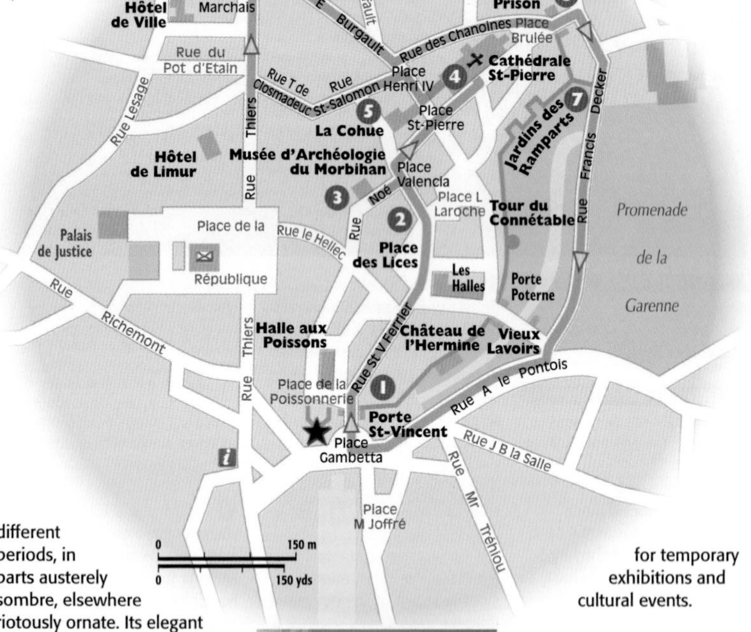

different periods, in parts austerely sombre, elsewhere riotously ornate. Its elegant rotunda chapel, in Italian Renaissance style, contains the tomb of St. Vincent-Ferrier.

Leave by the main west door, and walk across Place St-Pierre to La Cohue.

❺ This handsome old market hall is now used as Vannes' fine arts museum. Its permanent collections date back to the mid-19th century, and include many works by Breton artists. The spacious lower floor, which would have been crowded with traders' stalls in the 13th century, is now used for temporary exhibitions and cultural events.

A bridge spanning the stream at the foot of the ramparts

Turn left into Place Henri-IV, a postcard scene of ancient gabled buildings, and left again down rue St-Salomon. Rue des Halles, again to your left, is a typically atmospheric street with several good restaurants. Head along rue Closmadeuc until you reach busy rue Thiers, outside the original walls. Turn briefly left to admire the Hôtel de Limur, a grand late 17th-century town house in formal gardens. Retrace your steps and walk up rue Thiers to the imposing Place M. Marchais with its equestrian statue, flanked by the 19th-century Hôtel de Ville in Renaissance style. Take rue

Vannes and his Wife (above), and half-timbered mansions lining a square in the city (right)

Burgault on your right back into the old town, bearing left past the cathedral on rue des Chanoines towards the Porte Prison.

6 The Porte Prison, a machicolated gateway, dates from the 15th century, and is the oldest one left in Vannes. It was restored in the mid-1970s. You get the best view of it from beyond the walls.

Turn right outside the gateway and walk along rue Francis Decker. From here climb to the raised Promenade de la Garenne, above the road to your left. This walkway and the surrounding public gardens once belonged to the ducal castle, and both give splendid views of the city ramparts.

7 This is the most complete and picturesque stretch of the walls. Velvet lawns and jewel-like flowerbeds soften these stern fortifications, and stone benches sheltered from the wind are ideal places from which to admire them. Notable landmarks include the turreted Tour du Connetable (Constable's Tower), and the symmetrical façade of the Château de l'Hermine. Near the Porte Poterne (Postern Gate) stand some early 19th-century *lavoirs* (wash-houses), with picturesque slate roofs.

Continue past the Porte Poterne along rue Le Pontois, which brings you back to Place Gambetta and the Port de Plaisance.

WHERE TO EAT

Rue des Halles, off place des Lices, has three recommendable restaurants to suit all budgets in adjacent buildings. Alternatively, buy some picnic supplies in the market or from La Huche à Pains, and enjoy them in the rampart gardens.

Le Roscanvec
17 rue des Halles, Vannes
☎ 02 97 47 15 96
Jul–Aug Mon–Sat 12.15–1.30, 7.15–9.30; Sep–end Jun Tue–Sat 12.15–1.30, 7.15–9.30

Breizh Caffé
13 rue des Halles, Vannes
☎ 02 97 54 37 41
Summer daily 12–2, 7–10; reduced hours off-season

Brasserie des Halles
9 rue des Halles, Vannes
☎ 02 97 54 08 34
Jul–Aug daily 12–midnight; Sep–Jun 12–2.30, 7–12

Old wash-houses on the stream (the Marle) in the inner city

The Hotel de Ville

VANNES TO THE LANDES DE LANVAUX

Morbihan is the most southerly *département* in Brittany, an area full of interesting towns, pretty villages and fine countryside. The region's most popular attraction is the Golfe du Morbihan, and you can take a boat trip from Vannes to the small islands in the gulf. This drive heads inland, away from the gulf, to explore lesser-known places, slightly off the beaten track but well worth visiting.

A view from the castle at Rochefort-en-Terre (above), and an unusual carving at St-Gravé (below right)

THE DRIVE

Length: 97km (60 miles)
Allow: 1 day
Start/end: Vannes

★ The historic city of Vannes stands at the head of the Golfe du Morbihan, its medieval kernel still intact within a shell of protective ramparts (▷ 51). From the Port de Plaisance on Place Gambetta just beyond the city walls, the tree-lined Promenade de la Rabine follows the waterfront to the Parc du Golfe, 2km (1 mile) south of the town. This is one of the main departure points for ferries and excursion boats exploring the gulf and its islands.

From Place Gambetta, head eastwards out of the city following signs for Nantes and the N165. After about 2km (1 mile), take a brief detour to the right (signed Sené), then bear left to the Réserve Naturelle de Sené at Brouel-Kerbihan.

❶ The Réserve Naturelle de Sené is an expanse of marshes and mudflats, where fresh and salt water mingle. It is one of the best places in Brittany for birdwatching. The reserve has a visitor centre and several observation hides, where you may spot a number of resident and migratory species including spoonbills, egrets and herons.

Return to the main road and continue eastwards on the D779/N165, following signs to the village of Theix on your right.

❷ The pretty village of Theix has some interesting sights, including La Chapelle-de-la-Dame-Blanche, built in 1239 and one of the oldest chapels in the province. It has been restored several times. Nearby is the Château du Plessis-Josso, which dates from the 13th to the 18th centuries.

Pick up the D7, signed for le Gorvello and Questembert, and follow it to the market town of Questembert.

❸ Questembert's great covered market hall dates from the mid-16th century and is surrounded by a square with medieval houses.

From the middle of Questembert, follow the Toutes Directions signs onto the ring road, and then take the D777 for 10km (6 miles) to Rochefort-en-Terre.

❹ Pretty Rochefort-en-Terre is the capital of the moorlands of the Landes de Lanvaux. The town is on a ridge above the river Arz and most of it is medieval or dates from the 16th or 17th centuries. Aristocratic stone mansions line the cobbled streets, and some have been turned into shops and restaurants catering to the village's many visitors.

From Rochefort-en-Terre stay on the D777 to St-Gravé, turning left 1km (0.6 miles) before the village of St-Gravé and head north to Malestroit.

❺ The small town of St-Gravé stands between the winding river Oust and the moors of the Landes de Lanvaux. Its historic core is around Place du Bouffay and the church of St-Gilles. Look for the bizarre carvings on the houses here, such as a hare playing the bagpipes. A little to the west, in the village of St-Marcel, the Musée de la Résistance Bretonne tells the story of the Morbihan Maquis (French Resistance).

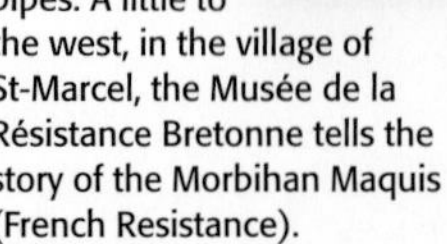

The road out of Malestroit, the D10, follows the river Oust for a short distance before veering off west towards Sérent.

❻ Sérent, a little village on the northern edge of the Landes de Lanvaux, has a number of fine houses and a church in the flamboyant Gothic style.

From Sérent take the D766 south to Elven.

The entrance to the Hotel de Ville

The feudal ruins of the Forteresse de Largoët

7 Elven has a church with a 16th-century choir, but the main attractions lie outside the town. To the north is the Château de Kerfily, in a park beside the Arz, while to the south is the Forteresse de Largoët.

After another 3km (2 miles), turn right to the Forteresse de Largoët.

8 The Forteresse de Largoët, also called Tours d'Elven, is an impressive feudal ruin in extensive wooded parkland. In 1488 the castle was burned down by the king of France, Charles XIII, and now the ruins make an atmospheric setting for sound-and-light shows.

With a height of 44m (145ft), the main tower, or *donjon*, of Largoët is the tallest medieval tower in France, with supporting walls 6–9m (20–30ft) thick.

Return to the D766 for 3km (2 miles), join the N166, and continue back into Vannes.

WHERE TO EAT

Le Canotier
Place du Docteur Queinnec, 56140 Malestroit
☎ 02 97 75 08 69
Apr–end Aug Tue–Sat lunch, dinner; Sep–end Mar Tue–Sat lunch

BASICS

Réserve Naturelle de Séné
☎ 02 97 66 92 76
Jul to end Aug daily 10–1, 2–7; Feb–Jun Sun and hols, afternoons only

Château du Plessis-Josso
☎ 02 97 43 16 16
Jul to end Aug 2–6.30

Musée de la Résistance Bretonne
☎ 02 97 75 16 90
Mid-Jun to mid-Sep daily 10–7; mid-Sep to mid Jun Wed–Mon 10–12, 2–6

Forteresse de Largoët
☎ 02 97 53 35 96
Jul–Aug daily 10.30–12.10, 2.20–6.30; Jun, Sep Wed–Mon 10.30–12.10, 2.20–6.30; Oct–end May Wed–Mon 2–6.30

THE CROZON PENINSULA

This drive takes you past some of Brittany's most exciting coastal scenery—giddy headlands, breathtaking beaches, a curvaceous estuary and one of the world's greatest natural harbours, the Rade de Brest. The entire peninsula and its inshore waters form part of the Armorique Regional Nature Park in recognition of its exceptional environmental status. This far-flung Finistèrian outpost has man-made attractions too, including boat trips and water sports, art galleries, excellent restaurants and some unusual sightseeing. But most of Crozon's appeal lies outdoors, so choose fine weather if you can. There are lots of good possibilities for walking (ask the tourist office in Crozon for suggestions) and it is excellent for birdwatching.

THE DRIVE

Length: 154km (96 miles)
Allow: 1 day
Start: Châteaulin
End: Le Faou

★Several major roads converge near Châteaulin, an appealing little town on the serpentine River Aulne, giving speedy access from most places in western Brittany.

Fill up with fuel (about the least expensive you'll find in this area) at Châteaulin's big Leclerc hypermarket signed just off the Crozon road, then head westwards on the D887. After 12km (7.5 miles) take a steep turning on your right (D83) to the summit of Ménez-Hom.

❶ Considering the modest height of Ménez-Hom (just 330m/1,082ft), the views from this isolated, gorse-clad hillock are surprisingly impressive, extending from Douarnenez Bay and the Sizun peninsula right across to the Rade de Brest. Ménez-Hom marks the western limit of the Montagnes Noires, a belt of hills stretching across central Finistère. A viewing table assists direction-finding; Ménez-Hom is exactly equidistant from Paris and London (483km/300 miles). The chapel of Sainte-Marie-du-Ménez-Hom at the foot of the hill contains an elaborate altarpiece.

Drive back to the main road and continue westwards, almost immediately turning left on to the D108 (signed Pentrez-Plage).

❷ The huge Lieue de Grève beyond St-Nic is an exquisite beach by any standards, facing southwest across Dournenez Bay between unspoiled headlands. Several little chapels (St-Côme, St-Nicaise) are worth tracking down nearby.

Hug the coastline along minor roads to Telgruc-sur-Mer, past more lovely beaches, then return to the main road (D887) and proceed to Crozon, 11km (7 miles) further on.

❸ Crozon is equipped with a helpful tourist office and a first-rate hotel-restaurant (▷ 157). Don't miss the church of St-Pierre, whose eye-popping altarpiece of the Ten Thousand Martyrs is one of the highlights of 16th-century Breton sculpture. The complexities of this obscure tale take some fathoming, but the overall effect, clarified by the church's obliging automatic lighting system, is stunning.

The bay at Morgat (above), and a detail of the calvary at Sainte Marie du Ménez-Hom (below)

From Crozon, several routes radiate to outlying headlands. You can skip one or two if you are short of time, but each has distinctive scenery. Follow the D887 southwards to Morgat 3km (2 miles).

❹ Morgat is an appealing little resort tucked into an east-facing bay and sheltered by pines. Its beach and harbour are popular for sailing and water sports. Sea caves eroded by wave action are the focus of summer boat trips.

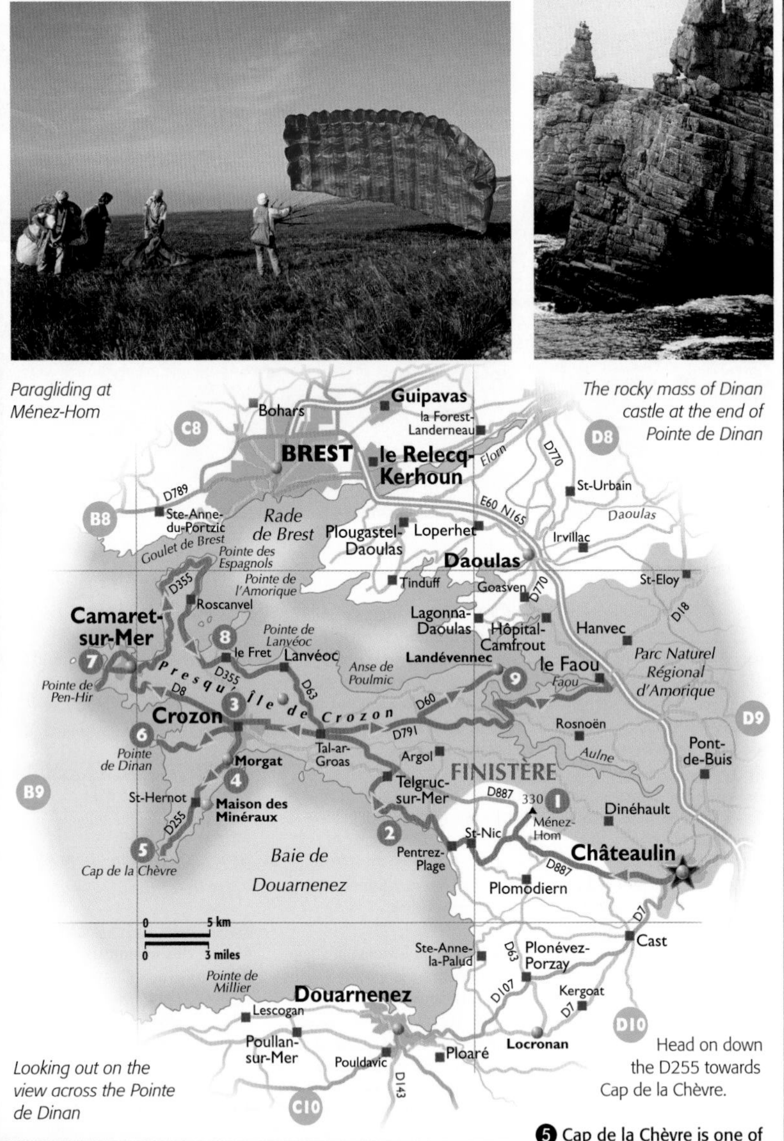

Paragliding at Ménez-Hom

The rocky mass of Dinan castle at the end of Pointe de Dinan

Looking out on the view across the Pointe de Dinan

Head on down the D255 towards Cap de la Chèvre.

❺ Cap de la Chèvre is one of the wildest of Crozon's rugged headlands. On the way, the Maison des Minéraux may divert you briefly with its curious fluorescent rocks.

Return to Crozon, then take signs for the Pointe de Dinan (6km/4 miles west).

❻ The spectacular heathery cliffs of the Pointe de Dinan rear 40m/132ft from the Atlantic breakers. A natural rock-arch connects the mainland with a striking formation called the Château

The quayside at the resort of Camaret

de Dinan just offshore (accessible on foot).

Return to Crozon again, then take the D8 to Camaret-sur-Mer and follow signs to the Pointe de Pen-Hir, perhaps the grandest of all the Crozon headlands, where a scattering of offshore rocks called Les Tas de Pois (pile of peas) adds to the coastal interest. Return into Camaret past the Alignements de Lagatjar (a group of roadside menhirs).

7 Camaret-sur-Mer is a quiet seaside resort renowned for spiny lobster, listed on local menus. A chapel and a Vauban fortress of toytown dimensions perch on a long sandspit (Le Sillon) protecting the harbour.

A circular drive around the verdant Pointe des Espagnols (on the D355) gives fine views of the Rade de Brest. Continue eastwards past the Ile Longue (a military naval base, no public access), following signs to Le Fret.

8 This charming little port has a summer ferry service to Brest. A waterfront hotel-restaurant overlooking the roadside makes the perfect lunch spot, but book ahead to reserve a table.

Return to the main road via Lanvéoc and the D63, taking the D791 towards Le Faou. At Les Quatre Chemins, turn left on to the D60 to Landévennec (6.5km/4 miles).

9 The main interest at Landévennec is a ruined Romanesque abbey on a lonely wooded peninsula at the mouth of the Aulne. A museum traces its history. Benedictine monks welcome visitors to their church nearby.

Return to the main road, turn left and cross the Aulne (admiring the views near the Térénez suspension bridge). Then head along the scenic corniche road to the pleasant village of Le Faou, where you can continue your journey on the N165.

WHERE TO EAT

Hostellerie de la Mer
Port du Fret
☎ 02 98 27 61 90
Feb–end Dec daily lunch, dinner (closed Jan)

BASICS

Musée des Minéraux
Route du Cap de la Chèvre, St-Hernot
☎ 02 98 27 19 73
Jul to mid-Sep daily 10–7; May to end Jun Sun–Fri 10–12, 2–5.30; Oct–end Dec, Feb–end Apr Sun–Fri 2–5; Jan Mon–Fri 2–5
Adult €4, child (8–14) €2.50

L'Ancienne Abbaye de Landévennec
☎ 02 98 27 35 90
Museum and abbey ruins: Jul to mid-Sep daily 10–7; May, Jun, mid–end Sep Sun–Fri 2–6; Oct–end Apr Sun 2–6 (Sun–Fri in school hols)
Adult €4; child (8–18) €2.50; new abbey free
Abbey shop sells regional products, some made by the monks

Part of the Alignements de Lagatjar, near Camaret-sur-Mer

4. WALK

AROUND HUELGOAT

At the heart of inland Brittany, within the Parc Naturel Régional d'Armorique, Huelgoat is surrounded by magnificent countryside combining a lake, an unruly river and a forest scattered with rocks piled in curious formations. It is excellent hiking country and this walk takes you through many changes of scenery.

THE WALK

Length: 5km (3 miles)
Allow: 2 hours
Start: Place Aristide Briand
End: La Roche Cintrée

HOW TO GET THERE

The village is 25km (15 miles) south of Morlaix and the N12 express road, in the northwest corner of Brittany.

The promenade alongside the lake at Huelgoat

★ Huelgoat (meaning 'high forest') is beside a lake, and this position, together with the nearby wooded hills, makes it a popular summer resort and a base for activity holidays.

Start from Place Aristide Briand at the heart of Huelgoat. Turn left at the northern end of the square, with the lake on your left. On the other side of the street, a well-marked path leads through the rocks.

❶ The huge boulders are piled in a chaotic formation because of the consistency of the granite: Soft inclusions crumble, isolating harder minerals, which eventually collapse onto one another. A Breton legend has it that the inhabitants of two nearby villages, wanting to settle a quarrel, hurled the stones at each other.

Continue along the path.

❷ Along the way you'll see the Chaos du Moulin and the Grotte du Diable, where you can go down a ladder and watch the river foaming against the rocks. On the other side of the river, the Roche Tremblante is a single boulder, weighing an estimated 100 tonnes, which rocks slightly when pushed. A little further on, the Ménage de la Vierge consists of several rocks looking like household utensils.

The pleasant allée Violette leads through the woods to the Pont Rouge and the D769A to Carhaix. Follow the road for approximately 100m (109 yards) and turn right onto a path in the form of a horseshoe, called the Promenade du Fer à Cheval. It dominates the Rivière d'Argent in a lovely setting before rejoining the road. Turn right and follow the road for another 300m (330 yards). A narrow staircase on the right goes down to Le Gouffre (the abyss) into which the river falls and disappears. Continue along the footpath past the Mare aux Fées (fairy pool), until you meet a gravel road where you should go right, following the road to the old mine.

❸ This is the site of an old silver mine, but there's little to see other than a clearing with a stream running through it.

Cross the stream and take the footpath up the hill following the signs *Huelgoat par le canal*. Halfway up the hill the route splits. Keep left and continue to the top, where you'll find a small hydroelectric station at the head of the canal.

❹ The canal is more of a channel, at just 1m (3ft) wide. It was created to bring water to the silver mines, worked since Roman times but abandoned at the end of the 19th century.

The Promenade du Canal follows the canal back to town, about 3.5km (2 miles) away. Just before you arrive, on the left, a road leads to La Roche Cintrée, with a good view of the town and the mountains.

WHERE TO EAT

Crêperie de l'Argoat
12 rue du Lac, 29690, Huelgoat
Apr–end Aug Wed–Sun 11–10, Mon 11–2; Sep–end Mar Wed–Sun 11–8, Mon 11–2

Dappled sunlight in Huelgoat Forest

5. DRIVE

THE EMERALD COAST

This drive takes in the fascinating Côte d'Émeraude, with its impressive cliffs, superb sandy beaches and the unforgettable Fort la Latte on a barren promontory. Inland, the Forêt de la Hunaudaye and the surrounding area provide an interesting contrast.

THE DRIVE

Distance: 92km (57 miles)
Time: Half to a full day
Start/end at: Le-Val-André

★ The beach at Le-Val-André is one of Brittany's finest. A road running around the promontory has lovely views of the beach and of the Île du Verdelet, a bird sanctuary accessible at low tide.

Forte la Latte (above), and the beach at Le-Val-Andre (below)

Follow the D34 to Planguenoual, then take the D59 to Lamballe.

❶ Lamballe, on a hillside beside a small river, is famous for its *haras national* (national stud farm), where you can take a guided tour. The Gothic Église Notre-Dame at the top of town has a finely carved rood screen and doorways.

Leave Lamballe eastwards by the D28, then bear right onto the D52A towards Plédéliac, 11km (7 miles) away. Turn left onto the D55 and drive for another 4km (2.5 miles), following the signs to Château de la Hunaudaye.

❷ The Château de la Hunaudaye dates back to the 12th century. It was battered into its present ruins during the Revolution. The most impressive parts are the Tour de la Glacière, the Renaissance manor house and the 15th-century keep, with a remarkable spiral staircase.

Turn left and left again along the D28 and drive through the Forêt de la Hunaudaye to the hamlet of St-Aubin, 6km (4 miles). Follow the D52 and turn right. Follow the D13 and D43 for 24km (15 miles) through Hénanbihen and Pléboulle to the Baie de la Frénaye and Fort la Latte.

❸ Fort la Latte is a medieval fortress perching on a rocky promontory. It offers magnificent views of Cap Fréhel to the west and the Côte d'Émeraude to the east. Two drawbridges span the deep cracks in the rock, filled by the sea at high tide. Inside, the oven heated cannonballs to set fire to enemy ships.

Drive round the Anse des Sévignés, 4km (2.5 miles), to Cap Fréhel (▷ 80), then follow the D34a to Sables-d'Or-les-Pins, 9km (5.5 miles). The scenic coast road winds through the wild Landes de Fréhel (Fréhel moors) to Pléhérel-Plage, with its beautiful beach.

❹ Most people come to Sables-d'Or-les-Pins (▷ 89) to

The headland at the Cap Fréhel Nature Reserve

The lighthouses (old and new) at Cap Fréhel

walk on the long golden beach. Strong currents make it unsuitable for swimming.

Continue on the D34 and turn right onto the D786 towards Erquy, 8km (5 miles).

❺ This resort and fishing port of Erquy is sheltered by the cliffs of Cap d'Erquy, 3km (2 miles) to the north, and is worth the detour. There are impressive views of the wide bay of St-Brieuc as far as the Île de Bréhat.

Continue on the D786 towards Le-Val-André for 5km (3 miles), past Château de Bienassis on your left.

❻ The late-medieval Château de Bienassis was rebuilt in the 17th century and furnished in Louis XIV and Breton Renaissance styles.

Continue on the D786 for 6km (4 miles) back to Le-Val-André.

WHEN TO GO

The Château de la Hunaudaye and Château de Bienassis are open in peak season only.

WHERE TO EAT

Beauséjour
21 rue de la Corniche, Erquy
☎ 02 96 72 30 39

BASICS

Château de la Hunaudaye
🕐 Jul–Aug daily 11–6.30 (Sat pm only)

Haras National
☎ 02 96 50 06 98
🕐 Guided tours mid-Jul to late Aug daily 10.30–11.30, 2.15–5.45

Fort la Latte
☎ 02 99 30 38 84
🕐 Guided tours Jul–Aug daily 10–7; Apr–end Jun, Sep daily 10–12.30, 2–6, Oct–Apr weekends 2.30–6.30
Adult €4.20, child (under 12) €2.30

Château de Bienassis
☎ 02 96 72 22 03
🕐 Mid-Jun to mid-Sep daily 10.30–12.30, 2–6.30

PLOUMANAC'H WALK

The seashore between Ploumanac'h and Perros-Guirec is the most remarkable stretch of the Pink Granite Coast, where the shapes and hues of the rocks are truly mesmerizing, especially towards sunset. Whatever you do, don't forget the camera. It is best seen on foot, from an old watch-path called the Sentier des Douaniers. This is one of the most popular sections of the GR34, a long-distance footpath that runs along most of Brittany's coast.

THE WALK

Length: 8.5km (5 miles)
Allow: Half a day
Start/end: La Chapelle de Notre-Dame de la Clarté

HOW TO GET THERE

La Clarté is signed near Ploumanac'h, off the main road (D788/Boulevard du Sémaphore) between Perros-Guirec and Trégastel on the Côte de Granit Rose (Côtes d'Armor). The spire makes it easy to spot. There is parking beside the chapel.

Looking out to sea at Perros-Guirec (above), and the coastguards' path along the rocky coast (below)

★ Notre-Dame de la Clarté (Our Lady of Light) stands on high land surveying the sea. The chapel consists of the attractive pink granite quarried from the hillsides behind the village. It dates from 1445, a thanksgiving (so the story goes) from a local nobleman who became lost in fog while sailing around the coast. He prayed for guidance and took his bearings from a sudden shaft of sunlight that fell on this spot. The weathered granite of the chapel porch is carved into low relief. An annual *pardon* attracts many pilgrims on 15th August.

Take the rue du Tertre from the north side of the chapel. It leads to a rocky knoll from which there's a wonderful view. Follow the path to the signal station (Sémaphore), and cross the main road (Boulevard du Sémaphore) on to rue des Fougères. Take a path to your left, which leads down towards the shore near a little beach (Grève St-Pierre). This connects you with the coastal footpath called the Sentier des Douaniers.

1 The Sentier des Douaniers, a former customs officers' trail, can be crowded in summer. The route is waymarked (with yellow signs) to discourage undue erosion; stick to the marked paths. The rocks may be slippery when damp. Bicycling is strictly forbidden.

Turn left and follow the path along the shoreline. Les Sept-Iles are visible on a clear day.

2 Les Sept-Iles, a rocky archipelago, is one of the most important seabird sanctuaries in France. Some 20,000 pairs and nearly 30 different species breed here annually, including puffins, along with a resident colony of grey seals. Motor launches take visitors around the islands from local resorts.

Pink granite rocks and coastal wild-flowers (above), and boats moored along the seafront at Ploumanac'h (below)

Carry on along the path westwards. At Pors Rolland the scenery suddenly becomes more dramatic, and you enter a conservation zone called Les Landes de Ploumanac'h.

3 At Les Landes de Ploumanac'h the granite boulders piled on top of one another assume startling shapes. Some of the most striking rock forms can be seen around the Pointe de Squewel. Many have been given fanciful names: the Tortoise, the Skull, the Devil's Castle.

Continue westwards around the headland, following the path through the astonishing rocky wilderness, splashed with gorse and heather and occasional pines. Within a few hundred metres (half a mile) you will reach Ploumanac'h's lighthouse, and near it the lifeboat station and the Maison du Littoral.

4 The Maison du Littoral is an information point in a typical pink granite building. It contains a permanent exhibition about the geology and ecology of this coastline, and the importance of granite to the local economy.

Walk along the path to Ploumanac'h's main beach, the Plage de St-Guirec.

5 Though quite small, the Plage de St-Guirec is one of the most attractive resort beaches anywhere in Brittany. On one of the rocks stands a tiny stone oratory containing a statue of the Celtic monk, St Guirec, who arrived here from Wales in the 6th century. The receding tide reveals yet another dazzling rockscape, leading the eye towards a tidal islet in the bay on which a Gothic mock castle—the Château de Costaëres—stands. The castle is privately owned, and not open to the public. Several panoramic restaurants by the entrance to the beach allow you to enjoy the scene at leisure.

The final section of the Sentier des Douaniers takes you to the pretty port of Ploumanac'h, past the landing stage for trips to Les Sept-Îles, and a crowd of anchored boats in the bay. Walk along the quai de Bellevue, then take the rue de la Plaine uphill to the rue de St-Guirec, which leads out of the village. Turn right, then almost immediately left on to the rue de Ranolien, where you will see the Christian Gad sculpture park on your right.

6 This public park contains a dozen modern sculptures in local pink granite, created for a festival in 1998. Here you'll spot L'Ankou (François Breton) and Dahud (Patrice Le Guen), inspired by Breton legends, and works by Pierre Székely.

Leave the park and cross the busy boulevard du Sémaphore. At the crossroads you will find a large shop selling biscuits and other regional products. Take rue Gabriel, passing a windmill on your right, and head back towards the spire of Notre-Dame-de-la-Clarté. A path off rue de la Vallée leads back into the car park beside the chapel.

WHERE TO EAT

Coste Mor
Plage St-Guirec, Ploumanac'h
☎ 02 96 91 65 55
Easter–Oct lunch and dinner

BASICS

Maison du Littoral
Chemin du Phare, Ploumanac'h
☎ 02 96 91 62 77
Mid-Jun to mid-Sep Mon–Sat 10–1, 2–6; school hols Mon–Fri 2–5
Free

ST-MALO AND DINAN

No visitor to Brittany should miss the two north-coast towns of St-Malo and Dinan. Although very different in character—St-Malo is a busy port and Dinan a splendidly preserved medieval town—both are beautiful. The river Rance flows past Dinan and out to sea at St-Malo, and is barred on the way by a great tidal dam.

The Tour Solidor on the Rance estuary at St-Servan-sur-Mer (above), and the old town of Dinan (below)

THE DRIVE

Length: 90km (56 miles)
Allow: 2 days
Start/end: St-Malo

★ St-Malo (⊳ 106–8) is a ferry port, yachting base and commercial port, with a walled citadel well worth exploring. Walk the ramparts for views of the town, the sea and nearby islands.

Follow signs for Rennes through the suburb of St-Servan-sur-Mer and, keeping the estuary of the Rance on your right, carry on past Tour Solidor.

❶ Medieval Tour Solidor, in the St-Servan district of St-Malo, was built in the late 14th century to protect shipping in the Rance from English pirates and Malouin corsairs. It was once the town jail and is now a museum with model ships and information about the mariners of Cape Horn.

Follow signs for Dinard, crossing the top of a huge dam, the Barrage de Rance, which generates electricity by harnessing the tidal current. Turn right onto the D266 into Dinard.

❷ Dinard is a fashionable seaside town, a resort of the smart set since the turn of the 20th century, when the Prince of Wales used to holiday here. There are good views over a forest of yacht masts to the walls of St-Malo. From here you can go on a boat trip up the Rance to Dinan.

Return to the D266, following signs for Dinan and Pleurtuit. After Pleurtuit turn left onto the D766 which will take you to the N176/E401. Head south on the N176 for 6km (4 miles) and exit for Dinan. Although the town is often crowded, it's usually possible to park in Place du Guesclin near to all the sights.

❸ Dinan is a place to explore on foot. Walk down to the banks of the Rance by rue du Jerzual, a steep street lined with medieval houses, including a spectacular three-floor half-timbered building, the Maison du Gouverneur. The riverside is lined with restaurants, great for lunch or dinner.

From Dinan, follow signs to the suburb of Lanvallay, east of Dinan, and pick up the D676. Fork left onto the D29 and head north past Pleudihen-sur-Rance. Continue north via the D74 and D76, following signs for Le Port as you come into Cancale.

❹ The oyster port and seaside resort of Cancale is tucked into a corner of the Baie du Mont-St-Michel. You can see the Mount itself on the far side of the bay. Oysters are bred out in the bay and are gathered from the flat-bottomed boats that you can see in the harbour. There are plenty of small restaurants along the wharf where you can sample the catch.

From Cancale harbour, follow the D201 northwards for 7km (4.5 miles) to the Pointe du Grouin (signed St-Malo par la côte).

❺ Pointe du Grouin is a nature reserve and bird sanctuary, with superb views over the bay to Mont-St-Michel and, to the south, to Mont-Dol near Dol-de-Bretagne. From the parking place there is a footpath up to the tip of the Pointe and from there another footpath leads along the coast to St-Malo.

Continue westwards along the picturesque coast road (still the D201) in the direction of St-Malo past the Baie du Guesclin and through the suburb of Rothéneuf.

❻ Rothéneuf is a pleasant suburb of St-Malo, next to a wide beach. Sights here include the coastal rocks carved by the Abbé Foure in the 19th century and the

Fresh oysters on sale at Cancale

A view of Mont-St-Michel from Mont-Dol

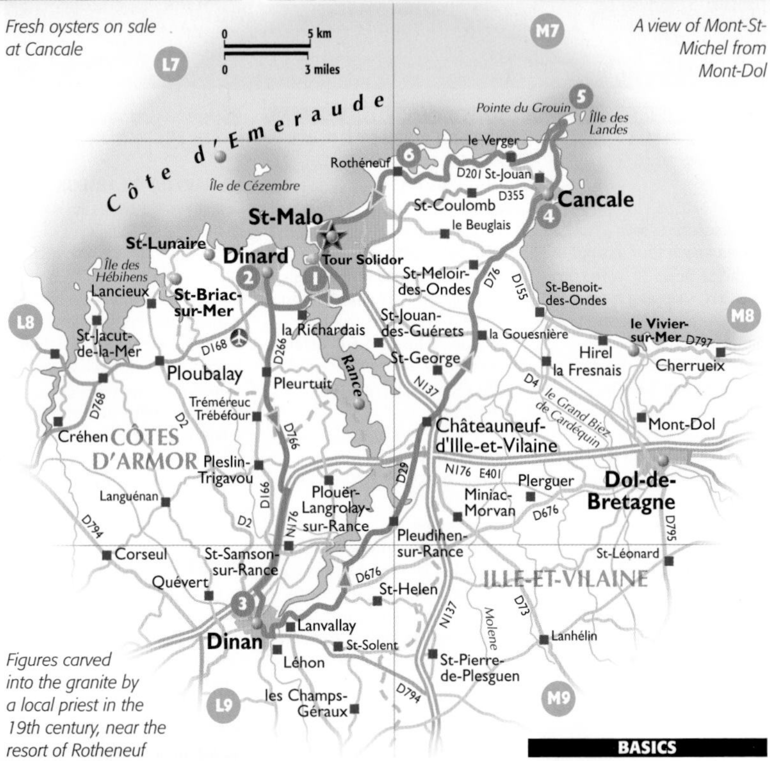

Figures carved into the granite by a local priest in the 19th century, near the resort of Rotheneuf

manor house lived in by the 16th-century explorer and discoverer of Canada, Jacques Cartier.

Pass through Paramé, and then along the waterfront and you reach the main gateway into St-Malo.

WHERE TO EAT

Les Terrasses
Dinan
☎ 02 96 39 09 60

WHERE TO STAY

Le Valmarin
7 rue Jean XXIII, 35400 St-Malo
☎ 02 99 81 94 76
www.levalmarin.com

BASICS

Tour Solidor
St-Servan, St-Malo
☎ 02 99 40 71 58
Apr–end Sep daily 10–12.30, 2–6; reduced hours in winter; closed Mon
Adult €5, child (8–23) €2.50

Maison du Gouverneur
24 rue Petit Fort, Dinan
☎ 02 96 39 29 97
Jun–Sep daily 10–6.30
Adult €1.70, child €0.90, under 12 free

Manoir de Limoëlou (Musée Jacques Cartier)
Rothéneuf
☎ 02 99 40 97 73
Jul–Aug daily 10–11.30, 2.30–6; closed Sun Sep–Jun; guided tours Mon–Sat 10 and 3

EXCURSIONS

Brittany excels in boat trips and outdoor activities such as water sports, bicycling, riding and walking. Details of these and suggestions for many kinds of self-guided discovery tour are readily available at any tourist office. Fully inclusive and escorted 'package tour'-style excursions, including transport from an easily accessed departure point, are less widespread. There is a general assumption that most visitors will have the use of a self-drive vehicle for touring in Brittany, and your options are certainly reduced without one. Below are some suggestions of worthwhile trips and activities you can do without a car.

MORBIHAN

LES CARS BLEUS
Quai Bonnelle, 56360 Le Palais, Belle-Île
Tel 02 97 31 83 56
www.lescarsbleus.com
Take a coach tour around the island of Belle-Île, with commentary, stopping for lunch on the Côte Sauvage (café or picnic), and visiting Port Goulphar, the Pointe des Poulains, and Sauzon.
All year

L'ETOILE DU BLAVET
Promenade des Estivants, St-Nicolas-des-Eaux, 56930 Plumeliau
Tel 02 97 51 83 09
You can take a two-hour trip up the tranquil valley of the Blavet, with commentary, from this pretty waterfront village near Pontivy. The boats are accessible for wheelchair-users.
Jul, Aug daily departures 2 and 4, subject to sufficient bookings; Mar–end Jun, Sep, Oct by arrangement
Adult €9, child (4–10) €5

PETITS-TRAINS DU MORBIHAN
Tel 02 97 24 06 29
Particularly suitable for children, you can take a 30-minute trip through Old Vannes and the rampart gardens on these 'toytown' road-trains, discover the wild west coast of the Quiberon peninsula, or trundle past the megaliths of Carnac and down to the beach.
Apr–end Sep daily 10–7 (except Wed, Sat am in Vannes) Adult €5 (Vannes) or €6 (Quiberon/Carnac), child (under 12) €3 for all locations

FINISTÈRE

LE LÉON À FER ET À FLOTS
Place des Otages, 29600 Morlaix
Tel 02 98 62 07 52
www.aferaflots.org
This enjoyable circular tour by boat and train takes in St-Pol-de-Léon, Roscoff and Morlaix Bay, escorted by a professional guide. Departures are from Morlaix or Roscoff. Full details from either tourist office.
Jun–end Oct Adult €20, child (4–11) €10

VIDEO MER
Quai de la Criée, 29900 Concarneau
Tel 06 80 26 34 25
www.videomer.fr
Tours of Concarneau's lively *criée*, led by Yvon Lachèvre, a journalist and documentary film-maker, take visitors to watch the unloading and sorting of the catch in the auction hall as the boats return each afternoon. Visits last an hour and a half, and include a wide-screen presentation of life on board. The commentary is only in French. Buy your tickets at the departure point at the quayside tourist office.
Easter–Oct at 5.30pm Adult €5, child €3

CÔTES D'ARMOR

LA MAISON DU LITTORAL
Chemin du Phare, 22700 Ploumanac'h
Tel 02 96 91 62 77
www.perros-guirec.com
On one of Brittany's most amazing stretches of coastline, this visitor centre near the lighthouses organizes a host of walks, talks and activities based around the geology and ecosystem of the Pink Granite Coast.
Mid-Jun to mid-Sep, school hols Mon–Sat Adult €3–€4

LA VAPEUR DU TRIEUX
Gare de Paimpol, avenue du Général de Gaulle, 22500 Paimpol
Tel 08 923 914 27 (premium-rate line €0.34 per min)
Take a steam-train ride (with multilingual commentary) along the scenic Trieux estuary to Pontrieux, with a halfway stop at a manor-house for music and refreshments. Advance booking is essential.
Jul, Aug almost daily; end–May, Jun, Sep mainly Wed–Sun Adult return €21, child (4–11) €10.50; one-way and family tickets available

ILLE-ET-VILAINE

LES COURRIERS BRETONS
Esplanade St-Vincent, 35400 St-Malo
Tel 02 99 19 70 80
www.lescourriersbretons.fr
This bus company organizes escorted day-trips to Mont-St-Michel, Dinan, Cap Fréhel, Île de Bréhat and other destinations from St-Malo. The booking agency is easy to find next to the tourist office.
All year

CROWN BLUE LINE
Port de Plaisance, 35480 Messac
Tel 02 99 34 60 11
www.crownblueline.com
House boats and cabin cruisers sleeping from two to twelve can be hired from this long-established firm for boating holidays on Brittany's inland waterways. There's another pick-up point at Dinan (Côtes d'Armor). No licence is required.
Apr–end Oct Mon–Sat; weekends off-season

This chapter lists places to eat and stay, broken down regionally, then alphabetically by town.

Eating and Staying

EATING OUT IN BRITTANY

Brittany is blessed. It is one of France's great agricultural regions, producing world-class vegetables such as potatoes, cauliflowers and onions; and wheat which turns humble *crêpes* and *galettes* into gourmet snacks. But perhaps Brittany's overriding highlight is the sea, washing 3,200km (2,000 miles) of coastline and giving innumerable fishing communities an unlimited harvest of the freshest seafood money can buy.

A selection of seafood (left), the art of eating an oyster (middle), and a café in Rennes (right)

In recent years, a move to lighter dishes and simpler techniques has acknowledged changing dietary habits. These days, many restaurants provide at least one completely vegetarian option, although notions of vegetarianism can be a little hazy. Meat stocks are often used in innocent-sounding vegetable soups, and lardons sprinkled on salads or omelettes. If you eat neither fish nor flesh, your choice will be rather restricted in north-western France. Ethnic restaurants are not nearly as widespread as in other regions, but you will find the odd North African or Asian restaurant in large towns like Rennes or Brest.

RESTAURANTS

Every town has its hallowed restaurants, quite different from the bistros and brasseries for every-day eating. In these, you'll find a more refined setting, with starched linen, polished glass and silverware and a sense of hushed reverence for the gastronomic offerings to come. Here, families celebrate birthdays and communions, promises are whispered and business deals settled over something even more important than a hand-shake. Dress smartly and reserve in advance. Northwestern France has its fair share of leading chefs, such as Olivier Roellinger in Cancale (▷ 162), Jacques Thorel in La Roche-Bernard (▷ 155), and Georges Paineau in Questembert (▷ 155). But you can find excellent regional food in many less grand dining rooms, especially in members of the Logis de France hotel group (▷ 176).

CRIÊPERIES

No Breton town or village seems to be without a *crêperie* or two, an inexpensive way to stave off hunger pangs. Imaginative, sometimes bizarre combinations of ingredients are used, both sweet and savoury, but exotic seafood fillings will cost much more than something simple like egg, cheese or mushrooms. *Crêpes* are useful fast-food options for children or vegetarians. An accompanying salad makes a meal of them.

BRASSERIES AND BISTROS

Brasseries were once brewery bars that served meals. Today, they are mostly informal restaurants that open long hours. Here you can enjoy local dishes, as well as familiar meals such as *steak-frites* (steak and chips/fries) and *assiettes de fruits de mer* (seafood platter). Bistros may be small, independent, family-run restaurants serving traditional cooking, with a modest wine list. Some also have a delicatessen.

CAFÉS AND BARS

Cafés and bars serve hot, soft and alcoholic drinks, snacks and sometimes light meals. Catering more for holidaymakers or leisure visitors than hard-pressed businessfolk, *salons de thé* or *glaciers* serve cakes and ice creams as well as drinks. They open from breakfast until late in the evening. As in all eating places, the smartness of the surroundings greatly affects the price you pay. Expect to pay a little more for your drink if you sit down rather than stand at the bar; and a coveted sea-view terrace table may be priciest of all.

CUTTING COSTS

If you are on a budget, have your main meal at lunchtime, when most restaurants serve an inexpensive *formule* or *menu du jour* (daily menu), of two or three courses with a glass of wine *(vin compris)* for around 50 per cent of the cost in the evening. Sometimes you can simply order a *plat du jour* (daily dish) and a drink for very low prices. On weekdays, lunch menus at even the most stellar establishments are often reasonably priced. Sticking to fixed-price or *table d'hôte* menus is almost always a much better deal than dining à la carte.

MENUS

A *menu* in a French restaurant is a set-price, multi-course meal, served at lunchtime and in the evening. If you want to see the menu, ask for *la carte*. A wine-list is a *carte à vins*. Take care you are presented with the bottle you ordered (it should be shown to you before it is opened). A *menu dégustation* or *menu gastronomique*, found in the finest restaurants, offers a sample of specialty dishes sometimes accompanied by a selection of appropriate wines, and is always expensive.

A Locronan crêperie *(left), bottles of local cider (middle), and freshly made galettes (right)*

OPENING TIMES

With few exceptions, restaurants and bistros tend to keep fairly strict serving times, though in popular holiday resorts all-day diners cater for the less disciplined habits of foreign visitors. Restaurants generally open at 12, close by 2.30, then reopen for dinner at 7.30. Except in large towns and resorts, restaurants mostly stop taking orders between 9pm and 9.30pm. In high season, however, you will find many places accept orders until at least 10pm. Many restaurants are closed at Saturday lunchtime, on Sunday evening and Monday, but may stay open every day or longer hours in July and August . Many establishments in remoter parts of Brittany's coast, or on islands, often close completely between November and Easter.

ETIQUETTE

Service is always included in the price of your meal, indicated by the words *service compris* or *s.c.*, but it is still customary to leave some change behind if the service has been exceptional. Only very exclusive restaurants in Brittany insist on a dress code, but it is courteous to dress up a little when dining in a smarter venue. Address staff as *Monsieur, Madame* or *Mademoiselle*. By law, all eating places in France must now provide non-smoking sections. Smoking is becoming less prevalent, but it's a slow process in a country where smoking is firmly entrenched.

BRETON MENU READER

Agneau de pré-salé: lamb raised on the coastal saltmarshes, for example around Ouessant.
Andouille: a smoked pork-tripe sausage consisting mainly of offal. Also called *chitterlings*.
Andouillette: similar to *Andouille*, but usually eaten hot.
Beurre blanc: butter whipped with white wine vinegar and shallots.
Cervoise: classic Breton beer, as drunk by the Gauls (including Asterix!).
Chateaubriand: a thick cut of tenderloin steak for two people with shallot, herb and white-wine sauce.
Cidre: cider, the local hooch of Brittany. *Doux* is sweet, *brut* is dry and *bouché* means fermented in the bottle.
Cocos de Paimpol: high-quality haricot beans produced around Paimpol and regarded as a great delicacy.
Cotriade: a fish stew, sometimes called the bouillabaisse of the north.
Chouchen: mead, a strong, sweet drink made with fermented honey.
Crêpes and galettes: pancakes are the staple diet of Brittany. A *crêpe* is made with a conventional wheat-flour batter and has a sweet filling, while a *galette* is traditionally made from heavier buckwheat or sarassin flour and has a savoury one. You can buy them ready-made in packets or tins, though they are much nicer warm and fresh. *Crêpes-dentelles* are wafer-thin pancakes.
Far breton: a thick, sweet tart with prunes or raisins, similar to a flan.
Galettes de Pont-Aven: not to be confused with pancakes, these are buttery biscuits.
Gigot à la Bretonne: roast leg of lamb with haricot beans.
Homard à l'armoricaine: lobster served flambéed in a cream and wine sauce.
Huîtres plates: flat or native oysters (as opposed to *huîtres creuses*, or hollow oysters).
Kig-ha-farz: a hearty stew containing ham or bacon.
Kouignamann: a traditional Breton cake made with sugar, butter and almonds, best eaten warm.
Lambig: a rare kind of Breton calvados (apple brandy).
Niniches: sugar-cane lollipops, especially popular in Morbihan.

MORBIHAN

PRICES AND SYMBOLS

The restaurants are listed alphabetically within each town. The prices given for lunch (L) and dinner (D) are for three courses for one person, without drinks. The wine price is for the least expensive bottle.

For a key to the symbols, ⊳ 2.

AURAY

L'EGLANTINE

17 Place St-Sauveur, Port St-Goustan, 56400 Auray
Tel 02 97 56 46 55

Bric-à-brac and historic portraits adorn the snug interior of this attractive salmon-washed period building overlooking the cobbled quayside, where tables are set on sunny days.

Widely regarded as the classiest restaurant along the St-Goustan waterfront, L'Eglantine specializes mainly in fish. Try a house bouillabaisse, or a salad of smoked fish à l'orange. Style and service are highly traditional, and the desserts are all home-made.

Thu–Tue 12.15–2, 7–10; also Wed in season

L €15, D €39, Wine €16

BELLE-ÎLE

ROZ-AVEL

Rue du Lieutenant-Riou, 56360 Sauzon
Tel 02 97 31 61 48

Just behind the church in the pretty fishing port of Sauzon, this elegant place is one of the best restaurants on the island. It offers sophisticated fare for adventurous diners (pig's trotters marinated with oysters or spiced crab claws), alongside perfectly prepared local lamb or a *panaché de poissons*. Terrace tables in summer.

Lunch and dinner; closed Wed and Jan, Feb

L €25, D €43, Wine €14

CARNAC

AUBERGE LE RATELIER

4 Chemin du Douët, 56340 Carnac
Tel 02 97 52 05 04
www.le-ratelier.com

A charming little place tucked away in a quiet but central enclave of Carnac Bourg, close to the church and museum. It's an old, creeper-covered house with a welcoming rustic feel.

Dishes ring the changes on seafood (scorpion fish in spinach and cider butter sauce, or a terrine of sea trout and vegetables). Meals start with a surprise *amuse-bouche*, and service couldn't be friendlier. The simple bedrooms here are very good value.

12–2, 7–9.30; closed Jan and Tue–Wed Oct–end Apr

L €25, D €34, Wine €14

LA CÔTE

Alignements de Kermario, 56340 Carnac
Tel 02 97 52 02 80

Close to Carnac's megaliths, this lively and enterprising place caters cheerfully for hundreds of multilingual visitors, but offers a great deal more than mere tourist fodder.

Pierre Michaud has built up a formidable reputation for his subtly flavoured *grande cuisine de la mer et du terroir*, blending meat and seafood flavours. The attractive two-part dining room has stone walls and a mix of modern and antique furniture. Outside are large gardens with play areas where children can roam happily.

Lunch, dinner Tue–Sun; off season closed Sun eve; also closed early Jan–early Feb

L €32, D €40, Wine €15

JOSSELIN

LA MARINE

8 rue du Canal, Josselin
Tel 02 97 22 21 98

True to its name, this waterfront *crêperie* has a blue-and-white nautical theme. Its flower-filled terrace overlooks the château and the River Oust. *Crêpes* reflect the seasons, for instance *L'Automne* has sweet chestnut purée and apple and pear jam. The local speciality, *La Josselinoise*, is filled with black pudding and fried apples. A lunch menu offers non-pancake alternatives.

Jul, Aug daily 12–1.45, 7–9; Sep–end Jun daily 12–1.45 and Sat 7–9; closed Wed dinner and 2 weeks in Nov

L €12, D €18, Wine €11

LA TABLE D'O

9 rue Glatinier, 56120 Josselin
Tel 02 97 70 61 39
www.latabledo.site.voila.fr

A town as attractive as Josselin deserves one or two classy restaurants, and this bright new venture looks set to raise the stakes in this area. It has a stylish contemporary interior decked with dark-red wicker chairs and fresh flowers. Dining room and balcony views stretch over the town and river. The lunchtime *formule gourmande* is excellent value. Sample dishes include *carré d'agneau aux herbes* (best end of lamb with herbs) or beef in a foie gras sauce.

Mon–Sat 12–1.30, 7.30–9.30; closed Tue eve and Wed eve off-season; annual hols 1 week begin Jul, 2 weeks Nov, 2 weeks Feb

L €14, D €33, Wine €14

MALESTROIT

LE CANOTIER

Place du Dr-Queinnec, 56140 Malestroit
Tel 02 97 75 08 69

This unpretentious but highly recommendable place on the main square serves a flexible and varied menu with strong leanings towards seafood—red mullet, salmon and scallops. Adventurous meat-eaters might try the foie gras fried with honey, or you can simply choose an omelette without feeling pressured. The ochre dining room with wood panels is comfortable, and in summer you can eat on the terrace.

Tue–Sat 12–2, 7.15–9.15, Sun 12–2
L €15, D €30, Wine €8.50

PORT-NAVALO

LE GRAND LARGUE

1 rue du Phare, Port-Navalo, 56640 Arzon
Tel 02 97 53 71 58
http://grand-largue.ifrance.com

The smart upper dining room of this nautically styled restaurant is definitely club class, with spectacular waterfront views over the entrance to the Golfe du Morbihan from huge glazed windows. But you can dine steerage in the less expensive cherry-wood cabins of the brasserie and oyster-bar downstairs, where menus suit all pockets. Seafood naturally predominates in many different guises, from spicy lobster to sea bass in balsamic vinegar. One elaborate speciality is *huîtres en gelée d'eau de mer à la chlorophylle d'algue* (oysters in seawater jelly with algae chlorophyll).

Wed–Sat 12.15–1.45, 7.30–9, Tue–Sun 12.15–1.45
L €33, D €62, Wine €29

QUESTEMBERT

LE BRETAGNE

13 rue St-Michel, 56230 Questembert
Tel 02 97 26 11 12
http://perso.wanadoo.fr/bretagne

Top chef Georges Paineau and his son-in-law Claude Corlouër cook up a storm of exotic gourmet fare in this traditional little market town. The creeper-covered corner-site building may look like a classic provincial auberge from outside, but there's nothing conventional about the shocking pink dining room decked with mine host's modern artworks. Be warned, it is very expensive, but a meal here is memorable for more reasons than the bill. Tranquil garden views aid digestion, and the on-site hotel rooms are splendidly luxurious.

Thu–Sun 12.15–1.45, 7.30–9, Tue–Wed 7.30–9; closed 3 weeks Jan, 1 week Mar, 1 week Nov
L €80, D €158, Wine €26

SPECIAL IN LA ROCHE-BERNARD

L'AUBERGE BRETONNE

2 Place Duguesclin, 56130 La Roche-Bernard
Tel 02 99 90 60 28
www.thorel.fr

The reputation of Solange and Jacques Thorel's exquisite Relais & Châteaux restaurant-with-rooms extends far beyond Morbihan's boundaries. It serves highly accomplished and ambitious cooking in an elegant, arty setting of sculptures, paintings and fountains. Needless to say, it isn't cheap, but the set menus at lunchtime make it worth reserving ahead for an outstanding treat. Try a *tourte de canard* (duck pie) or *baba à la mirabelle* (rum baba with plums). The hosts are kind and welcoming, and the bedrooms stunning.

12–1.30, 7.30–9; closed Mon and Tue, Thu, Fri eve; closed mid-Nov to Christmas and 3 weeks in Jan
L €55, D €105, Wine €30

QUIBERON

LA CRIÉE

11 quai de l'Océan, Port-Maria, 56170 Quiberon
Tel 02 97 30 53 09

If you're tired of over-elaborate food, you couldn't find anything more delicious or straightforward than Michel Lucas's superb fresh seafood direct from the fish market opposite his acclaimed restaurant on Quiberon harbour. You'll be served the catch of the day (on display at the adjacent *poissonnerie*), so no menus or prices are printed. Products from the chef's highly regarded smokery just up the road are also worth trying (▷ 119).

12.15–2, 7.15–9.30; closed Sun eve, Mon (lunch only Jul, Aug), first half of Dec and Jan
L €16, D €16, Wine €12

LA ROCHE-BERNARD

LE P'TIT MARIN

Quai de la Douane, 56130 La Roche-Bernard
Tel 02 99 90 79 41

This pretty *crêperie-moulerie* is sandwiched in a row of eateries down by the waterfront. Its terrace is filled with tables in summer, but otherwise you eat upstairs in an attractive little dining room. Inventive *crêpes* place an emphasis on seafood: Oysters go for €8 per half-dozen, a Cockpit contains scallops, and a Grande-Voile contains mussels, prawns and crab. A children's menu is available.

Open daily 12–2, 7–9.30
L €15, D €15, Wine €12

SARZEAU

L'HORTENSIA

47 route de La Grée, Penvins, 56370 Sarzeau
Tel 02 97 67 42 15
www.lhortensia.com

In a remote village on the Atlantic seaboard of the Rhuys peninsula, this secluded little restaurant attracts a surprising amount of trade. Hydrangea (*hortensia*) designs in blue fabrics, soft lighting and classical music create an atmosphere of refined, intimate charm in the twin dining rooms of this charming stonebuilt house. Menus, starting at around €20 (lunchtime only) but ranging much higher, show the chef's confident, inventive ways with both meat and shellfish. Specialities include *goujonettes* of sole in sesame or asparagus in parmesan.

Jul, Aug daily 12.15–1.30, 7.15–8.30; Sep–end Jun Wed–Sun 12.15–1.30, 7.15–8.30; closed 2 weeks Nov–Dec
L €20, D €58, Wine €21

LA-TRINITÉ-SUR-MER

OSTREA

Cours des Quais, 56470 La-Trinité-sur-Mer
Tel 02 97 55 73 23
www.hotel-ostrea.com

The enterprising seafood brasserie attached to a ship-shape little Logis de France hotel caters mainly for the marina-users of this popular sailing resort. Food is served all day every day from early breakfasts until late at night. Admire your yacht (or somebody else's) from the stylish glazed upper deck or terrace. Menus are sensibly priced from €16, and there are weekday *plats du jour* and *formules*, multifarious ice creams and fresh camembert. Specialities include *carpaccio de saumon* (thinly sliced salmon) and *choucroute de la mer* (seafood sauerkraut). The style is casually smart, and the atmosphere constantly buzzing. Downstairs, under the same management, is a good pizzeria.

Daily 8am–midnight
L €16, D €32, Wine €12

VANNES

BREIZH CAFFÉ

13 rue des Halles, 56000 Vannes
Tel 02 97 54 37 41

Hemmed in by similarly antique buildings in one of Vannes' oldest and quaintest streets, this fine brasserie is ideal for a quick lunch while sightseeing, though food is not served all day. Within the ancient stone-and-timber architecture, the interior is cool

and contemporary with bold splashes of primary colour. The traditional menu of regional dishes costs €18, but there's also a simple lunchtime *formule* including a main course, a cake and a hot drink, and a child menu too. À la carte selections include *moules* in lots of ways, and *assiettes composées* (cold cuts and salads). For pudding, try the house Mamich butter cake with apples, the iced nougat with raspberry sauce or a whole crottin de Chavignol goat's cheese.

Mon–Sat 12–2, 7–10.30
L €10, D €14, Wine €14

ROSCANVEC

17 rue des Halles, 56000 Vannes
Tel 02 97 47 15 96

A door or two away from the Breizh Caffé, this beamy old property is one of Vannes' most reputable and consistent restaurants.

The talented chef-patron serves ambitious and expensive fare, reflecting whatever's best in the nearby marketplace. You might sample the boned oxtail, or turbot in honey crust. The main dining room is upstairs, though you can see what's cooking at street level. It is not too grand to provide high chairs, and some items can be bought to take out.

Jul, Aug Mon–Sat 12.15–1.30, 7.15–9.30; Sep–end Jun Tue–Sat 12.15–1.30, 7.15–9.30; Sun 12.15–1.30; closed Christmas
L €17, D €24, Wine €23

FINISTÈRE

PRICES AND SYMBOLS

The restaurants are listed alphabetically within each town. The prices given for lunch (L) and dinner (D) are for three courses for one person, without drinks. The wine price is for the least expensive bottle.

For a key to the symbols, ▷ 2.

BREST

AMOUR DE POMME DE TERRE

23 rue des Halles, 29200 Brest
Tel 02 98 43 48 51

The humble *pomme de terre* assumes many varied guises at this young-at-heart, potato-themed restaurant. It's popular with hungry students, and sailors on shore leave. Ingredients are imaginatively combined, and often alcoholic, so the bill can mount higher than expected, but servings are huge, and fixed-price menus inexpensive. Specialities

include do-it-yourself chargrills, raclettes and deli-style salads.

Daily 12–2, 7.15–11, closed Sun lunch
L €15, D €21, Wine €8

MA PETITE FOLIE

Port du Moulin Blanc, 29200 Brest
Tel 02 98 42 44 42

This fine old crayfish boat permanently moored in the pleasure harbour near Océanopolis has been put to good use as a smart gourmet restaurant. As you might expect, seafood predominates on its menus (*soupe de poisson*, stuffed clams). You can

EATING

dine on either deck, but be sure to book ahead in high season.

Daily 12–2, 7.30–10; closed two weeks in Jan

L € 15, D €27, Wine €18.50

CONCARNEAU

L'AMIRAL

1 avenue Pierre Guéguen, 29900 Concarneau

Tel 02 98 60 55 23

www.restaurant-amiral.com

Smart bar-restaurant overlooking the Ville Close, nautically decorated with handsome panelling, designer lamps and models of old sailboats. The bar is decorated with a mosaic underwater scene. The menu changes daily, but always features top-notch seafood and home-made bread. Wines come by the glass, and the lunchtime *formules* are good value. Reserve ahead in summer; both French and British visitors love the place, which was once immortalized in a story featuring Georges Simenon's most famous character, Inspector Maigret.

Jul, Aug Tue–Sun 12–1.30, 7–9.30; Sep–end Jun Tue–Sat 12–1.30, 7–9.30, Sun 12–1.30; closed 2 weeks Jan–Feb and Sep–Oct

L €17, D €27, Wine €15

LE PETIT CHAPERON ROUGE

7 Place Duguesclin, 29900 Concarneau

Tel 02 98 60 53 32

This popular *crêperie* is shoehorned into a tiny square not far from the Ville Close. As the name implies, there's a Little Red Riding Hood theme here, so miniature baskets and rustic nick-nacks dangle everywhere. Its reputation, however, stems from its top-quality *crêpes* rather than the winsome interior. *La Blanchette* includes goat's cheese, spinach, ham and cream, while the house special, *Petit Chaperon Rouge*, contains chocolate fondue and

almonds. English-speaking staff make visitors very welcome.

Tue–Sat 12–2.30, 7–9.30; Sun 12–2.30; closed 2 weeks Mar, 2 weeks mid Jun, 3 weeks Oct

L €10, D €10, Wine €9

CROZON

HOSTELLERIE DE LA MER

Le Fret 29160 Crozon

Tel 02 98 27 61 90

www.hostelleriedelamer.com

You couldn't do better than arrive here at lunchtime (but reserve ahead!) for a ringside view of the Rade de Brest from the picture windows of this family-run hotel-restaurant. The dining room is spacious and light, with pink walls and carved Breton furnishings. As the lobster tank indicates, menus are mainly fishy.

Daily lunch, dinner

L€14, D €12, Wine €12, Cider €6

SPECIAL IN CROZON

LE MUTIN GOURMAND

Place de l'Église, 29160 Crozon

Tel 02 98 27 29 29

www.chez.com/mutingourmand

An elegant place decorated to reflect sunshine and seaside with exposed stonework, contemporary watercolours and clever use of mirror-glass. Acclaimed menus echo *mer* or *terre* (yellow pollack with black wheat pancakes, egg *chaud-froid* with sea urchin corals, pigeon pie with warm foie gras). There's an eye-popping wine-list. The attached hotel rooms reach equally high standards.

Tue 7–9, Wed–Sat 12–1.30, 7–9, Sun 12–1.30; closed 5 weeks starting 5 Jan

L €40, D €48, Wine €14

DOUARNENEZ

LE VIVIER

49 boulevard Camille Réaud, Le Port-Rhu, 29100 Douarnenez

Tel 02 98 92 73 72

Overlooking Port-Rhu and the floating boat museum, this stone-built restaurant is run by a charming Provençal couple. A central fish tank makes a talking point, and there are mezzanine tables. Menus include plenty of seafood with a hint of southern France: bouillabaisse, *bouquet de crevettes mayonnaise* or *calamar farci*. The atmosphere is pleasantly unstuffy, and many languages are spoken.

Wed–Mon 12–2.30, 7–9.30

L €22, D €29, Wine €14

GUIMILIAU

AR CHUPEN

43 rue du Calvaire, 29400 Guimiliau

Tel 02 98 68 73 63

This popular pancake restaurant occupies a renovated farmhouse by Guimiliau's famous parish close, decorated in *paysanne* style with copper pictures and antique furniture. The house special is artichokes with various accompaniments. A *Fermier* has ham, bacon, mushrooms and cream, while a *Léonard* or a *Royale* are based on seafood. Finish your meal with *chouchen* (mead served in a horn). When the restaurant fills up, the gregarious chef may come out of the kitchen to play his accordion.

Jun–Aug daily 12–10; Sun–Fri 12–2, Sat 12–10 rest of year

L €16, D €22, Wine €11

HUELGOAT

CRÉPERIE DE L'ARGOAT

12 rue du Lac, 29690 Huelgoat

Tel 02 98 99 71 72

www.creperie-argoat.com

This small *crêperie*, dating from 1949, has a rustic setting of wood furnishings. When the weather is pleasant you can sit out on the terrace overlooking the lake. Its large range of sweet and savoury *crêpes* include the Pirate (chitterling sausage and mustard) and the *Océane* (scallops with vegetables).

May–Sep daily 11–10; Mon 11–2, Wed–Sun 11–8 rest of year; closed for 2 weeks in Oct

L €10, D €15, Wine €8

LAMPAUL-GUIMILIAU

L'ESCAPADE

8 Place de Villers, 29400 Lampaul-Guimiliau
Tel 02 98 68 61 27

The best restaurant in the village stands by the town hall, its mellow dining space spread over two floors of an attractive yellow-painted house with green awnings. Specials include goulash soup and Finistère ostrich steaks. They also serve *crêpes* with unusual fillings such as prunes and smoked bacon. A *Lampaulaise* contains salmon and leek fondue, while *Le Forêt Noir* is a calorific concoction of cherry, Amarena, chocolate and whipped cream.

Tue, Thu, Fri 12–1.30, 7–8.30, Wed 12–1.30, Sat, Sun 12–1.30, 7–9; closed 3 weeks in Aug

L €10, D €34, Wine €12

MORLAIX

BRASSERIE DE L'EUROPE

Place Emile Souvestre, 29600 Morlaix
Tel 02 98 88 81 15
www.brasseriedeleurope.com

This bright, elegant two-tier café-brasserie shares premises with the hotel of the same name (▷ 169), but is separately managed. Stylish and sophisticated, it specializes mainly in seafood. You can have a full meal here, or simply graze on a *tarte salée*, a platter of smoked fish or half a dozen oysters. During happy hour (6–8pm) drinks are dispensed at half price in the downstairs wine-bar, including wines by the glass.

Mon–Sat 12–2, 7–10; bar open all day in season (Mon–Sat 10–1am)

L €17, D €23, Wine €12

L'HERMINE

35 rue Ange de Guernisac, 29600 Morlaix
Tel 02 98 88 10 91

There's no shortage of eateries on this picturesque cobbled *venelle* (alley), but this charming *crêperie* is unlikely to disappoint. In a quaint stone building, its rustic interior is decked with flowers, model boats and bric-à-brac. The welcome is warm, and service courteous (good English spoken). Pancakes are always freshly cooked and galettes made with genuine Breton buckwheat. Try a *Forestière* (lardons in bechamel sauce), or one of the house specials made with seaweed. There's terrace dining in fine weather.

Daily 12–2; 7–9.30 (10 on Fri and Sat, and every day in high season)

Crêpes €4–9.50, Wine €12

PONT-AVEN

TAHITI

21 rue de la Belle Angèle, 29930 Pont-Aven
Tel 02 98 06 15 93

Drawing on the Gauguin theme, this small restaurant run by a Breton–Tahitian couple offers an exotic combination of local and South Sea island cuisine. The pretty dining room is decorated with fresh flowers and Polynesian pictures. Dishes include Tahitian-style fish and *Tai Pen Lou* (Chinese fondue). Try Hinano beer, an island brew. A takeout service is available.

Wed–Sat 12.15–1.30, 7.15–9.30, Sun 7.15–9.30 (also open Tue in season); closed first 2 weeks in Feb and first 2 weeks in Nov

L €13, D €20, Wine €11

QUIMPERLÉ

BISTRO DE LA TOUR

2 rue Dom-Morice, 29300 Quimperlé
Tel 02 98 39 29 58
www.hotelvintage.com

This atmospheric restaurant and wine cellar stands on a street crammed with similar ancient timbered buildings. It has two split-level dining rooms, one on the ground floor in art deco style, and an upstairs one decked with paintings by the Pont-Aven school. Dishes include oysters or a Breton *cassoulet* with *andouille* sausages. Allow yourself enough time to read through the wine list, which has a staggering 700 entries. Takeout cooked dishes are available.

Tue–Fri 12.15–1.45, 7.30–9, Sat 7.30–9, Sun 12–1.45

L €17, D €29, Wine €15

RIEC-SUR-BÉLON

CHEZ JACKY

Port de Bélon, 29340 Riec-sur-Bélon
Tel 02 98 06 90 32
www.chez-jacky.com

This well-known seafood-rearing enterprise has a popular on-site brasserie overlooking the Bélon waterfront. In these idyllic surroundings, you can sample home-grown oysters, lobsters and shellfish on sturdy wooden benches and tables, then take some away with you. Reserve ahead in high season. Children are welcome, but don't ask for a steak here.

Easter–end Sep Tue–Sat lunch and dinner, and Sun lunch

L €17, D €36.50, Wine €15.50

ROSCOFF

CHEZ JANIE

Le Port, 29680 Roscoff
Tel 02 98 61 24 25
www.chezjanie.com

This informal, convivial bar-restaurant on Roscoff's old port has long been a popular watering hole for locals and visitors alike. It is now managed by the Chapalain family (Hôtel Brittany, ▷ 169), and offers an undaunting mix of drinks and snacks *(rillettes de saumon, tartare de poissons)*, salads, oysters and good-value *plats du jour*. Children's menus might include a *steak haché* (hamburger) or *jambon frites* (ham and chips). The practical, modern bedrooms at the attached Hôtel du Centre are terrific value.

Jul–Aug daily 12–2, 7–9.30; Mon, Wed–Sat 12–2, 7–9.30, Sun 12–2 rest of year. Closed mid Nov–mid Dec and 5 Jan–1 Feb

L €15, D €15, Wine €15

ST-POL-DE-LÉON

AUBERGE DE LA POMME D'API

49 rue Verderel, 29250 St-Pol-de-Léon
Tel 02 98 69 04 36

This 16th-century building has an elegant interior with a large fireplace and exposed stone walls. The food is a treat, but you'd better brush up on your French as dishes are elaborately concocted and equally elaborately named; *dos de bar, cuit sur peau* (sea bass), *légumes oubliés* (forgotten vegetables!) and *cèpes et saucisse de Morteau* (cep mushrooms and smoked sausage). Fish dishes include wild turbot or local lobster. Vegetarian and children's options are available.

Tue–Sat 12–2, 7.30–9, Sun 12–2

L €22, D €60, Wine €15

CÔTES D'ARMOR

PRICES AND SYMBOLS

The restaurants are listed alphabetically within each town. The prices given for lunch (L) and dinner (D) are for three courses for one person, without drinks. The wine price is for the least expensive bottle.

For a key to the symbols, ▷ 2.

DINAN

CAFÉ TERRASSES

2–4 rue du Quai, 22100 Port de Dinan
Tel 02 96 39 09 60

On the port beside the bridge, this bright all-day bistro is deservedly popular, as much for its flexible range of straightforward, well-prepared food and friendly welcome as its enticing location. A tented terrace with cane chairs caters for fine weather. Inside is a *petit zinc* style bar with banquette seating, enlivened with typical café posters. A lunchtime *formule* might include *steak frites* followed by an ice cream. Alternatively you could choose oysters or *crevettes roses* with an aperitif, or have an omelette or pasta with salad.

Jul, Aug daily 8am–1am; Sep–end Jun daily 9am–1am

L €25, D €35, Wine €14

SPECIAL IN DINAN

CHEZ LA MÈRE POURCEL

3 Place des Merciers, 22100 Dinan
Tel 02 96 39 03 80

Occupying a splendid old merchant's house on one of Dinan's quaintest squares, this restaurant is a long-established temple of gastronomy. The lovely winding staircase is a listed monument in its own right. The best tables are the round ones near the fireplace, with Louis XIII-style chairs. La Mère Pourcel specializes in *pré-salé* lamb fresh from Mont-St-Michel, available from April to the end of September. Other temptations are lobster, local fish and scallops in autumn and winter. Reservations are essential in high season.

Jul, Aug daily 12–2, 7–9.30; mid-Mar to end Jun, Sep Tue–Sat 12–2, 7–9.30, Sun 12–2; Oct to mid-Mar Wed–Sat 12–2, 7–9.30, Sun 12–2

L €20, D €62, Wine €13

LE ROMARIN

11 Place des Cordeliers, 22100 Dinan
Tel 02 96 85 20 37

These welcoming tea rooms in the heart of the old town are run by a mother-and-daughter team. The interior is tastefully decorated in rustic style with dried flowers and sheaves of corn. The delicious cake display will make your mouth water, but the superb feather-light tartes salées served with crisp salads deserve a try. A special dessert is a *macaron fourré au caramel*. The house wine is also excellent. In summer, Le Romarin opens in the evenings too. Takeout service.

Jul–Aug Sun–Fri 9–6, Sat 9am–9pm; Sun–Fri 11–6, Sat 11–9 rest of year

L €10, D €15, Wine €15

ERQUY

L'ESCURIAL

29 Boulevard de la Mer, 22430 Erquy
Tel 02 96 72 31 56
www.lescurial.com

Easily spotted on the seafront road next to the tourist office, this is one of the best restaurants in the area. The dining room is furnished with comfortable seating in green-and-white leather. Renowned for seasonal scallops (an Erquy special), it serves many other classic seafood dishes. Menus range from €22 to €56.

Jul, Aug Tue–Sun lunch 12–2.30, dinner 7.30–9.30; Sep–end Jun Tue–Sat lunch, dinner, Sun lunch; closed 2 weeks in Jan

L €20, D €56, Wine €18

ÎLE DE BREHAT

L'OISEAU DES ÎLES

Rue du Port, 22870 Île de Bréhat
Tel 02 96 20 00 53

This popular *crêperie* is in a blue-shuttered building just 10 minutes from the port, distinguished by a large puffin sign. Inside, the bare walls of pink granite complement the blue windows and doors. In fine weather you can eat on the terrace. Besides basic *crêpes* (ham, cheese, mushroom), it serves specials such as *andouille* (Breton sausage) and salads. Reservations recommended in summer.

Tue–Sun 12–2, 7–10 late Jun–mid Oct; closed mid Oct–late Jun exc school hols, hours as above

L €10, D €10, Wine €12

MÛR-DE-BRETAGNE

AUBERGE GRAND'MAISON

1 rue Léon-le-Cerf, 22530 Mûr-de-Bretagne
Tel 02 96 28 51 10

This highly regarded restaurant-with-rooms near the church is about as far from the sea as you can get in Brittany, but Jacques Guillo still seems to include plenty of fish in his inventive repertoire. House specials include Erquy lobster with wild mushrooms, and *langoustines royales*. Eating here is a serious gastronomic undertaking, so don't expect low prices. But for a treat, this is well worth tracking down. Reserve ahead.

Jul, Aug Tue–Sat lunch 12.30–2.30, dinner 7–9, Sun lunch; Sep–end Jun closed also Tue

L €76, D €140, Wine €30

PAIMPOL

LA COTRIADE

16 quai Armand Dayot, 22500 Paimpol
Tel 02 96 20 81 08
www.la-cotriade-paimpol.com

A well-kept stone building with a terrace overlooking the harbour. Inside lie double-decker dining rooms (smoking permitted upstairs) with bright stripy plates. Expect some decent fish cookery here, with the catch of the day ending up in dishes such as *marmite Paimpolaise*. Menus are named after classic sailing ships—a *Vieux Copain* costs €23 and a *Belle Poule* €43. Afterwards, try a *confit de*

pommes façon tatin with *crème fraiche battue au Calvados.*
Tue–Thu, Sun 12–2, 7–9, Fri 12–2, Sat 7–9; also open Fri 7–9 in season
L €24, D €32, Wine €18

L'ECLUSE
Quai Armand Dayot, 22500 Paimpol
Tel 02 96 55 03 38
Hidden amid the boatyards and chandleries by the harbour lock-gates, this light, airy shed-like building attracts discerning locals. Here fresh seafood is cooked before your eyes on an open hearth, and a roll of kitchen towel takes the place of a napkin. Breton sea shanties or soft jazz plays in the background, and nautical netting drapes around the ceiling fans. Blackboard suggestions show what's just swum in; the bread is fresh and warm and puddings are reassuringly familiar *(tarte tatin, poire belle Hélène)*. A real find, so don't tell anyone.
Jul–Aug daily 12–3, 7–11; Sep–end Jun daily 12–2, 7–10; closed Wed in June
L €9.50, D €32, Wine €10

PERROS-GUIREC

LA CRÉMAILLÈRE
13 Place de l'Église, 22700 Perros-Guirec
Tel 02 96 23 22 08

The two dining rooms are in a 17th-century building on the main square by the church, where dark tones, low ceilings and a rustic interior give a warm atmosphere. The menu changes with the seasons and is based around fresh seafood and chargrilled meat. Dishes to try include scallop kebab with smoked duck breast, roast beef and coffee tart with a citrus marmalade. In summer it's best to reserve a table.
Mon, Sat 7–10, Tue–Fri, Sun 12–2, 7–10
L €16, D €16, Wine €14

PLANCOËT

JEAN-PIERRE CROUZIL
20 Les Quais, 22130 Plancoët
Tel 02 96 84 10 24
www.crouzil.com
Foodies track down this restaurant some way inland to sample Jean-Pierre's top-flight cooking. It's a classy place with elegant glass and china, sculpted bronzes and designer flowers, but the welcome is warm and unpretentious. You might order foie gras with onion jam and grenadine, milk-fed lamb, lobster in Belgian beer, or hot oysters in a Vouvray zabaglione. Puddings ring the changes on chocolate, and the bread is all home-made. A virgin-pure brand of mineral water is bottled here, and some beautiful hotel rooms preclude the need to stagger any distance from the table.
Jul–Aug Mon 7.30–9.30, Tue 7.30–9.30, Wed–Sat 12.30–2.30, 7.30–9.30, Sun 12.30–2.30; Sep–Jun Wed–Sat lunch, dinner, Sun lunch (times as above); closed early Oct, mid-Jan
L €60, D €120, Wine €35

PLOUMANAC'H

COSTE MOR
Plage de St-Guirec, 22700 Ploumanac'h
Tel 02 96 91 65 55
Despite its name, this restaurant offers remarkable value in a matchless location overlooking the beach at St-Guirec, surely one of Brittany's most amazing seascapes (▷ 146–7). Enjoy a glass of wine and a *plateau de fruits de mer* at the stone tables and benches on the terrace, or some hot *soupe de poissons* inside. Child menus available.
Apr–Oct daily 12–2, 7.30–9.30; closed mid Nove–end Mar
L €13, D €13, Wine €13

ST-BRIEUC

AUX PESKED
59 rue du Légué, 22000 St-Brieuc
Tel: 02 96 33 34 65
www.auxpesked.com
Look for the grotesque fish on the hill leading from the heart of the city down to the port. The modern building overlooks the valley, with terrace tables outside in summer. It's a sophisticated, arty setting for accomplished contemporary cuisine. Much use is made of seafood, but classic Breton dishes also include local specials such as *cocos de Paimpol* (haricot beans) or *andouille*. The cellar has a daunting array of some 15,000 bottles (particularly Loire wines). Puddings are ornate and extravagant.
Tue–Fri lunch, dinner, Sat dinner, Sun lunch; closed first half of Jan, a week in early May and another in early Sep
L €42, D €52 Wine €16

TRÉGUIER

LE HANGAR
Port de Plaisance, 22220 Tréguier
Tel 02 96 92 47 46

Next to the harbourmaster's office down at the marina, this battered old wooden boatshed is suitably nautical in style. It serves no-nonsense fare such as *moules, tartes* and *assiettes de fruits de mer*. You could have a *brandade de morue* (cod puree) here, or stuffed clams from the Chausey islands. Local Dremmwell beers have a keen following.
Jul, Aug daily 12–2, 7–9.30; Sep–end Jun Wed–Sun lunch, dinner (times above)
L €15, D €20, Wine €11

LES TROIS RIVIÈRES
Port de Plaisance, 22220 Tréguier
Tel 02 96 92 97 00
www.aiguemarine.fr

There's a talented young chef at the restaurant belonging to the Aigues Marine Hotel (▷ 172) down on the quayside. Seafood predominates in

its light, modern dining-room, for example a double fillet of sole in a Viennese crust or some roast langoustines. Afterwards, you might toy with a crumble of William pears, or a *tarte fine aux pommes*. Prices are surprisingly reasonable for a four-star hotel, and child menus are available.
Mon–Fri 12.30–1.30, 7.30–9, Sat 7.30–9, Sun 12.30–1.30
L €27.50, D €52, Wine €15

LE VAL-ANDRÉ

ART & SAVEUR

28 quai des Terre-Neuvas, Port de Dahouët, 22370 Pléneuf-Val-André
Tel 02 96 63 19 17

In a converted sail-loft overlooking Val-André's old port of Dahouët, this enjoyable and deceptively sophisticated place is an art gallery, daytime café and wine-bar-cum-bistro, serving a lively mix of simple but interesting menus with an

oriental tang. Light meals (*tartines,* mixed platters, cheeses and puddings) can be ordered with wines by the glass. It also does breakfasts, popular with marina users. There are board games and cards, books and magazines, and arty happenings from time to time (jazz soirées or art exhibitions).
Jul, Aug daily 10am–10pm; closed Sun eve rest of year
L €15 (main courses €7–€14), D €20, Wine €16

ILLE-ET-VILAINE

PRICES AND SYMBOLS

The restaurants are listed alphabetically within each town. The prices given for lunch (L) and dinner (D) are for three courses for one person, without drinks. The wine price is for the least expensive bottle.

For a key to the symbols, ▷ 2.

CANCALE

MAISONS DE BRICOURT

See Special Panel ▷ 162

LE SURCOUF

7 quai Gambetta, 35260 Cancale
Tel 02 99 89 61 75

This is not the least expensive of the restaurants lining the picturesque old port of La Houle, but definitely one of the

best. The small granite building with its apron terrace, tastefully decked in blue and white, can offer you the *assiette de fruits de mer* of a lifetime, or an equally delicious roast lobster or house foie gras. Menus range from €18–€42, and much is made of local oysters. There are good wines from the Loire, and Breton cider too.
Jul–Aug 12–2.30; 7–10.30; Fri–Tue 12–2.30; 7–10.30 rest of year
L €40, D €50, Wine €19

COMBOURG

L'ECRIVAIN

Place St-Gilduin, 35270 Combourg
Tel 02 99 73 01 61

To find this place, head for the church on the main street. One dining room is panelled and candlelit; a larger salon faces the garden. Gilles Menier's reputation has crystallized over many years, but prices are still reasonable for such inventive, tasty cooking based on fresh local ingredients. Try the home-smoked fish or a *mille-feuille de canard au foie gras.* Set menus range from €14.60, or you can just have a *plat du jour* with a glass of wine. You can buy cakes to eat in or take out. The literary theme stems from local writer Chateaubriand.
Mid Jul–mid Aug Fri–Wed 12–2, 7–10; Fri–Sat 12–2, 7–9.30, Sun 12–2, Mon–Tue 7–9.30, Wed 12–2 rest of year
L €15, D €35, Wine €11

DINARD

DIDIER MÉRIL

6 rue Yves Verney, 35800 Dinard
Tel 02 99 46 95 74

The dynamic young chef who gives his name to this restaurant has made quite a hit in this exclusive Emerald Coast enclave. The modern premises are fashionably sleek and minimalist, with an elegant terrace close to the beach and casino. Service is polished but affable. Regularly changing menus include plenty of seafood. The home-made rolls (eight types) are hard to resist, but save room for a pudding *(moêlleux au chocolat, caramel à l'orange)*. There's a good-value weekday lunch *formule* (€20).
Thu–Tue lunch, dinner (also open Wed in school hols); closed Dec–Jan
L €30, D €50, Wine €17

FOUGÈRES

LE BUFFET

53 bis, rue Nationale, 35300 Fougères
Tel 02 99 94 35 76

On the main street by the church of St-Léonard in the upper town, this modest little establishment is terrific value, and will set you up for tackling that steep hill to the castle. The interior is decked with old photos and pictures, ancient coffee grinders and similar relics, and a handsome stone fireplace dispenses a warm glow on chilly days. Choose from a generous buffet display of entrées, hors d'oeuvres and desserts. Several simple menus all include a quarter bottle of wine, and there's a *plat du jour*.

Mon–Sat 12–1.45, 7–9.15, Wed lunch only

L €16.50, D €19, Wine €9

REDON

L'AKÈNE

10 rue de Jeu-de-Paume, 35600 Redon
Tel 02 99 71 25 15

This little *crêperie* tucked away in a tiny alley in the old port is set in a charming stone house with red shutters. The atmosphere is welcoming and the pancakes very good value. An After Eight *crêpe* includes chocolate and *glace de menthe*. Besides pancakes, it does salads, ices and superb raclettes (minimum two people).

Jul–Aug daily 12–2, 6.45–9.30; closed Tue, Wed dinner, rest of year

L €10, D €15, Wine €8

LA BOGUE

3 rue des Etats, 35600 Redon
Tel 02 99 71 12 95

In a flower-decked old stone building on the main square by the church, this welcoming place has an excellent reputation for value and traditional country cooking. You might get a *blanquette de veau à l'ancienne façon du chef* (veal in cream and mushroom sauce) or a *soufflé chaud à l'orange au Grand Marnier*. The nterior is rustic and delightfully old-fashioned. Look out for interesting ways with chestnuts (a local speciality) in late autumn.

Mon–Wed, Fri, Sat lunch, dinner; Sun lunch

L €16, D €21.50, Wine €16

RENNES

CAFÉ BRETON

14 rue Nantaise, 35000 Rennes
Tel 02 99 30 74 95

Hidden away in a street near the *halles* off Place des Lices, the dark-blue frontage of this *bistrot* is thronged with locals most lunchtimes, so it's best to book. Bustling with life inside, the dining space is nicely broken up and full of interest with china displays in alcove shelving, and posters against sunshine-yellow walls.

Chalkboard specials might include a *tagine de saumon et cabillaud* (salmon and cod), or *rillettes de thon et salade* (tuna mayonnaise). Excellent wines. Its friendly owner-chef is very much in evidence.

Mon 12–4, Tue–Fri 12–3, 7–11, Sat 12–4; closed 3 weeks in Aug and 2 weeks in Mar

L €15, D €20, Wine €13

Sainte-Anne

SPECIAL IN CANCALE

MAISONS DE BRICOURT

1 rue Duguesclin, 35260 Cancale
Tel 02 99 89 64 76
www.maisons-de-bricourt.com

Olivier Roellinger conquered the heights of France's gastronomic scene years ago,

and operates several celebrated enterprises around Cancale (▷ 94). His family home, a gracious 18th-century *malouinière* in a quiet residential street, is now a theatre for the *maître cuisinier's* most accomplished productions. Local seafood is naturally part of his stock in trade, but the subtle admixture of flavours and spices have travelled the world (for example John Dory steamed in seaweed and coconut milk). Reserve ahead for a memorable experience.

Jul, Aug Wed–Mon 12–1.30, 7–9; closed mid Dec–mid Mar; telephone for availability Sep–Jun

L €92, D €158, Wine €95

LE BOCAL-P'TY RESTO

6 rue d'Argentré, 35000 Rennes
Tel 02 99 78 34 10

Jars *(bocaux)* filled with shells and glass beads give this friendly restaurant its name. Inventive dishes run to fare like seafood muffins or *crumble au moment*, and the menu changes frequently. *Petit plats* cost €7.50; and there are *formules* from €10 at lunchtime. The well-chosen wines are all served by the glass. Upbeat young staff.

Tue–Fri 12–2, 7.30–10.30, Sat 7.30–11

L €16, D €22, Wine €12.50

République

LE KHALIFA

20 Place des Lices, 35000 Rennes
Tel 02 99 30 87 30

An agreeable Moroccan restaurant on lively Place des Lices, serving hearty platefuls of couscous, brochettes and delicately scented tagines at remarkable prices (a midday *formule* goes for as little as €8). Small wonder it's often full of hungry students. The levantine pastries are worth trying for dessert. North African furnishings and music, smiling

staff and a complimentary glass of sangria will put you in a good mood. The service is prompt and friendly.
Tue–Sun 12–2, 7–11; closed 3 weeks in Aug
L €16, D €20, Wine €12
Sainte-Anne

AU MARCHÉ DES LICES
3 Place du Bas des Lices, 35000 Rennes
Tel 02 99 30 42 95

An excellent *crêperie* in the marketplace, handily placed for shopping and sightseeing. The simple, rustic dining room has an open fireplace and a display of old coffee-pots. An Argoat contains *andouille,* cream and cheese, and strong cider is served in breakfast cups. If you're fed up with pancakes, the *plat du jour* (a classic beef stew with carrots, perhaps) is excellent value at lunchtime, but there are no starters or formal menus. Friendly service.
Mon–Sat 12–7, closed 3 weeks Aug, 2 weeks Jan
Crêpe and a pudding around €10; a pitcher of cider from €7.20
Sainte-Anne

ST-LUNAIRE

LE DÉCOLLÉ
1 pointe du Décollé, 35800 St-Lunaire
Tel 02 99 46 01 70
Panoramic views over the Emerald Coast enhance this popular seafood place on a scenic rocky promontory. The nearby *crêperie* and a disco in a thatched cottage provide other reasons to make your way here. In the glazed dining room or summer terraces of Le Décollé you can try roast cod or a ragout of lamb. Menus range from €19 to €36.
Jul, Aug Tue–Sun lunch, dinner; Sep to mid-Nov, Feb–end Jun Wed–Sun lunch, dinner
L €19, D €36, Wine €16

ST-MALO

LA BRIGANTINE
13 rue de Dinan, 35000 St-Malo
Tel 02 99 56 82 82

Soothingly decorated in light colours with pictures of sailing ships on the walls, this pleasant *crêperie* has a well-established reputation. It occupies a stone building in the heart of the walled town. Pancakes cost as little as €1.55 at the simple end of the scale, up to €8.10 for a super *malouine* with egg, ham, cheese and much else besides. You can have omelettes, or warm Chavignol goat's cheese with a glass of sauvignon, if you prefer. A prix-fixe menu costs €9.65; a junior menu €5.15.
Jul, Aug daily 12–3, 6.30–11; Sep–end Jun Thu–Mon 12–3, 6.30–11; closed late Nov and most of Jan
L €10, D €15, Wine €9

LES EMBRUNS
120 chaussée du Sillon, 35400 St-Malo
Tel 02 99 56 33 57

Seafood dishes are served here in a salmon-pink painted dining room close to the beach, on Paramé's hotel strip. The menu follows the seasons, but some classics are fat scampi with mayonnaise, lightly salted salmon with asparagus and lamb's kidneys with purple Brive mustard. Alternatively you can choose your meal from the lobster tank on display. You could even come away with more than a good meal as the artwork on the walls is for sale.
Tue–Sat 12–2, 7–10, Sun 12–2, all year
L €19, D €19, Wine €15

VITRÉ

LE CHÊNE VERT
2 Place du Général de Gaulle, 35500 Vitré
Tel 02 23 55 14 62
The cheerful yellow awnings of this handy brasserie are one of the first things you'll see after you've parked (as most people do) at the station and visited the tourist office. The stylish interior, split into several bar-dining zones, uses bright modern furnishings, pictures, mirrors and flowers to good effect. Menus offer a flexible range of simple but imaginative fish and meat dishes and a *vin du mois* (wine of the month). Tasty *tartines*, salads, omelettes and soups set you up for exploring the old town. The pleasant young team provide prompt, agreeable service. There's also a sunny terrace.
Daily 9am–midnight
L €12, D €15, Wine €12

TAVERNE DE L'ECU
12 rue de la Baudrairie, 35500 Vitré
Tel 02 99 75 11 09
This restaurant is in a beautiful 16th-century building with two dining rooms, each with a large fireplace and exposed beams. The menu changes with the seasons, and everything is made on the premises, even the bread. You might be tempted by the roasted rabbit leg with white beans and dried Italian tomatoes, boar fillet with salad and spicy apple chutney or catch of the day with preserved tomatoes. Extensive wine list.
Thu–Mon 12.15–1.45, 7.30–9, lunch Tue, Jul–Aug; Thu–Sat 12.15–1.45, 7.30–9, Sun 12.15–1.45, Mon 12.15–1.45, 7.30–9, Tue 12.15–1.45 rest of year
L €23, D €30, Wine €12

STAYING IN BRITTANY

This popular holiday destination offers a wealth of accomodation to suit every budget, from small *pensions* in countryside villages to top–quality balneotherapy spas overlooking the sea. Brittany caters particularly well to self-catering family holidaymakers in *gîtes* and campsites. Chain hotels are less widespread than in other parts of France, but are well represented in ferry ports and some larger towns.

The River Leguer in Lannion (left), a waterside château (middle) and boats on the beach (right)

CLASSIFICATION

Registered hotels are inspected regularly and classified into six categories: no star, 1*, 2*, 3*, 4* and 4*L (Luxury). Don't attach too much importance to star-ratings. They give some idea of the level of facilities you can expect (such as a lift, or 24-hour reception), but are no guide whatever to how pleasant or interesting your stay will be. Some two-star hotels are much more appealing than four-stars, if less luxuriously equipped. For perfectly legitimate reasons, some excellent hotels choose not to register with the local tourist office, and may not be included in official listings.

TARIFFS

On the whole, hotels are much less expensive in France than in Britain, though this may not apply to other types of accommodation. Hotel tariffs are generally quoted per room and not per person, though this doesn't apply if meals are included. Breakfast is nearly always quoted as an optional extra, except of course in *chambres d'hôte* (bed-and-breakfast) accommodation. Young children can sometimes stay free of charge in parents' rooms, but extra beds for adults will attract a supplement, as will pets brought into hotels. Lone visitors nearly always have to pay the full price for a double room; single rooms are unusual and generally inferior.

Hotels must display their rates (including tax) both outside the hotel and in each bedroom. In Brittany, prices vary enormously according to season, and rise sharply in July and August *(haute saison)*. Some hotels give reduced rates for stays of more than one night. Many local authorities impose a small tourist tax, known as a *taxe de séjour*, on visitors staying overnight. This is nearly always quoted separately, and on average may add an extra euro or so to your daily room bill.

Most hotels accept major credit cards belonging to the Carte Bancaire scheme (Visa/Barclaycard, MasterCard/Eurocard), but American Express and Diners Club are less widely favoured. Service is always included in hotel bills; you are under no obligation to leave anything extra as a tip, though many guests leave the spare change if paying by cash.

RESERVATIONS

During busy holiday periods or major festivals, accommodation can be very difficult to find, especially in popular coastal areas. It is advisable to reserve ahead rather than taking pot luck. Advance bookings require some kind of deposit, generally in the form of a credit card number; you may be charged a penalty if you have to cancel or amend your reservation, and should always check the hotel's policy on refunds. The internet has made booking accommodation much easier, especially from overseas, but has its pitfalls. Most places will only guarantee to hold a room for you until a specified time (usually 6pm), so be sure to telephone if you are running late. Many tourist offices will help find local accommodation, but only if you arrive in person, not by phone. A small fee may be charged (deductable from your final bill). Tourist office staff are not allowed to make personal recommendations, and can only book officially registered establishments.

PACKAGES

Many agencies and holiday companies, including Brittany Ferries, organize inclusive package deals, sometimes at lower rates than you could arrange independently. Low-cost flights to small regional airports from the UK have widened the choice of short-break packages available. Many discounted deals are available over the internet.

LUXURY STAYS

Brittany has many fine château hotels. Some belong to well-known groups such as Relais & Châteaux or Châteaux & Hôtels de France (▷ 176). Also at the top end of the range are hedonistic spa resorts, the swanky casino hotels of the Lucien Barrière group, and a few glamorously designed boutique hotels. But these are the exception rather than the rule.

ON A BUDGET

Most hotels in this part of France cater to simple family holidays on the beach or in the countryside, or offer traditional *auberge* hospitality in small towns and villages. Most familiar of these are the Logis de France hotels—pick up a regional list at any tourist office. These small, family-run inns and hotels are individually owned, but subscribe to a charter of agreed standards and are regularly inspected. They pledge to offer a friendly welcome (especially to families and foreign visitors), regional authenticity, value-for-money and good cooking (www.logis-de-france.fr). Low-cost *(économique)* chain hotels are a convenient if far less interesting option (▷ 176).

The canopied entrance to a hotel(left), lemon-drizzled shellfish (middle) and a plush hotel bar (right)

DEALS ON MEALS

Half-board *(demi-pension)* or full-board *(pension)* terms are sometimes obligatory in high season and can often represent excellent value, but may be irksomely restrictive over longer stays. Hotel breakfasts are optional extras and often seriously overpriced; local cafés or bars serve coffee and croissants or pastries at a fraction of the cost.

BED AND BREAKFAST

Chambres d'hôte are France's answer to the traditional concept of bed-and-breakfast. You'll get croissants and jam for breakfast instead of bacon and eggs, but these may well be home-made. Some places offer *table d'hôte* evening meals by prior arrangement. Dining *en famille* is a sociable way to meet the locals, though a little stressful if you speak no French (many hosts near the Channel coast speak some English). Tourist offices all have lists of families who offer rooms to visitors, but some of the best *chambres d'hôte* are affiliated to the Gîtes de France organization (see next section), and graded from one to four ears of corn (*épis*), depending on the level of comfort and facilities. You may even find yourself mixing with the nobility at the upper echelons of the *chambres d'hôte* market. A consortium called Bienvenue au Château offers classy stays in grand private homes in western France (www.bienvenue-au-chateau.com), while Bienvenue a la Ferme lists more modest *chambres d'hote* accommodation on farms (www.bretagnealaferme.com).

SELF-CATERING

Self-catering accommodation includes gregarious holiday parks with lots of entertainment and organized activities, and low-key *gîtes* of all kinds. These self-contained cottages, villas and apartments are found mainly in rural areas, and range from basic to luxurious. *Gîtes* are generally rented on a weekly basis, and are advertised in national newspapers or listed by tourist offices. For a large selection of accredited gîtes see www.gites-de-france.fr.

CAMPING

Brittany has some of France's best campsites, especially along its popular holiday coasts. Campsites are graded up to 4*. Some have mobile homes and pre-pitched tents, and cater to visitors bringing their own caravans or camper-vans. Most sites are open from Easter to September. In high season (July and August) it is essential to reserve ahead; you may not park a motorhome or put up a tent except on a designated site. Consult the National Federation of Campsites (www.campingfrance.com) for a list. Camping Plus is a superior group of about 30 high-quality sites in Brittany (www.campingplus.com).

USING A LAPTOP

Most hotels of two stars and above provide modem points. You can easily connect to the internet providing this service is supported by your ISP (Internet Service Provider). Local telephone charges will apply. Remember that you may need a modem plug adaptor. Laptops should be compatible with the 220V current in France; otherwise you will need both a converter and an adaptor, or a French modem lead. A global modem should work in France.

MORBIHAN

PRICES AND SYMBOLS

Prices quoted are the range for a double with private facilities. The *tax de séjour* (▷ 164) is not included. Unless otherwise stated, breakfast is excluded from the price.

For a key to the symbols, ▷ 2.

ARRADON

LES VÉNÈTES

La Pointe, 56610 Arradon
Tel 02 97 44 85 85
www.lesvenetes.com

The waterfront location is the magic factor at this smart modern hotel. From the glazed restaurant you could be on an ocean liner, and definitely at the captain's table in elegant blue-and-white surroundings furnished in teak. The views over the Golfe du Morbihan from all the stylish bedrooms are equally sublime (some rooms have private terraces). Luxury bathrooms with corner baths are the norm. Half-board terms are available; breakfast can be served in your room at no extra charge.

Closed 2 weeks in mid-Jan
€90–€200 (breakfast €10)
10, including 2 suites
P

AURAY

LE MARIN

1 Place du Rolland, port de Saint-Goustan, 56400 Auray
Tel 02 97 24 14 58
www.hotel-lemarin.com

A beguiling little bed-and-breakfast quietly placed just a few paces back from Auray's historic quayside at Saint-Goustan. Recently refurbished, its jaunty nautical style and contemporary fittings fit well within the confines of a beamy old property. Some of its neat little bedrooms enjoy river views, and a couple have bunk beds suitable for families with children. There's no restaurant (just a convivial ground-floor bar-lounge reserved for hotel guests), but half a dozen eateries lie within a minute's walk along the waterfront.

Closed Jan to mid-Feb
€52–€80 (breakfast €6)
12, all non-smoking

BELLE-ÎLE

LA DESIRADE

Le Petit Cosquet, 56360 Bangor, Belle-Île
Tel 02 97 31 70 70
www.hotel-la-desirade.com

Local island architecture is evoked in this delightful, village-like complex of low-rise, shuttered buildings built around a swimming pool in flower-filled gardens. The owner-chef's seafood-based cooking is much praised. Enjoy breakfast on the pool terrace or by the fireside, depending on the weather. Reserve well ahead, as many regulars return each season. Bicycle or car rental can be arranged, along with picnic hampers for days out exploring the island. There are facilities for children, and access for visitors with reduced mobility.

Closed Oct–mid Mar
€113–€123 (breakfast €11.60); half-board terms only in high season
28
Outdoor
P

BILLIERS

DOMAINE DE ROCHEVILAINE

See Special Panel

CARNAC

HOSTELLERIE LES AJONCS D'OR

Kerbachique–route de Plouharnel, 56340 Carnac
Tel 02 97 52 32 02
www.lesajoncsdor.com

Watch for the signs to Kerbachique just off the Plouharnel road (D781) north-west of Carnac, and you'll soon find this charming stone-built farmhouse. If you have your own transport, it makes a lovely rural retreat, ideal for exploring the megaliths, or nipping off to the beaches of

Quiberon and Belle-Île. The large, shady gardens add to its air of seclusion.

Closed Nov–late Mar
€57–€79 (breakfast €7)
17
P

JOSSELIN

LA BUTTE ST-LAURENT

La Butte St-Laurent, 56120 Josselin
Tel 02 97 22 22 09
www.chambres-bretagne.com

Perched on top of a hill *(butte)* on the edge of the town, this bed-and-breakfast has a splendid view of the nearby château

SPECIAL IN BILLIERS

DOMAINE DE ROCHEVILAINE

Pointe de Pen-Lan, 56190 Billiers
Tel 02 97 41 61 61
www.domainederochevilaine.com

This super-luxurious Relais & Châteaux hotel complex of converted coastguard buildings enjoys ravishing views over a rocky peninsula. A 13th-century stone gateway leads to terraced gardens surrounded by several separate buildings housing a sybaritic spa and fitness studio, a beautiful restaurant with picture windows, and a mix of individually designed but palatial bedrooms, most with private terraces. Thalassotherapy and beauty treatments attract a well-heeled and glamorous clientele. Furnishings are a mix of Breton antiques and high-quality modern classics. Food and service are formal but outstanding.

€120–€340 (breakfast €17; €10 for children under 10)
36, including 4 suites
Heated outdoor seawater; indoor spa with hot tub and sauna
P

and village, and a large garden which is great for children. The comfortable attic rooms, named after the owners' children, have a bathroom with a shower and/or bath. There is also a family room that sleeps up to four people. Credit cards are not accepted.

Closed mid-Sep to Jun

€52–€55, including breakfast (reductions for stays of 3 nights or more)

4, all non-smoking

LARMOR-BADEN

AUBERGE DU PARC FÉTAN

17 rue de Berder, 56870 Larmor-Baden
Tel 02 97 57 04 38
www.hotel-parcfetan.com

This exceptionally welcoming and dynamically managed new venture is on the road leading to Larmor-Baden's tiny port, with glimpses of sea from some rooms. A cluster of attractively designed chalet-style apartments for two to five people stands around the heated pool in the hotel grounds. These have kitchenettes, and two are suitable for visitors with disabilities. Tasty, simple menus and half-board terms are available.

€40–€95 (breakfast €7)

20, plus 14 apartments

Outdoor

Off-road parking

LOCMARIAQUER

HÔTEL DES TROIS FONTAINES

Route d'Auray, 56740 Locmariaquer
Tel 02 97 57 42 70
www.hotel-troisfontaines.com

Very close to Locmariaquer's impressive prehistoric antiquities, this hotel has all the advantages of thoughtful contemporary design. The interestingly curved block is set back from the road near the entrance to the village, in tidy gardens with shrubs and flower beds. The spacious interior has an airy, uncluttered feel; the soundproofed, cabin-style bedrooms are simply furnished but tasteful with plain walls, light colour schemes and laminate flooring. Some have sea views.

Closed Nov to late Mar (except Christmas and New Year)

€70–€125 (breakfast €10)

18

QUIBERON

LE NEPTUNE

4 quai de Houat, Port-Maria, 56170 Quiberon
Tel 02 97 50 09 62

Close to the *criée* and the *gare maritime* in lively Port-Maria, this typical Logis hotel (owned by the same family for over 50 years) couldn't be handier for an early-morning getaway to

Belle-Île. It's very friendly and well managed, representing excellent value in an oversubscribed location. All bedrooms have both bath and shower, and are surprisingly well finished. A dozen have balconies overlooking the port, but you may prefer to trade sea views for a quieter rear room. Seafood cooking prevails in the restaurant.

Closed Jan

€58–€78 (breakfast €7)

21

A few reserved spaces on the street

LA ROCHE-BERNARD

AUBERGE DES DEUX MAGOTS

1 Place du Bouffay, 56130 La Roche-Bernard
Tel 02 99 90 60 75

Three adjoining period houses at the heart of this historic little town create a charming picture on a quaint square, where steep steps plunge to the riverbank. In essence it's a simple, family-run restaurant-with-rooms (expect some interesting regional cooking from Joël Morice), but the bedrooms are as good value as the food. A mystery bird hidden in a covered cage may fool you with a cheery *Bonjour* at breakfast time.

Closed late Dec to mid-Jan; also late Jun and mid-Oct; Sun eve and Mon off-season (restaurant and hotel reception closed Sun eve and Mon in low season)

€43–€60 (breakfast €6.20)

15

ROCHEFORT-EN-TERRE

CHÂTEAU DE TALHOUËT

56220 Rochefort-en-Terre
Tel 02 97 43 34 72
www.chateaudetalhouet.com

Up a long bumpy private drive off the Malestroit road (D774), this romantic Breton manor founded by a crusader family promises a highly superior *chambre d'hôte* experience. The handsome stone building dates from the 16th century, and has been lovingly restored by its present owner Jean-Pol Soulaine. The beautifully furnished interior is full of antiques, books, Persian rugs and plush sofas; bedrooms are on a suitably grand scale, and so too are exquisite dinners (available by prior arrangement).

Closed Jan and late Nov

€120–€200, including breakfast

8

VANNES

LE MARINA

4 Place Gambetta, 56000 Vannes
Tel 02 97 47 22 81

Near the marina and the main gateway to the walled city, this modest little place above a bustling brasserie called L'Océan (where breakfast is served) couldn't be more convenient for exploring the old town. Double-glazed bedrooms have views over the port or the ramparts. These are simple and some are rather scuffed in places. In this central location, a little noise and a few imperfections may be forgiven. Parking is available nearby at the port, and there's a wide choice of bars and restaurants close at hand.

€57–€61 (breakfast €5.90)

14

PRICES AND SYMBOLS

Prices quoted are the range for a double with private facilities. The *tax de séjour* (▷ 164) is not included. Unless otherwise stated, breakfast is excluded from the price.

For a key to the symbols, ▷ 2.

BÉNODET

ARMORIC

3 rue Penfoul, 29950 Bénodet
Tel 02 98 57 04 03
www.armoric-hotel.com

After a change of ownership, this reliable, white-painted hotel near the entrance to the resort has taken on a sprightly new lease of life and a more contemporary interior. It is still just as welcoming and well managed, with English-speaking reception staff. Its large gardens, heated pool and self-contained garden rooms have a special appeal for families with children. Bedrooms are smartly refurbished with well-designed bathrooms. Half-board terms are available.

€55–€140 (breakfast €10)
30
Outdoor
Open-air and garage parking

BREST

CITOTEL DE LA GARE

4 boulevard Gambetta, 29200 Brest
Tel 02 98 44 47 01
www.hotelgare.com

This neatly kept little place in the Citotel group represents excellent value if you need a night in central Brest. It lies within an easy stroll of the bus and railway stations, the Quartz arts centre and the tourist office. Bedrooms are functional in style, but spick and span, completely refurbished and well soundproofed, with all mod cons, including a wide choice of cable TV channels. From some rooms, there's a pleasant outlook over Brest harbour (the best view is from a room on the fifth floor). The management is friendly and the hotel is open 24 hours.

€48–€65 (breakfast €6.50)
38
Garage

CONCARNEAU

AUBERGE DE JEUNESSE

Quai de la Croix, 29181 Concarneau
Tel 02 98 97 03 47

This youth hostel has a lovely position right by the sea within easy walking distance of the rest of the town. It stands beside the Marinarium to the west of the Ville Close. Accommodation is fairly basic, in bunk-bedded dormitories of varying sizes, with separate showers and toilets, but refurbishment is in progress. The management is helpful and friendly. There is no age limit, but to stay here you need an international youth hostel card (which can be purchased on arrival). This would be good for groups (under-16s must be accompanied by an adult).

Open all year (reception 9–12, 6–8)
€12.30 per person, including breakfast. Groups of more than 10 must stay demi-pension and take the evening meal (€20.50 per person dinner, bed and breakfast)
Sleeps 76, in rooms for 4, 6, or 10

CROZON

JULIA

43 rue du Tréflez, 29160 Crozon
Tel 02 98 27 05 89

Up a quiet side street leading to the sea, this appealing Logis de France has ocean views, attractive gardens and a family atmosphere. Well kept inside and out, it offers a friendly welcome, tasteful interior and regional cooking in its pleasantly traditional restaurant. Bedrooms vary in style, but all reach a good standard and are well maintained. A steady process of refurbishment continues.

Closed Nov to mid-Mar, except Christmas, New Year; reception closed Mon off season
€37–€58 (breakfast €7.50)
19
P

DOUARNENEZ

CLOS DE VALLOMBREUSE

7 rue d'Estienne-d'Orves, 29100 Douarnenez
Tel 02 98 92 63 64
www.closvallombreuse.com

Grandstand views over Douarnenez Bay can be seen from this impressive Belle-Époque villa in large, secluded grounds. The elegant parterres and terraces are particularly attractive in summer. The interior has many interesting features, such as fine panelling and plasterwork, handsome fireplaces and regal furnishings. The restaurant serves ambitious and reputable fare, mostly based on fresh fish from the port a few minutes away. To find it, look for the church at the top of the hill.

€52–€120 (breakfast €9)
25
Outdoor
P

LE GUILVINEC

POISSON D'AVRIL

19–21 rue de Men-Meur, 29730 Le Guilvinec
Tel 02 98 58 23 83

This sophisticated new venture is an unexpected find on the remote Penmarc'h peninsula. It's a restaurant-with-rooms overlooking the *criée* of Le Guilvinec, one of Brittany's most active fishing ports. Parisian connoisseurs are already making their way here to sample Jean-Marie Le Quellec's expertly prepared seafood in its stylish dining room. Above the restaurant, a handful of imaginatively designed bedrooms are accessible via an exterior spiral staircase. These spacious refined affairs make dramatic

STAYING

use of colour and accessories. One or two have private terraces with stunning views over the waves. Breakfasts include delicious fresh pastries. You can borrow binoculars to watch the seabirds foraging for fish scraps. Street parking is available nearby.
€85–€105 (breakfast €6.50)
9

LANDEDA

BAIE DES ANGES

See Special Panel

LOCRONAN

HOSTELLERIE DU BOIS DU NÉVET

Route du Bois du Névet, 29180 Locronan
Tel 02 98 91 83 12
www.hostellerie-bois-nevet.com

This modern hotel snakes through extensive wooded grounds about 10 minutes' walk from the historic village of Locronan (leave your car here to avoid parking charges). The comfortable rooms have no special charm, but the secluded setting is very peaceful and the reception welcoming. Accommodation includes several family apartments sleeping up to five people, and some duplex (split-level) suites. Two rooms are equipped for guests with disabilities. It has no restaurant.
Closed Nov–Easter
€55–€€3 (breakfast €7.50)
35, including 5 apartments, 6 duplex suites
P

MORLAIX

HÔTEL DE L'EUROPE

1 rue d'Aiguillon, 29600 Morlaix
Tel 02 98 62 11 99
www.hotel-europe-com.fr

This reassuringly traditional, personally managed 200-year-old hotel is filled with antique furnishings and some fine carved woodwork, particularly on the staircase. Bedrooms are large, tastefully decorated and well soundproofed, though quite variable in style; the suites sleep up to four people. A buffet breakfast is served in the Napoleon III dining room. The adjacent restaurant (Brasserie de l'Europe) has an internal connection with the hotel but is independently run (▷ 158). Public parking is in the nearby main square.
Closed Christmas, New Year
€60–€120 (breakfast €8)
60 (10 non-smoking)

SPECIAL IN LANDEDA

BAIE DES ANGES

350 route des Anges, Port de l'Aber-Wrac'h, 29870 Landéda
Tel 02 98 04 90 04
www.baie-des-anges.com

An entrancing location on the Côte des Abers in northwestern Finistère does much for this lovely place, and the chic maritime interior of seagrass, wicker and driftwood makes it just as seductive inside. There are lovely views from the breakfast tables and the breakfast is very good. Bedrooms are an airy combination of ivory walls and crisp blue-and-white stripes or checks. The owners are charming and speak excellent English. A sauna, jacuzzi and hydromassage are available. Annexe studios can be rented by the port. One room is suitable for visitors in wheelchairs.
Closed Jan, Feb
€68–€148 (breakfast €13)
20, including 2 suites
P

PONT-AVEN

HÔTEL DES MIMOSAS

22 square Théodore Botrel, 29930 Pont-Aven
Tel 02 98 06 00 30
www.hotels-pont-avon.com

A charming little place at the far end of the harbour, whose brightly lit bar-bistro attracts a convivial crowd of non-residents to dine on steaks or flambéd lobster amid parlour palms, bentwood chairs and polished wooden tables. It is especially popular with British visitors. There's a nautical theme, reinforced by a design of lifebelts and yachts on the fabric wall-coverings. The bedrooms are very pleasant and cosy, and all have views of the port. Staff and owners are young and informal. There's parking at the quayside.
€53–€65 (breakfast €6.50)
10

QUIMPER

DUPLEIX

34 boulevard Dupleix, 29000 Quimper
Tel 02 98 90 53 35
www.hotel-dupleix.com

This central business hotel stands on the south bank of the Odet, an easy stroll from the old town. Its plate glass and concrete are a sharp contrast to Quimper's historic buildings, but it has some architectural merit and is pleasantly landscaped. Public rooms include a large, comfortable lounge and terrace, while the spacious bedrooms are bland but quiet with pleasant river and cathedral views. Three rooms have private terraces; family rooms sleep up to six. Reception is open 24 hours. A charge is made for parking.
€70–€82 (€9)
29
P Open-air and garage parking

ROSCOFF

LE BRITTANY

Boulevard Sainte-Barbe, 29680 Roscoff
Tel 02 98 69 70 78
www.hotel-brittany.com

Under the stewardship of the charming Chapalain family, this 17th-century manor is popular with ferry travellers and has strong Anglophile connections. It stands in secluded grounds with views towards the Île de Batz. The interior is stylish and spacious, furnished with Breton antiques and elegant fabrics. Imposing fireplaces and original beams give it a snug but distinguished feel. Some bedrooms have private terraces. The restaurant (Le Yachtman) serves delicious *cuisine du terroir*.
Closed mid-Nov to late Mar
€108–€198 (breakfast €13)
25, including 2 suites (3 non-smoking)
Covered; sauna, solarium
P

PRICES AND SYMBOLS

Prices quoted are the range for a double with private facilities. The *tax de séjour* (▷ 164) is not included. Unless otherwise stated, breakfast is excluded from the price.

For a key to the symbols, ▷ 2.

BRELIDY

CHÂTEAU DE BRELIDY

22140 Brelidy
Tel 02 96 95 69 38
www.chateau-brelidy.com

This creeper-covered, turreted manor stands some way inland (signed off the D8 between Tréguier and Guingamp), in a pastoral setting of woods and fields where a feudal castle once stood. The extensive grounds encompass rivers and ponds with private fishing rights. The style of hospitality combines the comfort and grandeur of a country house hotel with the intimacy of a family home. Fires crackle in elegant, timbered salons filled with antiques. A cottage in the gardens makes an ideal self-contained unit for families.

Closed Jan–mid Mar
€91–€117 (breakfast €12)
15, including two suites and a garden annexe
Espace forme in the grounds; jacuzzi Outdoor but covered
P

CAP FRÉHEL

LE RELAIS DE FRÉHEL

Route du Cap, 22240 Plévenon, Cap Fréhel
Tel 02 96 41 43 02

Under enterprising new management, this beautifully renovated *longère* (a typical Breton longhouse) looks set to flourish. The building stands in large wooded grounds just 2km (1 mile) from the stunning Fréhel coastline (signed off the D16 near Fort La Latte). Accommodation consists of *chambres d'hôtes* (*table d'hote* dinners by arrangement) and *gîtes* sleeping up to four people. All the rooms are generously sized and comfortable with handsome Breton *armoires* (wardrobes) and beamy ceilings. The breakfast room is in a renovated stable, and afternoon tea is served by the fireside or in the gardens. A *rhumerie* bar and a tennis court add to the peaceful house-party atmosphere.

€50, including breakfast; 2 gîtes from €230 per week
5, plus 2 gîtes
P

DINAN

D'AVAUGOUR

1 Place du Champ, 22100 Dinan
Tel 02 96 39 07 49
www.avaugourhotel.com

A smartly refurbished, personally managed hotel, ideally placed for exploring the old town. The entrance of this 18th-century building overlooks the main square (easy parking except on market day—Thursday). Guests make use of the idyllic rear gardens extending above parts of the castle ramparts for drinks or summer breakfasts. The interior has lots of character; each room is different and carefully designed, incorporating personal sound systems and top-range German plumbing. Some are suitable for families with intercommunicating doors, others have walk-in showers for visitors with limited mobility. There's no restaurant, but breakfast is splendid, and many eating places lie within strolling distance.

Closed mid-Nov to mid-Feb
€84–€157, including breakfast (€5 supplement for one-night stays on Fri, Sat in high season)
21, plus 3 suites. Guests are requested not to smoke.

JERZUAL

26 quai des Talards, Port Dinan, 22100 Lanvallay
Tel 02 96 87 02 02
www.bestwestern-jerzual-dinan.com

Down by Dinan's port on the banks of the Rance, this purpose-built modern construction is tastefully designed in stone and slate. The spacious interior is inoffensively decorated in a blondwood-and-pastel style, with comfortable furnishings and excellent facilities.
Soundproofed bedrooms include room safes and multilingual cable and satellite TV. The raftered restaurant makes an eye-catching rustic setting for a carvery-style restaurant. Terraces suggest waterfront sundowners. Bicycle rental is available at the hotel, and river trips, nature rambles, fishing and water sports are virtually on the doorstep.

€108–€152 (breakfast €12)
54, including 2 suites (10 non-smoking)
Outdoor
P

ERQUY

BEAUSÉJOUR

21 rue de la Corniche, 22430 Erquy
Tel 02 96 72 30 39
www.beausejour-erquy.com

This reliable, good-value Logis has an instantly welcoming air. The E-shaped, blue-shuttered building stands a few minutes' walk from the beach, but there are sea views from the large windows of the dining room, and from some of the well-kept bedrooms. One of the nicest is at the top of the house, with sloping ceilings tucked into the gables.
The interior is attractively decorated with cane-look furnishings and bright fabrics. Appetizing, plain-looking menus highlight Erquy's famous seasonal scallops, making this place a good bet for lunch (▷ 159), and obligatory half-board terms are no

STAYING

hardship in high season.
Closed mid-Nov to mid-Feb
€48–€64 (breakfast €7.50)
15
P

ÎLE DE BRÉHAT

BELLEVUE

Port Clos, 22870 Bréhat
Tel 02 96 20 00 05
www.hotel-bellevue-brehat.com

Lovely views stretch to the rocky shores from this pretty white building near Bréhat's landing stage. In summer, blue agapanthus lilies reflect the colours of the sea. Bedrooms are simple but in perfect order, some in traditional florals. Fresh seafood is served at its panoramic restaurant, decked with paintings by a local artist. Tables outside are always at a premium in this idyllic spot, so reserve ahead. Bicycles can be rented for exploring the island. Half- and full-board terms are available.
Closed mid-Nov to mid-Dec and early Jan–early Feb
€86–€110 (breakfast €9.30)
17

PAIMPOL

LE REPAIRE DE KERROC'H

29 quai Morand, 22500 Paimpol
Tel 02 96 20 50 13
www.chateauxhotelsfrance.com/kerroch

Seafaring seems etched on the smartly dressed stonework of this superior late 18th-century corsair's residence alongside Paimpol's harbour. The refurbished interior reveals original timbers and monumental fireplaces. Most of its handsome bedrooms have port views. All are decorated in dashing, vibrant styles, and named after the islands off Brittany's coast. The well-regarded restaurant and less formal bistro serve freshly caught seafood and regional produce.
Closed mid-Nov to early Dec
€50–€114 (breakfast €11)
13, plus a suite and an apartment (1 non-smoking)
P

PERROS-GUIREC

VILLA CYRNOS

10 rue de Sergent l'Hévédere, 22700 Perros-Guirec
Tel 02 96 91 13 36

Halfway between the harbour and the middle of town (about 20 minutes' walk from the

beach), this is one of the most expensive bed-and-breakfasts in town—but it's worth it. The large granite mansion has a ship-like veranda with a great view of the harbour. The spacious, comfortable rooms, which sleep up to four people, are tastefully furnished and have TVs. The friendly owner serves a formidable breakfast and there is parking. In case you're wondering, 'Cyrnos' is the Greek name for Corsica.
Closed mid-Sep to end Apr
€58–€115, including breakfast
5, all non-smoking
P

PLOUËR-SUR-RANCE

MANOIR DE RIGOURDAINE

Route de Langrolay, 22490 Plouër-sur-Rance
Tel 02 96 86 89 96
www.hotel-rigourdaine.fr

Unspoiled views stretch to the serene blue ribbon of the Rance estuary from this rambling stone property. It's an old manor farm, with a reception block in an airy converted barn, and bedrooms in double-decker outbuildings around the courtyard. Guests may come and go as they please. The interior is simple but elegant—rugs and period furnishings enhancing the natural qualities of oak and granite. Bedrooms have private terraces, and several are suitable for families. There is no restaurant; the nearest are in Plouer or Pleslin. Follow signs to Plouer and Langrolay from N176 (Dinan–Dol-de-Bretagne road).
Closed mid-Nov to Easter
€58–€82 (breakfast €7)
19
P

PLOUGRESCANT

MANOIR DE KERGREC'H

Kergrec'h, 22820 Plougrescant
Tel 02 96 92 59 13

Originally this impressive creeper-clad château was a bishop's palace, but since the Revolution it has been the ancestral home of the Viscounts of Roquefeuil. It stands in a huge estate near the mouth of the River Jaudy (signed near the St-Gonéry chapel with the crooked spire just south of Plougrescant). The present incumbents run a vegetable farm at this 17th-century granite manor as well as providing gracious *chambres d'hôte* hospitality. The large, light bedrooms are furnished with family antiques, rugs, prints and hangings, and have magnificent bathrooms. The tower room even has some medieval but perfectly operational plumbing.
€100, including breakfast
8, including 2 family rooms and 1 suite
P

ST-CAST-LE-GUILDO

PORT JACQUET

32 rue du Port, 22380 St-Cast-le-Guildo
Tel 02 96 41 97 18
www.port-jacquet.com

Set high above the bay, this delightful stone-built hotel not far from the port has some of the best sea views in town. A warm welcome adds to the attractions of its cheerful, nautically styled interior, where the Etoile des Mers restaurant dishes up seafood creations such as *moules de bouchot au cidre*. The recently refurbished bedrooms are bright and appealing, though not large. Pricier ones face the sea, but there are pleasant garden and courtyard views behind. Limited street parking nearby.
€36–€56 (breakfast €6)
17

ST-QUAY-PORTRIEUX

LE GERBOT D'AVOINE

2 boulevard du Littoral, 22410 St-Quay-Portrieux
Tel 02 96 70 40 09
www.gerbotdavoine.com

The style of this stone-built Logis is undeniably old-fashioned, but so too are the prices and the courtesy of its assured and friendly staff. It has a pleasingly traditional, family-run feel and is very good value, with spacious, comfortable rooms (some with partial sea views). At lunchtime, French visitors of all ages patronize its excellent restaurant. It stands within easy walking distance of both beach and casino, and just five minutes from the middle of town.

Closed mid-Nov to mid-Dec and most of Jan
€44–€55 (breakfast €7)
20
P

TRÉBEURDEN

SPECIAL IN TRÉBEURDEN

TI AL LANNEC

14 allée de Mezo-Guen, 22560 Trébeurden
Tel 02 96 15 01 01
www.tiallannec.com

Utter relaxation is promised at this long-established, family-owned Relais du Silence hotel on a small wooded hill just behind the port. Terraced gardens cascade through pine trees towards one of the most enchanting seascapes anywhere on the Pink Granite coast. Inside, the style is a French version of English country house, with rooms of all shapes and sizes charmingly furnished with warmth, care and taste, plus a generous sprinkling of antiques. Bedrooms are supremely comfortable, staff friendly. Health and beauty treatments add another dimension to this hotel, but most guests just enjoy relaxing, diverted by the odd game of billiards, boules or outdoor chess. There is also a hot tub and sauna.

Closed Dec–Feb
€148–€238 (breakfast €14)
33
P

TRÉGUIER

AIGUE MARINE

Port de Plaisance, 22220 Tréguier
Tel 02 96 92 97 00
www.aiguemarine.fr

This spacious modern construction is down by the port, so is very convenient for marina-users, but at the same time is only 10 minutes' walk from the main cathedral square. The light, airy reception bar-lounge overlooks a pool terrace set with palms. Bedrooms are stylish and well equipped, some with private balconies and some suitable for visitors with disabilities. One of the main attractions is the restaurant, Les Trois Rivières (▷ 160–1). Leisure facilities include a sauna, jacuzzi and fitness room, as well as a pool.

Closed Jan to mid-Feb
€70–€92 (breakfast €10.50)
48
Outdoor
P

LE VAL-ANDRÉ

GRAND HÔTEL DU VAL-ANDRÉ

80 rue Amiral Charner, 22370 Pléneuf-Val-André
Tel 02 96 72 20 56
www.grand-hotel-val-andre.fr

Easily found on the seafront road, this place has unrivalled views of Val-André's spectacular beach, with direct access through the French windows of its public rooms. The bar-lounge, restaurant and the most expensive bedrooms all enjoy glorious views of the sea. The English-speaking, hands-on owner is attentive and courteous. Bedrooms are spacious and comfortable with seasidey blue-and-white decorations. Tidy gardens surround the hotel, and the sun-deck terrace is set with tables shaded by stripy parasols and mature pines.

Closed Jan
€78–€97 (breakfast €9)
39
P

HÔTEL DE LA MER

63 rue Amiral Charner, 22370 Pléneuf-Val-André
Tel 02 96 72 20 44

Despite its name, this Logis de France hotel stands a block back from the seafront, with only partial sea views. Bedrooms are simple but practical, and perfectly agreeable and clean. One reason to stay here is the excellent seafood restaurant, where you might enjoy house foie gras or *magret de canard*. (The Nuit et Jour motel annexe, though cheaper, is further from the seafront, and rather stuffy and claustrophobic.) Half-board terms are obligatory in high season.

Closed Nov–Jan
€51–€64 (breakfast €7)
12, plus 8 '*studettes*' in annexe
P

VILLA MARGUERITE

34 rue des Garennes, 22370 Pléneuf-Val-André
Tel 02 96 72 85 88

This elegant old villa stands on a quiet residential hillside about 300m (327 yards) from the middle of the town. Four bedrooms are let on a *chambre d'hôte* basis, with old furnishings and restful colours. Three have little balconies enjoying fine sea views from this elevated site. This place has a very personal air and is excellent value.

Closed Oct–Easter
€58–€63, including breakfast
4
P

ILLE-ET-VILAINE

PRICES AND SYMBOLS

Prices quoted are the range for a double with private facilities. The *tax de séjour* (▷ 164) is not included. Unless otherwise stated, breakfast is excluded from the price.

For a key to the symbols, ▷ 2.

CANCALE

LE CONTINENTAL

4 quai Thomas, 35260 Cancale
Tel 02 99 89 60 16
www.hotel-cancale.com

Streetside dining space takes over most of the ground floor of this traditional restaurant-with-rooms overlooking Cancale's old harbour of La Houle. A recent facelift has updated the panelled 'English-style' restaurant with its seascape paintings. Diners on its canopied veranda get a ringside view of the fishing fleet setting off into the bay, and tractors bustling around the nearby oysterbeds. Needless to say, Cancale's prized molluscs appear on every menu. Front bedrooms enjoy panoramic views, and are understandably pricier, but all are very comfortable and tastefully furnished.

Closed mid-Nov to late Mar
€78–€138 (breakfast €8.50)
18

CHATEAUBOURG

PEN'ROC

See Special Panel

COMBOURG

HÔTEL DU CHÂTEAU

1 Place Chateaubriand, 35270 Combourg
Tel 02 99 73 00 38
www.hotelduchateau.com

Easy to spot at a junction near Combourg's impressive castle, this hotel is a superior Logis de France, well known for its restaurant. Bedrooms are very varied, some stylishly modern in muted minimalism, others more traditional with William Morris wallpapers, but all are very comfortable and generously heated even on the coldest of nights. Some are in an annexe facing the attractive rear gardens; others have views of the castle or the lake across the road. The restaurant is warm and intimate, and there's a comfortable bar-lounge with a piano. A generous buffet breakfast is served in a large, plainer room to the rear.

Closed mid-Dec to mid-Jan; reception closed Sun eve and Mon off-season
€52–€145 (breakfast €10)
35
2 rooms
P

DINARD

PRINTANIA

5 avenue George V, 35800 Dinard
Tel 02 99 46 13 07
www.printaniahotel.com

This winsome place is one of the oldest (1920s) and most beautiful hotels in Dinard. It virtually paddles in the Rance, and views of the estuary from many of its windows are superb. Inside, it has distinctive character and many fine old Breton antiques, including carved linen-presses and box beds. In the restaurant, waitresses wear traditional regional costume. It's a popular place for lunch, so reserve ahead. Street parking is available nearby.

Late Nov–late Mar
€55–€85 (breakfast €8.50)
56, including a suite

FOUGÈRES

BALZAC

15 rue Nationale, 35300 Fougères
Tel 02 99 99 42 46
www.balzachotel.com

A traditional, classic hotel on a main street, well placed for exploring the old town and very good value. It occupies a handsome period town house handy for shops, restaurants and the tourist office. Public space by the reception entrance includes an intimate little breakfast room from which you can watch passers-by on the cobbled street, and a sitting area with internet access. Bedrooms are variable, simple but clean and brightly furnished. Several are suitable for families, and the upper floor can be let as a complete unit. Half-board deals can be arranged using two well-regarded local restaurants. The friendly owner speaks fluent English.

€38–€52 (breakfast €6)
22

SPECIAL IN CHATEAUBOURG

PEN'ROC

La Peinière, St-Didier, 35221 Chateaubourg
Tel 02 99 00 33 02
www.penroc.fr

This former farm on a pilgrimage site in deep countryside has been substantially modernized and upgraded, but has kept its restful air. English-speaking owners Mireille and Joseph Froc (he the chef, she front of house) do their best to make guests feel welcome. The entire house is bright, tasteful and immaculate, and the grounds are beautifully kept. Some bedrooms have private terraces and whirlpool baths. Ambitious, varied menus ring the changes on fresh market produce—try the home-made apricot jam for breakfast.

Closed mid Dec–mid Jan
€78–€121 (breakfast €11)
29
Indoor; sauna
P Open-air or in garage

HÉDÉ

HOSTELLERIE DU VIEUX MOULIN

La Vallée des Moulins, 35630 Hédé
Tel 02 99 45 45 70

British visitors constitute some 25 per cent of the trade of this friendly, good-value Logis in a wooded valley. Set in an old granite watermill, the elongated, creeper-clad building with its mini-belltower at one end looks instantly inviting. Flower-filled gardens reach to the foot of the ramparts on which the main village stands. Inside, original timbers and stone fireplaces are still on show. The recently refurbished bedrooms are cheerful and bright, the restaurant a roomy oblong of red-and-gold seating. The Irish chef-patron might dish up oysters and foie gras, or a hearty beef casserole.

Closed part of Oct and Jan; reception closed Sun eve, Mon
€42–€48 (breakfast €7)
13
Open and garage parking

QUÉDILLAC

RELAIS DE LA RANCE

6 rue de Rennes, 35290 Quédillac
Tel 02 99 06 20 20

This classic *maison bourgeoise*, part of the Logis group, makes a useful touring base for the Forêt de Paimpont. The smartly kept, attractively lit stone house is easy to find on the main street of a pleasant if undistinguished little town on the Rennes–Brest road. The very French interior is full of personality, with the focus squarely on its spacious twin dining rooms (look out for the *menu du terroir*). Three generations of the Guitton family have run the place since 1946, transforming it from a modest café into an acclaimed restaurant with a reassuring air of continuity and tradition.

Closed Christmas–late Jan; restaurant and hotel reception closed Fri eve and Sun eve
€47–€62 (breakfast €8)
13
P

REDON

CHANDOUINEAU

1 rue Thiers, avenue de la Gare, 35600 Redon
Tel 02 99 71 02 04

The rather charmless location near the railway station gives no accurate picture of this opulently decorated restaurant-with-rooms. Chef-patron Jean-Marc Chandouineau's reputation has steadily developed over more than 30 years, and you may well find some captain of industry or local bigwig sitting on the next balloon-back at lunch- or dinnertime. The bedrooms reach the same high standards as the cooking, pleasantly decorated in soothing tones with smart, spacious bathrooms. All are well insulated against the sound of passing trains.

Closed 2 weeks in May, 2 weeks in Aug, 2 weeks in Jan
€79 (breakfast €10)
7
P

RENNES

HOTEL DES LICES

7 Place des Lices,
35000 Rennes
Tel 02 99 79 14 81
www.hotel-des-lices.com

This modern, unobtrusive hotel overlooks a famous old-town square lined with historic buildings, many now turned into bars or restaurants. The market is held here on Saturday mornings. Nearly all rooms have their own balconies, and are practical and contemporary with blondwood fittings, trendy lighting and English-language satellite TV. Plumbing, insulation and workspace have been carefully considered. The breakfast room is calm and elegant with fresh flowers. Public parking near the hotel costs €2.50 per night (spaces reserved for hotel guests).

€57–€59 (breakfast €7)
45 (30 non-smoking)
Sainte-Anne

ST-MALO

LE BEAUFORT

25 chaussée du Sillon, 35400 St-Malo
Tel 02 99 40 99 99
www.hotel-beaufort.com

Sea views are spectacular from the breakfast room and best bedrooms of this elegant mid-19th-century hotel, and there's direct access to St-Malo's main beach. The building is a handsome townhouse with balustrades and dormers, smartly painted in gold and blue. The interior is cool and restrained, using a sophisticated muted palette and stylish contemporary furnishings. No dinners are served, but you can relax in the piano bar in the evenings. It's about a 15-minute stroll along the beach to the old town.

€70–€200 (breakfast €12)
22

MANOIR DU CUNNINGHAM

9 Place Monseigneur Duchesne,
St-Servan, 35400 St-Malo
Tel 02 99 21 33 33
www.st-malo-hotel-cunningham.com

Overlooking Port des Sablons and the old citadel, this flamboyant hotel in the St-Servan district is within easy striking distance of both the marina and the ferry terminal. The cream-rendered exterior of the imaginatively renovated 17th-

STAYING

century building sports a cat's cradle of red faux timbering and open woodwork. Bedrooms are spacious and kitted out in a dynamic combination of colonial-looking mahogany and vibrant modern shades. Many enjoy magnificent views. One room is suitable for wheelchair users.
Closed mid-Nov to mid-Mar, except weekends
€90–€180 (breakfast €9)
13, including 3 suites
Enclosed and garage parking

QUIC EN GROIGNE
8 rue d'Estrées, 35400 St-Malo
Tel 02 99 20 22 20
www.quic-en-groigne.com

This sweet little place in the heart of the walled city makes the perfect first or last night in Brittany if you're travelling by ferry. It is exceptionally friendly and very good value for such a delightful location. Rooms, some sleeping up to 4, are prettily decorated and well finished with fitted furnishings and good bathrooms. Generous breakfasts are served in a light conservatory facing a tidy interior courtyard. Secure off-street parking is an unusual bonus in this part of town, though access is a little tricky.
Closed Christmas, 2 weeks mid-Jan
€57–€63 (breakfast €6)
15
Garage (€5 per night)

LE VALMARIN
7 rue Jean XXIII, 35400 St-Malo
Tel 02 99 81 94 76
www.levalmarin.com
An elegant 18th-century *malouinière* built by a wealthy ship-owner makes a distinguished setting for this hotel in the suburb of St-Servan. It stands in secluded, shady gardens on a hill near the church of Sainte-Croix. It's a lovely old place inside, its antique furnishings and period features suggesting a private country house rather than a hotel. The welcome is warm and the atmosphere utterly relaxing. Bedrooms are graciously individual and full of character. Breakfast can be served outside in fine weather. There's no restaurant, but plenty lie around nearby Port Solidor. Secure off-street parking is available (arrive before 10.30pm).
€95–€135 (breakfast €10)
12
P

ST-MELOIR-DES-ONDES

TIREL GUÉRIN
Gare de la Gouesnière, 35350 St-Méloir-des-Ondes
Tel 02 99 89 10 46
www.tirelguerin.com
This smart place is an unexpected find beside a tiny old-fashioned railway station on the main road south of Cancale. Now an acclaimed restaurant-with-rooms, both food and accommodation reach high standards. Immaculately kept throughout, it has beautiful gardens and superior leisure facilities, including a splendid indoor pool in an annexe wing. The classically elegant dining room is a popular venue for discerning patrons, especially at lunchtime. Bedrooms are spacious and very *soignée*, the suites and apartments much more expensive.
Closed mid-Dec to mid-Jan
€82–€110 (breakfast €11.50)
38, plus 6 apartments and 12 suites
Indoor; sauna, jacuzzi
P

LE CHÂTEAU RICHEUX
Le Point du Jour, 35350 St-Méloir-des-Ondes
Tel 02 99 89 64 76

Top chef Olivier Roellinger's family empire is based in Cancale, but this classy 1920s mansion lies about 5km (3 miles) down the coast (signed off the D155 near St-Benoît). It stands in a secluded clifftop park on the ruins of a medieval fortress, its huge windows framing wondrous vistas of the bay of Mont-St-Michel. Though grand and sophisticated, it's also very relaxing, with attentive and friendly staff. The lounge bar has smart tan furnishings and an eye-catching boat model (guests may charter the splendid Roellinger yacht in summer). The *bistrot marin* called Le Coquillage serves predictably super seafood in an informal atmosphere. Bedrooms are luxuriously comfortable, with CD players and mosaic bathrooms.
Closed mid-Dec to end Jan
€160–€310 (breakfast €16)
13, including 2 apartments
P

VITRÉ

LE PETIT BILLOT
5 bis Place du Général Leclerc, 35500 Vitré
Tel 02 99 75 02 10
www.petit-billot.com
You get a warm welcome from the cheerful *patronne* at this neat, clean place (part of the independent Citotel group) on the edge of the old town. It's a cream-painted building with blue shutters, on a main street within easy reach of the station and tourist office. Bedrooms are modern, but surprisingly varied in size and style. All have excellent little showers and are light and pleasing. Breakfast is served in a green-panelled room to the rear. The hotel shares premises with a recommendable restaurant called Le Potager. Though under separate management, good-value half-board terms can be arranged with this and another local restaurant.
Closed Christmas and New Year
€46 (breakfast €6)
21
Garage

HOTEL CHAINS

Name of hotel chain	Description	Website	Phone number
B&B	Rapidly expanding and improving chain; some have duplex (split level) rooms good for families; unstaffed at night.	www.hotelbb.com	08 92 78 29 29 (France)
Balladins	Budget chain in several grades.	www.balladins.com	08 25 08 84 53 (France)
Best Western	Vast worldwide marketing consortium of mostly mid-range hotels.	www.bestwestern.fr	0800 393 130 (UK) 1800 780 7234 (US) 08 00 91 40 01 (France)
Campanile	Widespread mid-range chain. Hotels have restaurants.	www.campanile.fr	08 25 00 30 03 (France) 020 7519 5045 (UK)
Châteaux and Hotels de France	An affiliation of luxury hotels and châteaux.	www.chateaux-hotels.com	08 92 23 00 75 (France)
Citotel	Varied but friendly group of independent hoteliers.	www.citotel.com	04 73 74 65 90 (France)
Etap	Budget chain with simple, practical rooms	www.etaphotel.com	08 92 68 89 00 (France)
Formule 1	No-frills budget accommodation; rooms sleep 3; separate shared shower/wc facilities (auto-cleaned after use). Unstaffed at night.	www.hotelformule1.com	08 92 68 56 85 (France)
Inter Hotels	A widespread, varied group of mid-range hotels with good standards.	www.inter-hotel.com	08 25 06 46 46 (France)
Ibis	Superior economy hotels with neat, compact rooms; most have on-site catering and 24hr reception.	www.ibishotel.com	0870 609 0963 (UK) 08 92 68 66 86 (France)
Logis de France	Independently owned, family-run hotels in traditional styles, offering good-value rooms, a pleasant welcome and regional cooking.	www.logis-de-france.fr	01 45 84 83 84 (France)
Mercure	Smart business hotels at several grades.	www.mercure.com	0870 609 0961 (UK) 1800 221 4542 (US) 08 25 88 00 00 (France)
Novotel	Mid-range and superior spa resort hotels.	www.novotel.com	0870 609 0962 (UK) 1800 NOVOTEL (US) 08 25 88 44 44 (France)
Les Pieds dans l'Eau	Attractive hotel-restaurants with direct access to the waterfront.	www.lespiedsdansleau.com	
Première Classe	Practical budget hotels, unstaffed at night.		08 92 68 81 23 (France)
Relais du Silence	A group of classy hotels in peaceful locations with good food.	www.relais-du-silence.com	020 7295 0301 (UK) 01 44 49 90 00 (France)
Relais & Châteaux	Luxury-bracket hotels and châteaux.	www.relaischateaux.com	00 800 2000 00 02 (UK) 1800 735 2478 (US) 08 25 32 32 32 (France)

Planning

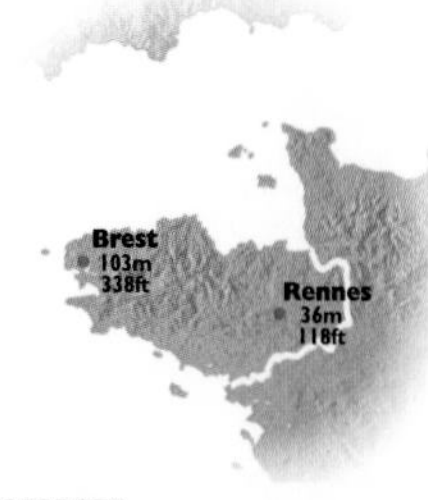

CLIMATE

- Brittany has a generally mild, dampish climate tempered by sea breezes. Some sheltered areas bathed by the Gulf Stream, such as the Golfe du Morbihan or the islands of Batz and Bréhat, enjoy a microclimate benign enough for vines and subtropical plants to flourish.
- Extremes of temperature are rare, but the weather is always unpredictable, and can change very quickly. Rain may occur at any time of year, but is most prevalent in autumn and winter. Short-lived bursts of frost and snow occasionally shock the flowering mimosa in winter, and gales assail the ocean coastline from time to time.
- Summer temperatures average just over 20° C (70°F), and are highest in August. Southern Brittany is warmest of all, with some 2,200 hours of sunshine a year, compared with just 1,700 on the Channel coast.
- The interior, whose gentle hills are high enough to puncture Atlantic rain-clouds, is generally wetter than low-lying coastal zones, and has wider temperature variations.
- For up-to-date weather information on Brittany, look up www.meteo.fr.

WHEN TO GO

- In July and August, the beaches and campsites of the popular coastal resorts overflow with French families taking their traditional summer break. Prices soar, and traffic clogs the roads. It can be difficult to find a bed for the night, or a restaurant table. But the resorts are at their liveliest, providing a seamless round of happenings—regattas and boat-trips, open-air concerts, fireworks and *son-et-lumière* shows. The biggest festivals attract huge gatherings.
- To miss the crowds, try to avoid school holidays (British or French), and check whether your destination plans any major festivals or events during your visit.
- Spring is always lovely in Brittany, when the cider orchards froth into blossom, hillsides are ablaze with gorse, and local markets display cornucopias of top-quality early vegetables. Autumn is a season of mellow fruitfulness, of apple-picking and mushroom-hunting. Late hydrangeas and geraniums still glow in gardens and window-boxes. Huge equinoctial tides continually reshape coastal views, and migrant birds stream through the skies.

TIME ZONES

City	Time difference	Time at 12 noon France
Amsterdam	0	12 noon
Berlin	0	12 noon
Brussels	0	12 noon
Chicago	-7	5am
Dublin	-1	11am
Johannesburg	+1*	1pm
London	-1	11am
Madrid	0	12 noon
Montréal	-6	6am
New York	-6	6am
Perth, Australia	+7*	7pm
Rome	0	12 noon
San Francisco	-9	3am
Sydney	+9*	9pm
Tokyo	+8*	8pm

Clocks in France go forward one hour on the last Sunday in March, until the last Sunday in October.
* One hour less during Summer Time.

- In the remote coastal locations of Brittany, or on offshore islands, many holiday establishments don't open until well after Easter, and pull down the shutters by the end of September.
- The enticing tropical appearance of Breton beaches can be deceptive. The shallow seas of Morbihan warm up a little by September, but in general sea temperatures stay cool all year.
- Many monuments and museums in France close on key national holidays (1 January, 1 May, 1 November, 11 November, 25 December), and bus and train services are much reduced.

BREST

TEMPERATURE

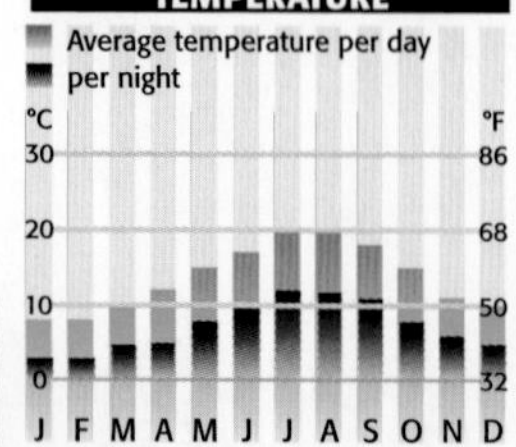

RAINFALL

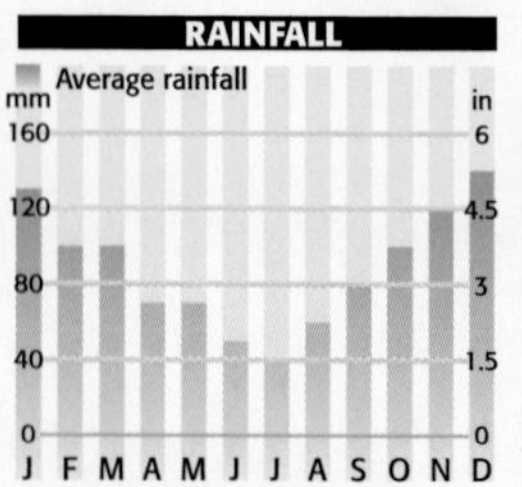

RENNES

TEMPERATURE

Average temperature per day
per night
°C 30 20 10 0 — °F 86 68 50 32
J F M A M J J A S O N D

RAINFALL

Average rainfall
mm 160 120 80 40 0 — in 6 4.5 3 1.5 0
J F M A M J J A S O N D

WHAT TO TAKE

- The key things to remember are travel and health insurance documents, money, credit cards and any medication you'll need. If you plan to drive in France, take your driving licence and, if using your own car, the vehicle registration and insurance certificates.
- A small rucksack or shoulder bag is useful for sightseeing. Bear in mind that these are attractive to pickpockets, so keep your money tucked away and an eye on your bag when you're in restaurants and other crowded places, especially in cities.
- Take the addresses and phone numbers of emergency contacts, including the numbers to call if your credit cards are stolen.

FRENCH EMBASSIES AND CONSULATES ABROAD		
COUNTRY	**ADDRESS**	**WEBSITE**
Australia	31 Market Street, St. Martin Tower, Level 26, Sydney, NSW 2000 Tel (02) 92 61 57 79	www.consulfrance-sydney.org
Canada	1 Place Ville Marie, Bureau 2601, Montréal, Québec, H3B 4S3 Tel 514 878-4385	www.consulfrance-montreal.org
Republic of Ireland	36 Ailesbury Road, Ballsbridge, Dublin 4. Tel 01 277 5000	www.ambafrance.ie
New Zealand	34–42 Manners Street, Wellington, 12th floor, PO Box 11-343 Tel 64 4384 2555	www.ambafrance-nz.org
UK	21 Cromwell Road, London, SW7 2EN. Tel 020 7073 1200	www.frenchembassy.org.uk
US (Los Angeles)	10990 Wilshire Boulevard, Suite 300, Los Angeles, CA 90024 Tel 310/235-3200	www.consulfrance-losangeles.org
US (New York)	934 Fifth Avenue, New York, NY 10021. Tel 212/606-3600	www.consulfrance-newyork.org

Make photocopies of your passport, insurance documents and tickets, in case of loss. Keep a separate note of your credit card numbers in case you need to report a theft to the police.

- Visitors from the UK and US will need adaptors for electrical equipment (▷ 180).
- There is a language guide on pages 191–6 of this book, but if you are keen to communicate in French you may find a separate phrasebook helpful.
- A first aid kit is a useful precaution.
- If you wear glasses, take a spare pair and your prescription.
- The strength of the sun can be masked by coastal breezes; take sunscreen and sunglasses during the holiday season.
- Much of your time may be spent outdoors, so take wet-weather gear, some warm, windproof clothing, and comfortable, robust footwear.
- When visiting churches or cathedrals, wear suitably modest clothing—beachwear and shorts are not acceptable.
- A lightweight pair of binoculars is worth stowing away, and possibly a bird or flower identification guide.

PASSPORTS/VISAS

- UK, US and Canadian visitors need a passport, but not a visa, for stays of up to three months. You should have at least six months' validity remaining on your passport. Citizens of EU countries that have National Identity cards need either a passport or National Identity card.
- For more information about visa and passport requirements, look up the French tourist office website (www.franceguide.com) or the French Embassy (www.frenchembassy.org.uk) or the General Consulate (www.consulfrance-newyork.org).
- Before you travel, check visa and passport regulations since these are subject to change.
- Take a photocopy of the relevant pages of your passport to carry around with you, so you can leave your actual passport in your hotel safe. Always keep a separate note of your passport number and a photocopy of the page that carries your details, in case of loss or theft.

Longer stays

- UK and other EU citizens who want to stay longer than three months no longer need a *carte de séjour*. US and Canadian visitors should apply for a *carte de séjour* and a visa. For information call the Immigration Department of the French Consulate (see chart).

TRAVEL INSURANCE

- Make sure you have full health and travel insurance before you set off.
- EU citizens (plus nationals of Iceland, Liechtenstein, Norway and Switzerland) are entitled to receive reduced-cost emergency health care within any member state if they have the relevant documentation. For Britons, this is the European Health Insurance Card (EHIC), which is being introduced in 2006 to replace the E111. However, comprehensive travel insurance is still advised for all visitors, whether from Europe or beyond.

CUSTOMS

From another EU country

Below are the guidelines for the quantity of goods you can bring to France from another EU country, for personal use:

- 800 cigarettes
- 400 cigarillos
- 200 cigars
- 1 kg of smoking tobacco
- 110 litres of beer
- 10 litres of spirits
- 90 litres of wine (of which only 60 litres can be sparkling wine)
- 20 litres of fortified wine

From a country outside the EU

You are entitled to the allowances shown below only if you travel with the goods and do not plan to sell them. If you come from outside the EU, check with your local customs and excise office what you can take home.

- 200 cigarettes or 100 cigarillos or 50 cigars or 250gms of tobacco
- 60cc/ml of perfume
- 250cc/ml of eau de toilette
- 2 litres of still table wine
- 1 litre of spirits or strong liqueurs over 22% volume; or 2 litres of fortified wine, sparkling wine or other liqueurs
- Up to €175 of all other goods

CONVERSION CHART		
FROM	TO	MULTIPLY BY
Inches	Centimetres	2.54
Centimetres	Inches	0.3937
Feet	Metres	0.3048
Metres	Feet	3.2810
Yards	Metres	0.9144
Metres	Yards	1.0940
Miles	Kilometres	1.6090
Kilometres	Miles	0.6214
Acres	Hectares	0.4047
Hectares	Acres	2.4710
Gallons	Litres	4.5460
Litres	Gallons	0.2200
Ounces	Grams	28.35
Grams	Ounces	0.0353
Pounds	Grams	453.6
Grams	Pounds	0.0022
Pounds	Kilograms	0.4536
Kilograms	Pounds	2.205
Tons	Tonnes	1.0160
Tonnes	Tons	0.9842

Driving is one of the best ways to see the Breton countryside

CAR RENTAL

- The absence of satisfactory public transport makes driving the only practical way to explore the rural villages and remote countryside of Brittany in depth, though it affords little pleasure in the larger cities. Congestion and parking can be a real headache in popular coastal areas in high season.
- It is often best to reserve a car in advance, making sure that full insurance is included in the package. You can also arrange car rental through some travel agents when you book your travel arrangements.
- See pages 27–9 for information on driving.

CHILDREN

- Look out for service stations (selling food and fuel, with play areas) or *aires* (scenic pull-ins with toilets and space to run around) on *autoroutes* and expressways, where restless children can stretch their legs.
- Most restaurants welcome children, although not many have highchairs and children's menus are not common outside family-friendly tourist resorts, so it's probably best to aim for family-style bistros where facilities are better and staff are more helpful.
- If you need special facilities in your hotel, such as a cot, or a child seat in your rented car, reserve them in advance.
- For baby-changing facilities while out and about, try the restrooms in department stores and the larger museums.
- Supermarkets and pharmacies sell nappies (diapers) and baby food, although they are often closed on a Sunday so make sure you stock up.
- Entrance to museums is often free to young children.

ELECTRICITY

- Voltage in France is 220 volts. Sockets take plugs with two round pins. UK electrical equipment will need an adaptor plug, which you can buy at airport and Eurostar terminals. American appliances using 110–120 volts will need an adaptor and a transformer. Equipment that is dual voltage should need only an adaptor.

LAUNDRY

- There are two options if you need a laundry service—a *laverie automatique* (laundrette) and a *pressing/nettoyage à sec* (dry-cleaners). Dry-cleaners are easier to find, but are more expensive. Some have an economy service, but this is not recommended for your best silk jacket.

LOCAL WAYS

- Greetings are often quite formal in France. Offer to shake hands when you are introduced to someone, and use *vous* rather than *tu*. It is polite to use *Monsieur, Madame* or *Mademoiselle* when speaking to people you don't know. For very young women and teenage girls use Mademoiselle, otherwise use Madame.
- The continental kiss is a common form of greeting between friends, and the number of times friends kiss each other on the cheek varies from region to region.
- Address waiters and waitresses as *Monsieur, Madame* or *Mademoiselle* when you are trying to attract their attention.
- Communicating in French is always the best option, even if you can manage only *bonjour, s'il vous plaît* and *merci* (hello, please and thank you). The French are protective of their language and your efforts to speak it will be appreciated. If your knowledge of French is limited, ask the fail-safe *Parlez-vous anglais?* and hope the answer is *oui*.
- Remember that it is traditional

Two Breton locals enjoying a chat and a joke

The local parish churches and closes are great attractions

to say hello as you enter a shop, bar or café, particularly in small towns and villages, and that you are greeting your fellow customers as well as the proprietor. For a mixed audience, a *Bonjour Messieurs Dames* is the appropriate phrase. When it is your turn to be served, greet the server with *Bonjour Madame* or *Bonjour Monsieur*, then don't forget to say *merci* and *au revoir* or *bonne-journée* as you leave.

MEASUREMENTS

- France uses the metric system. Road distances are measured in kilometres, fuel is sold by the litre and food is weighed in grams and kilograms.

PLACES OF WORSHIP

- Some of France's greatest architectural treasures are the idiosyncratic parish churches and closes of western Brittany.
- They have become so popular as visitor attractions that it's easy to forget that they are still active places of worship (western Brittany, in particular, is devoutly Catholic). It's important to respect these churches and worshippers by dressing appropriately. Men should wear long trousers rather than shorts and should avoid sleeveless shirts. Women should keep their knees and shoulders covered and men should remove hats on entering the building.
- Take photos only if it is permitted and don't forget to turn off your mobile phone.

SMOKING AREAS

- Smoking is banned in public places such as cinemas, buses and Métro stations.
- By law restaurants and cafés should provide a non-smoking section, although in reality it can be difficult to find a dining room, bar or café that is smoke-free. However, France is stepping up the pressure on smokers. Smoking is slowly becoming less prevalent in public places, not least because of the recent draconian tax rise in the price of cigarettes, and more places are willing to risk the unpopularity of banning smoking completely.

TOILETS

- Today's modern unisex public toilets are a vast improvement on previous facilities. Coin-operated and self-cleaning, you can find them in most large cities.
- In smaller towns and villages, free public toilets can normally be found by the market square or near tourist offices, although cleanliness varies.
- Facilities in museums and other visitor attractions generally reach a good standard, so take advantage of them while you can. Restaurants and cafés provide toilets for their customers—at least buy a drink if you intend using them.
- Ask for *les toilettes* or WC (pronounced *vay, say*).

VISITORS WITH DISABILITIES

- France has made some headway in recent years in providing access and facilities for visitors with disabilities. All new buildings must take the needs of people with special requirements into account, and, where possible, existing buildings such as town halls, airports and train stations must be adapted with ramps and automatic doors. But the cobbled, hilly streets of many picturesque historic towns and villages in Brittany and Normandy can be a trial for wheelchair-users.
- Some visitor offices, museums and restaurants that are in historic, protected buildings are still not fully accessible. A telephone call before going to a restaurant is a good idea to organize a more easily accessible table.
- For organizations that give advice to people with disabilities, see page 34.

CLOTHING SIZES

Use the clothing sizes chart below to convert the size you use at home.

UK	Metric	US	
36	46	36	SUITS (men)
38	48	38	
40	50	40	
42	52	42	
44	54	44	
46	56	46	
48	58	48	
7	41	8	SHOES (men)
7.5	42	8.5	
8.5	43	9.5	
9.5	44	10.5	
10.5	45	11.5	
11	46	12	
14.5	37	14.5	SHIRTS (men)
15	38	15	
15.5	39/40	15.5	
16	41	16	
16.5	42	16.5	
17	43	17	
8	36	6	DRESSES (women)
10	38	8	
12	40	10	
14	42	12	
16	44	14	
18	46	16	
20	46	18	
4.5	37.5	6	SHOES (women)
5	38	6.5	
5.5	38.5	7	
6	39	7.5	
6.5	40	8	
7	41	8.5	

MONEY MATTERS

THE EURO

- France is one of 12 European countries that has adopted the euro as the official currency. Euro notes and coins were introduced in January 2002, replacing the former currency, the French franc.

BEFORE YOU GO

- It is advisable to use a combination of cash, traveller's cheques and credit cards rather than relying on only one means of payment during your trip. Bear in mind that the number of banks and other outlets offering exchange facilities has plummeted since the introduction of the euro, so organize some euros in advance and take a credit card with you.
- Check with your credit and/or debit card company that your card can be used to withdraw cash from Automatic Teller Machines (ATMs) in France. It is also worth checking what fee will be charged for this and what number you should ring if your card is stolen.

TIPS

- Try to avoid using higher denomination notes when paying taxi drivers and when buying low-cost items in smaller shops.
- Never carry money or credit cards in back pockets, or other places that are easy targets for thieves.
- Keep your spare money and traveller's cheques in your hotel safe (*coffre-fort*) until you need them.
- Check the exchange rates for traveller's cheques and cash offered in post offices as well as in banks, as banks do not always offer the best rate.
- In France, Mastercard is sometimes known as Eurocard and Visa is known as Carte Bleue.
- Some smaller hotels and inns don't accept credit cards, so find out before you check in.

TRAVELLER'S CHEQUES

- Traveller's cheques are a safer way of bringing in money as you can claim a refund if they are stolen—but commission can be high when you cash them.

ATMS

- ATMs are common in France, often with on-screen instructions in a choice of languages. Among the cards accepted are Visa, MasterCard and Diners Club. You'll need a four-digit PIN number.
- Your card issuer will almost certainly charge you for withdrawing cash.
- Some British credit cards are still not accepted in certain automatic machines in France because the 'smart' technology doesn't match. It is hoped that the new wave of chip and pin cards will be more compatible.

BANKS

- Hours vary, but usual opening hours are Monday to Friday 8.30 or 9–12 and 2–5, although

BANKNOTES AND COINS

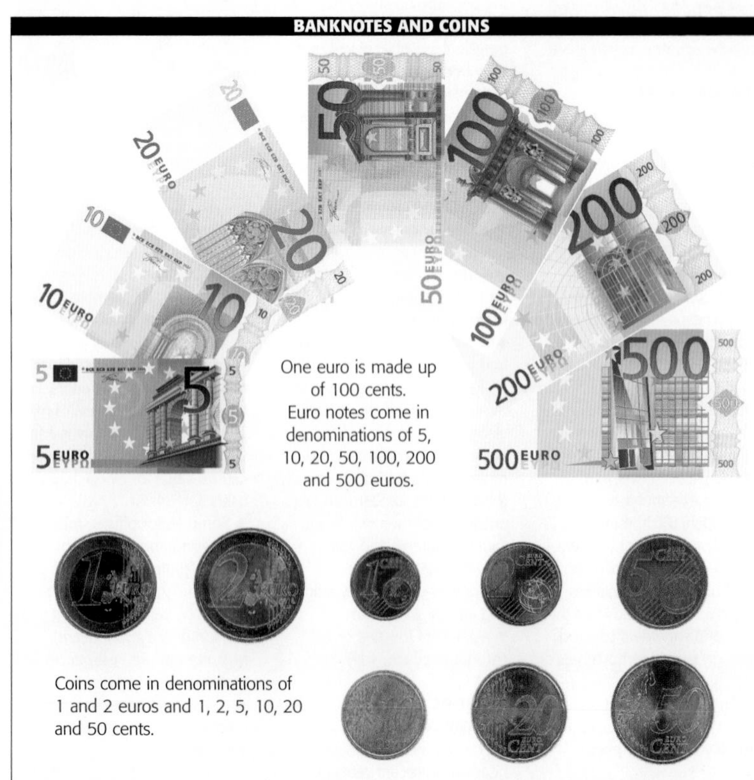

One euro is made up of 100 cents. Euro notes come in denominations of 5, 10, 20, 50, 100, 200 and 500 euros.

Coins come in denominations of 1 and 2 euros and 1, 2, 5, 10, 20 and 50 cents.

Look for the 'change' sign if you want to exchange money

banks in cities may not close for lunch.

- In smaller towns and villages banks often close on Mondays but open on Saturday mornings instead.
- Banks close at noon on the day before a national holiday, as well as on the holiday itself. Only banks with *change* signs change traveller's cheques or foreign currency and you'll need your passport to do this.

BUREAUX DE CHANGE

- Bureaux de Change have longer opening hours than banks, but the exchange rates may not be as good. You'll find them at airports, ferry terminals, large railway stations and in major cities.
- Avoid changing large amounts of traveller's cheques at hotels as the rates may not be competitive.

CREDIT CARDS

- Most restaurants, shops and hotels accept credit cards, although some have a minimum spending limit.

TAXES

- Non-EU residents can claim a sales tax refund *(détaxe)* of 12 per cent on certain purchases, although you must have spent more than €175 in one shop, at one time. Ask the store for the relevant forms, which the trader should complete and stamp. Give these forms to customs when you leave the country, along with the receipts, and they will be stamped. Post the forms back to the shop and they will either refund your credit card account or send you a cheque.
- Remember that you may have to show the goods to Customs when you leave France, so keep them within easy reach.
- Exempt products include food and drink, medicine, tobacco, unset gems, works of art and antiques.
- The company Global Refund offers a reimbursement service (01 41 61 51 51; www.globalrefund.com).

WIRING MONEY

- In an emergency, you can have money wired to you from your home country, but this can be expensive (as agents charge a fee for the service) and time-consuming.
- You can send and receive money via agents such as Western Union (www.westernunion.com) and Travelex (www.travelex.fr).
- Money can be wired from bank to bank, which takes up to two working days, or through Travelex and Western Union, which is normally faster.

CONCESSIONS

- If you are a student or teacher, apply to the International Student Travel Confederation (www.isic.org) in your own country for an International Student Identity Card (ISIC). This entitles you to various reductions during your visit.
- Seniors often get reduced-rate tickets on public transport and on admission to museums and sights by showing a valid identity card or passport.
- Small children often have free entry to sights.

TIPPING GUIDE

Restaurants (service included)	Change *
Hotels (service included)	Change *
Cafés (service included)	Change *
Taxis	10 per cent
Tour guides	€1–€1.50
Porters	€1
Hairdressers	€1
Cloakroom attendants	30c
Toilets	Change
Usherettes	30c

* Or more if you are impressed with the level of service

POST OFFICES

- Some post offices have ATMs.
- Cards accepted are listed on each dispenser and instructions are available in English.
- Money can be wired, through Western Union, via most post offices, and generally takes only a few minutes to receive.
- International Money Orders can be sent from all post offices (for a fee).
- Some larger post offices offer exchange services in the following currencies: American, Australian and Canadian dollars, yen, British pounds sterling, Swiss francs, Swedish kronor, and Danish and Norwegian kroner.

Most ATMs have instructions in a choice of languages

PRICES OF EVERYDAY ITEMS

Takeout sandwich		€2.50–€3.50
Bottle of mineral water	(from a shop, 0.5 litres)	€0.25–€0.45
Cup of coffee	(from a café, espresso)	€1.10–€2
	(*Crème*, larger cup with milk)	€2–€2.40
Beer	(*Un demi,* half a litre)	€2–€2.75
Glass of house wine		€2–€2.40
French national newspaper		€1–€1.20
International newspaper		€1.70–€2.50
Litre of fuel	(98 unleaded)	€1.15
	(diesel)	€0.90
Métro ticket	(single)	€1.30
	(per ticket, if you buy a *carnet*)	€1
Camera film	(36 pictures)	€7.50–€8.50
20 cigarettes	(on average)	€6.30

HEALTH

The sun can be strong in Brittany in the summer. Remember to pack a high-factor sun block

BEFORE YOU GO

• EU citizens receive reduced-cost healthcare in France with the relevant documentation. For UK citizens, this is the European Health Insurance Card (EHIC). An application form is available in post offices. A leaflet on health advice for travellers is also available, explaining in full the usage of EHIC, and including the appropriate form should you need to make a claim. Full health insurance is still strongly advised. For all other countries full insurance is a must.

• Make sure you are up to date with anti-tetanus boosters. Bring any medication you need with you and pack a first aid kit. In summer, always bring sun-protection cream.

IF YOU NEED TREATMENT

• The French national health system is complex. Any salaried French citizen who receives treatment by a doctor or public hospital can be reimbursed by up to 70 per cent. The same is true if you are an EU citizen and have a valid EHIC.

• If you are relying only on EHIC, rather than travel insurance, make sure the doctor you see is part of the French national health service (a *conventionné*), rather than the private system, otherwise you may face extra charges. In any case, you will have to pay up front for the consultation and treatment. To reclaim part of these costs, send the *feuille de soins* (a statement from the doctor) and your EHIC claim form to the Caisse Primaire d'Assurance-Maladie (state health insurance office) before you leave the country. Call 0820 904 175 to find the nearest office. You should also attach the labels of any medicine you have to buy.

• If you have to stay overnight in a public hospital, you will have to pay 25 per cent of the treatment costs, as well as a daily charge (*forfait journalier*). These are not refundable. It is far better to have full health insurance than to rely solely on the EHIC.

• Citizens of non-EU countries must have full health insurance.

• If you are hospitalized and have insurance, ask to see the *assistante sociale* to arrange reimbursement of the costs directly through your insurers.

• In an emergency, dial 15 for Service d'Aide Médicale d'Urgence (SAMU) unit (ambulance). They work closely with hospital emergency units and are accompanied by trained medical personnel.

• If you are able to get yourself to a hospital, make sure it has a casualty or emergency department (*urgences*).

FINDING A DOCTOR

• In a medical emergency, your hotel should be able to help find a hospital or an English-speaking doctor. The number of the regional SOS Médecins (a duty-rota of doctors on call) is in the phonebook, also listed in local newspapers; otherwise call 15 for an ambulance. Main hospitals with casualty (emergency) units are located in all major cities—ask for the nearest *centre hospitalier* or *services des urgences*.

• Any pharmacy should be able to direct you to a doctor (look for the green cross sign—if it is closed, a card in the window will tell you where the nearest one is). Pharmacists are trained to deal with minor medical problems and can provide first aid as well as over-the-counter medication.

FINDING A HOSPITAL

• Hospitals are listed in the phone book under *Hôpitaux*, and round-the-clock emergency services are called *urgences*.

• Private hospitals are a lot more expensive than public ones and treatment is not necessarily better. If you choose a private hospital, check that you are covered for the costs before receiving treatment.

DENTAL TREATMENT

• EU citizens can receive reduced-cost emergency dental treatment with their EHIC, although insurance is still advised. The reclaim procedure is the same as for general medical treatment.

Make sure any seafood you buy is fresh, particularly in summer

Pharmacies have an illuminated green cross outside

- Other visitors should check that their insurance covers dental treatment. It's a good idea to have a dental check-up before your trip.

PHARMACIES

- A pharmacy *(pharmacie)* will have an illuminated green cross outside. Most are open Mon–Sat 9–7 or 8, but when closed they usually post details on the door of another pharmacy that is open later (called the *pharmacie de garde*).
- Pharmacists are highly qualified and provide first aid, as well as supplying medication (some drugs are by prescription, or *ordonnance*, only). But they cannot dispense prescriptions written by doctors outside the French health system, so bring sufficient supplies of any prescribed drugs you need.
- Some pharmacists speak English and can direct you to local doctors or specialists.
- They also sell a range of health-related items, although it is less expensive to go to the supermarket for items such as soap, toothbrushes and razors.
- Some commonly used medicines sold in supermarkets at home (such as aspirins and cold remedies) can only be bought in pharmacies in France.

TAP WATER

- Tap water is safe to drink and restaurants will often bring a carafe of water to the table, although most French people opt instead for bottled water.
- In public places look for the sign *eau potable* (drinking water). Don't drink from anything marked *eau non potable*.

HEALTHY FLYING

- If you are visiting France from the US, Australia or New Zealand, you may be concerned about the effect of long-haul flights on your health. The most widely publicized concern is Deep Vein Thrombosis, or DVT. DVT occurs when a blood clot forms in the body's deep veins, particularly in the legs. The clot can move around the bloodstream and could be fatal.
- Those most at risk include the elderly, pregnant women and those using the contraceptive pill, smokers and the overweight. If you are at increased risk of DVT see your doctor before departing. Flying increases the likelihood of DVT because passengers are often seated in a cramped position for long periods of time and may become dehydrated.

To minimize risk:
Drink water (not alcohol).
Don't stay immobile for hours at a time.
Stretch and exercise your legs periodically.
Do wear elastic flight socks, which support veins and reduce the chances of a clot forming.

EXERCISES

1 ANKLE ROTATIONS **2 CALF STRETCHES** **3 KNEE LIFTS**

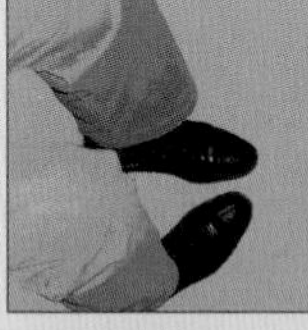
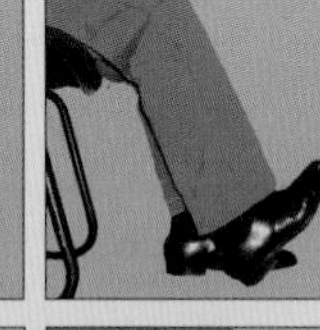
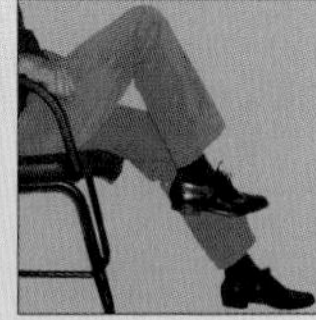

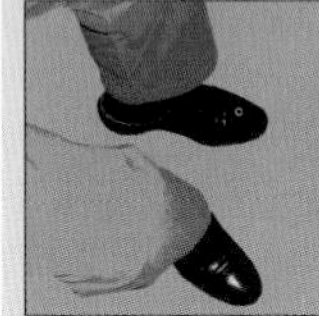
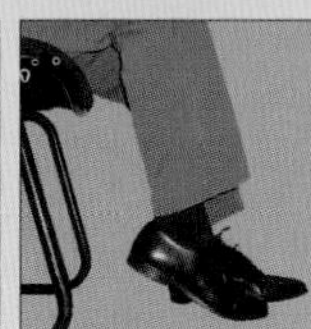

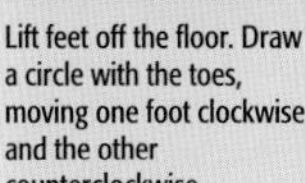

1 Lift feet off the floor. Draw a circle with the toes, moving one foot clockwise and the other counterclockwise

2 Start with heel on the floor and point foot upward as high as you can. Then lift heels high, keeping balls of feet on the floor

3 Lift leg with knee bent while contracting your thigh muscle. Then straighten leg, pressing foot flat to the floor

Other health hazards for flyers are airborne diseases and bugs spread by the plane's air-conditioning system. These are largely unavoidable, but if you have a serious medical condition seek advice from a doctor before setting off.

SUMMER HAZARDS

- The sun can be strong in Brittany between May and September, so pack a high-factor sun block. You may also like to take an insect repellent, although the insect bites you get in northwestern France are more likely to be irritating than dangerous.
- The likelihood of contracting food poisoning from shellfish is greater in the summer when ambient temperatures are higher. Toxic algal blooms (sudden proliferations of microscopic sea organisms) can sometimes affect fish—look out for local warnings.

ALTERNATIVE MEDICAL TREATMENT

- Alternative medicine, such as homeopathy, is generally available from most pharmacies.
- Alternative treatment is available and is on the increase, although chiropractics and reflexology are not widespread. Useful websites include www.chiropratique.org (the Association Française de Chiropratique), www.aea-org.com (Association Europe Acupuncture) and www.naturosante.com (a site about alternative medical treatments).

FINDING HELP

Most visits to northwestern France are trouble-free, but make sure you have adequate insurance to cover any health emergencies, thefts or legal costs that may arise. If you do become a victim of crime, it is most likely to be at the hands of a pickpocket, so always keep your money and mobile phones safely tucked away.

PERSONAL SECURITY

- Take a note of your traveller's cheque numbers and keep it separate from the cheques themselves, as you will need it to make a claim in case of loss.
- Don't keep wallets, purses or mobile phones in the back pockets of trousers, or anywhere else that is easily accessible to thieves. Money belts and bags worn around the waist are targets, as thieves know you are likely to have valuables in them. Always keep an eye on your bags in restaurants, bars and on the Métro, and hold shoulder bags close to you, fastener inwards, when you are walking in the streets.
- Thieves and pickpockets are especially fond of crowded places, such as rush-hour buses and trains, busy markets or popular festivals. Beware if someone bumps into you—it may be a ploy to distract you while someone else snatches your money.
- If you are the victim of theft, you must report it at the local police station *(commissariat)* if you want to claim on your insurance. Keep hold of the statement the police give you. You must also contact your credit card company as soon as possible to cancel any stolen cards.
- Keep valuable items in your hotel safe *(coffre-fort)*.
- When you park your car, don't leave anything of value inside. It's even risky leaving anything at all in view that may attract the interest of a thief. Carry your belongings with you or leave them behind.
- On trains, try to keep your luggage where you can see it.

LOSS OF PASSPORT

- Always keep a separate note of your passport number and a photocopy of the page that carries your details, in case of loss or theft. You can also scan the relevant pages of your passport and then email them to yourself at an email account that you can access anywhere (such as www.hotmail.com).
- If you do lose your passport or it is stolen, report it to the police and then contact your nearest embassy or consulate.

EMERGENCY NUMBERS
112 General emergency number
15 Ambulance
17 Police
18 Fire

POLICE

- There are various types of police officer in France. The two main forces are the Police Nationale, who are under the control of the local mayor, and the Gendarmerie Nationale, who you often see at airports.
- You are likely to encounter the armed CRS riot police only at a demonstration.
- In France, the police have wide powers of stop and search. It is wise to carry your passport in case a police officer stops you and requests your ID.

FIRE

- The French fire brigade deals with a number of emergencies in addition to actual fires. These range from stranded cats to road accidents and gas leaks. They are trained to give first aid.

EMBASSIES AND CONSULATES IN PARIS

- Most national embassies are in the capital (see chart). There is no UK consular assistance anywhere in Brittany, but the US has an American Presence Post at 30 quai Duguay-Trouin, 35000 Rennes, tel 02 23 44 09 60.

EMBASSIES AND CONSULATES IN PARIS

COUNTRY	ADDRESS	WEBSITE
Australia	4 rue Jean-Rey, 75015; tel 01 40 59 33 00	www.france.embassy.gov.au
Canada	35 avenue Montaigne, 75008 tel 01 44 43 29 00	www.amb-canada.fr
Germany	13–15 avenue Franklin Roosevelt, 75008; tel 01 53 83 45 00	www.amb-allemagne.fr
Ireland	4 rue Rude, 75116; tel 01 44 17 67 00	
Italy	51 rue de Varenne, 75007 tel 01 49 54 03 00	www.amb-italie.fr
Spain	22 avenue Marceau, 75008 tel 01 44 43 18 00	www.amb-espagne.fr
UK	35 rue du Faubourg-St-Honoré, 75008; tel 01 44 51 31 00	www.amb-grandebretagne.fr
US	2 avenue Gabriel, 75008 tel 01 43 12 22 22	www.amb-usa.fr

COMMUNICATION

TELEPHONING

French numbers All numbers in France have ten digits. The country is divided into five regional zones, indicated by the first two digits of the phone number (see chart below). You must dial these two digits even if you are calling from within the zone. Numbers in Brittany begin with 02.

International calls To call France from the UK dial 00 33, then drop the first zero from the 10-digit number. To call the UK from France, dial 00 44, then drop the first zero from the area code. To call France from the US, dial 011 33, then drop the first zero from the 10-digit number. To call the US from France, dial 00 1, followed by the number.

Call charges For calls within France, peak period is from 8am to 7pm, Monday to Friday. Numbers beginning with 08 have special rates. 0800 or 0805 numbers are free. 0810 and 0811 numbers are charged at local rate. Other 08 numbers cost more than national calls—sometimes considerably more.

GUIDE PRICES		
TYPE OF CALL	INITIAL CHARGE	EACH FURTHER MINUTE
Local, peak	€0.091 (1 min)	€0.033
Local, off-peak	€0.091 (1 min)	€0.018
National, peak	€0.112 (39 sec)	€0.091
National, off-peak	€0.112 (39sec)	€0.061
Calling the UK, off-peak	€0.11 (15 sec)	€0.12
Calling the US, off-peak	€0.11 (27 sec)	€0.15

PAYPHONES

- Nearly all public payphones in France use a phone card *(télécarte)* rather than coins. You can buy these at post offices, *tabacs*, newsagents and France Telecom shops, with 50 or 120 units. You do not need to pay if you are calling an emergency number.
- If the phone displays the blue bell sign, you can receive incoming calls.

Most public payphones use a phone card (télécarte)

MOBILE PHONES

You can usually use your own mobile, but there are a few points to check before leaving:

- Check the call charges, which can rise dramatically when you use your phone abroad for both incoming and outgoing calls.
- Make sure the numbers memorized in your directory are in the international format.

SENDING A LETTER

- You can buy stamps *(timbres)* for a letter *(lettre)* or a postcard *(carte postale)* at post offices and *tabacs*. Write *par avion* (by air) on the envelope or postcard.
- If you want registered post, ask at the post office for the letter to be sent *recommandé*. For a parcel *(colis)*, you can choose either *prioritaire* (priority) or the less expensive, but slower, *économique*.
- Mailboxes are yellow. In larger cities, some have two sections, one for the local *département*, and another for national and international mail *(autres départements/étranger)*. Mail sent from France should take up to five days to arrive.

POST OFFICES

- Post offices *(bureaux de poste)* are well signposted. The postal service is known as La Poste.
- Opening hours are generally Monday to Friday 8–5 or 6, Saturday 8–12. Some branches close for lunch.
- Facilities usually include phone booths, photocopiers, fax *(télécopieur)* and access to the Minitel directory service.
- Money can be wired through Western Union via most post offices, and international money orders can be sent from post offices (a charge is payable). Many also have exchange services in the following currencies: American, Australian and Canadian dollars, yen, British pounds sterling, Swiss francs, Swedish kronor, and Danish and Norwegian kroner.

COUNTRY CODES FROM FRANCE	
Australia	00 61
Belgium	00 32
Canada	00 1
Germany	00 49
Republic of Ireland	00 353
Italy	00 39
Monaco	00 377
Netherlands	00 31
New Zealand	00 64
Spain	00 34
Sweden	00 46
UK	00 44
US	00 1

PREFIXES	
00	International
01	Île-de-France (including Paris)
02	Northwest France
03	Northeast France
04	Southeast France
05	Southwest France
06	Mobile telephone numbers
0800/0805	Toll-free
08	Special-rate numbers

INTERNET ACCESS

- Many towns have internet cafés. Look for the Cyberposte sign in larger post offices, or check www.cyberposte.com. You buy a card at the counter, which can be recharged. Certain hotels, libraries, supermarkets, bars and tourist offices also have internet terminals., many operated by France Telecom using a *télécarte* (look for the word *Borne*).

POSTAGE RATES FOR LETTERS	
Within France	€0.53
To Western Europe	€0.55
To Eastern Europe	€0.75
To America	€0.90
To Africa	€0.75
To Asia	€0.90
To Australia	€0.90

OPENING TIMES AND TOURIST OFFICES

TICKETS

- Many popular tourist towns, for example, Vitré or Fougères in Brittany, provide a reduced-rate card or pass for entry to the main sights and museums. Some schemes include other benefits, such as low-cost transport, a free guided tour, a boat-trip or a *petit-train* ride. Ask the tourist office for details of any inclusive deals.
- For information on transport tickets, see pages 30–1.
- Students with an International Student Identity Card (ISIC) and seniors get reduced-price entry at some museums.
- For information on show and concert tickets, see page 116.

TOURIST OFFICES

- France has a complex but generally very efficient tourist information system. At the top end of the scale is the centralized regional office known as Comité Régional de Tourisme. In Brittany, the head office is in Rennes. This and their subordinate Comités Départementaux (one in each *département*) mostly handle postal, fax or telephone enquiries, some from overseas, rather than face-to-face encounters.
- Visitors are much more likely to have direct contact with the *offices de tourisme* or *syndicats d'initiative* in individual towns and villages, where you can collect all sorts of maps, leaflets and brochures on the attractions of the local area. Just about everywhere you may want to visit in France has some kind of tourist office (often well-signed or highly visible on the main square by the church).
- A useful document is a *Guide Pratique*, an informative listing of more or less everything a town has to offer from dentists to DIY shops, rather than glossy pictures. Accommodation brochures and public transport timetables are generally published separately, however.
- Most promotional information is free, but you may have to pay for guidebooks, detailed touring maps or walks guides. Some brochures are available in English (though occasionally the translation can be more baffling than the *version originale*).
- Tourist offices can book accommodation for you, and sometimes sell tickets for excursions or events. Some have internet points, or provide exchange facilities.
- A sign with a letter 'i' ('information' logo) on it may simply denote a display board with a local map and other information such as hotel listings, rather than an office.
- If you arrive when a tourist office is closed (perhaps on a Sunday), a local hotel may be able to provide a guide or map of the town, or information leaflets. These are sometimes available at museums or tourist attractions, and of course, passers-by may be only too happy to tell you about their home town.
- Other kinds of tourist office include small seasonal *Points d'Information*, commercially operated *Maisons du Tourisme* and *Pays d'Acceuil Touristiques*, which provide excellent regional information by post or email but are not generally open to the public.
- The French government tourist offices overseas are generally called Maisons de la France.

OPENING TIMES		
Banks	Usual opening hours are Monday to Friday 9–12, 2–5, but these can vary.	Banks close at noon on the day before a national holiday, as well as on the holiday itself.
Shops	Food shops are open Tuesday to Friday 7 or 8am–6.30 or 7.30pm.	Some close all day Monday while others will open in the afternoon only. On Saturday and Sunday they may open mornings only. Smaller shops tend to close at lunchtime from 12–2. Bakers (*boulangerie*) open on Sunday mornings and supermarkets and hypermarkets are open six days a week and have long business hours, opening at about 9am and staying open until 9 or 10pm, but closing on Sundays. Some also remain closed on Monday mornings.
Museums	Off-season, most municipal museums are closed on Monday, and some national museums close on Tuesday, but in high season they are generally open every day.	If you are planning to travel any distance for a special museum, ring in advance to check it is open. Sometimes public holidays, local festivals or renovation works may cause unexpected closures.
Restaurants	Lunch is generally served from 12–2 or 2.30 and dinner from 7.30–10 or 11.	Restaurants generally take at least one day off a week (often Sunday or Monday) except in high season (July and August), when they stay open longer hours. Except in larger business towns, many restaurants close completely from November to Easter.
Post offices	These generally open Monday to Friday 8–5, 6 or 7 weekdays and 8–noon on Saturday.	Small branches may close for lunch.
Pharmacies	Most are open Monday to Saturday 9–7 or 8.	They all display a list of local pharmacies that open later and on a Sunday.

USEFUL WEBSITES

www.aeroport.fr
Information on all of France's airports. (French)

www.fodors.com
A comprehensive travel-planning site that lets you research prices, reserve air tickets and put questions to fellow visitors. (English)

www.franceguide.com
Practical advice from the French Tourist Office on everything from arriving in France to buying a property. The site also has features on holidays and attractions. (French, English, German, Spanish, Italian, Dutch, Portuguese)

www.francetourism.com
The official US website of the French Government Tourist Office. (English)

www.lemonde.fr
Catch up on current events on the site of *Le Monde* newspaper. (French)

www.meteo.fr/meteonet
Weather forecasts for France. (French, English and Spanish)

www.monum.fr
Find out more about some of France's most historic monuments, on the site of the Centre des Monuments Nationaux. (French and English)

www.pagesjaunes.fr
France's Yellow Pages online. (French and English)

www.radio-france.fr
News, music and sport. (French)

www.theAA.com
The AA website contains a route planner, helpful if you are driving in France. You can also order maps of the country. (English)

www.tourist-office.org
Lists details of every tourist information office in France. (French)

Other websites are listed alongside the relevant sights and towns in the Sights section, and in the On the Move section.

Important ones include:
www.brittanytourism.com
www.fncrt.com
www.tourisme.fr
www.discoverbrittany.com
www.fco.gov.uk
www.cotesdarmor.com
www.finisteretourisme.com
www.bretagne35.com
www.morbihan.com
www.bretagne.com

MEDIA

TELEVISION

- France has five non-cable television stations, the nationally owned and operated channels 2 and 3, the privately owned 1 and 6, and the Franco-German ARTE (channel 5). Almost all the shows are in French. There are commercials on all terrestrial channels except ARTE.
- TF1 has news, recent American and French films, soaps and shows.
- France 2 has news, recent French and foreign films, soaps, shows and documentaries.
- France 3, a regional and national channel, has regional and national news, regional shows, documentaries, mostly French films and, once a week, a film in its original language.
- ARTE is a Franco-German channel operating with shows in French and German. International films are shown in their original language and there are also cultural documentaries.
- M6 shows a lot of low-budget films and past American sitcoms and soaps. There are also some interesting documentaries.
- Digital television has now taken off in France. More than 100 channels are on offer either through satellite or cable.
- If the TV listings mention VO *(version originale)*, the show or film will be in the language in which it was made, with French subtitles (Channel 3 usually screens a good VO film every Sunday at around midnight).
- Note that French television channels do not always keep exactly to schedule.
- Many hotels now provide a basic cable service; this may include Sky or Eurosport, BBC World and CNN. Cable channels now offer multilingual versions

CABLE TV

Depending on what cable option your hotel has, you may have some of the following channels:

BBC World	News and magazine reports of international interest
Canal+	Shows recent films (some in the original language)
MTV	Contemporary music channel
MCM	The French version of MTV
Eurosport or Infosport	For major sporting events
Planète	Nature and science documentaries
RAI Uno	Italian
TVE 1	Spanish
Euronews	A European all-news channel
LCI	All news in French
Canal Jimmy	Shows some British and American shows like *Friends* and *NYPD Blue* in English or multilingual versions
Paris Première	A cultural channel with some films in English
Canal J	With children's shows until 8pm
Téva	A women's channel that runs some English-language shows such as *Sex and the City*

PLANNING

of some shows. Ask at your hotel how to use this option as the mechanics vary. The commercial-free ARTE usually offers a choice between French and German for its cultural shows.

RADIO

- French radio stations are available mainly on FM wave lengths, with a few international stations on LW. All FM stations are in French.

Stations include:

- Chérie FM: 91.3 FM; French mainstream pop, news, reports.
- France Infos: 105.5 FM; news bulletins every 15 minutes.
- France Musique: 91.7 FM; classical and jazz music, concerts, operas, news.
- NRJ: 100.3 FM; French and international pop, techno, rap, R'n'B.
- Radio Classique: 101.1 FM; classical music.
- Skyrock: 96 FM; rap, hip-hop, R'n'B.
- BBC Radio 4 198 kHz MW; news, current affairs, drama, (reception is patchy in northwestern France).
- BBC Five Live 909 kHz MW; news and sport, (reception is patchy in northwestern France).
- BBC World Service 648 kHz LW.

NEWSPAPERS

- In tourist areas and the major cities you can buy the main English dailies, sometimes a day old, at a price premium.
- *The Economist*, *USA Today* and *The Wall Street Journal* can be found at news-stands in cities, along with *The European*, which presents a pan-European perspective in English, and the *International Herald Tribune*, which reports international news from a US standpoint.
- You may be disappointed to find an international edition of your preferred paper rather than the one you would get at home.
- Most French cities and regions have their own newspapers. In Brittany, you'll find the popular daily *Ouest France* and the Morlaix-based *La Télégramme*, plus regional periodicals like *Ar Men* and *Bretagne Magazine*.
- Leading local newspapers play an active part in pressure politics in their area, though the issues of some may seem parochial to the outsider.
- If you want to find out what's happening in a French city during your stay, consult the 'what's on' supplements that are issued with some newspapers.
- Listings magazines in Brittany include Côtes d'Armor's *Le Cri de l'Ormeau*. You'll often see these distributed free of charge in tourist offices, music stores, cafés and hotels.
- Weekly news magazines include *Le Nouvel Observateur*, *Le Point* and *L'Express*.
- When you want celebrity gossip and lots of pictures, buy *Paris Match*, *Voici* or *Gala*.

NEWSPAPERS

French daily newspapers have clear political leanings.

Le Monde
Until recently this stately paper, left-of-centre, refused to run photos and used illustrations.

Libération
This lively youth-focused paper is more clearly leftist.

L'Humanité
Left wing.

Le Figaro
Mainstream conservative daily.

Ouest France
A popular daily paper covering Brittany, Lower Normandy and Pays de la Loire

Journal du Dimanche
Sunday newspaper.

FILMS AND BOOKS

FILMS

- Watching a French film is a good way to get the feel of the place before you visit.
- For a classic, try *Les Enfants du Paradis* (1945) directed by Marcel Carné. For *nouvelle vague* (new wave) cinema—often filmed with a hand-held camera—try *Jules et Jim* (1962), directed by François Truffaut and starring Jeanne Moreau, or *À Bout de Souffle* (1959), directed by Jean-Luc Godard. The surreal *Belle de Jour* (1967), starring Catherine Deneuve, caused a scandal at the time due to its erotic subject matter. The 1987 weepie *Au Revoir les Enfants* tells the story of a Jewish boy in occupied France in World War II.
- No reference to French movies would be complete without mentioning Gérard Depardieu, the actor who conquered France and then Hollywood. His best-known works include *Cyrano de Bergerac* (1990) and *Jean de Florette* (1986).
- Jean-Pierre Jeunet's *Delicatessen* (1991) turns the controversial subject of cannibalism into a black comedy.
- Roman Polanski's *Tess* was filmed on location in Brittany, and the unforgettable *Babette's Feast*. came to international attention when it was shown at the Rouen Film Festival.
- Brittany's most famous cinematic coup was perhaps Alfred Hitchcock's spooky thriller *The Birds*, filmed in Dinard.
- The historical drama *The Vikings* put the romantic Emerald Coast setting of Fort La Latte to good effect. Now in Pays de la Loire, though it was still in Brittany when the film was made, the little village of St-Marc is where Jacques Tati's wonderful creation Monsieur Hulot had that hilarious holiday way back in 1953.

BOOKS

- For some modern novels with a sense of place, try *Flaubert's Parrot*, by Julian Barnes, a wander beside the Seine in Rouen, or *Odo's Hanging*, by Peter Benson, about the creation of the Bayeux Tapestry.
- Brittany can lay claim to associations with the Romantic writer René de Chateaubriand (*Mémoires*), Honoré de Balzac (*Les Chouans* – the royalist rebellion based in Fougères), Alexandre Dumas (*The Three Musketeers*—partly set on Belle-Île) and Pierre Loti (*Pêcheur d'Islande*—about the cod-fishing community of Paimpol). Madame de Sevigné wrote her letters about the French court from Vitré.

WORDS AND PHRASES

Even if you're far from fluent, it is always a good idea to try to speak a few words of French while in France. The words and phrases on the following pages should help you with the basics, from ordering a meal to dealing with emergencies.

CONVERSATION

What is the time?
Quelle heure est-il?

When do you open/close?
A quelle heure ouvrez/ fermez-vous?

I don't speak French.
Je ne parle pas français.

Do you speak English?
Parlez-vous anglais?

I don't understand.
Je ne comprends pas.

Please repeat that.
Pouvez-vous répéter (s'il vous plaît)?

Please speak more slowly.
Pouvez-vous parler plus lentement?

What does this mean?
Qu'est-ce que ça veut dire?

Write that down for me please.
Pouvez-vous me l'écrire, s'il vous plaît?

Please spell that.
Pouvez-vous me l'épeler, s'il vous plaît?

I'll look that up (in the dictionary).
Je vais le chercher (dans le dictionnaire).

My name is...
Je m'appelle...

What's your name?
Comment vous appelez-vous?

This is my wife/husband.
Voici ma femme/mon mari.

This is my daughter/son.
Voici ma fille/mon fils.

This is my friend.
Voici mon ami(e).

Hello, pleased to meet you.
Bonjour, enchanté(e).

I'm from ...
Je viens de ...

I'm on holiday.
Je suis en vacances.

I live in ...
J'habite à ...

Where do you live?
Où habitez-vous?

Good morning.
Bonjour.

Good evening.
Bonsoir.

Goodnight.
Bonne nuit.

Goodbye.
Au revoir.

See you later.
A plus tard.

How much is that?
C'est combien?

May I/Can I?
Est-ce que je peux?

I don't know.
Je ne sais pas.

You're welcome.
Je vous en prie.

How are you?
Comment allez-vous?

I'm sorry.
Je suis désolé(e).

Excuse me.
Excusez-moi.

That's all right.
De rien.

USEFUL WORDS

Yes **Oui**	There **Là-bas**	Who **Qui**	How **Comment**	Open **Ouvert**	Please **S'il vous plaît**
No **Non**	Here **Ici**	When **Quand**	Later **Plus tard**	Closed **Fermé**	Thank you **Merci**
	Where **Où**	Why **Pourquoi**	Now **Maintenant**		

SHOPPING

Could you help me, please?
(Est-ce que) vous pouvez m'aider, s'il vous plaît?

How much is this?
C'est combien?/Ça coûte combien?

I'm looking for …
Je cherche …

When does the shop open/close?
A quelle heure ouvre/ferme le magasin?

I'm just looking, thank you.
Je regarde, merci.

This isn't what I want.
Ce n'est pas ce que je veux.

This is the right size.
C'est la bonne taille.

Do you have anything less expensive/smaller/larger?
(Est-ce que) vous avez quelque chose de moins cher/plus petit/plus grand?

I'll take this.
Je prends ça.

Do you have a bag for this, please?
(Est-ce que) je peux avoir un sac, s'il vous plaît?

Do you accept credit cards?
(Est-ce que) vous acceptez les cartes de crédit?

I'd like … grams please.
Je voudrais … grammes, s'il vous plaît.

I'd like a kilo of …
Je voudrais un kilo de …

What does this contain?
Quels sont les ingrédients?/ Qu'est-ce qu'il y a dedans?

I'd like … slices of that.
J'en voudrais … tranches.

Bakery
Boulangerie

Bookshop
Librairie

Chemist
Pharmacie

Supermarket
Supermarché

Market
Marché

Sale
Soldes

NUMBERS

1 **un**	6 **six**	11 **onze**	16 **seize**	21 **vingt et un**	70 **soixante-dix**
2 **deux**	7 **sept**	12 **douze**	17 **dix-sept**	30 **trente**	80 **quatre-vingt**
3 **trois**	8 **huit**	13 **treize**	18 **dix-huit**	40 **quarante**	90 **quatre-vingt-dix**
4 **quatre**	9 **neuf**	14 **quatorze**	19 **dix-neuf**	50 **cinquante**	100 **cent**
5 **cinq**	10 **dix**	15 **quinze**	20 **vingt**	60 **soixante**	1000 **mille**

POST AND TELEPHONES

Where is the nearest post office/mail box?
Où se trouve la poste/la boîte aux lettres la plus proche?

How much is the postage to…?
A combien faut-il affranchir pour …?

I'd like to send this by air mail/ registered mail.
Je voudrais envoyer ceci par avion/en recommandé.

Can you direct me to a public phone?
Pouvez-vous m'indiquer la cabine téléphonique la plus proche?

What is the number for directory enquiries?
Quel est le numéro pour les renseignements?

Where can I find a telephone directory?
Où est-ce que je peux trouver un annuaire?

Where can I buy a phone card?
Où est-ce que je peux acheter une télécarte?

Please put me through to…
Pouvez-vous me passer …, s'il vous plaît?

Can I dial direct to …?
Est-ce que je peux appeler directement en …?

Do I need to dial 0 first?
Est-ce qu'il faut composer le zéro (d'abord)?

What is the charge per minute?
Quel est le tarif à la minute?

Have there been any calls for me?
Est-ce que j'ai eu des appels téléphoniques?

Hello, this is …
Allô, c'est … (à l'appareil)?

Who is speaking please …?
Qui est à l'appareil, s'il vous plaît?

I would like to speak to …
Je voudrais parler à …

DAYS/MONTHS/HOLIDAYS/TIMES

Monday **lundi**	January **janvier**	August **août**	spring **printemps**	morning **matin**	day **le jour**
Tuesday **mardi**	February **février**	September **septembre**	summer **été**	afternoon **après-midi**	month **le mois**
Wednesday **mercredi**	March **mars**	October **octobre**	autumn **automne**	evening **soir**	year **l'année**
Thursday **jeudi**	April **avril**	November **novembre**	winter **hiver**	night **nuit**	
Friday **vendredi**	May **mai**	December **décembre**	holiday **vacances**	today **aujourd'hui**	
Saturday **samedi**	June **juin**		Easter **Pâques**	yesterday **hier**	
Sunday **dimanche**	July **juillet**		Christmas **Noël**	tomorrow **demain**	

HOTELS

Do you have a room?
(Est-ce que) vous avez une chambre?

I have a reservation for … nights.
J'ai réservé pour … nuits.

How much each night?
C'est combien par nuit?

Double room.
Une chambre pour deux personnes/double.

Twin room.
Une chambre à deux lits/avec lits jumeaux.

Single room.
Une chambre à un lit/pour une personne.

With bath/shower/lavatory.
Avec salle de bain/douche/WC.

Is the room air-conditioned/heated?
(Est-ce que) la chambre est climatisée/chauffée?

Is breakfast/lunch/dinner included in the cost?
(Est-ce que) le petit déjeuner/le déjeuner/le dîner est compris dans le prix?

Is there a lift in the hotel?
(Est-ce qu')il y a un ascenseur à l'hôtel?

Is room service available?
(Est-ce qu')il y a le service en chambre?

When do you serve breakfast?
À quelle heure servez-vous le petit déjeuner?

May I have breakfast in my room?
(Est-ce que) je peux prendre le petit déjeuner dans ma chambre?

Do you serve evening meals?
(Est-ce que) vous servez le repas du soir/le dîner?

I need an alarm call at …
Je voudrais être réveillé(e) à … heures.

I'd like an extra blanket/pillow.
Je voudrais une couverture/un oreiller supplémentaire, s'il vous plaît.

May I have my room key?
(Est-ce que) je peux avoir la clé de ma chambre?

Will you look after my luggage until I leave?
Pouvez-vous garder mes bagages jusqu'à mon départ?

Is there parking?
(Est-ce qu') il y a un parking?

Where can I park my car?
Où est-ce que je peux garer ma voiture?

Do you have babysitters?
(Est-ce que) vous avez un service de babysitting/garde d'enfants?

When are the sheets changed?
Quand changez-vous les draps?

The room is too hot/cold.
Il fait trop chaud/froid dans la chambre.

Could I have another room?
(Est-ce que) je pourrais avoir une autre chambre?

I am leaving this morning.
Je pars ce matin.

What time should we leave our room?
A quelle heure devons-nous libérer la chambre?

Can I pay my bill?
(Est-ce que) je peux régler ma note, s'il vous plaît?

May I see the room?
(Est-ce que) je peux voir la chambre?

Swimming pool.
Piscine.

No smoking.
Non fumeur.

Sea view.
Vue sur la mer.

GETTING AROUND

Where is the information desk?
Où est le bureau des renseignements?

Where is the timetable?
Où sont les horaires?

Does this train/bus go to …?
Ce train/bus va à …?

Do you have a Métro/bus map?
Avez-vous un plan du Métro/des lignes de bus?

Please can I have a single/return ticket to …?
Je voudrais un aller simple/un aller-retour pour …, s'il vous plaît.

I'd like to rent a car.
Je voudrais louer une voiture.

Where are we?
Où sommes-nous?

I'm lost.
Je me suis perdu(e).

Is this the way to …?
C'est bien par ici pour aller à …?

I am in a hurry.
Je suis pressé(e).

Where can I find a taxi?
Où est-ce que je peux trouver un taxi?

How much is the journey?
Combien coûte la course?

Go straight on.
Allez tout droit.

Turn left.
Tournez à gauche.

Turn right.
Tournez à droite.

Cross over.
Traversez.

Traffic lights.
Les feux.

Intersection.
Carrefour.

Corner.
Coin.

No parking
Interdiction de stationner

Train/bus/Métro station
La gare SNCF/routière/la station de Métro.

Do you sell travel cards?
Avez-vous des cartes d'abonnement?

Do I need to get off here?
(Est-ce qu') il faut que je descende ici?

Where can I buy a ticket?
Où est-ce que je peux acheter un billet/ticket?

Where can I reserve a seat?
Où est-ce que je peux réserver une place?

Is this seat free?
(Est-ce que) cette place est libre?

Where can I find a taxi?
Où est-ce que je peux trouver un taxi?

MONEY

Is there a bank/currency exchange office nearby?
(Est-ce qu') il y a une banque/un bureau de change près d'ici?

Can I cash this here?
(Est-ce que) je peux encaisser ça ici?

I'd like to change sterling/dollars into euros.
Je voudrais changer des livres sterling/dollars en euros.

Can I use my credit card to withdraw cash?
(Est-ce que) je peux utiliser ma carte de crédit pour retirer de l'argent?

What is the exchange rate today?
Quel est le taux de change aujourd'hui?

COLOURS

brown **marron/brun**	blue **bleu(e)**
black **noir(e)**	green **vert(e)**
red **rouge**	yellow **jaune**

I'd like to reserve a table for … people at …
Je voudrais réserver une table pour … personnes à …heures, s'il vous plaît.

A table for …, please.
Une table pour …, s'il vous plaît.

We have/haven't booked.
Nous avons/n'avons pas réservé.

What time does the restaurant open?
A quelle heure ouvre le restaurant?

We'd like to wait for a table.
Nous aimerions attendre qu'une table se libère.

Could we sit there?
(Est-ce que) nous pouvons nous asseoir ici?

Is this table taken?
(Est-ce que) cette table est libre?

Are there tables outside?
(Est-ce qu') il y a des tables dehors/à la terrasse?

Where are the lavatories?
Où sont les toilettes?

Could you warm this up for me?
(Est-ce que) vous pouvez me faire réchauffer ceci/ça, s'il vous plaît?

Do you have nappy-changing facilities?
(Est-ce qu') il y a une pièce pour changer les bébés?

We'd like something to drink.
Nous voudrions quelque chose à boire.

Could we see the menu/wine list?
(Est-ce que) nous pouvons voir le menu/la carte des vins, s'il vous plaît?

Is there a dish of the day?
(Est-ce qu') il y a un plat du jour?

What do you recommend?
Qu'est-ce que vous nous conseillez?

RESTAURANTS

This is not what I ordered.
Ce n'est pas ce que j'ai commandé.

I can't eat wheat/sugar/salt/pork/beef/dairy.
Je ne peux pas manger de blé/sucre/sel/porc/bœuf/produits laitiers.

I am a vegetarian.
Je suis végétarien(ne).

I'd like ...
Je voudrais ...

Could we have some more bread?
(Est-ce que) vous pouvez nous apporter un peu plus de pain, s'il vous plaît?

How much is this dish?
Combien coûte ce plat?

Is service included?
(Est-ce que) le service est compris?

Could we have some salt and pepper?
(Est-ce que) vous pouvez nous apporter du sel et du poivre, s'il vous plaît?

May I have an ashtray?
(Est-ce que) je peux avoir un cendrier, s'il vous plaît?

Could I have bottled still/sparkling water?
(Est-ce que) je peux avoir une bouteille d'eau minérale/gazeuse, s'il vous plaît?

The meat is too rare/overcooked.
La viande est trop saignante/trop cuite.

The food is cold.
La nourriture est froide.

Can I have the bill, please?
(Est-ce que) je peux avoir l'addition, s'il vous plaît?

The bill is not right.
Il y a une erreur sur l'addition.

We didn't order this.
Nous n'avons pas commandé ça.

I'd like to speak to the manager, please.
Je voudrais parler au directeur, s'il vous plaît.

The food was excellent.
La nourriture était excellente.

FOOD AND DRINK

Breakfast
Petit déjeuner

Lunch
Déjeuner

Dinner
Dîner

Coffee
Café

Tea
Thé

Orange juice
Jus d'orange

Apple juice
Jus de pomme

Milk
Lait

Beer
Bière

Red wine
Vin rouge

White wine
Vin blanc

Bread roll
Petit pain

Bread
Pain

Sugar
Sucre

Wine list
Carte/liste des vins

Main course
Le plat principal

Dessert
Dessert

Salt/pepper
Sel/poivre

Cheese
Fromage

Knife/fork/spoon
Couteau/Fourchette/Cuillère

Soups
Soupes/potages

Vegetable soup
Soupe de légumes

Chicken soup
Soupe au poulet

Lentil soup
Soupe aux lentilles

Mushroom soup
Soupe aux champignons

Sandwiches
Sandwichs

Ham sandwich
Sandwich du jambon

Dish of the day
Plat du jour

Fish dishes
Les poissons

Prawns
Crevettes roses/bouquet

Oysters
Huîtres

Salmon
Saumon

Haddock
Aiglefin

Squid
Calmar

Meat dishes
Viandes

Roast chicken
Poulet rotî

Casserole
Plat en cocotte

Roast lamb
Gigot

Mixed cold meat
L'assiette de charcuterie

Potatoes
Pommes de terre

Cauliflower
Chou-fleur

Green beans
Haricots verts

Peas
Petits pois

Carrots
Carottes

Spinach
Épinards

Onions
Oignons

Lettuce
Laitue

Cucumber
Concombre

Tomatoes
Tomates

Fruit
Les fruits

Apples
Pommes

Strawberries
Fraises

Peaches
Pêches

Pears
Poires

Fruit tart
Tarte aux fruits

Pastry
Pâtisserie

Chocolate cake
Gâteau au chocolat

Cream
Crème

Ice cream
Glace

Chocolate mousse
Mousse au chocolat

TOURIST INFORMATION

Where is the tourist information office, please?
Où se trouve l'office du tourisme, s'il vous plaît?

Do you have a city map?
Avez-vous un plan de la ville?

Where is the museum?
Où est le musée?

Can you give me some information about …?
Pouvez-vous me donner des renseignements sur …?

What are the main places of interest here?
Quels sont les principaux sites touristiques ici?

Please could you point them out on the map?
Pouvez-vous me les indiquer sur la carte, s'il vous plaît?

What sights/hotels/restaurants can you recommend?
Quels sites/hôtels/restaurants nous recommandez-vous?

We are staying here for a day.
Nous sommes ici pour une journée.

I am interested in …
Je suis intéressé(e) par …

Does the guide speak English?
Est-ce qu'il y a un guide qui parle anglais?

Do you have any suggested walks?
Avez-vous des suggestions de promenades?

Are there guided tours?
Est-ce qu'il y a des visites guidées?

Are there organised excursions?
Est-ce qu'il y a des excursions organisées?

Can we make reservations here?
Est-ce que nous pouvons réserver ici?

What time does it open/close?
Ça ouvre/ferme à quelle heure?

What is the admission price?
Quel est le prix d'entrée?

Is there a discount for senior citizens/students?
Est-ce qu'il y a des réductions pour les personnes âgées/ les étudiants?

Do you have a brochure in English?
Avez-vous un dépliant en anglais?

What's on at the cinema?
Qu'est-ce qu'il y a au cinéma?

Where can I find a good nightclub?
Où est-ce que je peux trouver une bonne boîte de nuit?

Do you have a schedule for the theatre/opera?
Est-ce que vous avez un programme de théâtre/ d'opéra?

Should we dress smartly?
Est-ce qu'il faut mettre une tenue de soirée?

What time does the show start?
A quelle heure commence le spectacle?

How do I reserve a seat?
Comment fait-on pour réserver une place?

Could you reserve tickets for me?
Pouvez-vous me réserver des billets?

ILLNESS AND EMERGENCIES

I don't feel well.
Je ne me sens pas bien.

Could you call a doctor?
(Est-ce que) vous pouvez appeler un médecin/un docteur, s'il vous plaît?

Is there a doctor/pharmacist on duty?
(Est-ce qu') il y a un médecin/docteur/une pharmacie de garde?

I feel sick.
J'ai envie de vomir.

I need to see a doctor/dentist.
Il faut que je voie un médecin/docteur/ un dentiste.

Please direct me to the hospital.
(Est-ce que) vous pouvez m'indiquer le chemin pour aller à l'hôpital, s'il vous plaît?

I have a headache.
J'ai mal à la tête.

I've been stung by a wasp/bee/jellyfish.
J'ai été piqué(e) par une guêpe/abeille/méduse.

I have a heart condition.
J'ai un problème cardiaque.

I am diabetic.
Je suis diabétique.

I'm asthmatic.
Je suis asmathique.

I'm on a special diet.
Je suis un régime spécial.

I am on medication.
Je prends des médicaments.

I have left my medicine at home.
J'ai laissé mes médicaments chez moi.

I need to make an emergency appointment.
Je dois prendre rendez-vous d'urgence.

I have bad toothache.
J'ai mal aux dents.

I don't want an injection.
Je ne veux pas de piqûre.

Help!
Au secours!

I have lost my passport/ wallet/purse/handbag.
J'ai perdu mon passeport/ portefeuille/porte-monnaie/sac à main.

I have had an accident.
J'ai eu un accident.

My car has been stolen.
On m'a volé ma voiture.

I have been robbed.
J'ai été volé(e).

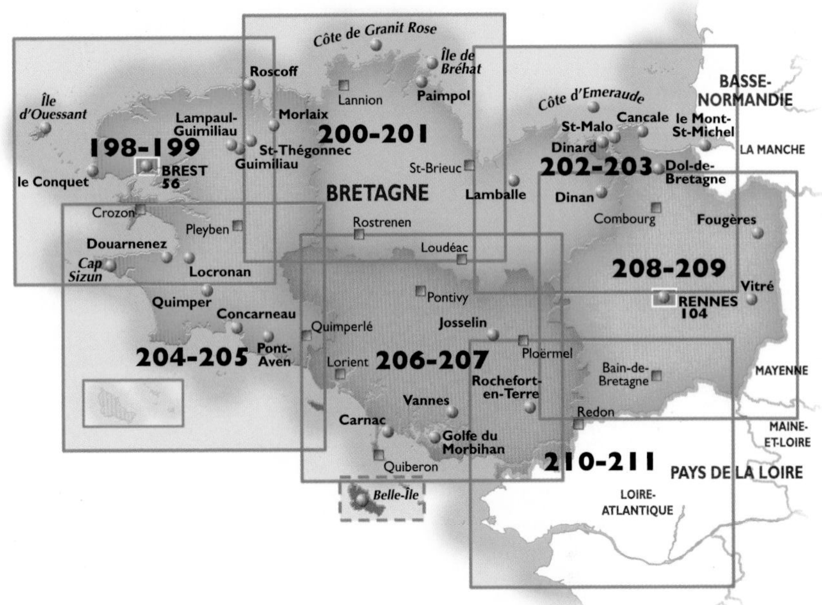

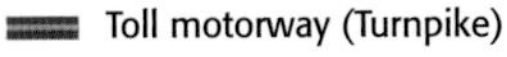

Toll motorway (Turnpike)

Motorway (Expressway)

Motorway junction with and without number

National road

Regional road

Other road

Railway

Administrative region boundary

Département boundary

City

Town / Village

National park

Featured place of interest

Other place of interest

Airport

621 Height in metres

Ferry route (vehicle)

Ferry route (passenger)

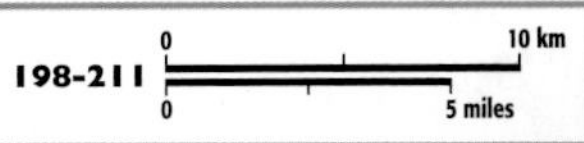

Maps

A
B
6
7
8
9
10
Côte des Légende
les Abers
Île Vierge
Île Stagadon
Lilia
Île Tariec
Île Guenioc
Vourch
Île du Bec
Île Garo
Landéda
Aber Benoît
Pointe de Landunvez
St-Pabu
D28
Tréglonou
Île Yoc'h
D27
Landunvez
Ploudalmézeau
Porspoder
Plouguin
D26
Île d'Ouessant
D28
Plourin
Pointe de Pern
Lampaul
Île Melon
Melon
D68
D168
Pointe de Porz Doun
Passage du Fromveur
Chenal de la Helle
Brélès
Lanrivoaré
Pays
Lampaul-Plouarzel
Aber Ildut
Milizac
Île de Bannec
Île Ségal
Plouarzel
D3
St-Renan
D5
Île de Balanec
Trézien
Guilers
Île de Molène
Lamber
Kerhornou
Ploumoguer
Île de Trielen
D28
D67
Plouzané
Pointe de Kermorvan
Trébabu
Locmaria-Plouzané
Île de Quéménès
Parc Naturel Régional d'Amorique
Chenal du Four
le Conquet
D789
Île de Beniguet
Porsmilin
Ste-Anne-du-Portzic
Plougonvelin
Pointe de St-Mathieu
Goulet de Brest
Pointe de Creac'h-Meur
Roscanvel
Pointe de Toulinguet
Camaret-sur-Mer
D355
Presqu'
Pointe de Pen-Hir
D8
Crozon
Pointe de Dinan
Morgat
Kerglintin
D255
Cap de la Chèvre
204
Chaussée de Sein
Pointe de Brézellec
Pointe du Van
Beuzec-Cap-Sizun
Baie des Trépassés
Cap Sizun
Cléden-Cap-Sizun
Île de Sein
Moulin-Castel
Pointe du Raz
Lescoff
D784
Plogoff
Primelin
Esquibien
Audierne
Plouhinec
Pointe de

C
D
E
6
7
8
9
10
Île de Batz
Roscoff
Île de Siec
Pointe de Beg Pol
Theven-Kerbrat
Santec
St-Pol-de-Léon
Pointe du D
Brignogan-Plage
Croazou
Plounéour-Trez
Kerlouan
Plouescat
Sibiril
Cléder
Plougoulm
Baie de Morlaix
St-Michel
Guissény
Ker-Emma
Tréflez
Lochrist
Goulven
Plouguerneau
le Grouannec
Plouider
Plounevez-Lochrist
Ste-Catherine
Henvic
Plouénan
Berven
Léon
Lannilis
Pont-du-Chatel
Kernilis
St-Vougay
Plouzévédé
Taulé
Penzé
Brévalaire
Lesneven
Lanhouarneau
Château de Kerjean
Plouvorn
200
le Folgoët
St-Méen
Plouvien
le Drennec
Ploudaniel
Plougourvest
Guiclan
Coatoulsach
Bourg-Blanc
Plabennec
Trémaouézan
Plounéventer
Landivisiau
St-Thégonnec
Kersaint-Plabennec
Plouédern
Pleyber-Christ
Guimiliau
Lampaul-Guimiliau
Landerneau
la Roche-Maurice
Guipavas
la Martyre
Ploudiry
Loc-Eguiner-St-Thégonnac
Kervian
la Forest-Landerneau
BREST
le Relecq-Kerhoun
FINISTÈRE
St-Sauveur
Plounéour-Menez
Tréflévénez
St-Urbain
Sizun
Commana
384 Roc'h Trévezel
Moulins de Kérouat
Daoulas
le Tréhou
Loperhet
Irvillac
Barrage du Drennec
Monts d'Arrée
Rade de Brest
Daoulas
la Feuillée
St-Cadou
Botmeur
St-Eloy
Tinduff
Goasven
Domaine de Menez-Meur
217 Pen-ar-Hoat
St-Rivoal
380 St-Michel
Réservoir de St Michel
Brennilis
Lagonna-Daoulas
Hôpital-Camfrout
Hanvec
Elez
Lanvéoc
Anse de Poulmic
Landévennec
le Faou
Parc Naturel Régional d'Amorique
Loquefret
274 Roc'h Begheor
Brasparts
Crozon
Lannédern
Rosnoën
Quimerch
Lopérec
Tal-ar-Groas
Argol
Aulne
Bassin de Châteaulin
le Cloitre-Pleyben
Telgruc-sur-Mer
Pont-de-Buis
330 Ménez-Hom
Dinéhault
Pleyben
Plounévez-du-Faou
Pentrez-Plage
Châteaulin
Baie de Douarnenez
Plomodiern
Lothey
Lennon
Gouézec
Cast
Ste-Anne-la-Palud
Plonévez-Porzay
205
Douarnenez
Groas-Brenn
Quéménéven
Kergoat
Laz
Poullan-sur-Mer
Pouldavic
Ploaré
Locronan
Briec
Edern
les M
Plogonnec
Trégourez
le Croëzou
Quilinep
Pouldergat
Guengat
Landudal
Langolen
Steir
Goyen
Nevet
Odet
199

E
F
6
7
8
9
10
les Sept Iles
Côte de
Île Renote
Pointe du Squéouel
Île Tomé
Ploumanac'h
Île Grande
Pointe du Château
Trévou-Treguign
Trégastel
Perros-Guirec
Île à Canton
Penvern
St-Quay-Perros
Trélévern
Louannec
Île de Batz
Baie de Lannion
Trébeurden
Pleumeur-Bodou
Pointe de Bihit
Kermaria-Sulard
D6
Roscoff
Pointe de Primel
Pointe du Diben
la Ville-Blanche
D786
St-Pol-de-Léon
Pointe de Séhar
Lannion
Rospez
Ploulec'h
Plougasnou
St-Jean-du-Doigt
Buhulien
Carantec
Trédrez
Locquirec
Ploubezre
Trég
Baie de Morlaix
Guimaëc
St-Michel-en-Grève
Ploumilliau
Confort
Henvic
Plouézoch
Lanmeur
Plestin-les-Grèves
Tonquédec
Cavan
Plouénan
Taulé
Dourdull
Yar
Pluzunet
Penzé
Ste-Geneviève
Lanvellec
Plufur
Plouaret
Douron
Coatoulsach
Morlaix
Plouigneau
Plouégat-Moysan
le Vieux-Marché
E50 N12
302 Ménez
Plounevez-Moëdec
Louargat
Plourin-lès-Mortaix
Guic
Plougonven
Belle-Isle-Benac'h
199
Pleyber-Christ
Guerlesquin
Loguivy-Plougras
Léguer
Cloitre-St-Thégonnec
Lannéanou
le Dresnay
Loc-Eguiner-St-Thégonnec
Gurunhuel
Kervian
Kermeur
Plounéour-Menez
Lohuec
Plougonver
Penze
Mendy
Squiriou
Bolazec
la Chapelle-Neuve
384 Roc'h Trévezel
Scrignac
FINISTÈRE
Calanhel
d'Arrée
Bulat-Pestivien
la Feuillée
Berrien
Botmeur
Callac
Réservoir de St Michel
Aulne
Fao
Brennilis
le Guilly
St-Servais
Huelgoat
Elez
Loc'h
Loqueffret
274 Roc'h Begheor
St-Herbot
Poullaouen
Plouyé
Hyère
Lannédern
Locarn
Collorec
Châteaulin
Kergrist-Moëlou
Cloitre-Pleyben
Goanes
Kergloff
Carhaix-Plouguer
Penquer Lois
Maël-Carhaix
Plounévez-du-Faou
St-Lubin
N164
la Pie
Landeleau
Cléden-Poher
Ancien
Canal
Nantes
Plouguernével
Lennon
Châteauneuf-du-Faou
205
Glomel
Rostrenen
Motreff
Etang du Coronc
Spézet
Brest
326 Roc de Toullaëron
Bonen
St-Goazes
290 Coat
Noires
Trégornan
200
Laz
Montagnes
Mellionnec
St-Nicolas
Ellé

H
J
6
7
8
9
10
Côte de Granit Rose
Pointe du Château
Îles d'Er
Sillon de Talbert
Île Modez
Phare du Paon
Île de Bréhat
l'Armor
Plougrescant
Pleubian
Lanmodez
Penvénan
Plouguiel
Pleumeur-Gautier
Loguivy de-la-Mer
Pointe de l'Arcouest
Ploubazlanec
Tréguier
Trédarzec
Lézardrieux
Côte de Goëlo
Paimpol
Pouldouran
Pleudaniel
Kerity
Pointe de Plouézec
la Roche-Derrien
Boloï
Trieux
Plouézec
Pointe de Minard
Pommerit-Jaudy
Plourivo
Pointe Berjule
Ploëzal
Lanloup
Quemper-Guézennec
Pontrieux
Pléhédel
Pointe de Plouha
Brélidy
Plouëc-du-Trieux
Plouha
Trévérec
Lannebert
St-Quay-Portrieux
Pléguien
Pommerit-le-Vicomte
Lanvollon
Plourhan
Etables-sur-Mer
Pabu
Goudelin
Tréguidel
Plouisy
Guingamp
Binic
la Corderie
Grâces
St-Agathon
la Ville-Louais
Pordic
les Rosaires
Ploumagor
Plouagat
Plélo
Baie de Saint-Brieuc
Pointe du Roselier
Châtelaudren
Coadut
Lanrodec
Plerin
Pointe des Guettes
Trémuson
St-Péver
Senven
St-Brieuc
Hillion
Bourbriac
Boqueho
Langueux
St-Donan
Ploufragan
Trégueux
Yffiniac
St-René
Plésidy
Cohiniac
CÔTES D'ARMOR
St-Julien
Urne
Pommeret
Norgant
Plaine Haute
Pledran
l'Hôpital
St-Gildas
le Fœil
Gouet
Quessoy
la Clarté
Kerpert
la Vieux-Bourg
Quintin
Carestremble
Plaintel
St-Brandan
St-Carreuc
Hénon
Moncontour
le-Haut-Corlay
Corlay
la Bodéo
l'Hermitage-Lorge
Ploeuc-sur-Lié
Plémy
la Porte-aux-Moines
Plussulien
Gausson
Blavet
Ste-Tréphine
Daoulas
Uzel
St-Hervé
Plouguenast
Gouarec
Laniscat
Plessala
St-Gelven
le Quillio
Caurel
Mur-de-Bretagne
St-Guen
Rigole d'Hilvern
La Motte
Etang des Salles
Lac de Guerlédan
Trévé
St-Caradec
MORBIHAN
Laurenan
E50
N12
E401
N164
D786
D767
D7
D15
D6
D8
D787
D9
D36
D700
D10
D1
D768
D765
D790
D44
D35
D5
D70
202
207
201
06

6
J
K
L
7
Côte d'Eme
Cap Fréhel
Anse des Sevignes
Forte la Latte
Île de Cézembre
Côte de Penthieve
Cap d'Erquy
Sables-d'Or-les-Pins
Pointe de St-Cast
Erquy
Plurien
Frèhel
Baie de la Frênaye
St-Cast-le-Guildo
St-Lunaire
D786
Pléboulle
Île des Hébihens
St-Briac-sur-Mer
Pointe de Pléneuf
le Val-André
Montbran
D14
Matignon
Lancieux
Pléneuf-Val-André
D13
St-Jacut-de-la-Mer
D168
Baie de Saint-Brieuc
la Bouillie
8
St-Alban
Fremur
D786
le Poirier
St-Jacques
D17
Hénanbihen
D794
Pleurtuit
Pointe des Guettes
Ploubalay
Hénansal
D13
St-Pôtan
Trémereuc
Trébéfour
D786
Planguenoual
Créhen
D768
St-Denoual
D2
Hillion
D768
Pluduno
Pleslin-Trigavou
Ponts-Neufs
St-Aaron
Langueux
Coëtmieux
D768
Plancoët
D791
Yffiniac
Gouessant
St-Symphorien
Languénan
D766
St-René
Arguenon
D2
D794
E50
E401
N12
Bourseul
Pommeret
Lamballe
Corseul
l'Hôpital
Evron
Meslin
Trégomar
Gast
D792
St-Michel-de-Plélan
Quévert
D1
Noyal
Plédéliac
Quessoy
D768
Landéhen
Plélan-le-Petit
Dinan
D14
Plestan
D765
Bréhand
E401
N176
Trélivan
la Malhourne
Hénon
Jugon-les-Lacs
CÔTES D'ARMOR
D1
Grand Etang de Jugon
9
Trédaniel
Penguily
le Hinglé
D44
D14
D792
Pléné-Jugon
Rosette
Megrit
D793
Brusvily
Guinefort
Plémy
D6
Gouessant
Rieule
D766
Yvignac
le Gouray
D39
D768
201
Tréfumel
Landes du Ménéz
Collinée
Broons
Plouguenast
208
St-Jacut-du-Mené
D793
Etang de Nea
Langourla
Plessala
Caulnes
Plouas
Rance
Eréac
St-Gilles-du-Mené
Lanrelas
Médréac
Plumaugat
D220
D792
St-Vran
Rance
Quédillac
St-Launeuc
E50
N12
Hivet
D6
D71
Laurenan
D166
N164
Plémet
Merdrignac
Trémorel
St-Méen-le-Grand
N164
207
N164
Moutauban-de-Bretagne
Ferrière
D793
Yvel
Meu
D125
D61
10
La Chèze
Illifaut
D14
Ménéac
Boisgervilly
Ninian
202
J
K
L
Gaël
D30
Muel
St-Ma
Lie
D793
MORBIHAN
D166
Meu
Iffendic

M
N
Quettreville-sur-Sienne
Lingreville
Trelly
6
Muneville-sur-Mer
Lengronne
Bricqueville-sur-Mer
Cérences
Illes Chausey
St-Martin-de-Bréhal
Bréhal
Grand Ile
Coudeville
le Loreur
Granville
D924
le Repas
St-Planchers
St-Jean-des-Champs
Folligny
St-Pair-sur-Mer
7
Kairon-Plage
La Haye-Pesnel
le Pont-Bleue
Jullouville
LA MANCHE
Carolles
Angey
Sartilly
Falaise de Champeaux
Ronthon
Dragey-Ronthon
Pointe du Grouin
Île des Landes
Rothéneuf
le Verger
St-Jouan
Marcey-les-Grèves
St-Coulomb
Cancale
Genêts
-Malo
le Beuglais
Baie du Mont Saint Michel
Avranches
le Val-St-Pierre
St-Meloir-des-Ondes
St-Benoit-des-Ondes
le Mont-St-Michel
Richardais
Bas-Courtil
St-Jouan-des-Guérets
la Gouesnière
le Vivier-sur-Mer
la Rive
Courtils
8
Rance
Hirel
Cherrueix
la Poultière
St-George
la Fresnais
Beauvoir
Précey
Marais de Dol
St-Broladre
Grand Biez de Cardéquin
Roz-sur-Couesnon
le Couesnon
Châteauneuf-d'Ille-et-Vilaine
Mont-Dol
Dol-de-Bretagne
Pontorson
Plerguer
Miniac-Morvan
Pleine-Fougères
La Croix-Avranchin
Baguer-Morvan
Bretagne
Pleudihen-sur-Rance
Epiniac
la Boussac
-Samson-r-Rance
St-Léonard
Trans
Montanel
St-Helen
ILLE-ET-VILAINE
Argouges
A84
nvallay
Molene
Bonnemain
Broualan
St-Solent
Lanhélin
St-Pierre-de-Plesguen
Cuguen
Antrain
Tronçon
Etang de Tremigon
les Champs-Géraux
Combourg
Trémeheuc
la-Selle-en-Coglés
Tremblay
Meillac
Bazouges-la-Pérouse
9
Pleugueneuc
St-Léger-des-Prés
St-Brice-en-Coglès
Evran
la Chapelle-aux-Filtzméens
Marcillé-Raoul
St-Domineuc
Quiou
Ille
St-Rémy-du-Plain
Dingé
Romazy
St-Marc-le-Blanc
Etang de Boulet
Minette
209
Tinténiac
Sens-de-Bretagne
Baillé
la Baussaine
Feins
St-Ouen-des-Alleux
St-Sauveur-des-Landes
St-Symphorien
Canal d'Ille et Rance
Montreuil-sur-Ille
St-Marc-sur-Couesnon
cherel
les Iffs
Hédé
Guipel
Neuville
Gahard
Mézières-sur-Coueson
St-Médard-sur-Ille
Irodouër
St-Aubin-d'Aubigne
Etang d'Ouée
Langan
Montreuil-le-Gast
Ercé-près-Liffre
St-Aubin-du-Corm
Vaunoise
Flume
Illet
Gosné
Romillé
Chasné-sur-Illet
Gévezé
la Mezière
Melesse
Veuvre
Chévaigné
Liffré
Pleumeleuc
la Chapelle-des-Fougereiz
10
Nouaye
Betton
Dourdain
la Bouëxière
Breteil
St-Gilles
St-Grégoire
Thorigné-Fouillard
Chevré
Pacé
l'Hermitage
203

Crozon
Morgat
Pointe de Dinan
Tal-ar-Groas
Argol
Telgruc-sur-Mer
Kerglintin
Cap de la Chèvre
Pentrez
Plomodiern
Baie de Douarnenez
198
Ste-Anne-la-Palud
Plonévez-Porzay
Pointe de Millier
Douarnenez
Lescogan
Beuzec-Cap-Sizun
Pointe de Brézellec
Pointe du Van
Baie des Trépassés
Chaussée de Sein
Île de Sein
Pointe du Raz
Cap Sizun
Cléden-Cap-Sizun
Moulin-Castel
Poullan-sur-Mer
Pouldavic
Ploaré
Locronan
Plogonnec
Lescoff
Plogoff
Primelin
Esquibien
Audierne
Confort
Pont-Croix
Pouldergat
Guengat
Plouhinec
Ty-Pic
Goyen
Pointe de Lervily
Landudec
Plozévet
Plogastel-StGermain
Pouldreuzic
Penhors
Tréogat
Plovan
Baie d'Audierne
Plonéour-Lanvern
St-Jean-Trolimon
Pont-l'Abbé
Pointe de la Porche
Plomeur
St-Guénolé
Plobannalec
Loctudy
Penmarc'h
Treffiagat
Pointe de Penmarc'h
Guilvinec
Présqu'Île de Penmarc'h
Lorient
Quiberon la Trinité
Quiberon
Passage de la Teignouse
Port-Navolo
Pointe des Poulains
Pointe du Cardinal
Sauzon
Pointe de Taillefer
Île d'Houat
Côte Sauvage
le Palais
Passage des Sœurs
Port de Donnant
Belle-Île
Kervilahouen
Bangor
Aiguilles de Port-Coton
Pointe de Kerdonis
Île d'Hœdic
Locmaria
la Turballe
Pointe de Pouldon
Pointe de l'Échelle

D
E
F
Châteaulin
Pleyben
Châteauneuf-du-Faou
Bassin de Châteaulin
Les Montagnes Noires
Gourin
MORBIHAN
FINISTÈRE
Quimper
Coray
Scaër
Rosporden
Bannalec
Concarneau
Fouesnant
la Forêt-Fouesnant
Bénodet
Beg-Meil
Pont-Aven
Quimperlé
Trégunc
Névez
Riec-sur-Belon
Moëlan-sur-Mer
Clohars-Carnoët
Guidel
le Pouldu
Plomer
Baie de Concarneau
Île aux Moutons
Îles de Glénan
Groix
Île de Groix
Pointe du Talut
Pointe de Bileric
199
200
206
9
10
11
12
13

Rostrenen
Gouarec
Laniscat
Motreff
Etang du Coronc
Bonen
St-Gelven
Caurel
Mur-de-Bretagne
Trégornan
200
Mellionnec
201
Lac de Guerlédan
St-Nicolas
Plouray
Kerguzul
Silfiac
le Corboulo
Langonnet
Langoëlan
Neuilliac
Séglien
Cléguérec
le Mouste
Poul-Grellec
Ploërdut
Priziac
le Croisty
Guéméné-s-Scorff
Locmalo
Malguénac
Stival
le Faouët
Lignol
Niziao-d'en-Bas
Pontivy
St-Fiacre
le Sourn
Guern
Meslan
Berné
Kernascléden
Pays de Pontivy
Querrien
Inguiniel
St-Thuriau
St-Fiacre
St-Armel
Melrand
St-Nicolas-des-Eaux
Roches du Diable
Bubry
Pluméliau
Tréméven
St-Yves
St-Barthélemy
Remungol
Arzano
Plouay
Quistinic
FINISTÈRE
Guénin
205
Rédené
Calan
St-Symphorien
Cléguer
Baud
Penquesten
Pont-Scorff
la Chapelle-Neuve
Inzinzac-Lochrist
Lambel
Camros
Coat-erMalo
Gestel
Hennebont
Languidic
Guidel
Queven
Locoal-Camors
Malachappe
Bienzy-Lanvaux
Brandérion
Lanester
Anse du Pouldu
Plomemeur
Kervignac
Pluvigner
Brandivy
Lorient
Landévant
Fort-Bloque
Merlevenez
Nostang
Landaul
Larmor-Plage
Locmiquelic
Ste-Hélène
Plumergat
Riantec
Brech
Pointe du Talut
Port-Louis
Plouhinec
Locoal-Mendon
Ste-Anne-d'Auray
Pointe de Gavres
Belz
Mériadec
Auray
Pluneret
Groix
Étel
Ploemel
Île de Groix
Locmaria
Erdeven
Plougoumelen
Bono
Ploeren
Pointe d'Erdeven
Crac'h
Baden
Plouharnel
Sauzon
Carnac
la Trinité-sur-Mer
Penthièvre
Sables Blancs
Locmariaquer
Ile de Gavrinis
Golfe
Portivy
Port-Navalo
Arzon
St-Pierre-Quiberon
Côte Sauvage
le Palais
Île Méaban
Presqu'Île de Quiberon
Baie de Quiberon
Quiberon
St-Gildas-de-Rhuys
Pointe du Conguel
Île d'Houat
206
F
G
H
204
Pointe des Poulains

CÔTES-D'ARMOR
MORBIHAN
Loudéac
Plémet
Merdrignac
Trémorel
La Motte
Trévé
St-Caradec
St-Gilles-du-Mené
St-Vran
St-Launeuc
Lanrelas
Eréac
Laurenan
202
10
11
12
13
208
210
J
K
la Chèze
la Ferrière
St-Barnabé
St-Gonnery
St-Maudan
St-Étienne du-Gué-de-l'Isle
Plumieux
la Trinité-Porhoët
Ménéac
Illifaut
St-Brieuc-de-Mauron
Mauron
St-Lery
Evriguet
Rohan
Bréhan
Mohon
Crédin
Guilliers
St-Malo-des-3-Fontaines
Néant-sur-Yve
Naizin
Pleugriffet
Lanouée
les Croix
Loyat
Réguiny
Josselin
Taupont
Etangu Duc
Moréac
Guégon
Ploërmel
Campéneac
Gourhel
St-Allouestre
Locminé
Bigan
Kerguéhennec
Guéhenno
Guillac
Augan
Porcaro
Moustoir-Ac
St-Jean-Brévelay
Lizio
le Roc-St-André
la Chapelle-Caro
Monteneuf
Caro
Réminiac
Plumelec
Colpo
Sérent
Malestroit
St-Marcel
Ruffiac
Grand-Champ
Trédion
Plaudren
St-Laurent
Locmaria-Grand-Champ
Locqueltas
Morbouleau
St-Guyomard
St-Congard
Monterblanc
Pleucadeur
Mont Hersé
80
Meucon
Elven
le Cours
Molac
St-Martin
St-Gravé
St-Nolff
St-Ave
Larré
Rochefort-en-Terre
Menimur
Theffléan
la Vraie-Croix
Bel-Air
Pluherlin
Malansac
Peillac
Vannes
Sulniac
Questembert
Arradon
Séné
le Gorvello
Berric
Limerzel
Thiex
Noyalo
Lauzach
Caden
Ile d'Arz
Morbihan
Île Ilur
Île Iluric
Noyal-Muziliac
Surzur
Péaule
St-Colombier
Sarzeau
Ambon
Muzillac
Ste-Cry
le Tour-du-Parc
Marzan
Nivillac
Kermoizan
Château de Suscinio
Penerf
Damgan
Arzal
la Bonne-Façaon
Pointe de Penvins
la Roche-Bernard
Pénestin
Camoël
Férel
207
Canal de Nantes à Brest
Forêt
Oust
Ninian
Claire
Arz
Vilaine
Trévélo
Loc'h
Runio
Yvel
Hivet
Rance
Lie
Arhor
Oyon
Leverin
Pehert
Meu
Landes de Lanvaux
N164
N24
N166
N165
E60
D700
D778
D768
D2
D14
D793
D16
D13
D766
D126
D10
D1
D4
D8
D11
D17
D764
D767
D775
D776
D777
D780
D774
D7
D20
D153
D140
D139
D34
D195

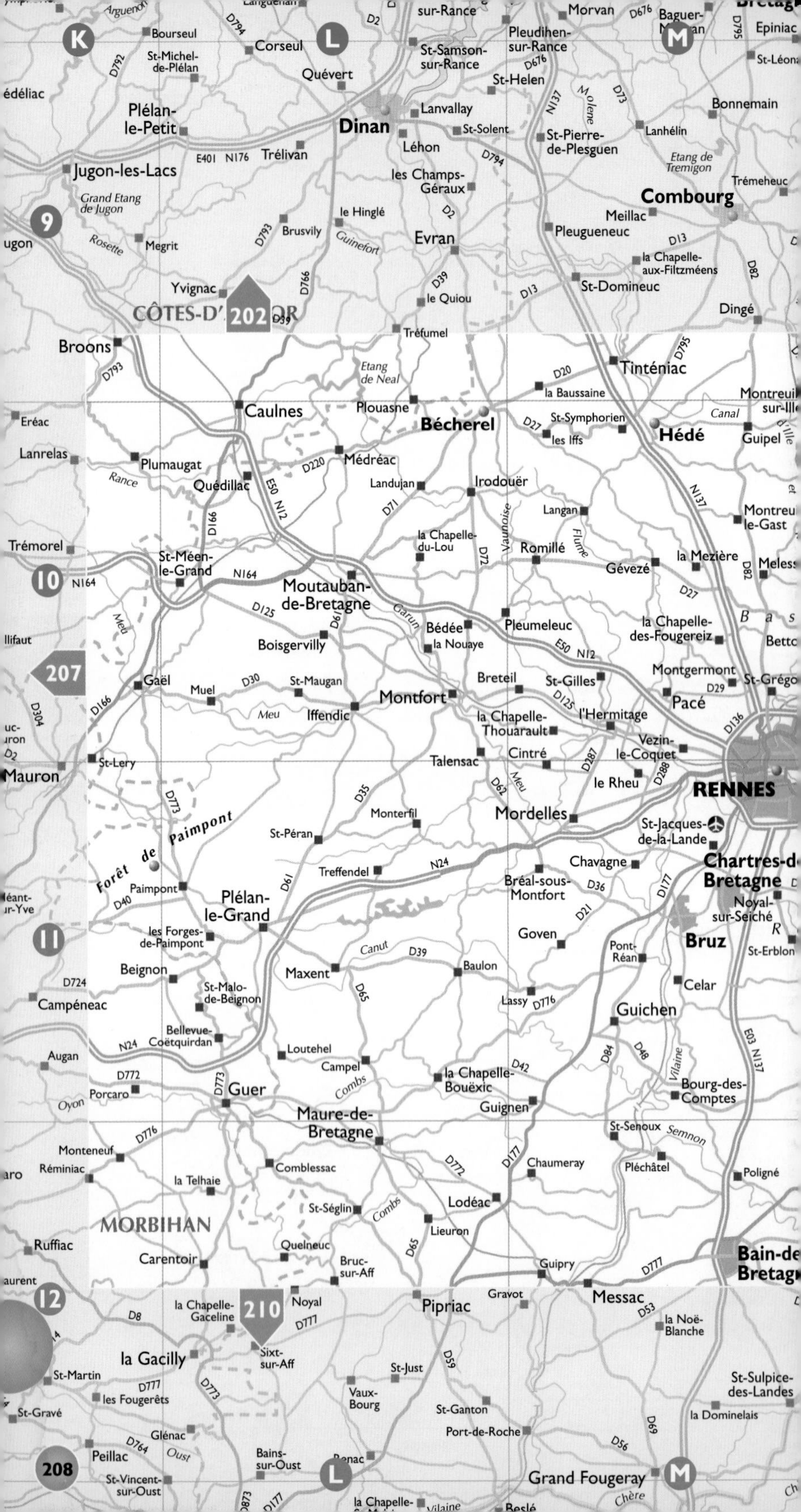

Arguenon
Bourseul
D794
Corseul
D2
sur-Rance
Morvan
D676
Baguer-Morvan
D795
Epiniac
K
L
M
St-Michel-de-Plélan
D792
Quévert
St-Samson-sur-Rance
Pleudihen-sur-Rance
D676
St-Helen
St-Léonard
Plélan-le-Petit
Dinan
Lanvallay
N137
Molene
D73
Bonnemain
St-Solent
Léhon
St-Pierre-de-Plesguen
Lanhélin
E401
N176
Trélivan
D794
Etang de Tremigon
Jugon-les-Lacs
les Champs-Géraux
Trémeheuc
Grand Etang de Jugon
D2
Combourg
9
le Hinglé
Meillac
Rosette
Megrit
D793
Brusvily
Guinefort
Evran
Pleugueneuc
D13
la Chapelle-aux-Filtzméens
D82
D39
D766
le Quiou
St-Domineuc
Yvignac
D13
CÔTES-D'ARMOR
202
D39
Dingé
Tréfumel
Broons
D795
Etang de Neal
D20
Tinténiac
D793
la Baussaine
Caulnes
Plouasne
Bécherel
D27
St-Symphorien
Hédé
Canal
Guipel
Eréac
les Iffs
Lanrelas
Plumaugat
D220
Médréac
Rance
Quédillac
E50
N12
Landujan
D71
Irodouër
Vaunoise
Langan
N137
Montreuil-le-Gast
D166
la Chapelle-du-Lou
D72
Flume
Romillé
la Mezière
D82
Trémorel
St-Méen-le-Grand
N164
Moutauban-de-Bretagne
Gévezé
10
N164
D27
Meu
D125
D61
Garun
Bédée
Pleumeleuc
la Chapelle-des-Fougereiz
Boisgervilly
la Nouaye
E50
N12
207
Montgermont
Gaël
D30
St-Maugan
Breteil
St-Gilles
D29
Pacé
D166
Muel
Montfort
D125
D304
Meu
Iffendic
la Chapelle-Thouarault
l'Hermitage
D136
Vezin-le-Coquet
Talensac
Cintré
Mauron
St-Lery
D287
le Rheu
D288
Meu
RENNES
D773
D35
D62
Monterfil
Mordelles
Forêt de Paimpont
St-Péran
St-Jacques-de-la-Lande
Chavagne
Chartres-de-Bretagne
Treffendel
N24
Paimpont
D61
Bréal-sous-Montfort
D36
D177
D40
Plélan-le-Grand
Noyal-sur-Seiché
D21
les Forges-de-Paimpont
Goven
Bruz
Canut
D39
Pont-Réan
St-Erblon
11
Beignon
Maxent
Baulon
D724
D65
Celar
St-Malo-de-Beignon
Lassy
D776
Campéneac
Guichen
Bellevue-Coëtquirdan
N24
Augan
Loutehel
D84
D48
E03
N137
Campel
D42
Vilaine
D772
D773
la Chapelle-Bouëxic
Bourg-des-Comptes
Porcaro
Guer
Combs
Oyon
Guignen
Maure-de-Bretagne
St-Senoux
Semnon
D776
Monteneuf
D177
Réminiac
Comblessac
D772
Chaumeray
Pléchâtel
Poligné
la Telhaie
Lodéac
St-Séglin
Combs
MORBIHAN
Lieuron
Ruffiac
D65
Quelneuc
Carentoir
Bruc-sur-Aff
Guipry
D777
Bain-de-Bretagne
12
Noyal
Gravot
Messac
la Chapelle-Gaceline
210
D8
D777
Pipriac
D53
la Noë-Blanche
la Gacilly
Sixt-sur-Aff
St-Martin
D777
D59
St-Just
St-Sulpice-des-Landes
D773
les Fougerêts
Vaux-Bourg
St-Ganton
St-Gravé
la Dominelais
Glénac
Port-de-Roche
D69
D764
Oust
D56
Peillac
Bains-sur-Oust
208
L
M
St-Vincent-sur-Oust
Grand Fougeray
D873
D177
Chère
la Chapelle-
Vilaine

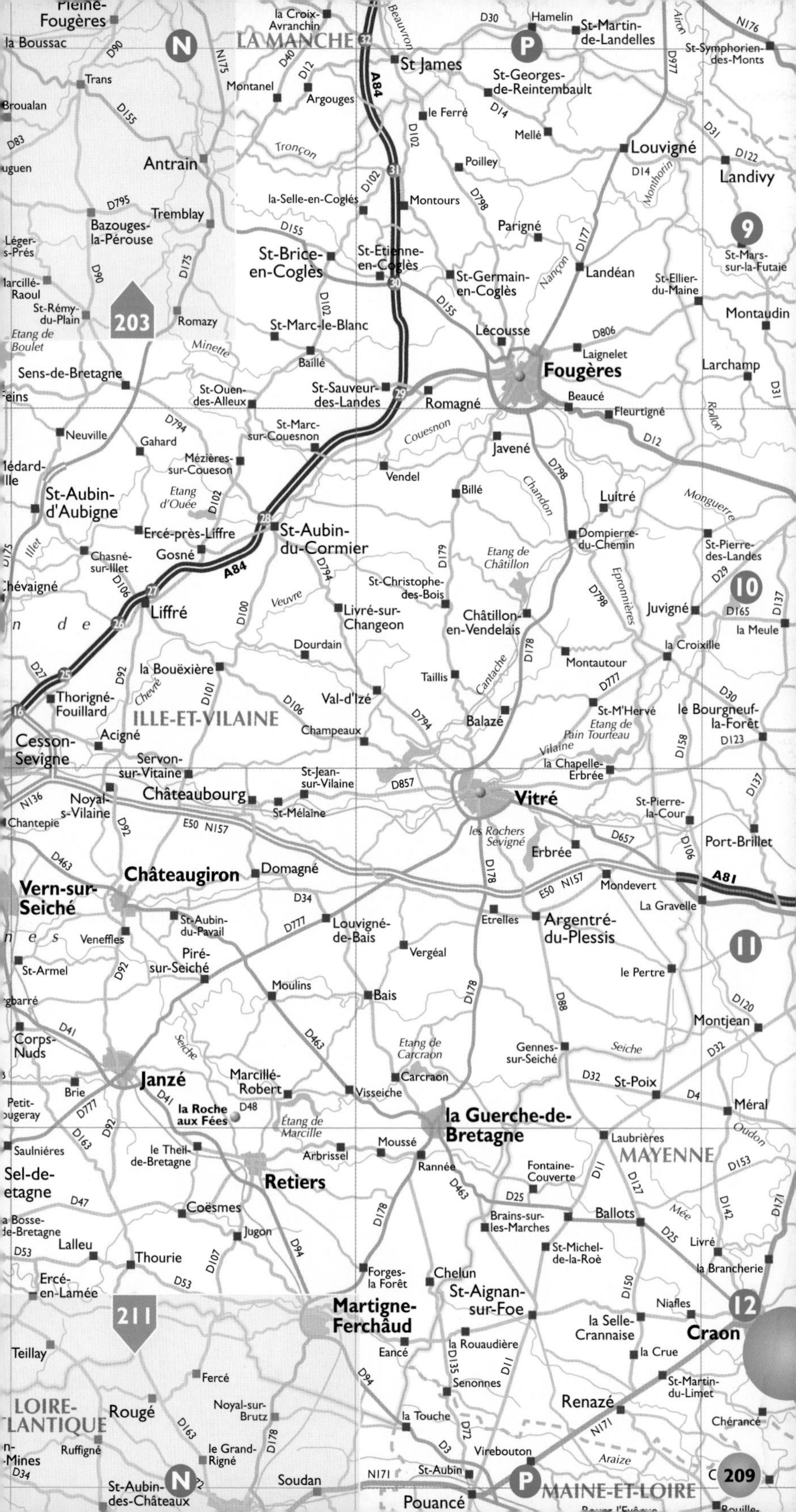

Fougères
la Boussac
LA MANCHE
N
P
St James
St-Georges-de-Reintembault
St-Martin-de-Landelles
St-Symphorien-des-Monts
Hamelin
la Croix-Avranchin
Montanel
Argouges
Trans
Broualan
Antrain
le Ferré
Mellé
Louvigné
Landivy
Poilley
Montours
la-Selle-en-Coglès
Tremblay
Bazouges-la-Pérouse
Parigné
9
St-Mars-sur-la-Futaie
St-Brice-en-Coglès
St-Etienne-en-Coglès
St-Germain-en-Coglès
Landéan
St-Ellier-du-Maine
Montaudin
Marcillé-Raoul
St-Rémy-du-Plain
203
Romazy
St-Marc-le-Blanc
Lécousse
Laignelet
Larchamp
Etang de Boulet
Baillé
Fougères
Sens-de-Bretagne
St-Ouen-des-Alleux
St-Sauveur-des-Landes
Romagné
Beaucé
Fleurtigné
Neuville
Gahard
St-Marc-sur-Couesnon
Javené
Mézières-sur-Coueson
Vendel
Billé
Luitré
St-Aubin-d'Aubigne
Etang d'Ouée
St-Aubin-du-Cormier
Dompierre-du-Chemin
St-Pierre-des-Landes
Ercé-près-Liffre
Gosné
Chasné-sur-Illet
Etang de Châtillon
St-Christophe-des-Bois
10
Chévaigné
Liffré
Livré-sur-Changeon
Châtillon-en-Vendelais
Juvigné
la Meule
Dourdain
la Croixille
Montautour
la Bouëxière
Taillis
Thorigné-Fouillard
Val-d'Izé
St-M'Hervé
Etang de Pain Tourteau
le Bourgneuf-la-Forêt
ILLE-ET-VILAINE
Balazé
Cesson-Sevigne
Acigné
Champeaux
Servon-sur-Vitaine
St-Jean-sur-Vilaine
la Chapelle-Erbrée
Châteaubourg
Vitré
Noyal-s-Vilaine
St-Mélaine
St-Pierre-la-Cour
Chantepie
les Rochers Sevigné
Port-Brillet
Erbrée
Châteaugiron
Domagné
Mondevert
Vern-sur-Seiché
La Gravelle
St-Aubin-du-Pavail
Louvigné-de-Bais
Etrelles
Argentré-du-Plessis
11
Veneffles
Vergéal
St-Armel
Piré-sur-Seiché
le Pertre
Moulins
Bais
Montjean
Corps-Nuds
Etang de Carcraon
Gennes-sur-Seiché
Janzé
Marcillé-Robert
Carcraon
St-Poix
Brie
Visseiche
la Guerche-de-Bretagne
Méral
la Roche aux Fées
Étang de Marcille
Laubrières
Saulnières
Mossé
le Theil-de-Bretagne
Arbrissel
MAYENNE
Rannée
Fontaine-Couverte
Sel-de-Bretagne
Retiers
Coësmes
Brains-sur-les-Marches
Ballots
Jugon
St-Michel-de-la-Roë
Livré
Lalleu
Thourie
Forges-la Forêt
Chelun
la Brancherie
Ercé-en-Lamée
211
Martigne-Ferchâud
St-Aignan-sur-Foe
Niafles
12
la Selle-Crannaise
Craon
Teillay
Eancé
la Rouaudière
la Crue
Fercé
Senonnes
St-Martin-du-Limet
LOIRE-ATLANTIQUE
Rougé
Noyal-sur-Brutz
Renazé
Chérancé
la Touche
Ruffigné
le Grand-Rigné
Virebouton
St-Aubin-des-Châteaux
Soudan
St-Aubin
Pouancé
MAINE-ET-LOIRE
A84
A81
E50
N157
N136
N171
N175
D178
D794
D798

J
K
L
12
13
14
15
208
207
Guéhenno
Guillac
Augan
D772
Porcaro
Oyon
Guer
Campel
Maure-de-Bretagne
D4
N166
D8
D773
Lizio
le Roc-St-André
la Chapelle-Caro
Monteneuf
D776
Caro
Réminiac
Comblessac
la Telhaie
D10
L a n v a u x
Sérent
D114
l'Oust
St-Séglin
Malestroit
Ruffiac
St-Marcel
Quelneuc
Carentoir
Trédion
Claire
D776
St-Laurent
St-Guyomard
D1
la Chapelle-Gaceline
Noyal
D777
D8
St-Congard
D112
D14
Elven
le Cours
Pleucadeuc
80
Mont Hersé
la Gacilly
Sixt-sur-Aff
D5
St-Martin
Molac
D774
D764
D777
Arz
Moustoir-Maria
St-Gravé
les Fougerêts
D773
Nolff
D1
D777
Glénac
D775
Rochefort-en-Terre
Peillac
D764
Oust
Bains-sur-Oust
Renac
Treffléan
la Vraie-Croix
Bel-Air
D777
Pluherlin
Malansac
St-Vincent-sur-Oust
Sulniac
D873
D177
D7
le Gorvello
D7
Questembert
D775
D14
Redon
Berric
Limerzel
Caden
Allaire
D775
Lauzach
D1
D774
Trévelo
MORBIHAN
D20
D164
Noyal-Muziliac
D153
D20
D140
Bocquéreux
Rieux
Péaule
Vilaine
Fégréac
D20
Ambon
Muzillac
D139
Pehert
D153
D774
Ste-Cry
D114
Isac
D164
D140
Damgan
Marzan
Nivillac
D34
St-Dolay
Sévérac
D128
Arzal
la Bonne-Façaon
D773
la Roche-Bernard
E60
N165
St-Gildas-des-Bois
D2
Guenrouet
Pénestin
D34
D2
D34
Camoël
Férel
D315
D4
Missillac
Drefféac
Brivé
D83
D82
Herbignac
la Chapelle-des-Marais
St-Anne-sur-Brivet
D17
Ste-Reine-de-Bretagne
D33
Île Dumet
Assérac
Mayun
St-Lomer
Quilly
Pont-d'Armes
D774
D47
D51
Pontchâteau
Balasson
l'Ebaup
Mesquer
Piriac-sur-Mer
Pompas
Crossac
D52
St-Molf
St-Lyphard
D50
D773
Campb
D33
D51
Parc Naturel
St-Joachim
Lerat
Régional
Revin
la Chapelle-Launay
la Turballe
Fourbihan
la Madeleine
Prinquiau
Trescalan
Ile-d'Aignac
Clis
D99
D47
de Brière
Montoir-de-Bretagne
N171
Savenay
Guérande
D100
Marais Salants
D92
St-André-des-Eaux
Trignac
Donges
le Croisic
Saillé
D3
N171
Brais
Lavau-Loire
Batz-sur-Mer
ST NAZAIRE
Loire
Paimbœuf
Grotte des Korrigans
Pornichet
D92
la-Baule-Escoublac
D723
D277
St-Brevin-les-Pins
St Vraud
Fros
D213
D86
St-Brevin-l'Ocean
D5
St-Père
P a y s
St-Michel-Chef-Chef
D78
la Sicauda
D5
D58
Tharon-Plage
le Feuillardais
D206
D97
D86
d e
D6
Chauve
R i
Préfailles
D13
D213
Pornic
la Croix
Haute Perche
Ste-Marie
Canal de Haute perche
D751

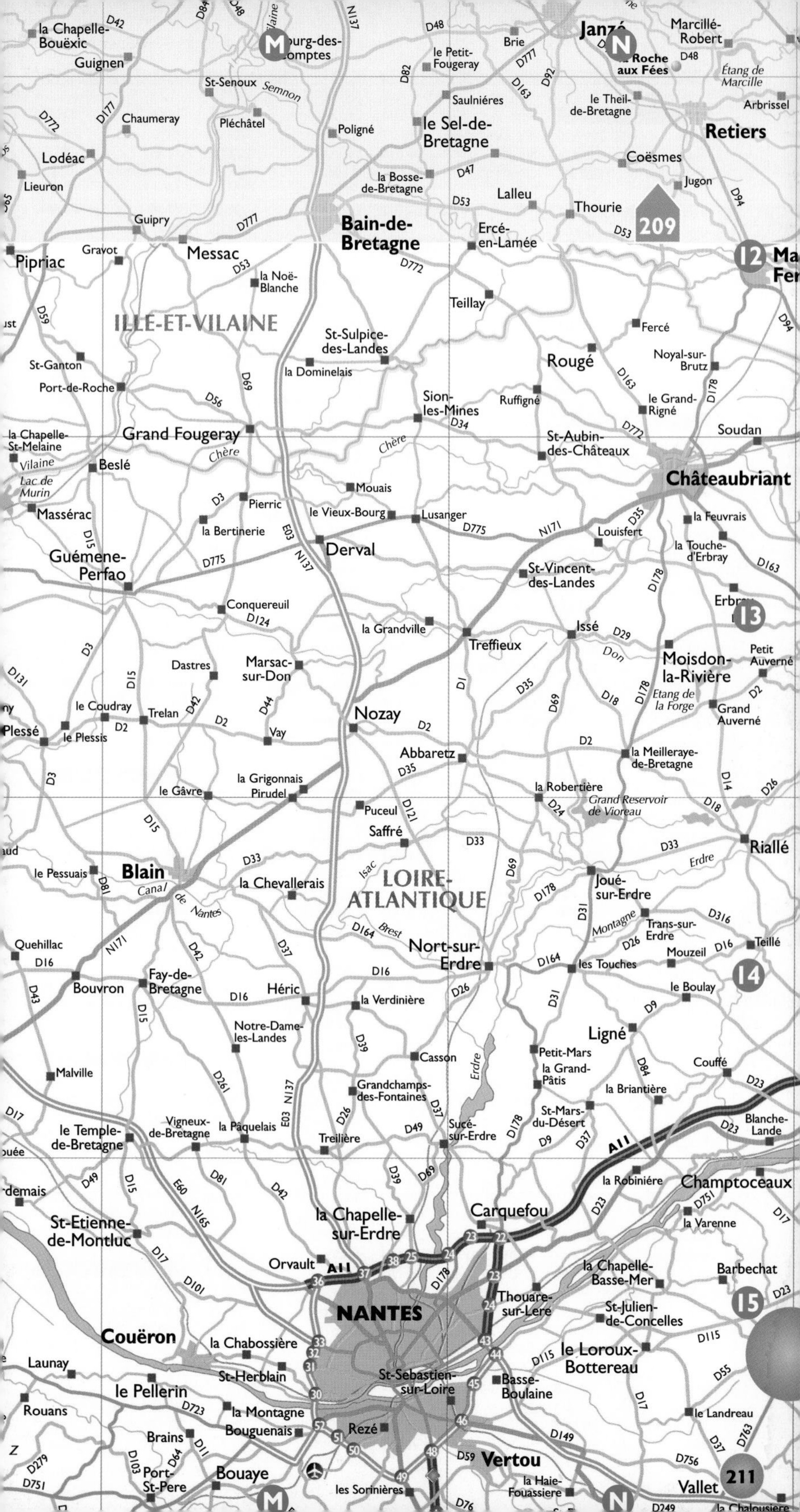

la Chapelle-Bouëxic
Guignen
Lodéac
Lieuron
Chaumeray
St-Senoux
Semnon
Pléchâtel
Poligné
le Sel-de-Bretagne
Saulniéres
le Petit-Fougeray
Brie
Janzé
la Roche aux Fées
Marcillé-Robert
Étang de Marcille
Arbrissel
le Theil-de-Bretagne
Retiers
Coësmes
Jugon
Lalleu
Thourie
la Bosse-de-Bretagne
Bain-de-Bretagne
Ercé-en-Lamée
209
Guipry
Pipriac
Gravot
Messac
la Noë-Blanche
Teillay
ILLE-ET-VILAINE
St-Sulpice-des-Landes
la Dominelais
Rougé
Fercé
Noyal-sur-Brutz
St-Ganton
Port-de-Roche
Sion-les-Mines
Ruffigné
le Grand-Rigné
Grand Fougeray
la Chapelle-St-Melaine
Vilaine
Lac de Murin
Beslé
Chère
St-Aubin-des-Châteaux
Soudan
Châteaubriant
12
Mouais
Pierric
Massérac
la Bertinerie
le Vieux-Bourg
Lusanger
la Feuvrais
Louisfert
la Touche-d'Erbray
Derval
Guémene-Perfao
St-Vincent-des-Landes
Conquereuil
Erbray
13
la Grandville
Treffieux
Issé
Don
Moisdon-la-Rivière
Petit Auverné
Dastres
Marsac-sur-Don
Etang de la Forge
Grand Auverné
le Coudray
Trelan
Nozay
Vay
Plessé
le Plessis
Abbaretz
la Meilleraye-de-Bretagne
la Grigonnais
Pirudel
le Gâvre
la Robertière
Grand Reservoir de Vioreau
Puceul
Saffré
Rialllé
Blain
le Pessuais
Canal de Nantes
la Chevallerais
Isac
LOIRE-ATLANTIQUE
Joué-sur-Erdre
Erdre
Brest
Montagne
Trans-sur-Erdre
Quehillac
Nort-sur-Erdre
Mouzeil
Teillé
les Touches
14
Bouvron
Fay-de-Bretagne
Héric
la Verdinière
le Boulay
Notre-Dame-les-Landes
Ligné
Malville
Casson
Petit-Mars
la Grand-Pâtis
Couffé
Grandchamps-des-Fontaines
la Briantière
le Temple-de-Bretagne
Vigneux-de-Bretagne
la Pâquelais
Treillière
Sucé-sur-Erdre
St-Mars-du-Désert
Blanche-Lande
la Robinière
Champtoceaux
St-Etienne-de-Montluc
la Chapelle-sur-Erdre
Carquefou
la Varenne
Orvault
Barbechat
la Chapelle-Basse-Mer
Thouare-sur-Lere
St-Julien-de-Concelles
15
NANTES
Couëron
la Chabossière
le Loroux-Bottereau
Launay
St-Herblain
St-Sebastien-sur-Loire
Basse-Boulaine
le Pellerin
Rouans
la Montagne
Bouguenais
Rezé
le Landreau
Brains
Port-St-Pere
Bouayé
Vertou
la Haie-Fouassiere
les Sorinières
Vallet
211
la Chalousière
A11
N137
E03
N171
N165
E60

Q

R

S

T

U

V

Y

Page numbers in bold indicate the main reference.

ACKNOWLEDGMENTS

Abbreviations for the picture credits are as follows:
AA = AA World Travel Library, **t** (top), **b** (bottom or below), **c** (centre), **l** (left), **r** (right), **c** (centre), **bg** (background)

UNDERSTANDING BRITTANY

5tl AA/P. Trenchard; **5tc** AA/R. Strange; **5tr** AA/P. Kenward; **5bc** AA/R. Strange; **6tr** AA/A. Kouprianoff; **6lc** AA/R. Strange; **7tl** AA/R.Victor; **7acl** AA/R.Strange; **7c** AA/A.Kouprianoff; **7bcl** AA/A. Kouprianoff; **7bl** AA/B. B. Smith; **7tr** AA/R. Strange; **7cr** AA/A.Kouprianoff; **7br** AA/R. Strange; **8tl** AA/A. Kouprianoff; **8bl** AA/R. Strange; **8tr** AA/R. Victor; **8acr** AA/J. Tims; **8cr** AA/R. Strange; **8br** AA/B. Smith

LIVING BRITTANY

9 AA/A. Kouprianoff; **10tl** AA/R. Victor; **10tc** & **tr** AA/S. Day; **10c** & **cl** AA/A. Kouprianoff; **10cr** Rex Features Ltd; **10bl** & **10/11 bg** AA/R. Strange; **11tl** AA/T. Oliver; **11tr** AA/A. Kouprianoff; **11tc** AA/R. Strange; **11lc** Rex Features Ltd; **11c** AA/J. Edmanson; **11rc** AA/A. Kouprianoff; **12tl** AA/R. Strange; **12lc** AA/P. Bennett; **12tr** AA/A. Kouprianoff; **12bc** AA/R. Strange; **12/13bg** AA/R. Strange; **13tl** AA/R. Strange; **13tr** AA/S. Day; **13lc** ©Annebicque Bernard/CORBIS SYGMA; **13c** AA/P. Bennett; **13ac** AA/A. Kouprianoff; **13rc** © Archivo Iconografico, S.A./CORBIS; **13br** © Michael Boys/CORBIS; **13bl** AA/P. Kenward; **14tl** AA/R. Strange; **14tr** AA/A. Kouprianoff; **14lc** © Chris Lisle/CORBIS; **14bl** AA/A. Kouprianoff; **14c** AA/R. Victor; **14rc** AA/R. Strange; **14br** © Charles & Josette Lenars/CORBIS; **14bg** AA/P. Bennett

THE STORY OF BRITTANY

15 AA; **16tc**, **bl** & **lc** AA; **16/17b** Biblioteca Marciana, Venice/Giraudon/Bridgeman Art Library, London; **16rc** Bibliotheque Nationale, Paris/Bridgeman Art Library, London; **16/17bg** AA/R. Strange; **17lc** AA/R. Strange; **17lac** Mary Evans Picture Library; **17rbc** AA; **17rc** AA/S. Day; **17c** AA/R. Moore; **17bc** AA/R. Strange; **17br** Mary Evans Picture Library; **18tl** © Collection Roger-Viollet/Topfoto.co.uk; **18lc** & **bl** AA/S. Day; **18rc** AA/S. Day; **18/19b** © Harlingue/Roger-Viollet/Topfoto.co.uk; **18/19bg** AA/R. Strange; **19tl** AA/A. Kouprianoff; **19tcl** AA/R. Strange; **19tcr** Mary Evans Picture Library; **19tr** & **bc** AA/R. Strange; **19cl** Musee d'Orsay, Paris/Giraudon/Bridgeman Art Library, London; **19br** Public Record Office/HIP/Topfoto.co.uk; **19c** ILN; **20tl** AA/R. Strange; **20bl** Rex Features Ltd., **20tr** AA/R. Victor; **20cr** © Emmanuel Pain/CORBIS SYGMA; **20b** AA/S. Day; **20bg** AA/R. Strange

ON THE MOVE

21 DigitalVision; **22/23t** DigitalVision; **22** DigitalVision; **23** DigitalVision; **24bl** AA/W. Voysey; **25c** AA/J. Tims; **25br** AA/S. Day; **24/25t** DigitalVision; **26t** & **cr** DigitalVision; **27t** DigitalVision; **27cr** AA/P. Kenward; **27** AA/P. Kenward; **28/29t** DigitalVision; **28tl** AA/K. Glendenning; **28tc** AA/J. Wyand; **28tr** & **cl** AA/R. Strange; **28c** AA/N. Setchfield; **28cr** AA/R. Moore; **28bl** AA/C. Sawyer; **28br** AA/K. Glendenning; **29c** AA/J. Tims; **28bc** AA/R. Victor; **30b** AA/A. Kouprianoff; **31c** AA/M. Jourdan; **30/31t** AA/P. Bennett; **32/33t** AA/J. Tims; **33c** AA/J. Tims; **34** AA/C. Sawyer

THE SIGHTS

35 AA/I. Dawson; **36/37t** AA/R. Strange; **37t** AA/A. Kouprianoff; **37lc** AA/A. Kouprianoff; **38t** AA/R. Victor; **38lc** AA/R. Strange; **38c** & **r** AA/A. Kouprianoff; **39** AA/R. Strange; **40t**, **c** & **cl** AA/R. Strange; **40cr** AA/A. Baker; **41** AA/A. Baker; **42tl** AA/A. Baker; **42tc** AA/R. Victor; **42tr** AA/R. Strange; **42bl** AA/R. Victor; **42/43t** AA/R. Strange; **43tl** AA/A. Kouprianoff; **43tr** © Chris Lisle/CORBIS; **43bc** AA/A. Kouprianoff; **44/45bg** AA/R. Strange; **44t** & **lc** AA/P. Bennett; **45tl** AA/A. Kouprianoff; **45tr** & **bl** AA/R. Victor; **46/47bg** AA/R. Strange; **46tl** AA/A. Kouprianoff; **46tc** AA/R. Strange; **46tr** AA/P. Bennett; **46bl** AA/A. Kouprianoff; **47tl** AA/P. Bennett; **47tr** AA/A. Kouprianoff; **48tl** AA/R. Strange; **48tr** AA/A. Baker; **48b/g** AA; **48bl** © Bildarchiv Monheim Gmbh/Alamy Images; **48br** AA/P. Kenward; **49t** AA/R. Strange; **49l** & **c** AA/A. Kouprianoff; **49r** AA/R. Strange; **50** AA/A. Kouprianoff; **51tl** AA/A. Kouprianoff; **51tc** & **tr** AA/R. Strange; **51bc** AA/A. Kouprianoff; **52/53bg** AA/R. Strange; **53tl** AA/A. Baker; **53c** AA/R. Strange; **53tr** AA/R. Strange; **54** AA/A. Kouprianoff; **55** AA/A. Kouprianoff; **56l** AA/B. Smith; **56r** AA/J. Tims; **57tl** AA/R. Victor; **57tc** & **tr** AA/R. Strange; **58/59bg** AA/R. Strange; **58t** AA/A. Baker; **58lc** AA/R. Strange; **59l** AA/R. Strange; **59c** AA/A. Baker; **59r** AA/A. Kouprianoff; **60/61tbg** AA/R. Strange; **60t** AA/A. Kouprianoff; **60cl** AA/R. Strange; **61tl**, **tr**, **62/63tbg** AA/R. Strange; **63l** AA/A. Kouprianoff; **63r** AA/R. Victor; **63tl** & **cl** AA/A. Kouprianoff; **63bl** AA/R. Victor; **64/65bg** AA/R. Strange; **64tl** AA/R. Strange; **64tc** AA/A. Kouprianoff; **64tr** AA/A. Kouprianoff; **65t** & **cr** AA/J. Tims; **66/67bg** AA/R. Strange; **66tl** AA/R. Victor; **66tr** AA/A. Baker; **67t** & **cr** AA/A. Kouprianoff; **68/69bg** AA/R. Strange; **68t** AA/A. Kouprianoff; **68cl** AA/R. Strange; **69tl** & **tc** AA/R. Strange; **69tr** AA/P. Bennett; **70/71bg** AA/R. Strange; **70tl**, **tr** & **b** AA/R. Strange; **71tl** AA/A. Kouprianoff; **71tr** & **cr** AA/R. Strange; **71b** AA/A. Kouprianoff; **72/73bg** AA/R. Strange; **72t** AA/R. Strange; **72cl** AA/R. Victor; **72b** AA/A. Kouprianoff; **73tl** & **tc** AA/R. Strange; **73tr** AA/A. Kouprianoff; **74t** AA/R. Victor; **74cl** A. Baker; **74c** AA/B. Smith; **74cr** AA/A. Kouprianoff; **75tl** AA/A. Kouprianoff; **75tr** AA/A. Baker;

75cr AA/A. Kouprianoff; **76/77bg** AA/R. Strange; **76t** & **cl** AA/A. Kouprianoff; **77tl** AA/R. Strange; **77tc** AA/R. Strange; **77tr** AA/A. Kouprianoff; **78bg** AA/R. Strange; **78t** AA/R. Strange; **78cl** AA/A. Kouprianoff; **79bg** AA/R. Strange; **80/81bg** AA/R. Strange; **80t** AA/A. Kouprianoff; **80cl** AA/R. Victor; **81t** AA/R. Strange; **81cr** AA/P. Bennett; **82** AA/A. Kouprianoff; **83t** & **cl** AA/S. Day; **83c** AA/A. Kouprianoff; **83cr** & **b** AA/S. Day; **84tr**, **bl** & **tl** AA/A. Kouprianoff; **84br** AA/S. Day; **85bg** AA/R. Strange; **85t** & **cr** AA/A. Kouprianoff; **86/87bg** AA/R. Strange; **86tl** AA/A. Kouprianoff; **86tr** AA/R. Strange; **87tl** & **tr** AA/A. Kouprianoff; **87b** AA/P. Bennett; **88/89bg** AA/R. Strange; **88tl** AA/P. Bennett; **88tr** AA/S. Day; **89tl** AA/S. Day; **89tr** AA/R. Strange; **90/91bg** AA/R. Strange; **90tl** & **bl** AA/R. Victor; **90tr** AA/A. Kouprianoff, **91tl** AA/R. Strange; **91tr** AA/A. Kouprianoff; **91b** AA/A. Baker; **92bg** AA/R. Strange; **91tl** AA/A. Kouprianoff; **92tr** AA/S. Day; **93bg** AA/R. Strange; **94/95bg** AA/R. Strange; **94tl** AA/R. Victor; **94tr** AA/S. Day; **95t** AA/A. Kouprianoff; **95cr** AA/S. Day; **96/97bg** AA/R. Strange; **96t** & **cl** AA/S. Day; **97t** AA/S. Day; **97cr** AA/S. Day; **98bg** AA/R. Strange; **98tl** AA/R. Victor; **98tc** AA/A. Baker; **98tr** AA/S. Day; **99t** AA/C. Sawyer; **99cl**, **c** & **cr** AA/Ian Dawson; **99b** AA/C. Sawyer; **100** R. Moore; **101tl** AA/I. Dawson; **101tr** & **cl** AA/C. Sawyer; **101c** AA/B. Smith; **101cr** & **b** AA/C. Sawyer; **102t** AA/A. Kouprianoff; **102cl** AA/S. Day; **102c** AA/B. Smith; **102cr** AA/S. Day; **103** AA/A. Kouprianoff; **104/5t** AA/A. Kouprianoff; **104lc** AA/S. Day; **105** AA/A. Kouprianoff; **106** AA/S. Day; **107** AA/S. Day; **108** AA/S. Day; **109bg** & **tl** AA/R. Strange; **109tc** & **tr** AA/S. Day; **110** AA/R. Strange; **110t** AA/S. Day; **110cl** AA/A. Kouprianoff

WHAT TO DO

111 AA/A. Kouprianoff; **112/113t** AA/A. Kouprianoff; **112cr** & **cl** AA/A. Kouprianoff; **112br** AA/J. Tims; **113cl** AA/R. Victor; **113cr** AA/R. Strange; **114/115t** AA/R. Strange; **114cl** & **cr** AA/A. Kouprianoff; **115cl** AA/A. Kouprianoff; **115cr** AA/P. Bennett; **115br** AA/R. Strange; **116t** AA/A. Kouprianoff; **117t** AA/J. Tims; **117c** AA/R. Strange; **118/119t** AA/J. Tims; **118c** AA/A. Kouprianoff; **119c** AA/P. Bennett; **120/121t** AA/J. Tims; **120c** AA/A. Kouprianoff; **121c** AA/P.Kenward; **122/123t** AA/R. Strange; **122c** AA/R. Victor; **123c** AA/P. Bennett; **124/125t** AA/R. Strange; **124c** AA/R. Strange; **126/127t** AA/P. Bennett; **126c** AA/A. Kouprianoff; **126c** AA/P. Kenward; **128/129t** AA/P. Bennett; **128c** AA/A. Kouprianoff; **130/131** A. Kouprianoff; **130c** AA/R. Moore; **131c** AA/J. Tims; **132t** AA/A. Kouprianoff

OUT AND ABOUT

133 AA/R. Victor; **134t** AA/R. Victor; **134c** AA/A. Kouprianoff; **134br** AA/P. Bennett; **135** AA/A. Kouprianoff; **136tr** AA/R. Strange; **136tl** AA/A. Kouprianoff; **136b** AA/A. Baker; **137tl** AA/A. Kouprianoff; **137tr** AA/A. Baker; **137bl** AA/R. Strange; **137br** AA/ A. Baker; **138l** AA/A. Kouprianoff; **138r** AA/R. Strange; **139l** AA/A. Kouprianoff; **139r** AA/R. Victor; **140t** & **b** AA/R. Strange; **141tl** AA/R. Victor; **141tr** AA/A. Kouprianoff; **141b** AA/A. Kouprianoff; **142t** & **b** AA/R. Strange; **143t** AA/A. Baker; **143b** AA/A. Kouprianoff; **144t** AA/A. Kouprianoff; **144b** AA/S. Day; **145l** & **r** AA/A. Kouprianoff; **146t** & **b** AA/A. Kouprianoff; **147t** AA/P. Bennett; **147b** AA/R. Strange; **148b** AA/S. Day; **148t** AA/S. Day; **149tl** AA/J. Tims; **149tr** AA/R. Moore; **149bl** AA/S. Day; **150l** AA/R. Strange; **150c** AA/C. Sawyer; **150r** AA/R. Strange

EATING & STAYING

151 AA/P. Kenward; **152l** Photodisc; **152c** & **r** AA/S. Day; **153l** AA/P. Kenward; **153c** AA/R. Strange; **153r** AA/R. Victor; **154-163** AA/J. Tims; **164l** AA/R. Strange; **164c** AA/R. Victor; **164r** AA/R. Strange; **165l** & **c** AA/R. Victor; **166-175** AA/J. Tims

PLANNING

177 DigitalVision; **180l** AA/P. Kenward; **180r** AA/S. Day; **181** AA/A. Kouprianoff; **183t** AA/R. Strange; **183b** AA/C. Sawyer; **184t** AA/R. Strange; **184b** Bananastock; **185** & **186** AA/J. Tims; **187** AA/I. Dawson; **189** AA/C. Sawyer

Project editor
Paul Mitchell

Design
Keith Russell

Picture research
Kathy Lockley

Internal repro work
Susan Crowhurst, Ian Little, Michael Moody

Production
Lyn Kirby, Helen Sweeney

Mapping
Maps produced by the Cartography Department of AA Publishing

Main contributors
David Halford (verifier), Lyndsay Hunt (Understanding Your Destination, On the Move, The Sights, What to Do, Out and About, Eating and Staying, Planning), Laurence Phillips (Living Brittany, The Story of Brittany), The Content Works (What to Do, Eating and Staying)

Copy editor
Stephanie Smith

Published by AA Publishing, a trading name of Automobile Association Developments Limited, whose registered office is Fanum House, Basingstoke, Hampshire, RG21 4EA. Registered number 1878835.

A CIP catalogue record for this book is available from the British Library.

ISBN-10: 0-7495-4819-3
ISBN-13: 978-0-7495-4819-3

Colour separation by Keenes
Printed and bound by Leo, China

Find out more about AA Publishing and the wide range of travel publications and services the AA provides by visiting our website at www.theAA.com/bookshop

A02404
Maps in this title produced from mapping © MAIRDUMONT / Falk Verlag 2005
Relief map images supplied by Mountain High Maps® Copyright © 1993 Digital Wisdom, Inc
Weather chart statistics supplied by Weatherbase © Copyright 2005 Canty and Associates, LLC

We believe the contents of this book are correct at the time of printing. However, some details, particularly prices, opening times and telephone numbers do change. We do not accept responsibility for any consequences arising from the use of this book. This does not affect your statutory rights. We would be grateful if readers would advise us of any inaccuracies they may encounter, or any suggestions they might like to make to improve the book. There is a form provided at the back of the book for this purpose, or you can email us at Keyguides@theaa.com

COVER PICTURE CREDITS

Front cover **t**: AA/S L Day, **c**: AA/R Strange, **l**: AA/R Strange, **b**: AA/P Kenward. Spine: AA/S L Day
Back cover **t**: AA/C Sawyer, **ct**: AA/R Victor, **cb**: AA/A Kouprianoff, **b**: AA/J A Tims

Dear Key Guide Reader

Thank you for buying this Key Guide. Your comments and opinions are very important to us, so please help us to improve our travel guides by taking a few minutes to complete this questionnaire.

You do not need a stamp (unless posted outside the UK). If you do not want to cut this page from your guide, then photocopy it or write your answers on a plain sheet of paper.

Send to: Key Guide Editor, AA World Travel Guides
FREEPOST SCE 4598, Basingstoke RG21 4GY

Find out more about AA Publishing and the wide range of travel publications the AA provides by visiting our website at
www.theAA.com/bookshop

ABOUT THIS GUIDE

Which Key Guide did you buy? ____________________

Where did you buy it? ____________________

When? _ _ month/ _ _ year

Why did you choose this AA Key Guide?

❑ Price ❑ AA Publication

❑ Used this series before; title ____________________

❑ Cover ❑ Other (please state) ____________________

Please let us know how helpful the following features of the guide were to you by circling the appropriate category: very helpful (**VH**), helpful (**H**) or little help (**LH**)

Size	**VH**	**H**	**LH**
Layout	**VH**	**H**	**LH**
Photos	**VH**	**H**	**LH**
Excursions	**VH**	**H**	**LH**
Entertainment	**VH**	**H**	**LH**
Hotels	**VH**	**H**	**LH**
Maps	**VH**	**H**	**LH**
Practical info	**VH**	**H**	**LH**
Restaurants	**VH**	**H**	**LH**
Shopping	**VH**	**H**	**LH**
Walks	**VH**	**H**	**LH**
Sights	**VH**	**H**	**LH**
Transport info	**VH**	**H**	**LH**

What was your favourite sight, attraction or feature listed in the guide?

Page ____________ Please give your reason ____________

____

Which features in the guide could be changed or improved? Or are there any other comments you would like to make?

____

____

ABOUT YOU

Name (*Mr/Mrs/Ms*) ______________________________

Address ______________________________

____

Postcode ______________ Daytime tel nos ______________

Please *only* give us your mobile phone number if you wish to hear from us about other products and services from the AA and partners by text or mms.

Which age group are you in?

Under 25 ❑ 25–34 ❑ 35–44 ❑ 45–54 ❑ 55+ ❑

How many trips do you make a year?

Less than1 ❑ 1 ❑ 2 ❑ 3 or more ❑

ABOUT YOUR TRIP

Are you an AA member? Yes ❑ No ❑

When did you book? _ _ month/_ _ year

When did you travel? _ _ month/_ _ year

Reason for your trip? Business ❑ Leisure ❑

How many nights did you stay? ______________________________

How did you travel? Individual ❑ Couple ❑ Family ❑ Group ❑

Did you buy any other travel guides for your trip? ______________________________

If yes, which ones? ______________________________

____

Thank you for taking the time to complete this questionnaire. Please send it to us as soon as possible, and remember, you do not need a stamp (*unless posted outside the UK*).

Titles in the Key Guide series:
Australia, Barcelona, Britain, Brittany, Canada, Costa Rica, Florence and Tuscany, France, Germany, Ireland, Italy, London, Mallorca, Mexico, New York, New Zealand, Normandy, Paris, Portugal, Prague, Provence and the Côte d'Azur, Rome, Scotland, South Africa, Spain, Venice, Vietnam.

Published in November 2006:
Thailand

The information we hold about you will be used to provide the products and services requested and for identification, account administration, analysis, and fraud/loss prevention purposes. More details about how that information is used is in our privacy statement, which you'll find under the heading "Personal Information" in our terms and conditions and on our website: **www.theAA.com**. Copies are also available from us by post, by contacting the Data Protection Manager at AA, Fanum House, Basing View, Basingstoke, Hampshire RG21 4EA.

We may want to contact you about other products and services provided by us, or our partners (by mail, telephone) but please tick the box if you DO NOT wish to hear about such products and services from us by mail or telephone. ❑